THE LEGAL FRAMEWORK OF THE OSCE

The Organization for Security and Co-operation in Europe (OSCE), the world's largest regional security organisation, possesses most of the attributes traditionally ascribed to an international organisation, but lacks a constitutive treaty and an established international legal personality. Moreover, OSCE decisions are considered mere political commitments and thus not legally binding. As such, it seems to correspond to the general zeitgeist, in which new, less formal actors and forms of international cooperation gain prominence, while traditional actors and instruments of international law are in stagnation.

However, an increasing number of voices – including the OSCE participating States – have been advocating for more formal and autonomous OSCE institutional structures, for international legal personality, or even for the adoption of a constitutive treaty. The book analyses why and how these demands have emerged, critically evaluates the reform proposals and provides new arguments for revisiting the OSCE legal framework.

Mateja Steinbrück Platise is Senior Research Fellow at the Max Planck Institute for Comparative Public Law and International Law in Heidelberg. She is also Lecturer at the University of Heidelberg and University of Frankfurt. Previously, she has worked as Legal Officer at the European Court of Human Rights, Lecturer at the Universities of Lille, Hamburg and Ljubljana, and as Research Assistant at the European Studies Centre of the University of Oxford. She received master and doctorate degrees from the Universities of Ljubljana and Oxford, and was awarded a Marie Curie Fellowship for her project on Responsibility of International Organisations for Human Rights Violations. She publishes on international institutional law, human rights law and international dispute settlement.

Carolyn Moser is Senior Research Fellow at the Max Planck Institute for Comparative Public Law and International Law in Heidelberg. In her previous position at the Basel Institute on Governance, she worked as a consultant on anti-corruption and rule of law projects in Asia, Europe and North Africa, inter alia for the World Bank, the European Parliament, the OSCE and national development agencies. She studied law and political science at Sciences Po Paris and The Fletcher School of Law and Diplomacy, Tufts University, and holds a PhD from Utrecht University. Her research interests relate to public governance and accountability as well as to foreign and security policy in Europe.

Anne Peters is Director at the Max Planck Institute for Comparative Public Law and International Law in Heidelberg, a Professor at the universities of Heidelberg, Freie Universität Berlin and Basel, and a William W. Cook Global Law Professor at the University of Michigan. She has been a member of the European Commission for Democracy through Law (Venice Commission) in respect of Germany (2011–2015) and served as the President of the European Society of International Law (2010–2012). Her current research interests relate to public international law including its history, global animal law, global governance and global constitutionalism.

The Legal Framework of the OSCE

Edited by

MATEJA STEINBRÜCK PLATISE

CAROLYN MOSER

ANNE PETERS

Max Planck Institute for Comparative Public Law and International Law

CAMBRIDGE
UNIVERSITY PRESS

CAMBRIDGE
UNIVERSITY PRESS

University Printing House, Cambridge CB2 8BS, United Kingdom

One Liberty Plaza, 20th Floor, New York, NY 10006, USA

477 Williamstown Road, Port Melbourne, VIC 3207, Australia

314–321, 3rd Floor, Plot 3, Splendor Forum, Jasola District Centre, New Delhi – 110025, India

79 Anson Road, #06–04/06, Singapore 079906

Cambridge University Press is part of the University of Cambridge.

It furthers the University's mission by disseminating knowledge in the pursuit of education, learning, and research at the highest international levels of excellence.

www.cambridge.org
Information on this title: www.cambridge.org/9781108483858
DOI: 10.1017/9781108594028

First published 2019

Printed and bound in Great Britain by Clays Ltd, Elcograf S.p.A.

A catalogue record for this publication is available from the British Library.

ISBN 978-1-108-48385-8 Hardback

Contents

Contributors

NIELS M. BLOKKER is Professor of International Institutional Law at Leiden University, Grotius Centre for International Legal Studies (Schermers Chair). In addition to his academic career, he has previously worked as Senior Legal Counsel and later as Deputy Legal Adviser at the Netherlands Ministry of Foreign Affairs. His publications include the books *International Institutional Law* (coauthored with Henry G. Schermers), *Proliferation of International Organizations* (coauthored with Henry G. Schermers) and *The Security Council and the Use of Force* (co-edited with Nico Schrijver). He is co-founder and Co-Editor-in-Chief of the journal *International Organizations Law Review*.

GLEB BOGUSH is Associate Professor at the National Research University – Higher School of Economics in Moscow. He is also Adjunct Associate Professor at the University of Luxembourg. He was as an Alexander von Humboldt Fellow at the Max Planck Institute for Foreign and International Criminal Law in Freiburg is an editorial board member of the *Criminal Law Forum*, the *Russian Law Journal*, the *International Justice Journal* and the *Journal of Constitutionalism and Human Rights*. His research relates to international criminal law, humanitarian law and human rights law.

LAURENCE BOISSON DE CHAZOURNES is Professor of International Law and International Organization at the University of Geneva and former Head of the Department of Public International Law and International Organization. She has been a visiting professor at numerous universities and has acted as an adviser to various international organizations, governments and law firms. She has served as chairperson of WTO arbitration panels, pleaded before the International Court of Justice and has been an arbitrator in ICSID arbitration. She is a member of the Permanent Court of Arbitration and of the Court of Arbitration for Sport, where she has been appointed arbitrator.

TANJA A. BÖRZEL is Professor of Political Science and holds the Chair for European Integration at the Otto-Suhr-Institute for Political Science of the Freie Universität Berlin. She also directs the Jean Monnet Center of Excellence 'Europe and its Citizens'. She previously taught at Humboldt University zu Berlin, University of Heidelberg and Harvard University. She is the director of the Cluster of Excellence "Contestations of the Liberal Script," together with Michael Zürn. Her most recent publications include *The Oxford Handbook of Comparative Regionalism* (co-edited with Thomas Risse).

ANDRZEJ GADKOWSKI is Postdoctoral Researcher at the University of Geneva and Adam Mickiewicz University in Poznań. He gained professional experience in Polish diplomatic and consular missions, international organisations and academic institutions. He was a SCIEX Fellow and subsequently a Teaching and Research Fellow at the Faculty of Law at the University of Geneva and Lecturer at the Faculty of Law and Administration at Adam Mickiewicz University in Poznań. He is the author of the book *Treaty-making Powers of International Organizations* and several articles on public international law, the law of international organisations and the law of the European Union.

LORENZO GASBARRI is postdoctoral researcher at Bocconi University. He was Research Fellow at University College London, working on the project 'Human Rights Beyond Borders'. Before, he has worked as Postdoctoral Researcher at the University of Helsinki on the project 'Towards a Credible Ethics for Global Governance', as Visiting Fellow at the Centre of Excellence iCourts at the University of Copenhagen and as Visiting Researcher at the Max Planck Institute for Comparative Public Law and International Law in Heidelberg. His research focuses on the law of international organisations, human rights and legal argumentation. He is junior Editor of the Oxford Database on the Law of International Organizations (OXIO).

PETRI HAKKARAINEN has been seconded as Senior Diplomatic Advisor by the Ministry for Foreign Affairs of Finland to the Geneva Centre for Security Policy. Previously, he served at the Finnish Embassy in Berlin and later was Deputy Director and then Acting Director for Policy Planning and Research at the Ministry in Helsinki. He also worked as Senior Fellow at the Institute for Advanced Sustainability Studies in Potsdam. He holds degrees in history and international relations from the University of Helsinki and the University of Oxford. His publications include the book *A State of Peace in Europe: West Germany and the CSCE, 1966–1975*.

OLIVIA HERMAN is a PhD fellow of the Research Foundation Flanders at the Leuven Centre for Global Governance Studies and Institute for International Law, KU Leuven. She is also an associated member of the

Leuven Institute of Criminology. Prior to joining the Centre, she was a trainee at the Delegation of the European Union to the State of Israel, where she assisted the Political and Operations Section on human rights, democracy and peace-related matters. She obtained her Bachelor and Master of Laws from KU Leuven and Master Degree in Human Rights and Democratisation from the European Inter-University Centre for Human Rights and Democratisation.

CAROLYN MOSER is Senior Research Fellow at the Max Planck Institute for Comparative Public Law and International Law in Heidelberg. In her previous position at the Basel Institute on Governance, she worked as a consultant on anti-corruption and rule of law projects in Asia, Europe and North Africa inter alia for the World Bank, the European Parliament, the OSCE and national development agencies. She studied law and political science at Sciences Po Paris and The Fletcher School of Law and Diplomacy (Tufts University), and holds a PhD from Utrecht University. Her research interests relate to public governance and accountability as well as to foreign and security policy in Europe.

CHRISTIAN NÜNLIST is Senior Researcher at the Center for Security Studies at ETH, Zürich and the Head of the team 'Swiss and Euro-Atlantic Security'. He is a member of the steering committee of the OSCE Network of Think Tanks and Academic Institutions. He studied history, international relations and international law and received his MA and his PhD from the University of Zürich. His publications include the book *The Origins of the European Security System: The Helsinki Process Revisited, 1965–1975*. His articles have appeared in *Cold War History*, *Journal of Transatlantic Studies* and *International Relations*, amongst others.

ANNE PETERS is Director at the Max Planck Institute for Comparative Public Law and International Law Heidelberg, Professor at Heidelberg, Freie Universität Berlin and Basel, and a William W. Cook Global Law Professor at the University of Michigan. She has been a member of the European Commission for Democracy through Law (Venice Commission) in respect of Germany (2011–2015) and served as the President of the European Society of International Law (2010–2012). Her current research interests relate to public international law including its history, global animal law, global governance and global constitutionalism, and the status of humans in international law.

INGO PETERS is Associated Professor and Executive Director of the Center of Transnational Studies, Foreign and Security Policy at the Otto Suhr Institute of the Freie Universität Berlin and Dean of Studies at the Department of Political and Social Sciences at the University. He studied political science at Freie Universität Berlin and the University of Lancaster. His research and teaching focuses on German foreign policy, European security and EU foreign policy, transatlantic relations, European security institutions and international relations theory. His recent project deals with the EU Crisis Response Policy, which is conducted as a EU collaborative research project (Horizon 2020).

ISABELLE PINGEL is Professor of Public Law at the Sorbonne Law School, University of Paris 1 (Panthéon-Sorbonne). Prior to that position she worked in the International Arbitration department of Shearman and Sterling LLP in Paris. She has published extensively on EU law and international law, including the book *Les Immunités des Etats en Droit International* and *Le multilinguisme dans l'Union européenne*. Her current research focuses on various aspects of language and law in the European Union and other major international organisations, most notably the Council of Europe and the United Nations.

CEDRIC RYNGAERT is Professor of Public International Law at Utrecht University and an Editor of the *Netherlands International Law Review, Human Rights and International Legal Discourse* and of the *Utrecht Law Review*. He is the Principal Investigator of two research projects on jurisdictional questions, one funded by the European Research Council and the other by the Dutch Organization for Scientific Research. He has published on a wide variety of international law topics, including his book *Jurisdiction in International Law*. His work on jurisdiction has been awarded by the Prix Henri Rolin, a prize for international law and international relations.

MATEJA STEINBRÜCK PLATISE is Senior Research Fellow at the Max Planck Institute for Comparative Public Law and International Law in Heidelberg. She is also Lecturer at the Universities of Heidelberg and Frankfurt. Previously, she worked as Legal Officer at the European Court of Human Rights, Lecturer at the Universities of Lille, Hamburg and Ljubljana, and as Research Assistant at the European Studies Centre of the University of Oxford. She received master and doctorate degrees from the Universities of Ljubljana and Oxford, and was awarded a Marie Curie Fellowship for her project on Responsibility of International Organisations for Human Rights Violations. She publishes on international institutional law, human rights law and international dispute settlement.

LISA TABASSI is the Head of the Office of Legal Affairs in the Secretariat of the Organization for Security and Co-operation in Europe (OSCE) in Vienna. Prior to this post, she held positions of Chief of the Legal Services Section of the Preparatory Commission for the Comprehensive Nuclear-Test-Ban Treaty Organisation in Vienna and as Legal Officer in the Organisation for the Prohibition of Chemical Weapons. She has also worked in private law firms in the Islamic Republic of Iran and the United States and in the Iran–United States Claims Tribunal in The Hague. Her publications relate to non-proliferation and disarmament, international criminal law and the law of international organisations.

HELMUT TICHY is Legal Adviser to the Austrian Federal Ministry for Europe, Integration and Foreign Affairs and Professor at the Institute of International Law and International Relations of the University of Graz. He held diplomatic postings in Belgrade, Geneva and Brussels, and served as Deputy Head of the Vienna Office of the United Nations High Commissioner for Refugees (UNHCR) and as Head of the General International Law Unit at the Office of the Legal Adviser of the Ministry. He holds law degrees from the University of Vienna (Dr. iur.) and the University of Cambridge (LLM).

RAMSES A. WESSEL is Professor of International and European Law and Governance and Co-Director of the Centre for European Studies at the University of Twente. He is also a Member of the standing Governmental Advisory Committee on Issues of Public International Law in The Hague and Member of the Governing Board of the Centre for the Law of EU External Relations in The Hague. His numerous editorial positions include Editor-in-Chief and founder of the *International Organizations Law Review*. He publishes extensively in the fields of international and European institutional law as well as EU external relations.

JAN WOUTERS is Full Professor of International Law and International Organizations, Jean Monnet Chair ad personam European Union and Global Governance, Director of the Institute for International Law and of the Leuven Centre for Global Governance Studies (both a Jean Monnet Centre of Excellence and a University Centre of Excellence) at KU Leuven, and President of the University's Board for International Policy. He is Adjunct Professor at Columbia University (New York) and Visiting Professor at Sciences Po (Paris), LUISS (Rome) and the College of Europe (Bruges). A Member of the Belgian Royal Academy and Of Counsel at Linklaters, he has published widely on international and EU law, international organizations and global governance. He is Coordinator of a large Horizon 2020 Project, RECONNECT (Reconnecting Europe with its Citizens through Democracy and Rule of Law). He advises and trains regularly international organizations and governments, and is often asked to comment international events in the media. In 2019 he is Visiting Professor at the University of Ottawa and the University of Trento.

Preface

The present book project was launched in 2016 when Germany, as one of the participating States of the Organization for Security and Co-operation in Europe (OSCE), took over the rotating one-year Chairmanship of the OSCE. We editors, who are researchers at the Max Planck Institute for Comparative Public Law and International Law in Heidelberg, have long been observing that the OSCE still lacks an established legal framework and that negotiation efforts to settle the OSCE's legal status have so far escaped close scholarly scrutiny, and have instead been conducted away from the public eye.

We believe that by opening up the debate to a broader international community, the decision-making process could become better informed, more inclusive and therefore more legitimate. After all, the OSCE is the largest regional security organisation in the world, comprising fifty-seven states from North America, Europe and Asia, and is responsible for stability, peace and democracy in relation to more than a billion people.

Several contributors to this Volume presented their initial proposals to other scholars, politicians, international civil servants, NGOs and media representatives at an international conference that we organised in 2016 in Berlin under the title 'Strengthening the OSCE Legal Framework'. For that purpose, we invited a number of experts of various profiles, who chaired the panels or held their own presentations. We would like to thank them all for bringing new ideas into the debate, for contributing to the exchange of arguments, and for moderating, at times, quite heated debates. In addition to the contributors to the present book, we are indebted in particular to Elena Ananieva, John Bernhard, Kristina Daugirdas, Tsvetana Kamenova and Antje Leendertse.

In organising the conference, we also received tremendous support from Lea Brinkman, Laura Flegel and Christian Müller. We thank them very much for their input into this project, which also benefited from the valuable help and advice from Alexandra Kemmerer and Sandra Sobol. We furthermore express our gratitude to Clara Schindowski and Florian Kriener, who joined our team once the present book started to take shape. Without their dedicated work and efficient assistance in handling the editing process, this volume would not have been possible. Likewise, our contributions greatly profited from the work of our diligent language editor Matthew James Milbourne as well as from the administrative assistance of Anette Kreutzfeld, whose support we very much appreciate.

Last, but not least, we also wish to thank the German Foreign Office for their financial support of our student assistants and for covering the material costs of the Berlin conference. Our acknowledgments go in particular to Dirk Stockhausen from the former Task Force for the OSCE Chairmanship 2016 for his enduring understanding that we, as scholars, maybe do and see things differently than many politicians have done thus far. We hereby make our modest own contribution to the discourse on strengthening the legal framework of the OSCE.

Heidelberg, September 2018

Mateja Steinbrück Platise

Carolyn Moser

Anne Peters

Abbreviations

APEC	Asia-Pacific Economic Cooperation
ARIO	Draft Articles on the Responsibility of International Organizations
ASEAN	Association of Southeast Asian Nations
ATF	Recueil des Arrêts du Tribunal Fédéral Suisse
BMEIA	Austrian Foreign Ministry
BVerfG	German abbreviation for the Federal Constitutional Court of the Federal Republic of Germany (Bundesverfassungsgericht)
CASM	Capacity Development Programme for Conventional Ammunition Stockpile Management for the Republic of Serbia
CERN	The European Organization for Nuclear Research
CiO	Chairperson-in-Office
CIS	Commonwealth of Independent States
CJEU	Court of Justice of the European Union
CoE	Council of Europe
CoE PA	Parliamentary Assembly of the Council of Europe
CRMS	Common Regulatory Management System
CSBMs	Confidence- and security-building measures
CSCE	Conference on Security and Cooperation in Europe
CSJN	Corte Suprema de Justicia de la Nación Argentina
CVCE	The Virtual Centre for Knowledge on Europe
DNA	Deoxyribonucleic acid
EC	European Community
ECJ	see CJEU
ECHR	European Convention on Human Rights
ECtHR	European Court of Human Rights

ENVSEC	The Environment and Security Initiative
EP	European Parliament
EST	European Security Treaty
EU	European Union
EULEX	EU Rule of Law Mission in Kosovo
EUR	Euro
EUROCONTROL	The European Organisation for the Safety of Air Navigation
FRY	Federal Republic of Yugoslavia
G20	Group of Twenty
GATT	General Agreement on Tariffs and Trade
GC	Grand Chamber of the European Court of Human Rights
HCNM	High Commissioner on National Minorities
HFA	Helsinki Final Act
HJIL	Heidelberg Journal of International Law
HRAP	Human Rights Advisory Panel
IACtHR	Inter-American Court of Human Rights
ICJ	International Court of Justice
ICJ Reports	Reports of the International Court of Justice
ICMP	International Commission on Missing Persons
ICRC	The International Committee of the Red Cross
ILA	International Law Association
ILC	United Nations International Law Commission
ILDC	Oxford Reports on International Law in Domestic Courts
ILO	International Labour Organization
INF	Intermediate Nuclear Forces
INTELSAT	International Telecommunications Satellite Organization
INTERPOL	International Criminal Police Organization
IO	International Organisation
IR	International Relations
ITC	International Tin Council
IWG	Informal Working Group on Strengthening the Legal Framework of the OSCE
KFOR	Kosovo Force
KSZE	German abbreviation for the Conference on Security and Cooperation in Europe (Konferenz über

	Sicherheit und Zusammenarbeit in Europa), see also CSCE
KVM	Kosovo Verification Mission
MC	Ministerial Council of the Organization for Security and Cooperation in Europe
MEP	Member of the European Parliament
MOU	Memorandum of Understanding
MPEPIL	Max Planck Encyclopedia of Public International Law
NATO	North Atlantic Treaty Organisation
NGO	Non-governmental organisation
NHRIs	National human rights institutions
NYIL	Netherlands Yearbook of International Law
OAS	Organization of American States
OCEEA	Office of the Co-ordinator of OSCE Economic and Environmental Activities
ODIHR	Office for Democratic Institutions and Human Rights
OHCHR	Office of the United Nations High Commissioner for Human Rights
OM	Observer Mission
OMiK	Organization for Security and Co-operation in Europe, Mission in Kosovo
OSCE	Organization for Security and Co-operation in Europe
OSCE PA	Parliamentary Assembly of the Organization for Security and Co-operation in Europe
OSZE	German abbreviation for Organization for Security and Co-operation in Europe (Organization für Sicherheit und Zusammenarbeit in Europa), see also OSCE
OTAN	French abbreviation for the North Atlantic Treaty Organization (Organisation du Traité de l'Atlantique Nord), see also NATO
PC	Permanent Council of the Organization for Security and Cooperation in Europe
PCIJ	Permanent Court of International Justice
PEMSEA	Partnerships in Environmental Management for the Seas of East Asia
pt.	part

REC	The Regional Centre for Central and Eastern Europe
SFRY	Socialist Federal Republic of Yugoslavia
SMM	Special Monitoring Mission
TEU	Treaty on European Union
TFEU	Treaty on the Functioning of the European Union
UAV	unmanned aerial vehicle
UK	United Kingdom of Great Britain and Northern Ireland
UN	United Nations
UNC	United Nations Charter
UNDP	United Nations Development Programme
UNECE	United Nations Economic Commission for Europe
UNEP	United Nations Environmental Programme
UNFCCC	United Nations Framework Convention on Climate Change
UNGA	United Nations General Assembly
UNHCR	United Nations High Commissioner for Refugees
UNJYB	The United Nations Juridical Yearbook
UNMIK	United Nations Interim Administration Mission in Kosovo
UNODC	United Nations Office on Drugs and Crime
UNPROFOR	United Nations Protection Force
UNSC	United Nations Security Council
UNSG	United Nations Secretary-General
UNTS	United Nations Treaty Series
USA	United States of America
VAT	Value-added tax
VCCR	Vienna Convention on Consular Relations of 1963
VCDR	Vienna Convention on Diplomatic Relations of 1961
VCLT	Vienna Convention on the Law of Treaties
WHO	World Health Organization
WP	Working Paper
WTO	World Trade Organization
ZaöRV	Zeitschrift für ausländisches öffentliches Recht und Völkerrecht (also named Heidelberg Journal of International Law)

PART I

INTRODUCTION

1

Legal Uncertainty and Indeterminacy: Immutable Characteristics of the OSCE?

Carolyn Moser and Anne Peters

1 NEW OPERATIONAL DYNAMISM FACING OLD LEGAL CONSTRAINTS: INSIGHTS FROM THE UKRAINE CRISIS

After having sat as a backbencher behind NATO and the EU for some years, the Ukraine crisis catapulted the Organization for Security and Co-operation in Europe (OSCE) again to the first row of European security players. When the crisis reached its height in early 2014, the OSCE seemed to be the forum of last resort for political dialogue, and the only entity capable of mediating between the conflict parties, including on the ground. In a remarkable decision of 21 March 2014, the Permanent Council – the principal decision-making body of the Organization for day-to-day business, comprising all fifty-seven participating States – agreed by consensus to launch a civilian Special Monitoring Mission (SMM) in Ukraine upon request of the Ukrainian government.[1] Under the principles of impartiality and transparency, the ongoing field operation in Ukraine is to contribute to 'reducing tensions and fostering peace, stability and security; and to monitoring and supporting the implementation of all OSCE principles and commitments'.[2] The operation's mandate underlines that, in the wake of the Ukraine crisis, the Organization has advanced from a supporting actor to one of the main players safeguarding European security.

Besides the field operation in Ukraine, which received much media attention, the OSCE covers a broad thematic and operational spectrum: from Vancouver to Vladivostok, the Organization's participating States work together on security issues, undertake joint economic and environmental efforts and develop common initiatives on human rights matters. Illustrative of the Organization's operational variety are selected field operations,

[1] OSCE, Permanent Council, Decision on Deployment of an OSCE Special Monitoring Mission to Ukraine, PC.DEC/1117, 21 March 2014.

[2] Ibid., para. 2.

programmes and projects. The ongoing OSCE Mission in Kosovo, for instance, is engaged in monitoring as well as in the promotion and support of human rights and democratic institutions, including training for police officers on curbing trafficking in human beings. Likewise, the OSCE Programme Offices in Astana (Kazakhstan) and Bishkek (Kyrgyzstan) both contribute to combatting corruption by organising, for example, workshops on law enforcement matters related to drug trafficking linked to the use of cryptocurrencies. Moreover, cyber security issues are discussed, inter alia during a sub-regional conference on the role of information and communication technologies in regional and international security in Tashkent (Uzbekistan). What is more, OSCE election observers regularly ensure that legislative processes and elections in participating States respect fundamental legal and democratic standards. One can add to this already impressive, but non-exhaustive, enumeration of OSCE activities the annually held Economic and Environmental Forum, last in September 2018 in Prague, dealing with 'Promoting economic progress and security in the OSCE area through innovation, human capital development, and good public and corporate governance'.

This multifaceted, pan-European OSCE cooperation, which is remarkable both in terms of geographic span and thematic breadth, started during the Cold War as a *détente*-effort. The aim was to build an East–West forum for political dialogue. Informal consultations paved the way for intensive exchanges of views in the framework of the Conference for Security and Co-operation in Europe (CSCE). At the end of two years of vivid debate and negotiation in Geneva, all thirty-five participating governments signed the final conference act, namely the Helsinki Final Act (1975).[3] The Act covered a large array of policy issues under so-called 'baskets': three substantive baskets addressed respectively politico-military affairs, economic and environmental issues and human rights matters, and the fourth basket dealt with follow-up meetings and implementation procedures. Indeed, regular diplomatic encounters succeeded the Helsinki meeting to uphold the East–West dialogue.[4] After the fall of the Berlin Wall, participating States decided to call a halt to this nomadic mode of functioning and endowed the CSCE with permanent structures when adopting the Charter of Paris (1990).[5] In particular, the Secretariat in Vienna was established as the bureaucratic

[3] CSCE, Helsinki Final Act, 1 August 1975, available at: www.osce.org/helsinki-final-act?download=true.

[4] Conferences were held in Belgrade (1977–8), Madrid (1980–3), Stockholm (1984–6) and Vienna (1986–9).

[5] CSCE, Charter of Paris for a New Europe, 21 November 1990, available at www.osce.org/mc/39516?download=true.

centrepiece of the institution. Some years later, the CSCE was renamed as the OSCE in the Budapest decision of 1994 – the conference became an organisation, at least by name.[6]

Over the years, the Organization has come to be a polyvalent European security actor. The OSCE serves as an intergovernmental platform for political dialogue and constitutes a transnational expertise hub for rule of law and human right issues; simultaneously, the Organization performs early warning tasks and sends numerous peacekeeping and peacebuilding missions to crisis zones, such as the previously mentioned Special Monitoring Mission in Ukraine. These plentiful activities are prepared and implemented by a variety of actors. In addition to the Secretariat in Vienna, established in 1990, there are three further OSCE institutions, namely the Office for Democratic Institutions and Human Rights (ODIHR) located in Warsaw, the High Commissioner on National Minorities (HCNM) based in The Hague and the Representative on Freedom of the Media (equally situated in Vienna). All in all, some 3,500 staff currently work for the OSCE: approximately 600 persons are active in the Secretariat and the three OSCE institutions, and an additional 2,900 experts are deployed in the Organization's sixteen field operations in South-Eastern Europe, Eastern Europe, the South Caucasus and Central Asia.[7] Furthermore, the OSCE family includes the OSCE Parliamentary Assembly, an autonomous interparliamentary body whose secretariat is situated in Copenhagen, and the Geneva-based Court of Conciliation and Arbitration (which has, so far, not become active).[8]

This institutional edifice and operational dynamism of different OSCE entities rests on shaky legal foundations. The practical implications thereof became significant in the Ukrainian context. Backed up by the Permanent Council decision of March 2014, staff began to operate on the ground shortly thereafter – but outside a clear legal framework. Indeed, the Memorandum of Understanding between the OSCE and the government in Kiev, determining inter alia the mandate and legal status of the mission and the privileges as well as immunities granted to the mission and its members, took some time to be concluded and to enter into force.[9] In the meantime – a period of twelve

6 CSCE, *Towards a Genuine Partnership in a New Era*, Budapest Decisions attached to the Budapest Document, 21 December 1994, available at: www.osce.org/mc/39554?download=true, point 29.

7 OSCE, 'Factsheet: What Is the OSCE?', 21 September 2018, available at: www.osce.org/whatistheosce/factsheet.

8 The Court was established in 1995 on the basis of the Convention on Conciliation and Arbitration within the OSCE of 15 December 1992, available at: www.osce.org/cca/111409.

9 The Memorandum of Understanding was signed on 14 April 2014 and ratified by the Ukrainian parliament on 29 May 2014, before entering into force on 13 June 2014.

weeks – the mission and its members were exposed to legal uncertainty, especially as regards their privileges and immunities. Thus, the deployed individuals took up their functions at risk of lacking legal protection. Very soon, this precarious situation would become problematic when several OSCE observers were abducted and held hostage by armed insurgents.[10] What was the legal status of OSCE observers in Ukraine in the absence of a bilateral agreement with Kiev? Were they entitled to (functional) immunity without any concluded Memorandum of Understanding? And who would pay for possible damages or injuries? These pressing questions resuscitated an age-old debate regarding the unsettled legal status of the OSCE.

2 OPERATING WITHIN A PATCHY LEGAL ENVIRONMENT

The legal status debate relates to several intertwined issues. First, the *legal nature* of the Organization is debated. The OSCE considers itself a 'regional arrangement' in the sense of Chapter VIII of the United Nations Charter (UNC), that is a regional peace and security actor.[11] Yet, the precise nature of the OSCE under public international law is unclear.

Generally, legal definitions of an international organisation – in the sense of a *public* international organisation – comprise two central elements. First, an international organisation is based on a constitutive act governed by international law concluded between one or more subjects of international law – usually states – which consciously decide to establish a forum of cooperation and coordination for a designated purpose. Secondly, an international organisation is vested with a functioning infrastructure – that is a seat, bodies (e.g. permanent secretariat, plenary and executive organs) and budgetary means – which are separate from the organisation's members.[12] Classic definitions additionally highlight that the entity must be capable of forming a will distinct from

[10] See, for instance, *BBC*, 'Ukraine Unrest: Abducted OSCE Observers Freed' (3 May 2014), available at: www.bbc.com/news/world-europe-27265927.

[11] Article 52(1) of the Charter of the United Nations, adopted 26 June 1945, 1 UNTS 16 (Chapter VIII) reads as follows: 'Nothing in the present Charter precludes the existence of regional arrangements or agencies for dealing with such matters relating to the maintenance of international peace and security as are appropriate for regional action provided that such arrangements or agencies and their activities are consistent with the Purposes and Principles of the United Nations.' The Budapest Summit Declaration (CSCE, 1994) (n. 6) qualified the OSCE as a 'security structure' (paragraph 3) and, more precisely, as a 'regional arrangement under Chapter VII of the United Nations Charter' (paragraph 26 of Annex I to the Declaration).

[12] See, e.g., Ruffert and Walter, *Institutionalised International Law*, 5; Archer, *International Organizations*, 31.

that of its member states ('*volonté distincte*').[13] This latter element echoes the nineteenth century doctrine on moral (legal) persons. While it remains obscure what 'will' exactly means, it seems to be a placeholder for legal personality.[14] Along these lines, some contemporary legal texts qualify an entity as an international organisation in the proper (legal) sense only if it possesses international legal personality.[15] The International Law Commission's Articles on the responsibility of international organisations are a case in point.[16] The narrow conception of international organisation makes sense for the purpose of assigning legal rights, legal duties and legal responsibility. The OSCE as it stands would prima facie not be an international organisation in that narrow legal sense. However, most legal scholars seem to espouse a broader conception of international organisation, even for a legal context, which encompasses entities that do not enjoy international legal personality. In other words, there are two types of international organisations: those with and those without international legal personality.[17] From that perspective, the OSCE could potentially qualify as an international organisation.

While the OSCE possesses many of the attributes normally ascribed to an international organisation – permanent headquarters and decision-making bodies; standing implementation structures and staff; financial resources – it lacks a fundamental normative characteristic: the OSCE has no legal constitutive act under international law. This absence of a constitutive treaty is no coincidence. To the contrary, 'the institutional ambivalence is built-in design'.[18] Indeed, all major OSCE documents – namely the Helsinki Final Act (1975), the Charter of Paris (1990) and the Summit Documents of Helsinki (1992) as well as Budapest (1994) – explicitly exclude the said documents from being registered at the UN Secretariat as international treaties according to Article 102 UNC.[19] These foundational documents, which set out the

13 Schermers and Blokker, *International Institutional Law*, 37; Charpentier and Sierpinski, *Institutions internationales*, 52; Schmalenbach, MPEPIL, para. 3; Klabbers, 'Formal Intergovernmental Organizations', 143–4.

14 Cf. Akande, 'International Organizations', 250.

15 Salmon, 'Organisation internationale gouvernementale', 793; Sands and Klein, *Bowett's Law of International Institutions*, 15.

16 'The term "international organization" refers to an organization established by a treaty or other instrument governed by international law and possessing its own international legal personality. International organizations may include as members, in addition to States, other entities' (Art. 2 lit. a ARIO, Yearbook of the International Law Commission [2011] vol. II, pt. 2).

17 Lagrange, 'La catégorie "Organisation internationale"', para. 86; White, *International Organisations*, 9.

18 Klabbers, 'Institutional Ambivalence by Design', 403, 408.

19 All documents stipulate that '[t]he Government of the [country hosting the respective conference or event] is requested to transmit to the Secretary-General of the United Nations the

institutional landscape and regulate the operational realities of the Organization, are referred to as politically but not legally binding.[20] And the same holds true for decisions and documents emanating from the OSCE: regardless of their addressee(s) being internal or external, they are regarded as political commitments deprived of legal bindingness. The Rules of Procedure of the Organization clearly stipulate that OSCE decisions and documents adopted by consensus by any OSCE decision-making body shall have a politically – in contrast to legally – binding character for the participating States.[21] As a matter of fact, the only two texts originating from the work of the OSCE having acquired the status of an international treaty are the Convention on Conciliation and Arbitration (1992) and the Treaty on Conventional Armed Forces (1990) – and neither of them is considered to be an OSCE document.[22] This intricate and ambivalent legal situation leads some legal scholars to conclude that the OSCE is a fully fledged international organisation,[23] while others describe the OSCE as an international organisation *in statu nascendi*[24] – in a perpetuated *statu nascendi*, one could add. Different authors again qualify the Organization as a 'soft organisation', meaning that it is based on soft law.[25] Finally, the OSCE is often regarded as a loose cooperation framework based on political commitments.[26] The Organization's international legal nature and status is thus controversial.

text of this [document], which is not eligible for registration under Article 102 of the Charter of the United Nations, with a view to its circulation to all the members of the Organization as an official document of the United Nations'. See the final provisions of the Helsinki Final Act 1 August 1975 (n. 3); final provisions of the Charter of Paris, 1990 (n. 5); para. 46 of the Helsinki Document 1992: The Challenges of Change, Helsinki Summit Declaration, 10–11 July 1992; para. 22 of the Budapest Summit Declaration, 1994 (n. 6).

20 OSCE, Chairmanship, Report to the Ministerial Council on Strengthening the Legal Framework of the OSCE in 2015, 1 December 2015, available at: www.osce.org/cio/205221, para. 2. See further OSCE, Panel of Eminent Persons, 'Final Report and Recommendations of the Panel of Eminent Persons on the Strengthening the Effectiveness of the OSCE, Common Purpose – Towards a More Effective OSCE', 27 June 2005, available at: https://www.osce.org/cio/15805, 30.b.

21 OSCE, Ministerial Council, Rules of Procedure of the Organization for Security and Co-operation in Europe, MC.DOC/1/06, 1 November 2006, pt. II (A) paras. 1 and 3.

22 See Fastenrath and Weigelt, 'Organization for Security and Co-operation in Europe (OSCE)', para. 35.

23 Sands and Klein, *Bowett's Law of International Institutions*, 203.

24 Schweisfurth, 'Die juristische Mutation der KSZE', 228.

25 Klabbers, 'Institutional Ambivalence by Design', 405; Seidl-Hohenveldern, 'Internationale Organisationen aufgrund von soft law', 239.

26 Manton, 'The OSCE Human Dimension and Customary International Law Formation', 197–8.

3 THE TRIAD OF INTERNATIONAL LEGAL PERSONALITY, DOMESTIC LEGAL CAPACITY AND PRIVILEGES AND IMMUNITIES

Closely tied to the open issue of the OSCE's legal–institutional nature is the conceptual triad regarding the Organization's international legal personality, domestic legal capacity and its privileges and immunities. This triad forms the title of the 'Draft Convention on the International Legal Personality, Legal Capacity, and Privileges and Immunities of the OSCE' of 2007.[27] As the OSCE-related documents have since 2000 conceptualised the issues along this triad, we shall briefly examine the three concepts.[28]

3.1 *International Legal Personality*

In international law, the concept of international legal personality is messy,[29] and the classifications and distinctions employed by legal scholars are not uniform.[30] In this chapter, we use the term 'international (legal) person' synonymously and interchangeably with 'subject of international law', in line with the case law of the International Court of Justice (ICJ).[31] By international legal personality (subjecthood) we understand the potential of an actor (e.g. the OSCE) to be a holder of international rights and duties. International legal personality precedes the ownership of rights and duties. Put differently, the attribution of a concrete right (e.g. arising from a treaty) or of an obligation to an actor implies as a precondition that the actor has international legal personality in the first place. While procedural powers and

27 Draft Convention on the International Legal Personality, Legal Capacity, and Privileges and Immunities of the OSCE, Annex to MC.DD/28/07, 29 November 2007.

28 See, for the shift of focus of codification proposals from the concepts 2 and 3 (domestic legal capacity and privileges and immunities) to concept 1 (international legal personality) in the reform debate, below text with note 51.

29 See for an excellent analysis Portmann, *Legal Personality in International Law*.

30 Other contributions to the book partly apply slightly differing terms, and these are explained by each author. For example, Blokker and Wessel put forward that 'legal personality concerns a *quality*, whereas legal capacity is an *asset*'. See Chapter 7 by Blokker and Wessel, 'Revisiting Questions of Organisationhood, Legal Personality and Membership in the OSCE: The Interplay between Law, Politics and Practice', in this Volume.

31 In its *Reparation for Injuries* Advisory Opinion, the ICJ equated the terms 'international person' and 'subject of international law' (ICJ, *Reparation for Injuries Suffered in the Service of the United Nations*, Advisory Opinion, ICJ Reports 1949, 174, 179). In contrast, older literature frequently distinguished between international legal subject and international legal personality (legal person). 'Legal person' was often used to designate a broader group of entities, while the quality of being an international legal subject was defined more narrowly and was limited to States.

lawmaking powers do not automatically flow from international legal personality, they cannot exist without the latter. In that way, the international legal personality (or subjecthood) of an actor is an empty legal vessel which is however the basis and legal precondition for acting under international law.[32]

What does the above imply for the OSCE and international legal personality? The Organization lacks an established international legal personality: it is nowhere explicitly qualified by its participating States as an international legal person (subject). There is also no authoritative decision which would have, in the style of the ICJ's Advisory Opinion *Reparations for Injuries* on the UN,[33] recognised an implied international legal personality of the OSCE. Therefore, the OSCE does not exist under international law as an entity which is *legally* distinct from (the sum) of its participating States, or which enjoys rights and is saddled with duties.

International legal personality does not say much about the real legal position of a concrete entity, for various reasons. First, the recognition of international legal personality does not automatically generate specific, concrete rights (e.g. a right to enter into diplomatic relations). Put differently, the personality must be filled by specific rights and/or duties, but is not constituted by them.[34] Secondly, we need to distinguish between having substantive rights and possessing the legal power to vindicate those rights before an

32 A. Peters, *Beyond Human Rights*, 58–9. See for a similar understanding Blokker and Wessel, 'Revisiting Questions of Organisationhood, Legal Personality and Membership in the OSCE', Chapter 7 in this Volume; Steinbrück Platise, 'Legitimate Governance as a Privilege and Price for the Autonomy of International Organisations', Chapter 14 in this Volume. In contrast, some authors claim that typical substantive rights (or what they sometimes call 'capacities') can be *derived* from international legal personality, especially the right to conclude treaties, the right to establish diplomatic missions, legal liability, and the right to participate in international organisations (e.g., Rama-Montaldo, 'International Legal Personality and Implied Powers of International Organizations', 116, 139–44). The same result emerges from the analytically converse strategy of other authors who qualify only those entities as international legal persons (subjects) that have certain rights or powers (capacities), e.g., the capacity to be held liable, the capacity to enjoy international privileges and immunities, and especially the capacity to conclude treaties (e.g. Dominicé, 'L'émergence de l'individu en droit international public', 122; Tomuschat, 'International Law: Ensuring the Survival of Mankind on the Eve of a New Century', 160). Independently of whether international legal personality defined in this way is considered as a precondition or as a consequence of the enumerated powers or substantive rights, both approaches associate international legal personality with a minimum set of rights or powers.

33 ICJ, *Reparation for Injuries* (n. 31), 179.

34 This is not to say that a person or entity not vested with international legal personality is not required to respect international law or governance standards. See Moser, 'Conceptualising Accountability in the Legal and Institutional Framework of the OSCE', Chapter 13 in this Volume, and Steinbrück Platise, 'Legitimate Governance as a Privilege and Price for the Autonomy of International Organisations', Chapter 14 in this Volume.

(international) court or tribunal or other monitoring body (which implies a legal power to perform procedural legal acts).[35] For example, even if the OSCE were entitled under international law to put together a mission, and a state would obstruct this, the OSCE could not automatically complain about such a legal violation in an international dispute settlement forum. Third, we need to distinguish between possessing rights and being empowered to make law: not every international legal person possesses lawmaking powers.[36] Therefore, international organisations could be considered as international legal persons without treaty-making power. However, customary international law has meanwhile established a presumption of international organisations' treaty-making power.[37] That power is, in the concrete case, defined and limited by the given organisation's law and practice. Moreover, it could be argued that the very *raison d'être* of all international organisations (namely to perform tasks in the common interest of its members) suggests that they need

35 Already the Permanent Court of International Justice held: 'It is scarcely necessary to point out that the capacity to *possess* civil rights does not necessarily imply the capacity to *exercise* those rights oneself.' (PCIJ, *Appeal from a Judgment of the Hungaro/Czecoslovak Mixed Arbitral Tribunal (The Peter Pázmány University* v. *The State of Czechoslovakia)*, Judgment of 15 December 1933, Ser. A/B, No. 61, 208, 231) (emphasis added). See also IACtHR, *Judicial Condition and Human Rights of the Child*, Advisory Opinion No. 17, 28 August 2002, resolutory point no. 1 of the opinion and concurring opinion of Cançado Trindade, paras. 6 and 8, which find that the child is a holder of (human) rights irrespective of the child's capacity to act, i.e., the capacity to exercise those rights. Justice Cançado Trindade in particular distinguished between 'juridical personality' in the sense of 'aptitude to be titulaire of rights and duties' and 'capacity' in the sense of 'aptitude to exercise'. Also in the *LaGrand* case, the ICJ assumed without further ado that the VCCR 'creates individual rights' that can (only) be asserted by the home State before the court. ICJ, *LaGrand Case* (*Germany* v. *United States of America*), ICJ Reports 2001, 466, para. 77. In *Reparations for Injuries* the ICJ had not clearly drawn this distinction. It posed the question of the potential international legal personality of the United Nations as follows: 'whether the Charter has given the Organization such a position that it possesses, in regard to its Members, *rights which it is entitled to ask them to respect*. In other words, does the Organization possess international personality?' (ICJ, *Reparation for Injuries* (n. 31), 178, emphasis added.) So here, the ICJ saw the power to assert own rights as a necessary component of legal personality.

36 For example, a human being is an international person enjoying human rights but does not have the capacity to conclude a peace treaty under international law.

37 See Brölmann, *The Institutional Veil in Public International Law*, 90–4. Under Art. 6 of the Vienna Convention on the Law of Treaties between States and International Organizations or between International Organizations, 21 March 1986 (available at: http://legal.un.org/ilc/texts/instruments/english/conventions/1_2_1986.pdf), which has not (at the time of writing) entered into force, '[t]he capacity of an international organization to conclude treaties is governed by the rules of the organization'. The Convention's preamble notes that 'international organizations possess the capacity to conclude treaties which is necessary for the exercise of their functions and the fulfilment of their purposes'. The 'rules of the organization' which are referred to in Art. 6 VCLT not only include the constituent instruments, but also secondary law and subsequent practice.

a minimum scope of treaty-making power, namely the power to conclude agreements on headquarters, on privileges and immunities and on arbitration. So if the OSCE were recognised as an international organisation endowed with international legal personality, a certain scope of treaty-making power could arguably be presumed.

Concomitantly, the lack of an international legal personality of the OSCE entails various legal consequences. The OSCE does not have the power to make international treaties, it does not have the power to invoke another legal person's responsibility and to bring claims before international bodies, and it cannot incur international legal responsibility. However, even without the power to make formal law (i.e. to conclude a treaty under international law), it may and does create informal law and adopt normative texts whose legal quality – both in terms of nature and effects – is ambiguous.[38]

It is worth mentioning that the OSCE is not the only international institution finding itself in an ambivalent situation regarding its international legal personality: The European Union equally lacked an explicit legal personality prior to the entry into force of the Treaty of Lisbon in 2009.[39] And before the establishment of the WTO in 1995, the GATT was in political terms a stable regime, but it was not managed by any formal institution. It was a treaty which had never entered into force due to the lack of international ratification, and was only 'provisionally' applied on a de facto basis.

3.2 *Domestic Legal Capacity*

The second element of the triad is legal capacity. The Draft Convention of 2007[40] contains an Article 4 on legal capacity: 'The OSCE shall possess such legal capacity as is necessary for the exercise of its functions, including the capacity to contract, to acquire and dispose of movable and immovable property, and to institute and participate in legal proceedings.' This is preceded by Article 3: 'The OSCE shall possess international legal personality.'

The distinction between personality and capacity is perfectly in line with the usages in modern founding instruments of international organisations. Those texts consistently employ the word 'capacity' to denote the status and

[38] See on the OSCE norm-making practice, Boisson de Chazournes and Gadkowski, 'The External Relations the OSCE', Chapter 10 in this Volume, and Herman and Wouters, 'The OSCE as a Case of Informal International Lawmaking?', Chapter 12 in this Volume. An analysis of the EU context is provided by Blokker, 'International Legal Personality of the European Communities and the European Union', 471–83.

[39] See below note 41.

[40] Draft Convention 2007 (n. 27).

powers of the organisation in domestic law. In contrast, they use the word 'personality' to describe the status and powers under international law.[41] The UNC of 1945 only addresses the UN's 'capacity'.[42] In most founding instruments, the word 'capacity' is not explicitly focused on or linked to the domestic legal orders of the member states, but the mentioning of contracts and the acquisition of property shows that the sphere of domestic law is meant – and this is also the case in Article 4 of the Draft Convention of 2007 quoted above.

The legal sphere in which the legal status of an actor unfolds and applies is distinct from the legal 'source' of that status. So the capacity of an international entity within the sphere of domestic law can flow from different sources. It can be regulated in national law, or in international law or in their interplay. For example, the Swiss Host State Act of 2007 is a national law[43] which regulates the domestic capacities of all kind of international legal actors,[44] such as acquisition of property, immunities and privileges, taxation and financial contributions. The Act explicitly states that 'privileges, immunities, facilities,

[41] Agreement establishing the World Trade Organization, 15 April 1994, UNTS Registration No. I-31874, Art. VIII: '1. The WTO shall have *legal personality*, and shall be accorded by each of its Members such *legal capacity* as may be necessary for the exercise of its functions. 2. The WTO shall be accorded by each of its Members such privileges and immunities as are necessary for the exercise of its functions' (emphasis added); Rome Statute of the International Criminal Court17 July 1998, UNTS Registration No. I-38544, Art. 4(1): '1. The Court shall have *international legal personality*. It shall also have such *legal capacity* as may be necessary for the exercise of its functions and the fulfilment of its purposes.' (emphasis added); Treaty on the Functioning of the European Union, 7 June 2016, available at: https://eur-lex.europa.eu/legal-content/EN/TXT/?uri=celex%3A12012E%2FTXT, Art. 335 (Lisbon version 2007): 'In each of the Member States, the Union shall enjoy the most extensive *legal capacity accorded to legal persons under their laws*; it may, in particular, acquire or dispose of movable and immovable property and may be a party to legal proceedings. (...)' (emphasis added). See for the complicated story of provisions on (domestic) legal capacity and international legal personality of the EU (and its precursors: the European Community/Communities, and the European Coal and Steel Community): Blokker, 'International Legal Personality of the European Communities and the European Union'. The international legal status of the EU (founded in 1992) under international law was codified only in 2007. Consolidated version of the Treaty on European Union, 7 February 1992, 1757 UNTS I- 30615, Art. 47 says: 'The Union shall have legal personality.' This provision was inserted only with the latest ('Lisbon') treaty revision of 13 December 2007 which entered into force on 1 December 2009.

[42] Art. 104 UN Charter (n. 11): 'The Organization shall enjoy in the territory of each of its Members such legal *capacity* as may be necessary for the exercise of its functions and the fulfilment of its purposes' (emphasis added).

[43] Switzerland, Federal Act on the Privileges, Immunities and Facilities and the Financial Subsidies granted by Switzerland as a Host State of 22 June 2007, RS 192.12.

[44] Ibid. Art. 2 of the Act states: 'The Confederation may grant privileges, immunities and facilities to the following institutional beneficiaries: a. intergovernmental organisations; b. international institutions; c. quasi-quasi-governmental international organisations'.

and financial subsidies arising under international law ... are unaffected' (Article 1 sentence 2, Host State Act). Unlike the Swiss Act, domestic arrangements can be specifically tailored to accommodate a particular organisation or entity. For example, in 2017, Austria replaced its legislation by a headquarters agreement with the OSCE on the legal status of OSCE institutions in Vienna.[45] The drawback of purely national or bilateral regulation (e.g. an agreement only between one participating State and the OSCE) is of course that the domestic capacities of one and the same international actor will differ in the various domestic legal orders, and potentially unfairly uneven treatment might result. This is the reason for the quest to harmonise the domestic legal status, either through similar or identical domestic laws, or by a multilateral international instrument. The state parties of that international instrument commit themselves to accord domestic capacities, as specified in the international instrument, by ratifying it.[46] They must then implement this commitment in their domestic laws.

An entity can be deprived of international personality, but enjoy domestic legal capacity. An interesting example is the scheme of international legal personality as opposed to domestic (or internal) legal capacity underpinning the civilian missions conducted by the European Union under the Common Security and Defence Policy. The EU enjoys international legal personality (Article 47 TEU), and can thus conclude Status of Mission Agreements with the respective host states, on whose basis civilian missions are deployed. In contrast to other EU entities (especially agencies[47]), civilian missions are but diplomatic missions which exercise the functions mentioned in Article 3 of the Vienna Convention on Diplomatic Relations.[48] Within the

45 Agreement between the Republic of Austria and the OSCE regarding the Headquarters of the Organization for Security and Co-operation in Europe, 14 June 2017, available at: https://www.ris.bka.gv.at/Dokumente/BgblAuth/BGBLA_2018_III_84/COO_2026_100_2_1531327.pdfsig.

46 See for example the provisions related to the WTO or the UN quoted in notes 41 and 42.

47 EU agencies are distinct legal entities endowed with legal personality. The founding documents of these agencies often leave the nature of the legal personality – domestic or international – undefined (e.g. European Aviation Safety Agency, the EU's law enforcement agency 'Europol', and Frontex, the EU Agency for the Management of Operational Cooperation at the External Borders of the Member States of the European Union). On this issue, see Blokker, 'International Legal Personality of the European Communities and the European Union', 480–2. In-depth analyses of the nature of (international) agreements concluded by these agencies bring to the fore that their legal personality is *domestic*, and that international treaty-making power (presupposing international legal personality) continues to rest with the Union, as does international legal responsibility. On this point, see Coman-Kund, The International Dimension of the EU Agencies: Framing a Growing Legal–Institutional Phenomenon.

48 Vienna Convention on Diplomatic Relations, 18 April 1961, 500 UNTS 95.

international law framework set out by the respective Status of Mission Agreement, civilian missions possess legal capacity. Indeed, from 2014 onwards, civilian missions have been endowed with the capacity 'to procure services and supplies, enter into contracts and administrative arrangements, employ staff, hold bank accounts, acquire and dispose of assets, discharge its liabilities and be a party to legal proceedings'.[49] As for many other EU documents dealing with legal personality and capacity questions, the drafters have left the nature of the capacity undetermined (international or domestic).[50] But it can be assumed that the legal capacity of civilian missions is above all domestic – unfolding in the legal orders of the host state. It probably also includes the capacity to appear before the Court of Justice of the European Union (but not necessarily before other international courts), because the entire EU legal order is viewed by the texts as an internal legal order separate from public international law.

So, what is the legal capacity of the OSCE and its institutions or field operations? Explicit and unequivocal rules are lacking. In 1993, a decision of the Ministerial Council held in Rome – the 'Rome Decision' – recommended to the participating States that they accord legal capacity to CSCE institutions 'subject to their constitutional, legislative and related requirements' – that meant at the national level.[51] (This was before the rebranding of the entity as OSCE by the Budapest decision of 1994.)[52] The recommendation was thus – already in 1993 – to grant domestic (in contrast to international) legal capacity to CSCE (OSCE) structures – and no mention was made of offering such capacity to the entity as such.[53] This shows that the (then CSCE's) OSCE's

49 This is the standard formulation in mission mandates regarding the provisions on 'legal arrangements'.

50 Blokker, 'International Legal Personality of the European Communities and the European Union', 474. However, Art. 335 TEU, for the EU as a whole, makes explicit that the term 'capacity' relates to the domestic law of the member states (see the wording of the provision).

51 CSCE, Fourth Meeting of the Council, CSCE and the New Europe – Our Security is Indivisible, Decisions of the Rome Council Meeting, CSCE/4-C/Dec.2, 1 December 1993, Annex 1 to Annex A, Provisions concerning the Legal Capacity of the CSCE Institutions and Privileges and Immunities. The stipulations on the *legal capacity* of the CSCE institutions reads as follows: 'The CSCE participating States will, subject to their constitutional, legislative and related requirements, confer such legal capacity as is necessary for the exercise of their functions, and in particular the capacity to contract, to acquire and dispose of movable and immovable property, and to institute and participate in legal proceedings, on the following CSCE institutions: The CSCE Secretariat; The Office for Democratic Institutions and Human Rights (ODIHR); Any other CSCE institution determined by the CSCE Council.'

52 See CSCE, Budapest Summit Declaration, 1994 (n. 6).

53 OSCE, Permanent Council, Decision No. 383: Report on OSCE Legal Capacity and on Privileges and Immunities to the Ministerial Council, PC.DEC/383, 26 November 2000, para. 14.

non-existence under international law does not prevent it from being granted legal capacity at the domestic level. In other words, the fact that the international legal personality of the OSCE has not been explicitly established does not per se hinder it – both in theory and practice – from performing legal acts (e.g. entering a contractual relation) vis-à-vis national institutions (and even international institutions). These acts might have a legal value (e.g. as sales or rent contracts under the domestic law of a hosting state, or as a detached 'transnationalised' contract) – without these legal acts being public international law instruments proper.

3.3 *Privileges and Immunities*

This brings us to the third element of the triad. In the absence of a unified international legal personality, the legal status of the OSCE and its members of staff depends on domestic law or, more precisely, on a patchwork of national legal regimes of various states.[54] Hence, it is in and through arrangements with states that the Organization's status, including privileges and immunities, is determined: next to national laws and bilateral agreements for standing OSCE institutions and bodies, Memoranda of Understanding are signed ad hoc with host states of field operations (but not always ratified).[55] Consequently, the OSCE operates within a fragmented legal framework consisting of varying national legal regimes and of diverse types of instruments. The regimes and instruments relate (1) to its permanent institutional structures (such as the Secretariat or the ODIHR; permanent missions of participating States to the OSCE), (2) to OSCE field operations and (3) to individuals (both to representatives of participating States working with or for the OSCE and to OSCE staff working at the Vienna Headquarters and in the field). This eclectic legal situation persists notwithstanding the abovementioned Rome Decision of 1993 which recommended to the participating States to confer – in accordance with their own legal order – privileges and immunities to enumerated CSCE institutions,[56] again not to the entity as such.[57]

54 See the careful assessment by Pingel, 'Privileges and Immunities of the OSCE', Chapter 9 in this Volume.

55 Simonet and Lübner, 'The OSCE and Its Legal Status', 293.

56 CSCE, Rome Decision, 1993 (n. 51). The section on *privileges and immunities* states that '[t]he CSCE participating States will, subject to their constitutional, legislative and related requirements, confer the privileges and immunities as set out in paragraphs 4–16 below [that is to OSCE institutions; to the permanent missions of the participating States; to the representatives of participating States; to the OSCE officials; and to the members of OSCE missions]'.

57 OSCE, Permanent Council, 'Report on OSCE Legal Capacity and on Privileges and Immunities to the Ministerial Council', 26 November 2000 (n. 53), para. 14.

The core issue of the triad of international legal personality, legal capacity and privileges and immunities is the legal uncertainty and the missing legal predictability – for the institution, for its staff members and for third parties – due to a legal patchwork of applicable regimes and arrangements which, in turn, results from lacking codification. This legal eclecticism can have severe negative consequences in and for practice. That problem has motivated attempts for formalisation to which we now turn.

4 OPTIONS FOR FORMALISATION

Historically, the three elements of the triad examined in the last section have received different degrees of attention. Initial efforts to revisit the legal status of the OSCE (then CSCE) focused on granting the Organization and/or its structures legal capacity and privileges and immunities (at the domestic level). Only from the mid-2000s onward, the quest for international legal personality was added to the quest for domestic legal capacity.[58] Since then, international legal personality has become the central issue of discussions (somehow superseding the quest for domestic legal capacity). Despite many formalisation attempts undertaken since the early 1990s, no consensus could be reached on the matter until the present day. The OSCE continues to lack a clearly established international legal personality and, moreover, a uniform regime regarding its legal capacity and privileges and immunities in participating States.

As regards further formalisation options, a deadlock is deeply entrenched: while some participating States (including the USA) favour the adoption of a convention on the international legal personality, legal capacity and privileges and immunities (as drafted in 2007),[59] other participating States (notably Russia)[60] insist on the

58 Compare, for instance, the CSCE, Rome Decision, 1993 (n. 51); the OSCE, Permanent Council, Report on OSCE Legal Capacity and on Privileges and Immunities to the Ministerial Council, 26 November 2000 (n. 53) – advocating for legal capacity and privileges and immunities only – and the Draft Convention 2007 (n. 27).

59 OSCE, Ministerial Council, Draft Convention on the International Legal Personality, Legal Capacity, and Privileges and Immunities of the OSCE, MC.DD/28/07, 29 November 2007, Annex. As for *legal personality*, article 3 of the said Draft Convention stipulates that '[t]he OSCE shall possess international legal personality'. Article 4 on *legal capacity* reads as follows: 'The OSCE shall possess such legal capacity as is necessary for the exercise of its functions, including the capacity to contract, to acquire and dispose of movable and immovable property, and to institute and participate in legal proceedings.'

60 See the interpretative statement under paragraph IV.1(A)6 of the OSCE, Rules of Procedure of the OSCE, MC.DEC/4/08, 2 December 2006. Reference is made to the Draft Charter, PC. DEL/897/07, 18 September 2007, proposed by the delegations of the Republic of Armenia, the Republic of Belarus, the Republic of Kazakhstan, the Kyrgyz Republic, the Russian Federation, the Republic of Tajikistan and the Republic of Uzbekistan.

adoption of a constituent treaty (a 'Charter of the OSCE'), as likewise drafted in 2007.[61]

The core of the discord is not the *objective* to be achieved – legal certainty and predictability – but the *means* to achieve this objective. The convention option as supported by EU states and now also favoured by the USA is limited to formalising the triad of legal aspects: namely international legal personality, domestic legal capacity and privileges and immunities. The scope of the competing Russian solution, a charter, is much broader. It implies the codification of the OSCE itself, including its objective, mandate, institutions and procedures. While the USA had given up its initial resistance to a draft convention, it still vehemently opposes codifying OSCE business beyond the three issues of legal personality, legal capacity and privileges and immunities.[62] The underlying fear is twofold. First, formalisation could change the nature of the OSCE framework – turning it from a politically to a legally binding framework. And secondly, codification could contribute to diluting existing commitments by the states, so that formalisation would lead to fewer obligations than the current informal arrangements entail. In opposition to this stance, the Russian Federation (together with some others states) inter alia bolsters its quest for an OSCE Charter with the argument that the Russian constitution would not allow the conferral of international legal personality and privileges as well as immunities to an (international) entity lacking a constitutive treaty (a charter).[63] The problem that other states see in the adoption of a constitutive treaty is that the development of the Organization's mandate and commitments which has, until now, been dynamic, could be cemented – thus leaving much less institutional and operational flexibility in the future.[64]

Against the backdrop of these conflicting positions, the alarming abduction of OSCE observers in Ukraine revived expectations within the Organization and among some participating States that the OSCE would eventually be granted international legal personality. This, it was believed, would facilitate the implementation of OSCE field operations and the overall functioning of the Organization. Indeed, formalisation efforts have been pursued in the past

61 OSCE, Permanent Council, Draft decision on the charter of the OSCE, PC.DEL/897/07, 18 September 2007, introduced in the Permanent Council on 18 May 2007 (PC.DEL/444/07).

62 See Tichy, 'The Role of the Participating States in Reforming the Legal Framework of the OSCE – Past Developments, Status Quo and Future Ambitions', Chapter 4 in this Volume. For further analysis, see Simonet and Lüber, 'The OSCE and Its Legal Status', 287.

63 On this point, see Bogush, 'Domestic Implications of the OSCE Legal Personality under the Russian Constitutional Law', Chapter 6 in this Volume.

64 I. Peters, 'Legitimacy and International Organizations – The Case of the OSCE', 204–6.

in a belief that endowing the OSCE with international legal personality and providing a uniform regime of privileges and immunities would ensure a coherent legal status and the necessary legal protection for the Organization and its staff, both in the Vienna Headquarters and in field operations.[65] International legal personality was also expected to facilitate the relations of the OSCE with both domestic and international public and private actors, therefore improving the Organization's effectiveness and contributing towards greater legal certainty.

Formalisation comes, however, at a risk.[66] So far, (hard) international law has consciously been kept at a safe distance from the Organization and its activities, apparently based on the assumption that 'to withhold [the OSCE] from the workings of international law would somehow contribute to the efficiency or effectiveness (or both) of its work'.[67] Precisely because the OSCE is seen by participating States as a political forum giving rise to politically – instead of legally – binding solutions, the Organization offers a platform for diplomatic encounters and political dialogue. Participating States can discuss sensitive topics and make (political) concessions on certain matters in the OSCE context without losing their face at home because decisions are said to be political and deprived of legal bindingness – implying that these decisions are felt to be less constraining. The consensual decision to deploy OSCE observers to Ukraine is a perfect case in point: despite their diverging points of view, Russia, all EU member states and the USA could agree in the OSCE context to deploy a monitoring mission to Ukraine. Formalisation bears the risk of tightening the legal and institutional framework of the OSCE from which the Organization has derived much credit and strength in the past.[68] Yet, the current informality generates much insecurity. There is thus an inherent tension between institutional flexibility, on the one hand, and legal certainty on the other hand.

65 See, on this point, Tabassi, 'The Role of the Organisation in Asserting Legal Personality: The Position of the OSCE Secretariat on the OSCE's Legal Status', Chapter 3 in this Volume, and Tichy, 'The Role of the Participating States in Reforming the Legal Framework of the OSCE – Past Developments, Status Quo and Future Ambitions', Chapter 4 in this Volume.

66 On the potential risks of formalisation, see Börzel and I. Peters, '"It's Politics, Stupid": An International Relations Perspective on Strengthening the Legal Framework of the OSCE', Chapter 5 in this Volume.

67 Klabbers, 'Institutional Ambivalence by Design', 408.

68 On the incremental development and (potential) reform of the legal–institutional framework of the OSCE, see Nünlist and Hakkarainen, 'Political Dynamics and Institutional Reforms in the OSCE', Chapter 2 in this Volume.

5 AIM AND CONTENT OF THE BOOK

Taking the observation of an inherent tension between institutional flexibility and legal certainty as a starting point, this book sets out to examine legal and political implications which arise from the OSCE's unsettled legal status. The endeavour is an interdisciplinary one, bringing together legal scholars and International Relations specialists, whose analysis is complemented by insights from practitioners. By tackling both the de jure and de facto aspects of the Organization's current situation, this book seeks to fill a gap in the literature, which currently lacks a thorough scholarly analysis of the questions surrounding the incomplete and fragmented legal framework of the OSCE.[69]

Beyond the crucial interrogation of the merits of the Organization's (in)formality, a range of questions arises as to the causes and consequences of the OSCE's current legal indeterminacy. Some questions deal with political or politicised matters which have repercussions on the legal status of the Organization. What are the interests and arguments of the parties involved? Which dynamics have been and are still at work when it comes to institutional reforms in the OSCE? What is the role of law, politics and practice for the legal status of the OSCE? Are legal uncertainty and indeterminacy perhaps immutable characteristics of the functioning and success of the OSCE? Other – more legal or even legalistic – interrogations circle around international legal personality and domestic legal capacity. On which legal basis can the OSCE's international legal personality rest? In the absence of conventional instruments, has the Organization perhaps already acquired international legal personality by means of customary law? If so, can there be persistent objectors to this customary international legal personality? Furthermore, one can ask how far the OSCE does exist autonomously from its participating States and which legal consequences would result from its possible autonomy. Can the OSCE conclude binding legal instruments with states or international organisations in the absence of a unified international legal personality? Can it do so on the basis of domestic legal capacity? Can such instruments thus be governed fully or in part by international law? And, importantly, which entity is or can be held responsible or liable for damages caused by the OSCE, and under which legal order?

69 Next to a handful of articles on legal status issues published in the OSCE Yearbook, the only comprehensive legal analysis of the matter is contained in an unpublished doctoral thesis by Hélène Cadet, entitled 'Le statut juridique de l'Organisation pour la sécurité et la coopération en Europe' and defended in 2012 at Paris 1 (Sorbonne). It is therefore not astonishing that a recent publication on the OSCE and its personnel makes reference to a number of contributions contained in this edited Volume. See Russo, 'Duty of Care', 2018.

Very similar questions can be addressed from the perspective of a different discipline, in the vocabulary of governance in the international realm: can and does the OSCE craft international rules and standards on the basis of informality? How far does the legal status and institutional design of the OSCE impact on its internal and external accountability? And does a strengthening of the Organization's international legal status necessarily require institutional reforms?

Another set of legal questions relates to the status and legal protection of members of staff. Which legal regime(s) or standards apply concretely when it comes to privileges and immunities of staff? Does the status and protection of individuals working in Headquarters differ from the protection offered to experts deployed to crisis contexts?

Under the title 'The Legal Framework of the OSCE', this book addresses the abovementioned questions in three transversal parts. The first part entails different perspectives on the quest for international legal personality of the OSCE. The first chapter by Christian Nünlist and Petri Hakkarainen underlines that the historical baggage of the OSCE is a crucial factor when discussing potential institutional reforms, including formalisation. They argue that a prerequisite to strengthening the legal framework of the OSCE is to revive the genuine political dialogue within the Organization. Subsequently, Lisa Tabassi portraits the implications of the Organization's current informality in the day-to-day business of the OSCE. Helmut Tichy then goes on to describes the numerous efforts made since the early 1990s to provide the OSCE with an internationally recognised legal personality as well as with internationally recognised privileges and immunities. His contribution does not stop at past developments, but also maps possible future options in this regard. While the chapters of Tabassi and Tichy consider the formalisation of the Organization's legal status as paramount to its (efficient) functioning, the fourth chapter in this part takes a more critical stance on this issue. In their contribution, Tanja Börzel and Ingo Peters argue that the weakening governance performance of the OSCE, which one could witness over the last decade, primarily results from disagreement among participating States over fundamental principles and the strategic role of the Organization, rather than from its uncertain legal status. The part closes with an analysis by Gleb Bogush, whose assessment of Russian constitutional law and case law suggests that the hurdles to the adoption by Russia of a draft convention on the legal status of the OSCE is rather more political than legal in nature.

The second part of the Volume deals with a range of cross-cutting issues tied to the manifestation of the OSCE's current legal position under international law. First, Niels Blokker and Ramses Wessel show that the present legal indeterminacy of the OSCE results from an interplay of law, politics and practice. Considering that the OSCE does not exist or operate in a legal vacuum, they contend that the Organization will sooner or later – despite the attempts of participating State to avoid this situation – be obliged to apply international rules. Then Cedric Ryngaert inquires as to the international law sources impacting on the international legal status of the OSCE. His analysis goes beyond the conventional–customary law debate and extends the discussion to the implications for participating States and the OSCE of the institutional principle of loyal cooperation. In a further chapter, Isabelle Pingel disentangles the panoply of domestic regimes and arrangements providing for privileges and immunities of the OSCE and its members of staff. Next to a study of the chaotic status quo, she assesses how far the adoption of an international treaty on the matter could improve the daily work of the Organization. In their ensuing contribution, Laurence Boisson de Chazournes and Andrzej Gadkowski map the variety of the OSCE's legal ties with other international institutions, states and private entities. They demonstrate that the absence of an established international legal personality has not hindered the OSCE from creating a dense web of external relationships of various types, but also show the limits to the current patchy system. The last chapter of this part, authored by Lorenzo Gasbarri, tackles the issue of international legal responsibility of the OSCE. He examines different options based on various legal personality–legal system constellations. While he argues that some options provide for international legal personality and thus for international legal responsibility of the Organization, others according to him do not.

The third part of the book addresses governance issues related to the legal status of the OSCE. Olivia Herman and Jan Wouters engage in an informal international lawmaking analysis of the OSCE. Their assessment provides for a nuanced picture of the informal nature of the OSCE in terms of process, actors and output formality and confirms that the OSCE is itself an international lawmaker, which in turn raises questions of accountability. Carolyn Moser continues the governance debate by arguing that accountability is crucial for the OSCE – independently of the conferral of international legal personality – not least because of reputational aspects. She contends that the current legal–institutional framework of the OSCE should be further enhanced to provide for more political and administrative accountability of actors both at the strategic and operational level. The third governance-related contribution addresses the topic of autonomy of the OSCE and the legal consequences thereof. Taking a legitimacy stance, Mateja Steinbrück Platise postulates that the capacity to exercise powers autonomously, which can adversely affect individuals and peoples at large, generates expectations towards international institutions such that they will respect core governance standards. Her finding is that these expectations also apply to the OSCE and that, eventually, it is the participating States' obligation to ensure that the Organization abides by certain basis human rights and rule of law standards.

In the fourth and final part of the book, Mateja Steinbrück Platise and Anne Peters revisit all the arguments presented by the authors in their respective chapters and provide conclusive answers to the complex questions surrounding the legal nature and status of the OSCE.

REFERENCES

Akande, Dapo, 'International Organizations', in Malcolm Evans (ed.), *International Law* 4th edn (Oxford: Oxford University Press, 2014), 248–79.

Archer, Clive, *International Organizations* 4th edn (London: Routledge, 2015).

Blokker, Niels, 'International Legal Personality of the European Communities and the European Union: Inspirations from Public International Law', *Yearbook of European Law* 35 (2016), 471–83.

Brölmann, Catherine, *The Institutional Veil in Public International Law: International Organisations and the Law of Treaties* (Oxford: Hart Publishing, 2007).

Charpentier, Jean and Sierpinski, Batyah, *Institutions internationales* 18th edn (Paris: Dalloz, 2012).

Coman-Kund, Florin, 'The International Dimension of the EU Agencies: Framing a Growing Legal–Institutional Phenomenon', *European Foreign Affairs Review* 23 (2018), 97–118.

Dominicé, Christian, 'L'émergence de l'individu en droit international public', in Christian Dominicé, *L'ordre juridique international entre tradition et innovation* (Paris: PUF, 1997), 109–23.

Fastenrath, Ulrich and Weigelt, Katja, 'Organization for Security and Cooperation in Europe (OSCE)', in Rüdiger Wolfrum (ed.), *Max Planck Encyclopedia of Public International Law* VII (Oxford: Oxford University Press, 2012), 1040–55.

Klabbers, Jan, 'Institutional Ambivalence by Design: Soft Organizations in International Law', *Nordic Journal of International Law* 70 (2001), 403–421.

'Formal Intergovernmental Organizations', in Jacob Katz Cogan, Ian Hurd and Ian Johnstone (eds.), *The Oxford Handbook of International Organizations* (Oxford: Oxford University Press, 2016), 132–51.

Lagrange, Evelyne, 'Chapitre 2: La catégorie "Organisation internationale"', in Evelyne Lagrange and Jean-Marc Sorel (eds.), *Droit des organisations internationales* (Paris: LGDJ, 2013), 35–70.

Manton, Eric, 'The OSCE Human Dimension and Customary International Law Formation', in Institute for Peace Research and Security Policy at the University of Hamburg (ed.), *OSCE Yearbook 2005* (Baden-Baden: Nomos Verlagsgesellschaft, 2006), 1–20.

Peters, Anne, *Beyond Human Rights* (Cambridge: Cambridge University Press, 2016).

Peters, Ingo, 'Legitimacy and International Organizations – The Case of the OSCE', in Dominik Zaum (ed.), *Legitimating International Organizations* (Oxford: Oxford University Press, 2013), 196–220.

Portmann, Roland, *Legal Personality in International Law* (Cambridge: Cambridge University Press, 2010).

Rama-Montaldo, Manuel, 'International Legal Personality and Implied Powers of International Organizations', *British Yearbook of International Law* 44 (1970), 111–55.

Ruffert, Matthias and Walter, Christian, *Institutionalised International Law* 2nd edn (Munich: C. H. Beck, 2015).

Russo, Deborah, 'Implementation of the Duty of Care by the OSCE', in Andrea de Guttry, Micaela Frulli, Edoardo Greppi and Chiara Macchi (eds.), *The Duty of Care of International Organizations towards Their Civilian Personnel – Legal Obligations and Implementation Challenges* (The Hague: TMC Asser Press, 2018), 265–292.

Salmon, Jean, 'Organisation internationale gouvernementale', in Jean Salmon (dir.), *Dictonnaire de droit international public* (Brussels: Bruylant, 2001), 793.

Sands, Philippe and Klein, Pierre, *Bowett's Law of International Institutions* 6th edn (London: Sweet and Maxwell, 2001).

Schermers, Henry and Blokker, Nils, *International Institutional Law: Unity within Diversity* 5th edn (Dordrecht: Martinus Nijhoff, 2011).

Schmalenbach, Kirsten, 'International Organizations or Institutions, General Aspects', in Rüdiger Wolfrum (ed.), *Max Planck Encyclopedia of Public International Law* (Oxford: Oxford University Press, 2014), 1126–53.

Schweisfurth, Theodor, 'Die juristische Mutation der KSZE: Eine internationale Organisation in statu nascendi', in Ulrich Beyerlin, Michael Bothe, Rainer Hofmann and Ernst-Ulrich Petersmann (eds.), *Recht zwischen Umbruch und Bewahrung: Festschrift für Rudolf Bernhardt* (Berlin/Heidelberg: Springer, 1995), 213–28.

Seidl-Hohenveldern, Ignaz, 'Internationale Organisationen aufgrund von soft law', in Ulrich Beyerlin, Michael Bothe, Rainer Hofmann and Ernst-Ulrich Petersmann (eds.), *Recht zwischen Umbruch und Bewahrung:*

Festschrift für Rudolf Bernhardt (Berlin/Heidelberg: Springer, 1995), 229–39.

Simonet, Loïc and Lüber, Hans Georg, 'The OSCE and Its Legal Status: Revising the Myth of Sisyphus', in Institute for Peace Research and Security Policy at the University of Hamburg (ed.), *OSCE Yearbook* 2016 (Baden-Baden: Nomos Verlagsgesellschaft, 2017), 277–314.

Tomuschat, Christian, 'International Law: Ensuring the Survival of Mankind on the Eve of a New Century', *Recueil des Cours* 1999, Académie de Droit International de La Haye 281 (The Hague, Boston, London: Martinus Nijhoff Publishing, 2001), 11–438.

White, Nigel D., *The Law of International Organisations* 3rd edn (Manchester: Manchester University Press, 2017).

PART II

THE QUEST FOR INTERNATIONAL LEGAL PERSONALITY

2

Political Dynamics and Institutional Reforms in the OSCE

Christian Nünlist and Petri Hakkarainen

1 INTRODUCTION

Regardless of the outcome, future attempts to revisit the legal status of the OSCE will not happen in a political vacuum. The institutional and historical context of European security, in addition to reflecting current geopolitical conditions, will continue to affect the fate of any reform endeavour.

Reforming an international institution in times of geopolitical turmoil is a wickedly difficult challenge. The difficulties in reforming the United Nations system amid the collapse of the post-Cold War era are likewise encountered in the context of the EU as it attempts to confront a number of existential crises while simultaneously furthering European integration. The OSCE is no exception. The Russian annexation of Crimea and the crisis in Ukraine represent a serious breach of the norms of European security and has had a twin impact on the OSCE: undermining the existing normative order and challenging the very foundations of the Organization. Yet the OSCE has expanded its role both at the diplomatic and operational level as it attempts to defuse tensions between its participating States. The harsh realities of operating a civilian OSCE monitoring mission during a civil war reveal how advances in the legal status of the OSCE are urgently needed. The Special Monitoring Mission (SMM) was deployed to Ukraine less than twenty-four hours after the OSCE Permanent Council's decision on 21 March 2014, but a Memorandum of Understanding on its deployment only came into force on 13 June 2014, twelve weeks after the initial deployment of OSCE observers.[1]

This chapter aims to shed light on the political dynamics of the OSCE in its fifth decade and on the historical baggage the Organization carries on its shoulders. In the first part, the special case of the CSCE–OSCE as an institution built in the middle of the Cold War, but not after a historic caesura,

[1] Simonet and Lüber, 'The OSCE and Its Legal Status', 299.

is discussed. Since the end of the Cold War, the evolution of the CSCE through the so-called 'Helsinki Process' from 1975 to 1990 is now being reinterpreted by scholars quite differently from contemporary assessments. The second part discusses the enduring, but so far unsuccessful, efforts to reform the OSCE into a strong organisation with legal personality. Although the OSCE has time and again adapted successfully to new and challenging circumstances, most OSCE participating States – the United States in particular – wish to preserve the Organization's flexible and unbureaucratic structure. The chapter concludes with some thoughts on possible ways to return to a genuine political dialogue in the OSCE, which ultimately is a prerequisite for strengthening its legal framework.

Whereas the OSCE can be understood as an international organisation in name only, it serves as the quintessential guardian of the jointly agreed norms, principles and rules that constitute the present European security order. Any discussion regarding fundamental institutional reforms of the OSCE therefore immediately touches upon the higher-level notion of order. Transforming the system may be required to uphold that order, but it could also be counterproductive. In any case, the legitimacy of the system needs to be maintained in all circumstances, lest parallel systems appear and threaten the security order as we know it.

The value of a rules-based security architecture becomes apparent with merely a superficial glance into history: successive alternatives to the established order of the day proved very costly. On the other hand, completely new institutions and systems were often formed in the wake of a terrible catastrophe. There would be no Westphalian Order without the Thirty Years War, no Concert of Europe without the Napoleonic Wars, no League of Nations without the First World War and no United Nations system without the Second World War. The gates of hell were opened as the preceding order collapsed.

2 HISTORY AND THE PRESENT

The CSCE–OSCE represents an interesting exception to this general rule that new orders and institutions are established only after drastic and major wars. The Conference on Security and Co-operation in Europe (CSCE) was created *amid* the Cold War, a conflict that endured for more than a decade after the CSCE's Helsinki Final Act was signed in 1975. Admittedly, the nature of the Cold War had changed by the early 1970s. The East–West conflict was no longer as acute as it had been at the time of the Korean War or the Berlin Wall and Cuban Missile crises. The 'little *détente*' between John F. Kennedy and Nikita Khrushchev in 1963, Charles de Gaulle's *détente* policy after 1964 and, above all, Willy Brandt's new 'Ostpolitik' after 1969 all paved the way for a broader East–West *détente*. After successful agreements between Bonn and Moscow (1970), between the Four Powers on Berlin (1971) and between the Federal Republic of Germany and the German Democratic Republic (1972), the German question had lost its volatility. However, the ideological rivalry between East and West continued after 1975, escalating further during the conflicts in Afghanistan (1979) and Poland (1981), as well as throughout the second Cold War in the 1980s, until Mikhail Gorbachev's arrival in 1985 helped bring about its end.

With the benefit of hindsight, the Helsinki process was dramatically reinterpreted after 1989. Many in the West readily forgot that the CSCE had originally been a Soviet initiative. The earliest conference proposal came from Soviet Foreign Minister Vyacheslav Molotov in 1954. With the convening of a pan-European security conference, Moscow wished to finalise a surrogate peace treaty that would formally conclude the Second World War. The West would thus recognise Europe's post-war borders, including a divided Germany, thereby also accepting Soviet predominance in central and eastern Europe.[2] Moscow's interests were in confirming the status quo.

Time and again the initiative for a conference had been rejected by the West. It only began to gain traction in 1969 when Finland offered to facilitate preparatory talks leading to such a conference. When the talks led to more concrete multilateral negotiations, the West realised that it could leverage the process in its favour and extract Soviet concessions for accepting the borders of 1945. In the three-year negotiation process that followed, starting at the Dipoli conference centre near Helsinki in 1972 and concluding in Geneva in 1975, the West succeeded in linking the notion of security with principles such as self-determination and individual human and civil rights.

In 1975, many in the West would have agreed with the view that Moscow held the upper hand in the negotiations. True enough, Soviet leader Leonid Brezhnev agreed to make critical concessions in the area of human rights in return for western recognition of Europe's territorial status quo. Yet Soviet concessions were made in part because Brezhnev did not feel committed to implementing any component of the Helsinki Final Act that he did not like. The document consisted only of political declarations of intent, not legally binding principles.[3]

2 Rey, 'USSR and the Helsinki Process'.
3 Maresca, *To Helsinki*; Thomas, *Helsinki Effect*.

For Brezhnev, 'Helsinki 1975' marked the climax of his political career and of his policy of *détente* towards the West. In the West, the Helsinki Final Act was mainly regarded as a victory for the Soviet Union. The *Wall Street Journal*, with its headline 'Jerry, don't go!', prompted US President Gerald Ford to refrain from flying to Helsinki and signing the document.[4] Scepticism was widespread elsewhere, too. Swiss diplomat Ernesto Thalmann spoke for many of his colleagues with his disillusioned prediction: 'As soon as the ink was dry on the signatures in Helsinki, the whole agreement would sink into oblivion.'[5]

Only later did the revolutionary potential of the Helsinki process become clear. In a stroke of genius, western Europeans had succeeded in broadening the definition of security to include much more than merely political and military perspectives. The innovative and visionary idea of the Helsinki Final Act was that arms control and disarmament alone were insufficient to accomplish genuine security. Achieving sustainable international security required, in addition to political and military dimensions, the promotion of economic development, the responsible stewardship of the environment and a guarantee of individual human rights. This holistic approach to cooperative security was avant-garde at the time and it remains equally important today, as the impact of economic crises and climate change demonstrates.

The early Helsinki process was mainly driven by the 'EC Nine' and marked an early phase of a common European foreign policy.[6] The United States, in contrast, remained extremely passive throughout the CSCE process until 1975 when Henry Kissinger repeatedly mocked Europe's insistence on including human rights in the agenda. In the end, however, western Europe succeeded in incorporating dynamic elements of change into the East–West *détente* process – a striking rejection of the US and Soviet preference for the bilateral status quo.[7]

As early as 1977, the supposed victory of the Soviet Union was revealed to have pyrrhic characteristics. The Helsinki principles of self-determination and individual human and civil rights were enthusiastically championed by dissidents in both the Soviet Union and eastern Europe.[8] The human dimension transformed the CSCE into a 'continuation of the Cold War with more subtle

4 Editorial, *'Jerry, don't go'*, *Wall Street Journal*, 23 July 1975, 14.

5 Cited in Nünlist, 'Expanding the East–West Dialog', 213 (translated from German by the author).

6 The nine member states of the European Communities (EC), the predecessor of today's European Union (EU), were France, West Germany, Italy, Belgium, the Netherlands, Luxembourg, Denmark, Ireland and the United Kingdom.

7 Möckli, 'EC Nine'.

8 Snyder, *Human Rights Activism*.

means', as a visionary British diplomat fittingly recorded in a telegram from Dipoli.[9] Therefore, Helsinki 1975 did indeed mark an important turning point in the Cold War. From that moment there was a multilateral dialogue forum on European security questions. Most importantly, the forum persisted despite the increasingly hostile phases that followed. The East–West confrontation was by no means over in 1975, and it continued to shape International Relations until 1989. The CSCE ensured that cooperation remained possible during times of strained relations and ideological competition.

However, no direct road led from Helsinki 1975 to the fall of the Berlin Wall in 1989. There are other elements than the impact of the Helsinki Final Act that better explain the *annus mirabilis* of 1989: the 'Gorbachev factor' and the economic and social problems of the Soviet Union, to be sure, but also US rearmament under President Ronald Reagan.[10]

Interestingly, the preferences for specific Helsinki principles have been radically altered since the end of the Cold War. The West increasingly champions territorial integrity, as Russia is considered to be challenging Europe's territorial status quo with its military interventions in Georgia and Ukraine, as well as the recognition of South Ossetia and Abkhazia. Moreover, Russia's annexation of Crimea represented the first interstate land grab in Europe since the Second World War. Ironically, Moscow now advocates for self-determination, in contrast to its traditional support for the principles of territorial inviolability and state sovereignty. The Russian perspective on current events, of course, is different. According to the dominant Russian narrative, the United States is committed to maintaining its unilateral predominance over European security through NATO, and NATO's eastern expansion and the West's recognition of Kosovar independence meant a betrayal of the 1990 Cold War settlement.[11]

Different interpretations of the history of the European security order are not solely an academic concern. The clash between Russia and the West's diametrically opposed narratives concerning the evolution of European security post-1990 has immediate implications for the present: these narratives continue to poison political discussions on a return to dialogue and diplomacy.

History also played a central role in shaping the two seminal CSCE documents. In the Helsinki Final Act of 1975, the preamble of the famous

9 Cited in Rosin, *Schweiz im KSZE-Prozess*, 322.

10 Brown, *Gorbachev Factor*.

11 Deudney and Ikenberry, 'Unravelling of the Cold War Settlement'. For a critical discussion, see Nünlist, 'Contested History'.

'Decalogue' – which outlined ten principles intended to guide relations between CSCE participating States – emphasised that 'a commitment to peace, security and justice . . . constitutes for each participating State a present and future responsibility, heightened by experience of the past'. This represented a subtle reminder that the Second World War had ended only thirty years earlier.[12]

The November 1990 Paris Charter for a New Europe reconfirmed the Helsinki principles, but the landmark document was marked by a different, more optimistic mood. Heavily influenced by Francis Fukuyama's 'end of history' argument and the desire for a 'Europe whole and free and at peace', the Paris Charter recorded 'a time of profound change and historic expectations'. The CSCE participating States were now ready to open a new chapter in the history of Europe: 'Europe is liberating itself from the legacy of the past.'[13]

The Paris Charter was infused with the positive spirit that surrounded the radical changes of 1989, which in hindsight could be construed as naïve. Twenty-five years later, Russia's annexation of Crimea and the subsequent Ukrainian crisis made it painfully clear that the historical patterns and rivalries that affected European security thinking still cast long shadows over today's relations between Russia and the West. History has returned: facts and accusations, perceptions and misperceptions, and different narratives characterise contemporary political discourse even at the highest level. An OSCE expert committee, chaired by German Ambassador Wolfgang Ischinger, published the report 'Back to Diplomacy' in 2015. The document underlined the extent to which different narratives about the evolution of European security still poison relations between Russia and the West.[14] Addressing these perceptions is a prerequisite for a return to real dialogue between Russia and the West, which in turn is a prerequisite for any institutional reform of the OSCE, including that of its legal framework.

3 OSCE REFORM: A 'NEVERENDING STORY'

The challenges of institutional reform have plagued the CSCE-OSCE since the Cold War. The CSCE-OSCE's protracted reform efforts have essentially

12 CSCE, Helsinki Final Act 1 August 1975, available at: https://www.osce.org/helsinki-final-act.

13 CSCE, Charter of Paris for a new Europe 19–21 November 1990, available at: https://www.osce.org/mc/39516?download=true.

14 Panel of Eminent Persons, *Back to Diplomacy*, 2.

become, borrowing the title of the 1979 children's novel by Michael Ende, 'The Neverending Story'.

From 1972 to 1993 the CSCE was a relatively loose multilateral forum for dialogue between the Cold War's two hostile blocs, where phases of preparatory talks (Dipoli–Helsinki, 1972–3), intense negotiations (Geneva, 1973–5) and follow-up meetings (Belgrade, 1977–8; Madrid, 1980–3; and Vienna, 1986–9) alternated with periods of relative inactivity.

In the early Helsinki process (1972–5), attention was mostly focused on the famous 'three baskets', or three dimensions of security: (I) politico-military, (II) economic and environmental and (III) human. However, it was the largely forgotten 'fourth basket' that changed the original Helsinki conference into the quasi-permanent Helsinki process. Basket IV dealt with the question of any 'follow-up meetings' of the CSCE. Soviet ideas to establish permanent conference features (including a secretariat) were initially met with western resistance. During talks in Geneva (1973–5), even the Soviet Union seemed to have lost interest in an institutionalisation of the CSCE. However, from 1974 onwards neutral countries like Finland and Switzerland began to support the idea of follow-up conferences. While they were still very hesitant to create a tool with which the Soviet Union could impose its will upon western Europe, the neutral states realised that continued CSCE meetings would also act as valuable forums to influence human rights debates within the eastern bloc. Moreover, it was believed that such a forum could also be used to help Moscow's eastern European satellites gain greater autonomy from the Soviet Union. Innovative features including the intensification of human contacts, improved dissemination of information and the establishment of military codes of conduct could only be realised and improved upon if the CSCE continued after 1975.[15]

In early 1975, the neutral and non-aligned countries – who had come to see the CSCE as a beneficial framework that gave them a voice in East–West relations – began to push for follow-up conferences. Their main objective was to prevent the CSCE from ending up as a one-off, backwards-oriented episode. They felt that the Helsinki Final Act would benefit from a follow-up process that emphasised the future direction of the new, comprehensive security approach. Because the western countries remained sceptical, the neutrals only lobbied for regular follow-up conferences without the need for a permanent institution or even a permanent secretariat. Ultimately, an influential Danish proposal prompted the CSCE delegations to agree on a two-year pause

[15] Rosin, *Die Schweiz im KSZE-Prozess*, 119 *et seq*.

after Helsinki, but to reconvene in Belgrade in 1977 to guarantee a continuation of the Helsinki process.[16]

In retrospect, the insistence of the neutrals to link basket III (human rights commitments) with basket IV (follow-up meetings) was a brilliant and visionary idea.[17] Western fears that the Soviet Union would use follow-up conferences as propaganda forums to cement the territorial status quo in Europe according to the 1945 borders proved unfounded. In fact, the CSCE meetings in Belgrade, Madrid and Vienna essentially became human rights tribunals on the situation in the eastern bloc. Dissidents from all over eastern Europe demanded that their governments implement the Helsinki commitments. Thus, the Helsinki process indeed proved to be the 'final nail in the coffin of Marxism and Communism', to quote a later bon mot of former US President Gerald Ford.[18]

It was a deliberate choice of the CSCE participating States not to create permanent institutions in 1975. However, the Helsinki process nevertheless contributed to and influenced a 'continuous CSCE identity' through mandated CSCE conferences, expert workshops and preparatory work between meetings. In the words of one participant, the CSCE became a kind of 'travelling circus'.[19] The Stockholm (1984–6) and Vienna (1986–9) meetings additionally created arms control inspection and human rights monitoring regimes, which expanded the original purpose of the CSCE from outlining noble aims to creating mechanisms and concrete activities, thereby generating continuous work between follow-up meetings. However, ideas like the establishment of a CSCE youth symphony orchestra in 1989 were still rejected in an attempt to dispel the impression of too much institutionalisation.[20]

During the period of transition from the Cold War to the post-Cold War era, the CSCE played a key role in discussions concerning a Cold War settlement and a common vision for a new security architecture in Europe. In retrospect, the inclusive spirit of 1990 seems counter-intuitive after decades of mutual mistrust. At the time, however, optimism reigned supreme and most political leaders in Europe were ready to close the chapter of the Cold War amicably and embark on a new era of cooperation. In the 1990 Paris Charter, CSCE participating States declared that 'the era of confrontation and division of Europe has ended'.[21]

16 Ibid., 121 *et seq*.

17 Nünlist, 'Expanding the East–West Dialog', 215 *et seq*.

18 Ford made his famous statement in 1995 in Helsinki, celebrating 20 years of the Helsinki Final Act. See US Congress, *Congressional Record* 2000, 10109.

19 Lehne, *The CSCE in the 1990s*, 10.

20 Ibid., 13.

21 CSCE, Charter of Paris 1990 (n. 13); see Maresca, *Helsinki Revisited*, 116–35.

Yet for all the optimistic talk of an end to enmity and the rise of indivisible security in a new age of peace, Russia's new place within the European security system did not result in the level of security the former superpower desired. Early western promises to grant the pan-European CSCE a leading role in the new security system were not realised. The United States in particular was unwilling to give the CSCE the necessary powers and instruments required to fulfil such a role, preferring instead to centre the new security system around NATO. A crucial component of the institutional status quo of the Cold War was thus preserved.[22]

Consequently, Moscow's hopes that post-Cold War European security would be based on the CSCE model were quickly dashed. In fairness, the Paris Charter did establish new structures and institutions supporting a stronger CSCE, including a permanent Secretariat, a Conflict Prevention Centre and an Office for Free Elections. Russia also sought to legally incorporate the CSCE as a regional security organisation by creating a legally binding charter and an Executive Council comparable to the UN Security Council. The Russian proposals were ultimately rejected by the West when the CSCE was transformed into the OSCE at the Budapest Summit in 1994.[23] Nevertheless, similar proposals found support from individual western countries. For example, German Foreign Minister Hans-Dietrich Genscher proposed the establishment of a CSCE Security Council as early as 1990. In May 1994, Germany and the Netherlands floated the idea of 'CSCE First': a proposal that suggested the CSCE would act as the institution of first resort in tackling regional conflicts.[24]

At the 1994 CSCE Summit in Budapest, western leaders made it clear that NATO (without Russia) would form the foundation of European security, rather than the CSCE, in which Russia enjoyed equal participation. It was during the same Summit that the CSCE was transformed into the OSCE, but a close reading of Budapest Decision No. 1 on 'Strengthening the CSCE' makes clear that this name change was not intended to correlate with stronger institutionalisation. Rather, the document reads: 'The change in name from CSCE to OSCE alters neither the character of our CSCE commitments nor the status of the CSCE and its institutions.'[25]

22 See Nünlist, 'Contested History', 18 *et seq*.

23 Kropatcheva, 'Evolution of Russia's OSCE Policy', 11. These Russian proposals were also a reaction to western discussions on NATO expansion, which had picked up speed in 1994.

24 Zellner, 'Russia and the OSCE', 392.

25 CSCE, Decision No. 1, 'Strengthening the CSCE', Budapest Document 21 December 1994, available at: www.osce.org/mc/39554?download=true, para. 22.

With no meaningful strengthening of the Organization's institutions, the emergence of the OSCE in 1995 again disappointed Russian hopes for a pan-European security organisation that could provide an equal say for Moscow. The OSCE created various institutions and mechanisms, but in Russia's view European security was built on the bedrock of NATO and the EU – placing Brussels rather than Vienna at the heart of the new European security architecture.

Russia's constructive engagement with the OSCE gradually declined and gave way to disillusionment, disengagement and a lack of ownership. Two rounds of NATO enlargement in 1999 and 2004 furthered Russia's sense of isolation and marginalisation in European security matters. Instead of advocating for a new OSCE-based pan-European security system, after 1995 Russia argued for a 'Charter on European Security' based on the three institutional pillars of the OSCE, NATO and the UN. Such a security document was indeed adopted at the 1999 Istanbul Summit, but the Istanbul Charter did not reach the level of influence achieved by the two landmark documents of Helsinki (1975) and Paris (1990). Moreover, the OSCE's theoretical and abstract discussions about the future of the Organization during this time were clearly overshadowed by the events in Kosovo, and Russia lost confidence in the Organization after the failure of its 1998–9 policing field operation in Kosovo (KVM).[26]

The 1999 Istanbul Charter nevertheless strengthened the OSCE's operational capabilities by achieving agreement to develop the Organization's role in peacekeeping and create rapid response teams for field operations. The Charter also proposed closer ties and cooperation between the OSCE and other international institutions, including NATO and the EU. Contrary to Russian wishes, however, it did not provide for an institutional overhaul. A clear majority of OSCE participating States still felt that the Organization should not depart from its traditional pragmatism and flexibility, and so the traditional consensus rule remained the basis for OSCE decision-making.[27]

The OSCE reform debate was revitalised with the launching of a Panel of Eminent Persons in December 2004 to analyse possible ways to strengthen the effectiveness of the Organization. The seven members of the panel published their thirty-two page report 'Common Purpose' in 2005, which included over seventy recommendations designed to strengthen the OSCE's long-term effectiveness.[28] The report suggested that the OSCE should focus on issues

[26] Ibid., 393. Within the OSCE, the reform debates in 1995–6 were labelled 'security model discussions'.

[27] Ghebali, 'The OSCE's Istanbul Charter for European Security', 23 *et seq*.

[28] Panel of Eminent Persons, *Common Purpose*; see also Bakker and Pietersma, 'OSCE in Search'.

and areas in which it has a comparative advantage: including political dialogue, early warning and conflict prevention, post-conflict rehabilitation, arms control and confidence- and security-building measures (CSBMs). Additionally, the panel found that the OSCE could also make meaningful contributions to the fight against terrorism, border management, the stimulation of regional economic cooperation and the promotion of good governance. Other priority areas included election observation, the protection of media freedoms and the promotion of tolerance and non-discrimination. Related to the OSCE's structure, the panel suggested a stronger role for the Secretary-General, particularly regarding operational management and identifying long-term strategies and objectives.

The most recent effort to reform the institution started in Berlin with a surprising Russian proposal presented by President Dmitri Medvedev in June 2008. Medvedev suggested convening a pan-European summit to negotiate a new European Security Treaty, a legally binding non-aggression treaty that would emphasise arms control, the renunciation of violence and the indivisible nature of security.[29] The Russian proposal intended to radically change the OSCE and reduce US influence in Europe by giving the OSCE legal competence, or even a veto, over NATO and the EU. It was a return to the original Soviet idea of a European security pact in 1954 and to the Russian reform proposals of the mid-1990s. The August 2008 war in Georgia, however, changed the circumstances of this discussion dramatically.

Nonetheless, the Finnish and Greek chairmanships in 2008–9 seized upon Medvedev's initiative, which would have replaced the OSCE with a new legally binding pan-European security treaty, and integrated it into an internal reform process of the Organization. Russia's active involvement in the so-called Corfu Process in 2009 was a major success for the OSCE.[30] The reform process succeeded in reconvening an OSCE Summit in Astana in 2010, the first summit for eleven years. The Astana Declaration reaffirmed earlier settled CSCE–OSCE principles and reiterated that existing human and civil rights were non-negotiable. The Summit failed, however, to enact a working plan outlining concrete next steps for the achievement of a 'free, democratic, common, and indivisible security community from Vancouver to Vladivostok'; the United States, Georgia and Moldova vetoed the initiative after participating States failed to reach a consensus regarding frozen conflicts.[31]

[29] Medvedev, 'European Security Treaty' available at: http://en.kremlin.ru/events/president/news/6152; see also Zagorski, 'Russian Proposal', 44; and Nünlist, 'Helsinki +40', 205 et seq.

[30] Lynch, 'State of the OSCE', 12.

[31] Zellner, 'OSZE-Gipfeltreffen in Astana', 26.

The cumbersome OSCE reform process persisted and was renamed 'Helsinki +40' in late 2012. In 2013, expectations began to build that another OSCE summit meeting could be convened by mid-2015 to celebrate the achievements of the 1975 Helsinki Final Act. The attempt to use the fortieth anniversary of Helsinki 1975 as an incentive to stimulate institutional reform was ultimately killed off by Russia's intervention in Crimea and the crisis in Ukraine that followed. The Helsinki +40 process lingered on and several working groups discussed ideas on how to strengthen the OSCE. The renewed confrontation between Russia and the West did not allow for sufficient progress to legitimise an OSCE summit in 2015. In July of that year, only a brief commemorative event was held in Helsinki, without high-level representation.[32]

In summary, the OSCE has successfully adapted to new circumstances and challenges over time. Despite very limited resources (including within the Secretariat),[33] the Organization flexibly set up institutions and operations on the ground to respond to the new post-Cold War challenges. The majority of OSCE participating States – the United States in particular – wished to preserve the OSCE's flexible and unbureaucratic structure and thus have categorically opposed reform proposals that would establish the OSCE as an international organisation with legal personality. In addition, many western states have tried to limit opportunities for the renegotiation of past OSCE documents and commitments.

4 THE WAY AHEAD: BACK TO DIALOGUE

The slow death of the Helsinki +40 reform process in 2014–15, however, did not undermine the fact that the Ukraine crisis also acted as a trigger for more serious debates concerning the future role of the OSCE. The difficulties experienced by OSCE monitors in Ukraine in March and April 2014, where they operated without privileges or immunities in the absence of a concluded Memorandum of Understanding, further highlighted the challenges inherent in the Organization's current structure. The apparent necessity of providing an international legal personality for the OSCE prompted further calls for reform. OSCE staff were deployed to Ukraine a full ten weeks before legal

32 Nünlist, 'Helsinki +40', 199 *et seq.*, 207.

33 The OSCE had a budget for 2016 totalling EUR 141 million. In 2016, the Organization employed 550 people in its institutions and around 2,330 in its field operations. Seconded staff members are funded by their national administrations. The field operation in Ukraine is funded by a separate budget, which for the period of 1 April 2016 to 31 March 2017 was EUR 98.8 million.

arrangements necessary for the successful implementation of the mandate and the protection of observers were in place.[34]

An open-ended and informal working group on strengthening the legal framework of the OSCE has tried for many years to solve these challenges. Despite consensus at the expert level having been achieved in 2007, a Draft Convention on international legal personality, legal capacity and the privileges and immunities of the OSCE has not been adopted.[35] Several OSCE participating States link the proposed convention to a legally binding OSCE Charter. As the idea of such a charter inspires great debate among members, the broader Draft Convention it is associated with remains unresolved. Thus far, the legal fundament of the OSCE's activities in participating States remains rooted in the 1993 Rome 'Decision on Legal Capacity and Privileges and Immunities of the CSCE'.[36] Notably, the decision is only implemented by roughly one quarter of participating States. In addition, there is a lack of uniformity within the OSCE region in the application of the legal status of the OSCE in domestic law, as a survey in 2014 made clear.[37]

As an unexpected consequence, the Ukraine crisis put the OSCE back into the spotlight as a meaningful player in the modern security system: the all-but-forgotten organisation proved its usefulness and agility once again with its management of the worst security crisis to strike Europe in decades. In late 2014, the Swiss chairmanship launched a new 'Panel of Eminent Persons' and tasked the experts, led by Wolfgang Ischinger, to explore lessons learnt from the OSCE's engagement in Ukraine, both for the Organization and for the European security order. The Panel's final report was published in November 2015 and suggested setting in motion a robust political and diplomatic process to overcome the crisis between Russia and the West, focusing first on measures to reduce the risk of military incidents. The Panel took inspiration from the stillborn Helsinki +40 process and recommended the use of a future OSCE summit meeting as a lure to propel reform efforts forward.[38]

Innovative academic 'track 2 initiatives' (i.e. non-state actors acting outside official government channels) also contributed fresh ideas for institutional reform to the ongoing debate. A 2015 report by the OSCE Network of Think

34 Neukirch, 'Special Monitoring Mission to Ukraine'.

35 OSCE, Draft Convention on the International Legal Personality, Legal Capacity, and Privileges and Immunities of the OSCE, CIO.GAL/48/07/Rev.6, 23 October 2007.

36 CSCE, Decision on Legal Capacity and Privileges and Immunities, CSCE/4-C, 2 December 1993.

37 OSCE, Report to the Ministerial Council on Strengthening the Legal Framework of the OSCE in 2014, MC.GAL/5/14/Corr.1, 3 December 2014. For a concise chronology covering the years from 1993 to 2009, see Brander, 'Making a Credible Case'.

38 Panel of Eminent Persons, *Back to Diplomacy*, 13 *et seq.*

Tanks, for example, advised increasing the frequency of ministerial council meetings and cultivating greater flexibility within the consensus rule applicable to decision-making within the Organization. It also, quite revolutionarily, suggested changing the annual cycle of the OSCE from calendar to school year to avoid additional interruptions created by the traditional summer break.[39]

In 2016, the OSCE Network of Think Tanks produced another report with recommendations for how OSCE participating States could prompt a return to diplomacy through interim rules for the security, economic and social spheres.[40] These interim guidelines would be based on current realities and currently shared interests. To facilitate the return to at least pragmatic transactional cooperation, it advocated for the resumption of a comprehensive dialogue between Russia and the West. The report argued that no alternatives to such transactional cooperation which is selective and interest-based – whether it be a strategy of containment, a new Yalta-type deal,[41] or the Astana vision of a norm-based security community[42] – is currently receiving support from OSCE participating States. The report suggested a kind of Code of Conduct for facilitating a diplomatic process, consisting of measures aimed at lowering the intensity of the confrontation, strengthening communication between the sides and re-establishing cooperation. It also recommended a Programme of Urgent Action that would normalise the current status quo, restructure dialogue, devise a list of immediate steps (including an agreement to avoid military incidents and accidents), further the implementation of the Minsk Protocol (2014), and elaborate on a set of economic and environmental confidence-building measures. The said Protocol, which recapitulates the consultation results reached by the trilateral contact group composed of representatives from Ukraine, Russia and the OSCE, was signed in Minsk on 5 September 2014 by representatives of Ukraine, the Russian Federation, the Donetsk People's Republic, the Luhansk People's Republic and the OSCE. It set out a twelve-point plan, including an immediate bilateral ceasefire to be monitored and verified by the OSCE.

39 Tiilikainen, 'Reviving Co-operative Security', 15.

40 Zellner *et al.*, *European Security*.

41 In 1945, allied leaders Roosevelt, Churchill and Stalin concluded a deal in Yalta to define and recognise boundaries and spheres of interests.

42 In December 2010, the OSCE adopted the 'Astana Commemorative Declaration towards a Security Community' at the Summit meeting in Astana: OSCE, Astana Commemorative Declaration towards a Security Community, 3 December 2010, available at: www.osce.org/mc/74985?download=true.

The Panel of Eminent Persons published another report in 2016 with alternative ideas on how to renew dialogue on European security.[43] It also bemoaned the lack of communication between Russia and the West, arguing that this could lead to dangerous misjudgements and miscalculations during a crisis situation. As a means to map out areas of convergence and divergence between the two sides, the report innovatively suggested an update to the OSCE's December 2003 'Strategy to Address Threats to Security and Stability in the Twenty-First Century'.[44] In undertaking such a task, the similarities of participating States should be highlighted as well as the need for multilateral cooperation in addressing national security challenges. While the 2016 report stressed that reviving dialogue with Russia without meaningful progress towards the implementation of the Minsk Protocol risks the perception of a return to 'business as usual', or even as a reward for so-called 'bad behaviour', it argued that it is precisely in times of crisis that dialogue is most needed. Talking only to one's friends is bad diplomacy.

Such a return to selective, interest-based cooperation with Russia would incrementally help build trust as the basis for more sustainable cooperation. A first step in this direction was undertaken with the relaunch of conventional arms control in Europe by OSCE Chairperson-in-Office Frank-Walter Steinmeier in August 2016. The OSCE Ministerial Council held in Hamburg in December 2016 achieved a consensus and approved the advancement of Steinmeier's initiative within the OSCE in an informal yet structured dialogue on threat perceptions and mutual security policy interests.[45] In April 2017, discussions on mutual threat perceptions among senior officials from the capitals and ambassadors of OSCE participating States at Kahlenberg, Vienna, marked the beginning of this dialogue on current and future challenges and risks. The aim is to address challenges in the wider politico-military sphere and explore possibilities of overcoming divergences. Besides fostering a better understanding of threat perceptions, future meetings are expected to address recent developments in military doctrines and trends in military force postures.[46]

43 Panel of Eminent Persons, *Renewing Dialogue*.

44 OSCE, Strategy to Address Threats to Security and Stability in the Twenty-First Century, 2 December 2003, available at: www.osce.org/mc/17504?download=true.

45 Nünlist, 'The OSCE and the Future of European Security', 4.

46 OSCE, OSCE to Explore Common Ground on Current and Future Security Challenges, Press Release, 7 April 2017, available at: www.osce.org/chairmanship/310481. The OSCE Structured Dialogue on current and future challenges and risks was chaired by the Ambassadors Eberhard Pohl (2017, Germany) and Paul Huynen (2018, Belgium).

Since 2014, the comprehensive and inclusive approach of the OSCE has appeared particularly valuable in difficult times. Its format allows for a dialogue with Russia despite presently strained relations. The OSCE is well equipped to gradually build the basis for a new *modus vivendi* despite deep ideological and political divisions. This is the way forward, and the historical Helsinki process could serve as a highly instructive model for this endeavour. If pragmatic, confidence-building measures and an open dialogue on both diverging threat perceptions and conflicting interests were possible at the height of the Cold War, they should certainly be possible today.[47]

Communication is important for de-escalation, and dialogue is an important prerequisite for *détente*. Moreover, it needs to be emphasised that dialogue is not the same as appeasement, and attempting to listen to and understand the other side is not synonymous with taking their arguments at face value.[48] Much like the CSCE during the Cold War, the OSCE today seems to be the most suitable forum for a continuous exploration of practical ways to carefully manage the current volatile confrontation with Russia, while firmly defending western interests and values.

5 CONCLUSION

Within the OSCE, there is certainly a fatigue from open-ended reform processes designed to strengthen the effectiveness of the Organization. The OSCE and its predecessor, the CSCE, evolved flexibly and pragmatically. Ironically, the title of the very first CSCE landmark document made clear that nobody at the time expected the pan-European security conference meetings in Dipoli and Geneva to result in a quasi-permanent, albeit loosely structured, forum for East–West dialogue. The 'Helsinki Final Act', in name, seemed to signal that the European security conference, as desired by Moscow since 1954, was a one-time event that concluded with a rather weak, politically binding document with no legal basis. In 1975, East and West did not adopt a charter under the form of a treaty; no organisation or strong institution was constructed.

When the CSCE changed into the OSCE in December 1994, it graduated to a proper organisation in name only. In essence, the conference-style institution did not transform into a fully fledged international organisation and the issue of its international legal status remains unresolved today. The lack of legal commitments, a constitutional treaty or an international legal

47 Hakkarainen and Nünlist, 'Trust and Realpolitik', 1, 4.
48 Nünlist, 'Contested History', 24 et seq.

personality leaves the OSCE rather weak in its influence. Its documents and decisions are not legally binding, and so rely on the political and moral commitments of the fifty-seven participating States.

The OSCE has always been an evolutionary process and the political will to use OSCE tools is still more important than legally binding agreements or a new security charter. When the political will was present, a rapid expansion of missions and institutions reinvigorated the OSCE. Over time, with NATO and the EU taking the lead in European security, the OSCE remained a useful pan-European security forum where Russia could vote and make itself heard.

Starting in 1999, the OSCE became less relevant in the European security sphere and was increasingly thought of as a relic of the Cold War. Both the US and Russian presidents failed to attend the OSCE Summit in 2010, which demonstrated just how neglected the Organization had become. The Ukraine crisis in 2014 and the resulting confrontation between Russia and the West led to a remarkable revival of the Organization. Its 'convening power' and inclusive setting distinguished the OSCE from other security organisations and made it useful once again as a forum for dialogue and crisis management.

The OSCE's legitimacy, however, rests largely on its historical legacy and the unanticipated success of the Helsinki process. During the period of *détente*, political leaders in the early 1970s succeeded in transforming the confrontational style of their strategic rivalry into a cooperative one by emphasising compromise and reconciling diverging interests. It remains to be seen, however, if the political will can be found on both sides of the current conflict between Russia and the West to prompt a return to dialogue and diplomacy, and mutually to increase security in Europe through cooperation.

REFERENCES

Bakker, Edwin and Pietersma, Hinke, 'The OSCE in Search of a Meaningful Reform Agenda', *Atlantisch Perspectief* 29 No. 7–8 (2005), 23–9.

Brander, Sonya, 'Making a Credible Case for a Legal Personality for the OSCE', *OSCE Magazine* 18 (2009), 18–23.

Brown, Archie, *The Gorbachev Factor* (Oxford: Oxford University Press, 1996).

Deudney, Daniel and Ikenberry, John, G. 'The Unravelling of the Cold War Settlement', *Survival: Global Politics and Strategy* 51, No. 6 (2009–2010), 39–62.

Ghebali, Victor-Yves, 'The OSCEs Istanbul Charter for European Security', *NATO Review* 48 No. 1 (2000), 23–6.

Hakkarainen, Petri and Nünlist, Christian, 'Trust and Realpolitik: The OSCE in 2016', *Policy Perspectives* 4, No. 1 (2016).

Kropatcheva, Elena, 'The Evolution of Russia's OSCE Policy: From the Promises of the Helsinki Final Act to the Ukrainian Crisis', *Journal of Contemporary European Studies* 23 No. 1 (2015), 6–24.

Lehne, Stefan, *The CSCE in the 1990s: Common European House or Potemkin Village?* (Vienna: Braumüller, 1991).

Lynch, Dov, 'The State of the OSCE', *The EU-Russia Centre Review: Russia, the OSCE and European Security*, No. 12, 5–13.

Maresca, John, *To Helsinki: The Conference on Security and Cooperation in Europe 1973–1975* (Durham: Duke University Press, 1987).

Helsinki Revisited: A Key U.S. Negotiator's Memoirs on the Development of the CSCE into the OSCE (Stuttgart: Ibidem, 2016).

Möckli, Daniel, 'The EC Nine, the CSCE, and the Changing Pattern of European Security', in Andreas Wenger, Vojtech Mastny and Christian Nünlist (eds.), *Origins of the European Security System: The Helsinki Process Revisited*, 1965–75 (London: Routledge, 2008), 145–63.

Neukirch, Claus, 'The Special Monitoring Mission to Ukraine: Operational Challenges and New Horizons', in Institute for Peace Research and Security Policy at University of Hamburged, *OSCE Yearbook 2014* (Baden-Baden: Nomos Verlagsgesellschaft, 2015), 183–97.

Nünlist, Christian, 'Expanding the East–West Dialog beyond the Bloc Division: The Neutrals as Negotiators and Mediators', in Andreas Wenger, Vojtech Mastny and Christian Nünlist (eds.), *Origins of the European Security System: The Helsinki Process Revisited*, 1965–75 (London: Routledge, 2008), 201–21.

'Helsinki +40 in the Historical Context', *Security and Human Rights* 25 (2014), 198–209.

'Contested History: Rebuilding Trust in European Security', *Strategic Trends* (2017), 9–32.

'The OSCE and the Future of European Security', CSS Analyses in Security Policy No. 202 (2017).

Panel of Eminent Persons, *Common Purpose: Towards a More Effective OSCE* (Vienna: OSCE 2005).

Back to Diplomacy (Vienna: OSCE 2015).

Rey, Marie-Pierre, 'The USSR and the Helsinki Process, 1969–75: Optimism, Doubt, or Defiance?', in Andreas Wenger, Vojtech Mastny and Christian Nünlist (eds.), *Origins of the European Security System: The Helsinki Process Revisited*, 1965–75 (London: Routledge, 2008), 65–81.

Rosin, Philip, *Die Schweiz im KSZE-Prozess 1972–1983: Einfluss durch Neutralität* (Munich: Oldenbourg, 2014).

Simonet, Loïc and Lüber,Hans Georg, 'The OSCE and Its Legal Status: Revisiting the Myth of Sisyphus', in Institute for Peace Research and Security Policy at University of Hamburg (ed.), *OSCE Yearbook 2016* (Baden-Baden: Nomos Verlagsgesellschaft, 2017), 277–314.

Snyder, Sarah, *Human Rights Activism and the End of the Cold War* (New York: Cambridge University Press, 2011).

Thomas, Daniel, *The Helsinki Effect: International Norms, Human Rights, and the Demise of Communism* (Princeton: Princeton University Press, 2001).

Tiilikainen, Teija (ed.), *Reviving Co-operative Security in Europe through the OSCE* (Vienna: OSCE, 2015).

US Congress, Congressional Record: Proceedings and Debates of the 106th Congress vol. 146, part 7 (Washington: GPO, 2000).

Zagorski, Andrei, 'The Russian Proposal for a Treaty on European Security: From the Medvedev Initiative to the Corfu Process', in Institute for Peace Research and Security Policy at University of Hamburg (ed.), *OSCE Yearbook 2009* (Baden-Baden: Nomos Verlagsgesellschaft, 2010), 43–59.

Zellner, Wolfgang, 'Russia and the OSCE: From High Hopes to Disillusionment', *Cambridge Review of International Affairs* 18 No. 3 (2005), 389–402.

'Das OSZE-Gipfeltreffen in Astana im Jahr 2010', in Institute for Peace Research and Security Policy at University of Hamburg (ed.), *OSCE Yearbook 2010* (Baden-Baden: Nomos Verlagsgesellschaft, 2011), 23–31.

3

The Role of the Organisation in Asserting Legal Personality: the Position of the OSCE Secretariat on the OSCE's Legal Status

Lisa Tabassi

'The existence of personality is not a matter of recognition but a matter of objective reality.'

Judge Rosalyn Higgins[1]

International legal personality is usually understood as the capacity to have rights and duties.[2] In the case of international organisations this is consistent with the principle of speciality – that international organisations are not all created equal – they only enjoy those powers (rights and duties) expressly conferred upon them by the states that created them or those powers that are implied by necessity for achieving their objectives or that are essential for performing their duties.[3] For the Organization for Security and Co-operation in Europe (OSCE), such necessity is to be interpreted in the widest sense: within its region the OSCE's three-dimensional approach to security is as extensive as the Charter of the UN[4] and is carried out by an unarmed civilian operation of more than 3,500 officials, across fifty-seven states, including conflict zones where its vulnerability is fully exposed.

The present chapter sets aside the doctrinal debate regarding the international legal personality of international organisations[5] and instead examines the practical consequences of operating within the OSCE paradigm where the OSCE's legal status has been debated and, at least for the past twenty years,

1 Higgins, *Problems & Process: International Law and How We Use It*, 47–8.

2 See for more detail Anne Peters, *Beyond Human Rights*, 37–38, with further references; see also Moser and A. Peters, 'Legal Uncertainty and Indeterminacy: Immutable Characteristics of the OSCE?', Chapter 1 in this Volume.

3 ICJ, *Legality of the Use by a State of Nuclear Weapons in Armed Conflict*, Advisory Opinion of 8 July 1996, ICJ Reports 1996, 66, 78.

4 With due regard to the primacy of the Charter of the UN and the mandate of the Security Council in matters of international peace and security.

5 See Blokker and Wessel, Revisiting Questions of Organisationhood, Legal Personality and Membership in the OSCE: the Interplay Between Law, Politics and Practice'; Gasbarri, 'The International Legal Responsibility of the OSCE', both in this Volume.

openly disputed by states. The present author writes in her role as a practitioner, who on a daily basis works in the grey zone of that paradigm, defending the OSCE while at the same time facing the manifold consequences of the lack of formal recognition, or active denial, of its international legal personality and its lack of legal capacity in most national jurisdictions. The following sections therefore analyse, in brief: (1) the source of the dilemma, (2) the evolving institutionalisation of the formally undefined OSCE, (3) the fragmentation of the OSCE through ad hoc mandates and legal arrangements, (4) financial effects, (5) the OSCE's accountability and duty of care as an employer, (6) the possible impact on status neutral engagement, (7) weaknesses made visible in the OSCE deployment to Ukraine, (8) the implications for future OSCE operations, (9) practical applications of theory, (10) de facto international legal personality, (11) functional independence as a prerequisite and finally (12) the recourse to short-term, interim stop-gap measures to fully function and meet the expectations of its participating States.

The present author concludes by arguing that the accumulation of instruments adopted by its decision-making bodies has resulted in establishing a living constitution in the most flexible sense for the OSCE, which enjoys de facto international legal personality as well as privileges and immunities on a customary basis. Rather than simply being a beneficiary of international law, international legal personality allows the OSCE to be the possessor and creator of rights and obligations under international law, something which it in fact does, resulting in the OSCE paradigm. While that paradigm is a fascinating topic for academic scrutiny, the present author concludes with a reminder that, ultimately, legal protection is essential for the human lives engaged in the achievement of OSCE mandates.

1 SOURCE OF THE DILEMMA

The core documents adopted by the CSCE–OSCE over a forty-year period reflect the consistent intention of OSCE participating States that the Organization will have a political constitution in international relations, not a legal constitution under international law. The intention to create the Organization as a political actor rather than a legal one has been explained by two commentators as reflecting 'the assumption that common and comprehensive security is best assured through political consensus rather than legal conditions'.[6] In the view of another, its soft law character not only

[6] Galbreath and Brosig, 'OSCE', 271.

enabled the Helsinki norms to be articulated more broadly than they would have been in a treaty but enabled the very creation of the Organization, which otherwise would not have been achieved.[7] In practice, the absence of formal legal constraints and legal clearance processes for its decisions has resulted in an organisation that is flexible and able to move remarkably quickly to respond to crises or other needs in its region, is relatively small in view of its broad mandates, is not overly bureaucratic and is cost-effective.[8] This flexibility is viewed by some as critical for the preservation of the effectiveness of the OSCE, and a formal alteration of the OSCE's legal basis poses a risk to that flexibility. This is the core of the active debate in the OSCE: the advocates for flexibility are juxtaposed against those who argue that international legal personality of an international organisation can only be acquired on the basis of a formal constitution.

While the intentions concerning the nature of the Organization's political status have remained consistent, the nature of the Organization's structure and operations have gradually transformed as a result of the increasingly complex operational functions mandated to it and the structures created to perform them. The Conference on Security and Co-operation in Europe (CSCE), as the OSCE was initially called, was no longer a diplomatic conference convening on an ad hoc basis in various capitals.[9] In the early 1990s, 'structures' began to be created, including institutions and field operations, as well as mechanisms with the aim of conflict prevention, including confidence- and security-building measures in the military sphere – like the 1990 Vienna Document.[10] Through mandates for election monitoring, ceasefire monitoring, arms control verification and quiet diplomacy, the OSCE necessarily began to exercise independence and a will of its own.

In 1993, the CSCE Ministerial Council met in Rome and decided that it was appropriate to grant legal status and privileges and immunities to the CSCE institutions, albeit by national legislative means and not a multilateral

7 Schlager, 'A Hard Look at Compliance with "Soft" Law' 2000, 371–2.

8 Total budget amounts to EUR 245 million in 2017, including operations in Ukraine, see OSCE, 'Funding and Budget', available at: www.osce.org/funding-and-budget.

9 One commentator classified the CSCE as a permanent pan-European organ, see Smouts, 'Les suites institutionnelles de la Conférence sur la Sécurité et la Coopération en Europe' 1974, 1232. Another explains the CSCE–OSCE as a new form of international organisation consisting of a forum for transgovernmental networking, led by heads of state, which may ripen, or not, into a more traditional organisation, see Slaughter, *A New World Order* 2004, 50–1.

10 Bloed, 'Two Decades of the CSCE Process' 1993, 1–118.

treaty.[11] Notably absent in that Rome Council Decision was the definition of, and necessity to attribute legal status to, the CSCE itself. In 1994, the CSCE Budapest Summit decided upon the change of name to the OSCE but stipulated that it 'alters neither the character of our CSCE commitments nor the status of the CSCE and its institutions. … The CSCE will review implementation of the Rome Decision … and explore if necessary the possibility of further arrangements of a legal nature. Participating States will furthermore examine possible ways of incorporating their commitments into national legislation and, where appropriate, of concluding treaties.'[12]

In 2007, consensus was reached at the expert level on the text of the 2007 Draft Convention on the International Legal Personality, Legal Capacity and Privileges and Immunities of the OSCE. The three footnotes inserted during the conclusion of the negotiations made the adoption of the text conditional on the existence of a legally binding Charter setting forth the OSCE's basic goals, principles, commitments and structure.[13] Such a Charter has not been realised.[14] In 2009, the open-ended Informal Working Group on Strengthening the Legal Framework of the OSCE (IWG) was convened by the OSCE Chairmanship.[15] Since then it has met three times a year to revisit the options tabled and to receive an operational update on the impact of the debacle, so far without result.[16]

The largely academic, though deeply politicised, debate over its international legal personality has not prevented the OSCE from, in fact, establishing agreed mandates and structures to carry out those mandates, concluding agreements with host governments as the 'OSCE' and responding in any dispute proceedings as the 'OSCE'. Nevertheless, the lack of a recognised

11 CSCE, '*Provisions Concerning the Legal Capacity of the CSCE Institutions and Privileges and Immunities. Legal Capacity of the CSCE Institutions* ("Rome Council Decision")', CSCE/4-C/Dec.2, 1 December 1993, Decision 2, Annex 1, available at: www.osce.org/mc/40401?download=true. For discussion of the negotiating history of the 1993 Rome Council Decision, see Sapiro, 'Changing the CSCE into the OSCE: Legal Aspects of a Political Transformation', 634–6.

12 CSCE, Towards a Genuine Partnership in a New Era, Budapest Decisions attached to the Budapest Document, 21 December 1994, available at: www.osce.org/mc/39554?download=true.

13 OSCE, 'Letter from the Chair of the Informal Working Group at Expert Level to the OSCE Chairmanship', CIO.GAL/159/07, 22 October 2017, Annex: Draft Convention on the International Legal Personality, Legal Capacity, and Privileges and Immunities of the OSCE.

14 See further Helmut Tichy, Chapter 4 in this Volume.

15 Ibid.

16 See Helmut Tichy, Chapter 4 in this Volume and in the most recent annual OSCE 'Chairmanship Report to the Ministerial Council on Strengthening the Legal Framework of the OSCE', MC.GAL/7/17, 2017.

legal personality has been identified as one of the most visible weaknesses of the OSCE.[17]

2 EVOLVING INSTITUTIONALISATION OF THE FORMALLY UNDEFINED OSCE

It should be noted that the OSCE, as a unitary institution, is not defined in any document. As will be shown below, the OSCE is amorphous in the sense that one structure is formally autonomous, while three others are treaty bodies with different memberships. Not all participating States agree that those are part of the OSCE although they seem to have been accepted as forming part of the 'Helsinki Process', a holistic term used to explain the aftermath of the 1975 Helskinki Final Act. The OSCE's fragmented structure comprises the following:

(a) Political roles, i.e. the OSCE Chairperson-in-Office; the Troika; Personal Representatives of the Chairperson-in-Office, at least one of which functions as a field operation; and the Secretary General.
(b) Executive Structures, i.e. the Secretariat; the three Institutions (Office for Democratic Institutions and Human Rights (ODIHR) in Warsaw; the High Commissioner on National Minorities (HCNM) in The Hague, the Representative on Freedom of the Media (RFOM) in Vienna); and seventeen field operations.

Each is accountable for their programme delivery to the decision-making bodies, which are described in the OSCE Rules of Procedure as:

(c) Meeting of Heads of State or Government (Summit); Ministerial Council; Permanent Council; and the Forum for Security Co-operation.

In addition, there is:

(d) The OSCE Parliamentary Assembly.
(e) Three entities established by separate treaties, i.e. the OSCE Court of Conciliation and Arbitration, established by the 1992 Stockholm Convention on Conciliation and Arbitration; the Joint Consultative Group, established by the 1990 Treaty on Conventional Armed Forces in Europe; and the Open Skies Consultative Commission, established

[17] Panel of Eminent Persons on European Security as a Common Project, 'Lessons Learned for the OSCE from its Engagement in Ukraine: Interim Report and Recommendations', June 2015, Recommendation 3, available at: www.osce.org/networks/164561?download=true.

by the 1992 Open Skies Treaty. The treaty bodies of the last two entities meet at OSCE premises and are serviced under its auspices.[18]

3 FRAGMENTATION OF THE OSCE THROUGH AD HOC MANDATES AND LEGAL ARRANGEMENTS

The grant on a national basis of legal status and privileges and immunities pursuant to the 1993 Rome Council Decision has resulted in the legal fragmentation of the already structurally fragmented OSCE. The twenty-four separate structures in twenty-two different countries operate under a very broad variety of national legal arrangements.

The host states of the permanent structures of the OSCE (Secretariat and Institutions) have granted privileges and immunities comparable to those granted to the UN. Austria enacted federal legislation in 1995, which granted legal capacity to the OSCE institutions headquartered in Austria and extended application of the UN Headquarters Agreement in Austria to the OSCE institutions, *mutatis mutandis*, as well as privileges and immunities to the OSCE institutions and all OSCE officials present in Austria on official business.[19] The Czech Republic, as host state to the initial CSCE Secretariat (now Documentation Centre in Prague), adopted an Act in respect of the CSCE Secretariat and Institutions in 1992.[20] In the case of the HCNM, the Dutch parliament adopted an Act in 2000 granting legal personality and privileges and immunities to the HCNM, as well as privileges and immunities to all OSCE officials present in the Netherlands on official business.[21] To host the OSCE Parliamentary Assembly, Denmark concluded a headquarters agreement with the OSCE Parliamentary Assembly in 1993.

In the most recent and significant development, Austria concluded a headquarters agreement with the OSCE on 14 June 2017 that comprehensively covers all structures, as well as officers, representatives and officials.[22] The Agreement received parliamentary approval and entered into force in

[18] CSCE, Summit, 'Helsinki Document: The Challenges of Change', 9-10 July 1992, Decision V on the Forum for Security Co-operation, para. 43, available at www.osce.org/helsinki-final-act?download=true.

[19] Austria, Federal Act on the Legal Status of OSCE Institutions in Austria, 30 July 1993 as amended 1995 and 2002, Federal Law Gazette (*Bundesgesetzblatt*) No. 511/1993.

[20] Czech Republic, Act No. 125/1992.

[21] The Netherlands, Act of 31 October 2002 containing provisions concerning the legal personality and privileges and immunities of the High Commissioner on National Minorities.

[22] See further, Tichy and Quidenus, 'Consolidating the International Legal Personality of the OSCE' 2017.

2018, replacing the Austrian Federal Act mentioned above. Concurrently, Poland concluded an Arrangement with the OSCE on 28 June 2017, providing equally comprehensive coverage to the OSCE as well as additional provisions necessary to cover the hosting of the headquarters of ODIHR in Warsaw; it was also ratified by parliament and entered into force in 2018.[23] Registration of both agreements is being pursued with the UN Secretariat under Article 102 of the UN Charter.

In line with the 1993 Rome Council Decision, and in addition to the Austrian, Czech and Dutch legislation mentioned above, the following states adopted legislative or other national measures in favour of the OSCE, which vary as to scope and content: Germany, Hungary, Italy, Norway, Slovakia, Sweden, Switzerland, the United Kingdom and the United States.[24]

[23] Arsić-Đapo, 'Another Brick in the Wall,' 2017.

[24] (1) Federal Republic of Germany, *Verordnung über Vorrechte und Immunitäten der Organisation für Sicherheit und Zusammenarbeit in Europa* (OSZE), 18 February 2016, Federal Law Gazette (*Bundesgesetzblatt*) II No. 4 of 2016, 138 *et seq.*; (2) Hungary, Act on Extension to Institutions, Officers and Employees of the Conference on Security and Cooperation in Europe, Representatives of Participating States and Members of CSCE Missions of the Privileges, Exemptions and Mitigations Granted under the Vienna Convention on Diplomatic Relations dated April 18, 1961, 1994, Act LXXXV of 1994; (3) Italy, Law no. 301 of 1998, 30 July 1998, Official Gazette number 196 of 24 August 1998; (4) Norway, Regulation FOR-2000–01-07–14 *Forskrift om immunitet og privilegier mv. for personer, eiendom og aktiva tilknyttet Organisasjonen for Sikkerhet og Samarbeid i Europa (OSSE), og for personer som foretar inspeksjoner og evaluering under Wien-dokumentet av 1994* (Regulations relating to immunities, privileges, etc., for persons attached to and property and assets connected with the OSCE, and for persons conducting inspections and evaluations in accordance with the Vienna Document of 1994) 1994, available at: https://lovdata.no /dokument/SF/forskrift/ 2000–01-07–14; (5) Czech Republic and Slovak Republic, Act number 125 of 1992, 1992 (n. 19). The act was passed by Czechoslovakia in advance of the 1994 Rome Council Decision; (6) Sweden, *Lag (1976:661) om immunititet och privilegier i vissa fall* (Act on Privileges and Immunities in Certain Cases), 1 July 1994, § 2 (b) and Sweden, *Lag (1994: 716) om rättslig ställning för institiutioner inom Konferensen om säkerhet och samarbete i Europa (ESK)* (Act 1994: 716 on the Legal Capacity of CSCE Institutions), 9 June 1994; (7) Switzerland, Federal Act on the Privileges, Immunities and Facilities and the financial Subsidies granted by Switzerland as a Host State, 22 June 2007, RS 192.12 and Switzerland, Ordinance to the Federal Act on the Privileges, Immunities and Facilities and the Financial Subsidies granted by Switzerland as a Host State, 7 December 2007, RS 192.121; (8) United Kingdom of Great Britain and Northern Ireland, International Organisations Act, 2005, available at: www.legislation.gov.uk/ukpga/2005/20/contents, Chapter 20, Section 4 'The Organization for Security and Co-operation in Europe'; and (9) United States of America, Foreign Relations Authorization Act, Fiscal Years 1994 and 1995, Public Law 103-236, Section 422 and United States of America, Implementing, for the United States, the Provisions of Annex 1 of the Decision Concerning Legal Capacity and Privileges and Immunities, Issued by the Council of Ministers of the Conference on Security and Cooperation in Europe on 1 December 1993, 3 December 1996, Executive Order 13029.

Bilateral Memoranda of Understanding (MOU) or other instruments have been concluded by the OSCE with Armenia (ratified by parliament), Kazakhstan, Kyrgyzstan (ratified by parliament), Montenegro, Serbia, Tajikistan, Turkmenistan, two with Ukraine (both ratified by parliament) and Uzbekistan. In the early instances, the specific field operation itself concluded the instrument with the host government, i.e. with Albania, Bosnia and Herzegovina, Moldova and the former Yugoslav Republic of Macedonia.

In Kosovo,[25] the OSCE operates the field operation under UN Security Council Resolution 1244 (1999) and subsidiary regulations issued by the UN Interim Administration Mission in Kosovo (UNMIK), which explicitly refer to the OSCE as an integrated component of UNMIK for institution-building.

The differences in form have also resulted in broad differences in treatment. The two recent agreements with Austria and Poland are comprehensive; the twelve examples of national legislation or executive orders cover either the 'OSCE' as such or only a particular OSCE structure, the bilateral instruments for fifteen structures cover only that particular structure, one structure derives status and privileges and immunities from a UN Security Council resolution and subsidiary legislation, and one enjoys nothing at all except a Cabinet decision ordering facilitation by relevant ministries.

When status has been granted solely to the particular structure and the officials serving there, other OSCE structures and their officials are unrecognised. When present on official business, they have no formal protection. This includes the Secretary General and heads of other structures who routinely travel throughout the OSCE region on OSCE internal business with no formal arrangements made with the host state i.e., as tourists. In most cases officials are travelling on ordinary passports and, depending on their nationality and the destination, with or without a visa. The Secretary General and various others entitled to do so by their state of nationality possess diplomatic passports issued by that state but, in the exercise of functional independence, are not accredited anywhere by that state. The Vienna Convention on Diplomatic Relations, which has been made applicable *mutatis mutandis* to the structure in most MOUs even though its purpose is to regulate interstate relations, does not cover this situation; it accords protection to diplomatic personnel only in the country of accreditation and in transit.[26] It does not offer protection for the diplomat who is accredited nowhere. In some

25 All references to Kosovo should be understood to be in full compliance with United Nations, United Nations Security Council, Resolution 1244, 1999.

26 Vienna Convention on Diplomatic Relations, 18 April 1961, 500 UNTS 96.

circumstances, the official might be offered treatment as a courtesy, enjoying the status of an official visitor[27] or customary treatment codified in the Convention on Special Missions.[28] This solution, while having no legal certainty, is also not available in most instances: normally for such courtesies to be extended the host state must be notified about the official's visit, which obviously does not occur for routine travel on OSCE internal business.

Regardless of the format or signatures, for the OSCE Secretariat all instruments are considered to be binding and enforceable. In asserting so, it notes the opinion of the International Court of Justice (ICJ) which, when considering the 1946 Convention on the Privileges and Immunities of the United Nations,[29] concluded that 'it is difficult to see how such a convention could operate except upon the international plane and as between parties possessing international personality'.[30] Regarding instruments that have been ratified by the respective parliament, the presumption is that the instrument is *legally* binding and enforceable. However, in respect of the unratified instruments, the national position on their enforceability is not clear to the Secretariat. Notably, serious issues rarely arise, since the political willingness underlying the OSCE consensus decisions to carry out activities in that country seems also to carry over into the host states' political willingness to facilitate operations and resolve any problems.

The patchwork practice of the granting of status and privileges and immunities by national measures not only leaves weaknesses in coverage and gaps but also carries the risk that the measures can disappear overnight, as happened in 2015: a host state unilaterally and formally notified the OSCE through a *Note Verbale* that the MOU for a field operation (a MOU which had been ratified by parliament) was terminated with immediate effect and the OSCE was given one month to wind up its operations and repatriate its international members. Although the Permanent Council decision establishing that field operation and its approved mandate continued until the end of 2015, and although it was questionable whether the provisions of the agreement ratified by parliament could be terminated by a Ministry's *Note Verbale*,

27 Wood, 'The Immunity of Official Visitors' 2012, 35–98.

28 Convention on Special Missions, 8 December 1969, 1400 UNTS 232. See further Michael Wood, 'Convention on Special Missions', United Nations Audio Visual Library, 2012, available at: http://legal.un.org/avl/pdf/ha/csm/csm_e.pdf. For an analysis of the application of the Convention on Special Missions to the OSCE under customary international law, see Hirsch, 'OSCE Legal Personality: Implications for Field Operations' 2017.

29 Convention on the Privileges and Immunities of the United Nations, 13 February 1946, 1 UNTS 16.

30 ICJ, *Reparation for Injuries Suffered in the Service of the United Nations*, Advisory Opinion of 11 April 1949, ICJ Reports 1949, 174, 179.

the message was clear that the field operation was no longer welcome and the privileges and immunities granted would no longer be supported by the Ministry. The OSCE had no recourse but to acquiesce, discontinue operations, liquidate a sixteen-year presence under pressure and extract all international officials, assets and archives within the one-month deadline.[31] The granting of privileges and immunities by means of a multilateral treaty would be more onerous to withdraw from, thus providing more security to the OSCE and its officials regarding the continuity of legal protection, including for an orderly withdrawal.

The strongest statement in support of a unitary OSCE possessing international legal personality are the two comprehensive headquarters agreements concluded in June 2017 by Austria and Poland (mentioned above). As stated by the Legal Adviser to the Austrian Foreign Ministry, such an agreement represents clear recognition by Austria that it considers the OSCE to have obtained international legal personality on the basis of far-reaching – although not general – state practice accepted as law, that is, on the basis of customary international law.[32] Similarly to the process for piecemeal acquisition of statehood, the OSCE may begin to acquire its international legal personality through formal step-by-step recognition, agreement by agreement.[33]

4 FINANCIAL EFFECTS

The tenuous immunity described above (which is arguably not enforceable) and potential legal liability in national courts which could arise from high-risk activities (for example, patrolling or monitoring in conflict zones and high-risk projects involving destruction of surplus armaments and related materials) are a particular concern in terms of financial risk.[34] As immunity from jurisdiction for the persons engaged in those activities may not be successfully recognised by a national court, scrutiny is ongoing in respect of the possible ways to

[31] On this point, cf. ICJ, *Interpretation of the Agreement of 25 March 1951 between the WHO and Egypt*, Advisory Opinion of 20 December 1980, ICJ Reports 1980, 73 & 97, in which the ICJ considered that a reasonable notice was due for the termination of the existing situation, because of all practical arrangements needed to effect an orderly and equitable transfer.

[32] Tichy and Quidenus, 'Consolidating the International Legal Personality of the OSCE' 2017 (n. 24).

[33] Arsić-Đapo, n. 22; cf. Hafner, 'Did the FR Yugoslavia Make the OSCE an International Organization?', 53, who characterises the 1998 Agreement concluded by the Federal Republic of Yugoslavia (FRY) with the OSCE as a unilateral act by the FRY which had no stretch beyond the Agreement itself.

[34] Zhun, 'Operational Aspects of Patrolling/Monitoring' 2016, 12–14.

mitigate potential liabilities through insurance and to fill these gaps to the extent that the OSCE and its officials are protected.

A recent case was scrutinised by the OSCE Secretariat in particular, due to the important financial implications that arose from litigation against an organisation found lacking in exercising its duty of care. That case did not involve an international organisation but rather an NGO not enjoying immunity. However, if OSCE immunity were to fail in a particular jurisdiction, it could find itself in a similar situation before national courts, if an injured party were to sue the OSCE and the OSCE was recognised as having legal standing, based on recognition granted elsewhere, but not recognised as possessing immunity. In the NGO case the staff member was awarded damages of EUR 750,000 over and above the EUR 185,000 he was entitled to (i.e. an increase of 402 per cent over the normal entitlements).[35]

Immunity is granted on the assumption that an international organisation will make appropriate arrangements for settlement of disputes, for example an internal regulatory framework to deal with staff disputes and provisions for arbitration to settle third party disputes. The OSCE internal regulatory framework establishes a financial package for its officials, including social security, roughly commensurate with that offered by other international organisations, with the upper limit being that of the UN common system[36] and provides for arbitration in its General Conditions of Contract. If a scenario arose in which OSCE activities otherwise caused damage to a third party, it would be handled on an ad hoc basis through internal or independent investigation, consultation with the Chairmanship or Troika or relevant decision-making body, etc. This is the general norm among international organisations which rely on public monies contributed by their member states. However, bearing in mind the NGO example, if OSCE immunity were to fail and the dispute heard outside the OSCE's self-contained regime, such a case in national courts could expose the OSCE to significant financial risk under domestic law, presumably a consequence unintended by the OSCE participating States.[37]

If the OSCE cannot be sued, victims injured by the OSCE might initiate legal action against the individual(s) involved. In particular, such legal action might be brought personally against the official who was responsible, i.e. the

35 There was a finding of gross negligence against the NGO; Oslo District Court, *Steven Patrick Dennis* v. *Stiftelsen Flyktninghjelpen* [the Norwegian Refugee Council], Case No: 15-032886TVI-OTI R/05, Judgment of 25 November 2015.

36 OSCE, 'Staff Regulations and Staff Rules', DOC.SEC/3/03, 1 January 2017, Staff Regulation 5.00.

37 Tabassi, 'Operational Update: Legal Liability for Patrolling/Monitoring; Crisis Response; Tax Exemption', SEC.GAL/159/16, 19 October 2016.

Secretary General, Head of Institution or Head of Mission, in a jurisdiction where that official holds assets. If such an event were to occur, the OSCE would ordinarily have the duty to protect the official, either by requesting the respective Ministry of Foreign Affairs to intervene or by securing legal counsel to defend the individual and satisfy any eventual judgment. This is an irregular situation that an international organisation enjoying the standard legal protections would not normally face.[38]

The OSCE regularly concludes commercial contracts with third parties for goods and services in order to carry out its activities, including in states where it has no legal status under domestic law. The OSCE General Conditions of Contract make reference to the OSCE's privileges and immunities, although in most states the existence of them would be disputed and not enforceable, as they are lacking any basis in treaty or domestic law. Alternatively, the individuals acting on behalf of the OSCE would likely be named in the suit. OSCE assets held by them could be seized to satisfy any eventual judgment. Again, this personal liability would ordinarily never arise for officials of an international organisation. International organisations as a matter of course provide in their General Conditions of Contract that dispute settlement shall be by arbitration; in the OSCE paradigm it is particularly important to ensure so.

In addition to the above hypothetical scenarios for potential financial liability, the OSCE's legal status has actual financial consequences on the budget of the OSCE, primarily in terms of taxation. When tax and customs exemption has not been granted in the host country arrangement, direct and indirect taxes (VAT) and duties are paid by the OSCE. Taxes are also paid in locations where no structure is maintained, raising the costs of project implementation by 18–23 per cent.[39]

There is also an impact through taxation of the salaries of OSCE officials. Although the states hosting the CSCE institutions had granted tax exemption on CSCE salaries, the 1993 Rome Council Decision explicitly excluded the issue and specified that, other than functional immunity, participating States are not obliged to grant privileges and immunities to their nationals and permanent residents. Later MOU made the 1961 Vienna Convention on Diplomatic Relations applicable to field operations and its members, *mutatis mutandis*. This resulted in assertions by the host states concerned that the respective field operation is only entitled to the treatment accorded to embassies, not international organisations. In examining that position under the

38 Zhun, 'Operational Aspects of Patrolling/Monitoring' 2016 (n. 44), 12–14.

39 Stribis, 'Operational Update: Lack of Clarity of the Status of the OSCE: Impact on Project Implementation', SEC.GAL/204/15, 15 July 2015.

Vienna Convention, it is noted that of the fifty-three Articles of the Vienna Convention, twenty-seven of them – over half – are irrelevant to the functioning of an international organisation and cannot be applied. One of them relates to the right retained by the receiving state to tax its nationals who are employed in the embassy of the sending state. However, in contrast to embassies, such a practice violates the fundamental and essential principle of the international civil service that salaries are to be tax exempt.[40]

Nevertheless, several host states are asserting their right to tax the salaries of OSCE officials who possess their nationality and serve in a structure in the host state (for example, locally recruited OSCE officials). So far, the tax advances included in the OSCE Unified Budget to remedy such taxation is heatedly disputed by non-taxing and taxing states, some of which argue against treating the OSCE as an international organisation and correspondingly granting tax exemption until such time as the OSCE possesses treaty-based international legal personality. The resources spent by the Secretariat and affected field operations to assert tax exemption and avoid the application of national tax and labour law to the OSCE and its officials is a significant burden in terms of resources and time. Taxation is visible and its financial and resource impact is calculable. The other hypothetical scenarios discussed above, however, carry a far greater and uncertain financial risk than taxation and expose OSCE officials to personal risk.

5 THE OSCE'S ACCOUNTABILITY AND DUTY OF CARE AS AN EMPLOYER

The gaps in the legal framework impose upon the OSCE an additional burden to meet its obligations towards its officials. In 1949, the ICJ concluded that effective protection of international civil servants (in that particular case, UN officials) is an essential *duty*: 'the Organization may find it necessary, and has in fact found it necessary, to entrust its agents with important missions to be

40 For example, the following judgments recognised the principle of tax exemption in the international civil service: Administrative Tribunal of the International Labour Organization, *In re Krutzsch*, Judgment 2032, 31 January 2001, para. 17, available at: www.ilo.org/dyn/triblex/triblex main.fullText?p_lang=en&p_judgment_no=2032&p language_code=EN, & Administrative Tribunal of the International Labour Organization, *ML* v. *Organisation for the Prohibition of Chemical Weapons*, Judgment 2256, 16 July 2003, available at: www.ilo.org/dyn/triblex/ triblexmain.fullText?p_lang=en&p_judgment_no=2256&p_language_code=EN; European Court of Justice, Judgment of 3 July 1974 in Case 7/74 at 760, 762, 764; World Bank Administrative Tribunal, *de Merode case*, 1981, WBAT Reports 1981, Decision number 1; OECD Appeals Board, *Decision No. 111*, 8 July 1988, available at: www.oecd.org/administrative tribunal/Recueil%20de%20décisions%2010 3%20à%20118.pdf, 65–82.

performed in disturbed parts of the world. Many missions, from their very nature, involve the agents in unusual dangers to which ordinary persons are not exposed ... Both to ensure the efficient and independent performance of these missions and to afford effective support to its agents, the Organization must provide them with adequate protection ... In order that the agent may perform his duties satisfactorily, he must feel that this protection is assured to him by the Organization and *that he may count on it*.'[41]

The OSCE's duty of care as an employer has been explicitly incorporated into the OSCE's internal regulatory framework. Staff Regulation 2.07 on Functional Protection provides as follows: 'OSCE officials shall be entitled to the protection of the OSCE in the performance of their duties within the limits specified in the Staff Rules.' In this regard, the OSCE is committed to ensuring the safety and security of its officials through provisions of the OSCE Staff Regulations and Staff Rules[42]. The OSCE has established internal and external procedures for addressing eventual disputes and it has entered into contractual relationships with the aim of providing the necessary insurance coverage as well as paramedic and medical evacuation services.

The scope of OSCE-mandated activities is broad and includes high-risk projects such as demining, or the destruction of ammunition, arms and highly flammable and toxic rocket fuel. OSCE officials may be injured, detained or suffer in many ways. A lack of status, protection and security guarantees raises financial and legal risks that overall may impede and limit the OSCE's ability to resolve crisis situations. Taking into account that in May 2014 two groups of OSCE monitors were abducted and detained for thirty-one and twenty-six days respectively (see further in section 7 below), and that in April 2017 an OSCE mission member was tragically killed,[43] the risks to the health and well-being of OSCE staff is not a hypothetical or academic scenario.

If the OSCE's legal capacity is questionable, who would be held responsible for an accident? Would it be the officials carrying out the activity in the

[41] ICJ, *Reparation for Injuries* (n. 32), 183 [emphasis added]. The UN General Assembly had already articulated the duty to protect its officials in UN, General Assembly, UNGA/Res/258 (III), 1948.

[42] Inter alia, Staff Regulation 2.07 on Functional Protection; Staff Regulation 6.01 on the OSCE Social Security scheme; Staff Regulation 6.05 on the emergency medical evacuation insurance scheme, Article IX on Disciplinary Procedures, Article X on Appeals and the OSCE Code of Conduct, as well as security instructions and other administrative issuances.

[43] OSCE, 'OSCE Special Monitoring Mission to Ukraine patrol member killed in explosion near Luhansk', 23 April 2017, available at: www.osce.org/special-monitoring-mission-to-ukraine/312951; International Humanitarian Fact-Finding Mission, 'International Humanitarian Fact-Finding Commission to lead an independent forensic investigation in Eastern Ukraine', 19 May 2017, available at: www.ihffc.org/index.asp?page=news.

national territory? If they were assigned to an OSCE field operation, would it be the Head of Mission responsible for the activity and instructing the officials there? Would it be the Secretary General as Chief Administrative Officer? Would it be the participating States who approved the Permanent Council decision to mandate the activities and deploy there? If seconded officials were involved, would it partially be the states who seconded them to the OSCE, due to the triangular nature of the employment relationship with secondees?[44] If extra-budgetary, would it be the donors who funded the project? All these questions are in many ways debatable, and lead to legal uncertainty and legal risk, exposure and contingent liability.[45]

It remains to be seen whether the OSCE would be held internationally responsible in a concrete case. Certainly it operates as a unitary institution, its 'executive structures' administratively functioning under one Secretary General, sharing the OSCE internal regulatory system and one array of decision-making bodies. The OSCE has given no indication that it considers itself anything other than an accountable actor, and proceeds to take precautionary steps to mitigate financial liability through insurance, for example.[46] Nevertheless, the adamant, persistent objections to its personality by some states weaken that conclusion, along with the varying scholarly views of commentators.

6 POSSIBLE IMPACT ON STATUS-NEUTRAL ENGAGEMENT?

While the establishment of legal capacity and privileges and immunities at the national level would resolve the localised issues related to OSCE operations in

[44] It should also be clarified that 'seconded officials' in the OSCE, of which 90 per cent of international officials in the field operations are, do not hold a special status, or in many cases any status, with the government which seconded them. 'Secondment' in the OSCE sense merely means that a participating State introduced the application of the individual concerned during the recruitment process. The OSCE Staff Regulations stipulate that seconded officials serve at no cost to the OSCE other than a board and lodging allowance received by those assigned to field operations. Beyond that there is no insight since this triangular secondment employment relationship is unregulated in the OSCE. Consequently, no special protection by the seconding state can be presumed except the customary diplomatic protection the state of nationality may assert under international law if one of its nationals is injured.

[45] For different possible scenarios with respect to the OSCE responsibility, see Gasbarri, 'The International Legal Responsibility of the OSCE', Chapter 11 in this Volume. For questions concerning the OSCE legitimacy arising thereof more generally, see Steinbrück Platise, 'Legitimate Governance as a Privilege and Price for Autonomy of International Organisations', Chapter 14 in this Volume.

[46] See however Moser, 'Conceptualising Accountability in the Legal and Institutional Framework of the OSCE', Chapter 13 in this Volume.

that particular country, the fragmented legal framework and lack of consensus on the international legal personality of the OSCE gives rise to a very serious implication which has not yet been debated. Setting aside for a moment accountability and liability, let us turn now to the political and legal impact of one single activity that occurs in various OSCE operations: unavoidable interaction with de facto 'authorities' in disputed territories or areas not under governmental control while avoiding any suggestion that the interaction implies recognition of them in any way, i.e., 'status-neutral engagement'.

Clearly, when an OSCE mandate requires the field operation to carry out activities in such territories, the mission members necessarily interact with persons in those territories, some of whom assert various forms of authority. Particularly in terms of safety and security, the OSCE cannot rely on the provisions of the MOU concluded with the host government when the government has lost control over the area at issue. The OSCE necessarily interacts with de facto authorities to the extent necessary for safety and security and furthermore may have no alternative but to make arrangements, at least oral or tacit, to obtain goods and services which are necessary for the mission's operations.

OSCE officials have relied on the consistent legal advice from the Secretariat that such 'status-neutral engagement' has no legal consequences for the recognition of such de facto authorities or disputed areas under international law – i.e. only states can recognise states. However, if one holds the view that the OSCE does not possess international legal personality, it is deprived of an independent will. Such a view would suggest that the OSCE merely carries out the consensus-based decisions of OSCE participating States and would logically lead to a conclusion that the OSCE is not an independent entity; rather, it is the instrument through which the fifty-seven participating States exercise their collective will. As a consequence, when OSCE officials are engaging with de facto authorities and agreeing on practical arrangements for access, safety, security, goods, services and so on, it is doing so *not* as an international organisation exercising its functions and acting independently. Rather, it is doing so in the exercise of the joint and several will of the fifty-seven participating States. That conclusion, presumably, is not one that the OSCE decision-making bodies have intended, nor the participating States themselves, and is a political minefield.[47]

[47] Tabassi, 'Update on the Operational Consequences of the Lack of a Clear Legal Status of the OSCE', SEC.GAL/26/17, 10 February 2017.

7 WEAKNESSES MADE VISIBLE IN THE OSCE DEPLOYMENT TO UKRAINE

The operational problems that can arise from the OSCE legal framework became quickly visible in the deployment to address the conflict in and around Ukraine. To address that crisis, the Permanent Council adopted Decision No. 1117 of 21 March 2014, establishing a new OSCE field operation: the Special Monitoring Mission to Ukraine (SMM). In that decision, the Permanent Council tasked the Secretary General to deploy an advance team within twenty-four hours of the decision being adopted. The Secretary General did so, which is a testimony to the effectiveness, flexibility and capacity of the OSCE to react rapidly to a crisis.

Due to the fragmented structure of the OSCE, a new MOU had to be concluded. Negotiations between the OSCE Secretariat and the Ukrainian Government commenced as soon as adoption of the mandate by the Permanent Council became likely (March 2014). The MOU was signed on 14 April 2014, providing for provisional application of all articles of the MOU except those related to privileges and immunities; was ratified by the parliament of Ukraine on 29 May 2014; and it entered into force on 13 June 2014. Start to finish the process took a total of twelve weeks from the date of deployment.

Even so, for the first three weeks (from deployment on 22 March until signature and provisional application on 14 April 2015), the SMM was operating with no formal legal status or capacity. And for the first twelve weeks (22 March until entry into force of the MOU on 13 June 2014), SMM monitors had no formal privileges or immunities covering their official activities nor the formal protection of the security guarantees by the host state other than, perhaps, courtesy to official visitors or customary Special Mission treatment. It is important to note that during those twelve weeks in which the OSCE and the SMM were carrying out the mandated activities, they were in principle accountable for any injury caused and – in view of the unclear legal status – the SMM and its members were exposed to an uncertain liability for any damage caused.

Furthermore, during that period, eight SMM monitors were abducted and held incommunicado for one month by armed groups, giving rise to speculation within the OSCE as to how liability would manifest if injuries were suffered. Until the MOU was signed and provisionally applied, Ukraine was formally under no obligation to afford special protection, other than its obligations as State Party to the 1973 Convention on the Prevention and Punishment of Crimes against Internationally Protected Persons, including

Diplomatic Agents,[48] which provides for protection *ex post facto* of any incident.[49]

Moreover on the practical operational level, the SMM's effective operation was initially hampered in the first three weeks by its lack of formal legal capacity, preventing it from being entitled to open bank accounts, enter into contracts or import much-needed equipment and vehicles, especially armoured vehicles, to enable it to travel safely throughout Ukraine. These difficulties had to be resolved on an ad hoc and sub-optimal basis, such as officials temporarily assigned to SMM entering Ukraine with OSCE vehicles on a personal basis and then encountering difficulties when they tried to leave without them.

Additionally, in the OSCE's existing patchwork system of granting privileges and immunities on a limited case-by-case basis, while the MOU ensures that the SMM monitors are now protected in Ukraine, other OSCE officials who undertake official travel to Ukraine such as the Secretary General and Secretariat staff; the High Commissioner on National Authorities and his staff; the ODIHR or Parliamentary Assembly human rights or election monitors and other officials, are deprived of formal legal status, privileges, immunities or security guarantees in Ukraine. Consequently, to a certain extent legal risk persists.

The establishment of the Observer Mission at the Russian checkpoints of Gukovo and Donetsk[50] (OM) on the Russian–Ukrainian border posed particular difficulties, since the Russian Federation repeatedly declared its position in the IWG and elsewhere that, in accordance with its constitution, it cannot recognise the OSCE as a 'fully-fledged' regional organisation until it is established by treaty ratified by its parliament. The OM is hosted by the Russian Federation pursuant to the Permanent Council Decision 1130 (2014) and a Russian Federation Cabinet Order of 15 October 2014; nevertheless, the OM lacks domestic legal capacity. Consequently, the OM has no bank account, no locally recruited employees and its members have been encouraged to bear diplomatic passports accredited to the embassy (in Moscow) by their respective home state (albeit assuring no consequences for reciprocity at the bilateral level). As a procedure for issuing diplomatic passports on such

48 Convention on the Prevention and Punishment of Crimes against Internationally Protected Persons, including Diplomatic Agents, 14 December 1973, 1035 UNTS 168.

49 Although the SMM monitors enjoyed no privileges and immunities in Ukraine, the offers and acceptances of their Letters of Appointment as OSCE officials had taken place in the Secretariat in Vienna under the Austrian Federal Law on the OSCE, conferring on them the status of 'privileged persons' in Austria at the time of deployment to Ukraine.

50 OSCE, Permanent Council, 'Deployment of OSCE Observers to two Russian Checkpoints on the Russian–Ukrainian Border', PC.DEC/1130, 24 July 2014.

a basis is not available in some states, such a solution is not implementable for all and some OM members enjoy no special protection. It has not been clarified whether they may be considered official visitors, or whether the OM may be considered to be a Special Mission under customary international law. If the OSCE does not exist as a legal person there, it is not clear who would be held accountable.

8 IMPLICATIONS FOR FUTURE OSCE OPERATIONS

The 1992 Helsinki Summit Decision III provides the OSCE with a mandate to carry out civilian as well as military peacekeeping.[51] However, the Organization has not yet deployed a peacekeeping operation, whether 'formed' police or formed military units. In the context of military peacekeeping by the OSCE, conceptually there is only one concrete example: the 1994 Budapest Summit Decision II on the Nagorno-Karabakh conflict foresaw that,

> '. . . the conclusion of the agreement mentioned above [a political agreement on the cessation of the armed conflict] would also make it possible to deploy multinational peacekeeping forces as an essential element for the implementation of the agreement itself. They [the participating States] declared their political will to provide, with an appropriate resolution from the United Nations Security Council, a multinational CSCE peacekeeping force.'[52]

While it has been foreseen in the 1994 Budapest Decision II that OSCE peacekeeping would involve a UN Security Council resolution,[53] could such a resolution, if adopted under Chapter VII, resolve the constitutional and legal obstacles that may prevent a peacekeeping operation composed of formed police or military units to be placed under the authority of the OSCE in an OSCE operation? It could potentially provide the solution, if one looks to the example of Security Council Resolution 1778 (2007) on the violence occurring in Chad, the Central African Republic and the sub-region. In that case, acting under Chapter VII, the Security Council authorised the EU to deploy an operation and to take all necessary measures. The UN Security Council called upon all parties to cooperate fully in the deployment and running of the EU operation, including by guaranteeing the security and freedom of movement of their personnel. It urged all the UN member states to facilitate the delivery

[51] See further the legal analysis in Ronzitti, 'OSCE Peacekeeping' 1997, 237–55.

[52] CSCE, Summit, 'Budapest Document 1994: Towards a Genuine Partnership in a New Era,' Decision II, paragraph 4, 21 December 1994.

[53] For a general discussion, see Burci, 'Division of Labour between the UN and the OSCE in connection with Peacekeeping', 289 –313.

to Chad and the Central African Republic freely and without obstacles or delay of all personnel, equipment, provisions, supplies and other goods, including vehicles and spare parts, intended for the EU Operation. Significant (and encouraging) in this respect is that although the Treaty of Lisbon establishing the EU's international legal personality was not yet in force, the UN Security Council nonetheless authorised the EU and required all states to cooperate with it, including non-EU member states.

Conceptually, a 'peace operation' does not necessarily mean peacekeeping and has not yet been articulated in the OSCE. It could include the more readily recognisable needs for effective operations in conflict zones: (a) unarmed unmanned aerial vehicle (UAV) system capabilities operated by militarily trained technicians and analysts, (b) a military field hospital operated by military personnel or (c) small police contingents to assist in the rule of law, particularly in post-conflict rehabilitation.[54] The legal obstacles that could arise should not be underestimated or minimised by the notion that they can be effectively overcome with sufficient political will. The secondment and deployment of formed units may give rise to constitutional and/or legislative restrictions on the side of both the contributing and the host states. In many jurisdictions, such obstacles cannot be resolved without pursuing parliamentary approval processes, which are ordinarily time-consuming and not conducive to crisis responses.

To illustrate the possible legal impediments, there is the precedent from 2014 of the failed attempt by a group of OSCE participating States to conclude the legal arrangements necessary to loan to the OSCE military UAVs and the military personnel to operate them. That effort failed despite the political will to carry it forward and efforts by the authorities in capital cities to secure the necessary legal clearances. In this specific case, SMM was seeking to enhance its effectiveness through remote aerial surveillance by unmanned aerial vehicles (UAVs) of the area it was monitoring. Offers from participating States to provide the equipment and technological capacity were received; however, legal obstacles prevented the offers from being accepted because such equipment and experts from the potentially contributing states belonged to the military, which could not make loans to an entity not enjoying international legal personality, as there could be no assurances of the proper immunity at the international level. Consequently, the SMM has had to obtain such services through a commercial contractor, at significant expense, through open tender in accordance with the OSCE Financial Regulations.

54 Tabassi, 'Operational Update: The Legal Aspects of OSCE Peace Operations' SEC.GAL/205/15, 5 October 2015.

The Package of Measures for the Implementation of the Minsk Agreements, signed in Minsk on 12 February 2015 by 'the participants of the Trilateral Contact Group', i.e. the OSCE, the Russian Federation and Ukraine,[55] envisage that the OSCE will carry out effective monitoring and verification of the ceasefire regime in Ukraine and the withdrawal of heavy weapons with the use of all necessary technical means, including satellites, UAVs, radar systems and so on. It is not yet entirely clear to what extent or by what means the OSCE will be able to obtain all those technological capacities. If such support is to be contributed as formed military or police units or technical equipment with military or police operators, legal obstacles, similar to those experienced in Ukraine with the loan of UAVs and the relevant analysts, could again come into play.

9 PRACTICAL APPLICATIONS OF THEORY

Given the broad scope of the OSCE's sphere of activities and its importance in the region for the European security architecture, it could even be said that despite the statement that the renaming of the CSCE to the OSCE in 1994 had no substantive effect, the acquisition of international legal personality was inherent[56] in that Summit decision.[57] The small group of states advocating for a Charter as a precondition for such personality faces the other equally small group promoting the 2007 Draft Convention, while the majority remain silent, presumably awaiting consensus to emerge at some point. The OSCE's internal debate on its legal personality has been externally analysed in sporadic legal commentaries.[58]

Nevertheless, the solution is not to be found in the academic definitions of 'international organisation', which are not consistent.[59] One commentator has remarked that the grant of immunity is not indicative of the existence of international legal personality, noting that Switzerland has granted immunity to the

55 UN Security Council, Package of Measures for the Implementation of the Minsk Agreements, S/RES/2202, 17 February 2015, Annex I.

56 See discussion of the inherent powers approach in Klabbers, *An Introduction to International Organizations Law*, 68 and White, *The Law of International Organisations*, 87–9.

57 This is the conclusion of Bertrand, 'La nature juridique de l'Organisation pour la Securite et la Cooperation en Europe (OSCE)', 387–405; and Sands and Klein, *Bowett's Law of International Institutions*, 201; cf. the contrary, Sapiro, 'Changing the CSCE into the OSCE', 631–7, and Martha, *The Legal Foundations of Interpol* 2010, 199, who concludes that in order for an organisation to acquire international legal personality, there must be, inter alia, evidence of an *animus* to create a new subject of law.

58 See bibliography to the present chapter.

59 See, ILC, 'Draft Articles on the Responsibility of International Organisations, with Commentaries', UNGA/66/10, 2011, commentary on Article 2(a); Amerasinghe, *Principles of the Institutional Law of International Organizations*, 10; Bouwhuis, 'The International Law Commission's Definition of International Organizations', 452–4.

OSCE, making a distinction between 'international organisations' – which possess international legal personality, and 'international institutions' – which do not.[60] The same commentator argues that 'an international organization can be granted domestic legal personality not in order to comply with an international obligation but on the basis of political commitment or even expedience. This is the position, for instance, of the UK with regard to the OSCE.'[61] Recognition of the OSCE solely on the basis of its legal personality established in domestic law has the effect of enabling it to carry out functions as a legal person in that jurisdiction; it does not create or impact its recognition on the international plane.

In noting that the OSCE has a fact-finding capacity and can conduct peacekeeping activities, one commentator has explained the legal basis for such powers as 'the sum of those customary rights possessed by individual member States in the areas of consensual pacific settlement'.[62] Following the 'objective' theory of international legal personality, Judge Higgins has noted that the classic attributes of legal personality for an international organisation are '(1) an ability to contract, (2) an ability to sue and be sued, (3) an ability to own property, and (4) a *volonté distincte* – in other words, a capacity to take decisions which bind the membership, perhaps even when not all of the members have favoured the decision concerned ... If the attributes are there, personality exists. It is not a matter of recognition. It is a matter of objective reality.'[63]

On the other hand, Judge Crawford indicated that 'the primary test is functional' and has explicitly included the OSCE as an example of an international organisation that has derived its legal personality from 'government consensus reached at international conferences'.[64] Arguably the OSCE also meets the three criteria summarised by him for an organisation to objectively possess legal personality: it is an association with aims and organs, possesses a distinct will and exercises powers on the international plane.[65] The OSCE does all that, albeit in its own way and phrased terminologically differently.

60 Gazzini, 'Personality of International Organisations' 2011, 42–3.
61 Gazzini, 'Personality of International Organisations' 2011 (n. 66), 45. See further, United Kingdom International Organisations Act 2005, 2005 (n. 26).
62 White, *The Law of International Organisations* 2005 (n. 69), 52–3.
63 Higgins, *Problems & Process: International Law and How We Use It*, 46–8. Note that consensus is achieved in most instances by allowing participating States to attach 'interpretative statements', which they regularly do. Some of those resemble reservations although in practice are not treated as such. It seems that in some cases such interpretative statements are indicative of the strong views of a state which later may develop into opposition to any further decisions in the same vein.
64 Crawford, *Brownlie's Principles of Public International Law*, 170.
65 Ibidem, 169.

Klabbers has criticised the notion that 'soft organisations' like the OSCE exist in a legal limbo outside the scrutiny of the judiciary or parliament, considering this a fiction since there is no difference between the OSCE and a formal (treaty-based) organisation in terms of efficacy. Consequently, it is of little relevance whether its decisions are considered to be legally binding or not.[66] In particular, he considered that 'law is the normative order governing political behaviour: our political agreements become law, whether we intend them to or not, precisely because "politics" is not (and can hardly be) a separate normative order'.[67] He further states that to argue that such a status is needed for the purposes of flexibility and effectiveness can be unhelpful, illusory and affect its legitimacy.[68]

In terms of Portmann's recent analysis, the OSCE falls most neatly into the actor conception, i.e. 'all actors actually taking part in authoritative decision-making processes of an international kind are participants of the international legal order irrespective of the cause for participation, based on legal realism and international realism'.[69] Portmann concludes that 'recognition of international legal status may have considerable evidential value but is not in itself necessary or sufficient for constituting personality in international law . . . the sole consequence of being an international person is to be able to invoke international responsibility and to be held internationally responsible as far as applicable secondary rules exist'.[70] This aspect has not yet been tested, although the reactions in respect of the death of a mission member on 23 April 2017 strongly suggest that accountability would lie with the Organization if fault were to be identified.[71]

66 Klabbers, 'Institutional Ambivalence by Design', 407–13, 421, citing also on page 419; Schweisfurth, 'Die juristische Mutation der KSZE', 228. See also I. Peters, 'Legitimacy and International Organizations – The Case of the OSCE', 196–220, in particular 203–6.

67 Gautier also agrees. He concludes that law is not based on will; legal consequences may attach to political agreements. See Gautier, 'Accord et Engagement Politique en Droit des Gens a Propose de l'Acte Fondateur sur les Relations, La Coopération et la Sécurité Mutuelles entre l'OTAN et la Fédération de Russie, signe à Paris le 27 Mai 1997', 89. Cf. Hafner, n. 32, 35–57, who argues that the OSCE remains outside the legal realm.

68 Klabbers, 'Institutional Ambivalence by Design' 2001 (n. .73), 407–13.

69 Portmann, *Legal Personality in International Law*, 212–13. Unfortunately, the author omitted any discussion of the OSCE in his analysis.

70 Ibid., 282–3.

71 The Secretary General immediately established an internal investigation into compliance with regulations, rules and standard operating procedures; the Chairmanship tasked the Secretary General to form and deploy an independent team of experts to conduct a forensic post-blast scene investigation; and the Permanent Council endorsed these and demanded that all those responsible be held to account (OSCE, Permanent Council, 'Declaration of Support for the Special Monitoring Mission to Ukraine following the tragic Incident that occurred on 23 April 2017', PC.DOC/1/17, 27 April 2017.

10 DE FACTO INTERNATIONAL LEGAL PERSONALITY

The aims of the OSCE are ambitious – in terms of specialty, the Helsinki Final Act conceptualised a uniquely comprehensive approach to security, encompassing politico-military (First Dimension), environmental and economic (Second Dimension), and human rights and fundamental freedoms (Third Dimension), plus certain cross-dimensional threats (gender equality, border management, policing, human trafficking, violent radicalisation, terrorism and so on). A deficit in any one of those dimensions is considered to be a security threat, prompting the OSCE to react. The Helsinki Final Act also established ten fundamental principles ('the Decalogue'), all of which appear in the Charter of the UN (albeit articulated differently),[72] against which 'compliance' is measured and discussed in the OSCE bodies. The course of action available within the OSCE realm to respond to non-compliance by participating States is dispute resolution by political means, not legal proceedings.[73] All this is indicative of the very broad sphere the OSCE operates in and the serious matters in which it is engaged, despite its fragmented legal status.

Due to the critical need for legal status and privileges and immunities in order for the OSCE to function, the OSCE Secretariat is left with no other choice but to pragmatically assert that the OSCE enjoys them on a de facto or customary basis across the OSCE region. Although there is almost no scholarly support for such an assertion[74] and the argument can easily be dismissed by those opposing it, the Secretariat has no alternative. In doing so, it relies upon the 1949 Advisory Opinion of the ICJ, rendered when the international legal personality of the UN was disputed. In that case, the ICJ concluded that in order for the UN to achieve its ends, the attribution of international personality to the UN was indispensable:

> [T]he Organization is a political body, charged with political tasks of an important character, and covering a wide field namely, the maintenance of international peace and security, the development of friendly relations among nations, and the achievement of international co-operation in the

72 For a discussion of the OSCE commitments as legal rules, see Odello, 'The Organization for Security and Co-operation in Europe and European Security Law', 302–10.

73 See further Bothe, 'The Various Dispute Settlement Procedures – General International Law and OSCE Practice', 367–79; and Lohmann, 'Dispute Settlement Procedures in the OSCE – Genesis and Overview', 343–65.

74 See Wood, 'Do International Organizations Enjoy Immunity Under Customary International Law?', 316–18.

> solution of problems of an economic, social, cultural or humanitarian character ... and in dealing with its Members it employs political means .... In the opinion of the Court, the Organization was intended to exercise and enjoy, and is in fact exercising and enjoying, functions and rights which can only be explained on the basis of the possession of a large measure of international personality and the capacity to operate upon an international plane .... It must be acknowledged that its Members, by entrusting certain functions to it, with the attendant duties and responsibilities, have clothed it with the competence required to enable those functions to be effectively discharged. Accordingly, the Court has come to the conclusion that the Organization is an international person.[75]

Taking into account the scope of the OSCE principles and commitments, the multitude of instruments and documents that have been adopted in its three dimensions, and the decisions that have been taken to establish the mandates and tasks of the OSCE and the structures to carry them out, the above conclusion of the ICJ is relevant to the OSCE paradigm. This is despite it having no constitutive treaty, which would expressly grant it legal capacity, privileges or immunities, the way the UN Charter grant these to the UN in Articles 104 and 105, nor a convention that would elaborate on these issues the way the UN Convention on the Privileges and Immunities does with respect to the UN. The relevance of the ICJ findings for the OSCE is underscored by the reliance of participating States upon the OSCE as a primary instrument for providing early warning of conflict in the region[76] and its establishment of multiple field operations and other deployments over twenty-five years to address crises before and during conflict and to carry out post-conflict rehabilitation and capacity-building in all areas affecting human security, and concluding agreements with it, which normally would only be concluded with a subject of international law.

Furthermore, it would appear that the OSCE's possession of international legal personality is accepted by many states and international organisations.[77] Although the politicised debate blocks progress in the IWG, it has not blocked

75 ICJ, *Reparation for Injuries* 1949 (n. 32), 179.

76 OSCE, Ministerial Council, 'Elements of the Conflict Cycle, related to Enhancing the OSCE's Capabilities in Early Warning, Early Action, Dialogue Facilitation and Mediation Support, and Post-Conflict Rehabilitation', MC.DEC/3/11, 7 December 2011.

77 The OSCE regularly collaborates with other international organisations as implementing partners or in cost-sharing agreements. For these purposes it has concluded agreements, MOUs, exchanges of letters or other instruments with the UN and its Specialized Agencies and Programmes, the EU, the Council of Europe, Interpol and other international organisations, universal and regional. See further Laurence Boisson de Chazournes and Gadkowski, 'The External Relations the OSCE', Chapter 10 in this Volume.

the operations of the OSCE, which have proceeded as if the OSCE enjoys a unitary international legal personality.

The legal arrangements concluded between the OSCE and countries hosting OSCE structures are markedly similar to the treatment accorded to other regional and universal international organisations. A few of the agreements for the first field operations were concluded in the form of Exchanges of Letters or Articles of Understanding. Since then, however, a practice has developed that all of the later host country agreements bear the nomenclature of MOU, which in some legal systems would suggest that the instruments are politically, not legally binding. Nevertheless, the texts of these agreements are very similar in content to the usual host country agreements concluded as treaties with treaty-based international organisations. This type of agreement is necessarily legally binding for the very reason that the provisions need to be enforceable under national law and often cannot be granted as a courtesy. As indicated in Section 3 above, some of the OSCE MOUs have been ratified by the respective parliament of the host country in order to give effect to them within that national law, which suggests that they may qualify as treaties in the national legal order.

The Secretariat approaches this situation pragmatically, since the OSCE must carry out its mandates and functions on the ground and achieve its purposes. In doing so, the Secretariat assumes that the OSCE enjoys international personality and invokes status and privileges and immunities across the OSCE region whether they have been formally granted or not. Since the OSCE operates with the consensus of its participating States, these assertions have not been challenged and have not become problematic. The legal basis for allowing the Secretary General to assume this power is to be found in his duty of care as Chief Administrative Officer, accountable to the Permanent Council for protection of OSCE officials and OSCE assets, as stipulated in his approved mandate and the OSCE CRMS, in both the Staff and Financial Regulations. Furthermore, in legal terms, such a longstanding silent acceptance of this by participating States indicates that *per facta concludentia* states recognise the Secretary General with the power to conclude such agreements with states, which by now has become a well-established practice.

Even if the intention of OSCE participating States remains *not* to create an international legal person, the acts of the decision-making bodies have had the de facto consequence of doing just that, as OSCE operations and treatment are otherwise not explainable. The mandates and tasks assigned by consensus to the OSCE have clear *operational* aspects that manifest on the territories of OSCE participating States. The operational dimension of OSCE activities is at least as important as the deliberative one. Echoing the ICJ in terms equally applicable to the OSCE, 'it must be acknowledged that its Members, by entrusting certain functions to it, with the attendant duties and responsibilities, have clothed it with the competence required to enable those functions to be effectively discharged. Accordingly, the Court has come to the conclusion that the Organization is an international person.'[78]

11 FUNCTIONAL INDEPENDENCE AS A PREREQUISITE

The grant of legal status and privileges and immunities by multilateral treaty ensures consistency and prevents unilateral revocation without notice or recourse. This is important because legal status and privileges and immunities are essential to the functioning of international organisations and are a prerequisite for their independence. The fundamental importance of independence has been articulated at the highest levels: by the ICJ,[79] the International Civil Service Commission,[80] and the Administrative Tribunal of the International Labour Organization.[81] Consistent with that, the OSCE Code of Conduct provides that 'OSCE officials shall neither seek nor accept instructions regarding the performance of their duties, from any government or from any authority external to the OSCE.'[82] OSCE Staff Regulation 2.03 stipulates that privileges and immunities shall be enjoyed by OSCE officials. The 1993 Rome Council Decision elaborated that appropriate treatment is to be implemented by participating States.

In the OSCE paradigm, the OSCE exercises its independence unquestioned, without legal underpinnings in most cases other than custom. There is no suggestion that any state or organisation challenges the OSCE's expectation that it will be granted the necessary facilities to carry out its mandates. In fact, the Secretary General from time to time has received requests for waivers of immunity when national or international investigators have wished to introduce OSCE documents as evidence in judicial proceedings or

78 ICJ, *Reparation for Injuries* 1949 (n. 32) 179.

79 Ibidem, 183.

80 International Civil Service Commission, 'Standards of Conduct for the International Civil Service', Paragraph 8, available at: http://icsc.un.org/resources/pdfs/general/standardsE.pdf. The standards were approved by the UN General Assembly United Nations common system: Report of the International Civil Service Commission, UNGA/Res/ 67/257, 3 June 2013.

81 Administrative Tribunal of the International Labour Organization, *JMB* v. *Organisation for the Prohibition of Chemical Weapons*, Judgment 2232, 16 July 2003, para. 16.

82 OSCE, 'Staff Regulations and Staff Rules', DOC.SEC/3/03, 1 January 2017 (n. 37), Appendix 1, Section 2.

otherwise needed access to present or former OSCE officials as witnesses. Some such requests have been received from states where the OSCE and its officials enjoy no formal immunity. Those instances can only be explained on the basis of a customary basis for legal status and privileges and immunities.

12 SHORT-TERM INTERIM STOP-GAP MEASURES

Since the Secretary General, as Chief Administrative Officer, is faced on a daily basis with the operational impact of the OSCE's current legal status, and given the fact that there is no apparent solution anticipated to emerge from the IWG in the near future, he initiated a short-term interim stop-gap measure: the model Standing Arrangement.[83] The model was proposed to all participating States in July 2015 and, if concluded by each of them, would recognise the legal status of the OSCE and its officials in national jurisdictions in a comprehensive and harmonised manner, filling in the patchwork of arrangements across in the OSCE region as envisaged by the 1993 Rome Council Decision. It is also consistent with Staff Regulation 2.03, which provides that OSCE officials shall enjoy the privileges and immunities to which they may be entitled by national legislation or by virtue of bilateral agreements concluded by the OSCE relating to this matter.

The text of the model Standing Arrangement is formulated to address the Secretary General's duty of care towards OSCE staff and his accountability to the Permanent Council for the sound management of the OSCE's assets. It is an interim solution, purely based on the serious operational need to protect OSCE officials and assets in states where no national measures in favour of the OSCE exist. It is a separate track from the political–legal discussions ongoing in the IWG. This initiative also serves to demonstrate that the Secretary General does not acquiesce to the present legal situation in which the OSCE operates.

The text of the Standing Arrangement grants, inter alia: legal capacity to the OSCE, inviolability of its premises and archives, immunity from jurisdiction and tax and customs exemptions; as well as privileges and immunities to

[83] Such a concept was originally developed by the Austrian Chairmanship and the Secretariat in 2000 and tabled in an open-ended working group on OSCE legal capacity. Initial provisions published as CIO.GAL/170/00 dated 22 August 2000 and developed further into a draft following meetings of the group in September and October (on file in the Secretariat). The 2015 model Standing Arrangement was published in OSCE document SEC.GAL/135/16, 8 September 2016. Its revised version has been issued in 2017 in SEC.GAL/117/17, 11 September 2017.

representatives of participating States participating in OSCE meetings, members of the Parliamentary Assembly and officials of its Secretariat, experts on mission and OSCE officials without distinction as to nationality, consistent with their status as international civil servants as stipulated in Staff Regulation 2.01 and section 3 of the OSCE Code of Conduct. Once the Standing Arrangement is concluded and in force, it would cover the OSCE and any of its activities in the host state's territory, including, among others, project implementation, meetings and election monitoring.

13 CONCLUSION

The rapid deployment in Ukraine brought sharp focus to the legal and operational consequences of the lack of consensus on the international legal personality and the scope of privileges and immunities to be enjoyed by the OSCE, its structures and officials. The Ukraine experience, however, is not unique nor is it an anomaly. Although not as dramatic, similar consequences are experienced routinely in the daily operations of the OSCE in its other executive structures, including the Secretariat and the Institutions and the other field operations. This tension created by the OSCE paradigm has recently prompted bolder unilateral action by participating States, notably the agreements concluded as treaties by Austria and by Poland with the OSCE in June 2017. The strongest statement in support of a unitary OSCE possessing international legal personality is the combination of those two agreements. The Austrian Legal Adviser found this to imply Austrian recognition of the OSCE's customary law-based international legal personality.[84] Similarly to the process for piecemeal acquisition of statehood, the OSCE may begin to acquire its international legal personality through formal step-by-step recognition, agreement by agreement.[85]

Within the OSCE, decisions are routinely relied upon for legal interpretation of its rights and obligations. The Secretariat argues that the accumulation of Summit, Ministerial and Permanent Council decisions comprise the OSCE's Constitution as a living instrument in the most dynamic sense,[86] its

[84] Tichy and Quidenus, (n. 24).

[85] Arsić-Đapo, 'Another Brick in the Wall'; cf. Hafner, (n. 35), 53, who characterises the 1998 Agreement concluded by the Federal Republic of Yugoslavia (FRY) with the OSCE as a unilateral act by the FRY which had no stretch beyond the Agreement itself.

[86] See further Odello, 'The Developing Legal Status of the Organisation for Security and Co-operation in Europe', 372–7, referring also to Amerasinghe, *Principles of the Institutional Law of International Organizations*. Gautier considers that based on the OSCE's evolution and effectiveness, it has become an international organisation despite its lack of

international legal personality has been de facto established and privileges and immunities are enjoyed on a customary basis – arguments which are easily disputed.

The OSCE's fifty-seven participating States, through consensus-based political arrangements, have over a period of forty years created an international organisation, assigned it functions and mandates, dispatched it into conflict zones, and seconded their citizens to staff it. While there may be a lack of clarity on the formal legal status and privileges and immunities of the OSCE and its officials, there is *full clarity* on the operational activities it is expected to perform as an international entity, carrying out its activities as if it enjoyed the privileges and immunities that treaty-based international organisations normally need and are formally granted.

The commemoration of the forty years since the signature of the Helsinki Final Act, the founding document of the OSCE, was well timed for achieving progress on the issue of strengthening the legal framework of the OSCE. Politically, however, consensus was more elusive than ever. Nevertheless, a clear legal status of the OSCE is essential for enabling the OSCE to perform effectively and efficiently the mandates assigned to it by its decision-making bodies in a proper legal framework, ensuring the centrality of its role in the European security architecture.

While this may be a matter of academic interest, let us not forget that what we are speaking of here is legal protection for human safety and security, both of the more than 3,500 individuals who are dedicated to delivering the OSCE's mandate, as well as the 1 billion individuals who are hoping to be the beneficiaries of the OSCE's principles and commitments: peace and security across the OSCE region – from Vancouver to Vladivostok – economic development, environmental protection, democracy and human rights. The tragedy relating to the death of an OSCE mission member in 2017 is compounded further by the fact that while the lawyers in the IWG in Vienna dithered over whether the OSCE legally exists or not, the OSCE mission member died in the pursuit of its aims. As a former Special Adviser to the OSCE Chairmanship on the Legal Framework admonished on several occasions, '[T]his problem is not just a theoretical one or a playground for lawyers . . . It is clearly unacceptable that common and clear rules about status,

a constituent treaty and functions on the basis of instruments of equivalent effect; see Gautier, 'Accord et Engagement Politique en Droit des Gens a Propose de l'Acte Fondateur sur les Relations, la Coopération et la Sécurité Mutuelles entre l'OTAN et la Fédération de Russie, signe à Paris le 27 Mai 1997', 91–2. Bekkers argues that any document may constitute a constituent instrument: Bekkers, *The Legal Position of Intergovernmental Organizations*, 56.

privileges and immunities are not already in place when the OSCE has to act so rapidly.'[87]

REFERENCES

Amerasinghe, Chittharanjan, *Principles of the Institutional Law of International Organizations* 2nd edn (Cambridge: Cambridge University Press, 2003).

Arsić-Đapo, Jasna, 'Another Brick in the Wall: Building Up the OSCE as an International Organization One Agreement at a Time', *International Organisations Law Review* 14 (2017), 414–29.

Bekkers, Peter, *The Legal Position of Intergovernmental Organizations: A Functional Necessity Analysis of Their Legal Status and Immunities* (Dordrecht: TMC Asser Institute, 1996).

Bertrand, Christine, 'La nature juridique de l'Organisation pour la Sécurité et la Coopération en Europe (OSCE)', *Revue Generale de Droit International Public* (April–June 1998), 366–406.

Bloed, Arie, 'Two Decades of the CSCE Process: From Confrontation to Co-operation', in Arie Bloed (ed.), *The Conference on Security and Co-operation in Europe: Analysis and Basic Documents, 1972–1993* (Dordrecht: Kluwer Academic Publishers, 1993), 1–118.

Bothe, Michael, 'The Various Dispute Settlement Procedures – General International Law and OSCE Practice', in Michael Bothe, Natalino Ronzitti and Allan Rosas (eds.), *The OSCE in the Maintenance of Peace and Security: Conflict Prevention, Crisis Management and Peaceful Settlement of Disputes* (The Hague: Kluwer Law International, 1997), 367–79.

Bouwhuis, Steven, 'The International Law Commission's Definition of International Organizations', *International Organizations Law Review* 9 (2012), 451–65.

Burci, Gian Luca, 'Division of Labour between the UN and the OSCE in connection with Peacekeeping', in Michael Bothe, Natalino Ronzitti and Allan Rosas (eds.), *The OSCE in the Maintenance of Peace and Security: Conflict Prevention, Crisis Management and Peaceful Settlement of Disputes* (The Hague: Kluwer Law International, 1997), 289–313.

Crawford, James, *Brownlie's Principles of Public International Law* 8th edn (Oxford: Oxford University Press, 2012).

[87] OSCE, John Bernard, Chairperson of the Informal Working Group on Strengthening the Legal Personality of the OSCE during 2010–2016, 'Statement to the OSCE Parliamentary Assembly, Helsinki +40 Seminar', 28 April 2015, available at: www.osce.org/pa/154186.

Dominicé, Christian, 'L'émergence de l'individu en droit international public', in Christian Dominicé (ed.), *L'ordre juridique international entre tradition et innovation* (Paris: PUF, 1997), 109–23.

Galbreath, David J. and Brosig, Malte, 'OSCE', in Knud Erik Jørgensen and Katie Verlin Laatikainen (eds.), *Routledge Handbook on the European Union and International Institutions: Performance, Policy, Power* (London: Routledge, 2013), 271–81.

Gautier, Philippe, 'Accord et engagement politique en droit des gens a propose de l'Acte fondateur sur les relations, la coopération et la sécurité mutuelles entre l'OTAN et la Fédération de Russie, signe à Paris le 27 mai 1997', *Annuaire Français de Droit International XLIII* (1997), 82–92.

Gazzini, Tarcisio, 'Personality of International Organisations', in Jan Klabbers and Åsa Wallendahl (eds.), *Research Handbook on the Law of International Organisations* (Cheltenham: Edward Elgar, 2011), 33–53.

Hafner, Gerhard, 'Did the FR Yugoslavia Make the OSCE an International Organization?', in Wolfgang Benedek, Hubert Isak and Renate Kicker (eds.), *Development and Developing International and European Law: Essays in Honour of Konrad Ginther on the Occasion of His 65th Birthday* (Frankfurt am Main: Peter Lang, 1999), 35–57.

Higgins, Rosalyn, *Problems & Process: International Law and How We Use It* (Oxford: Clarendon Press, 1994).

Hirsch, Christian, 'OSCE Legal Personality: Implications for Field Operations', *OSCE Legal Digest* (2016–2017).

Klabbers, Jan, *An Introduction to International Organizations Law* 3rd edn (Cambridge: Cambridge University Press, 2015).

'Institutional Ambivalence by Design: Soft Organizations in International Law', *Nordic Journal of International Law* 70 (2001), 403–21.

Lohmann, Torsten, 'Dispute Settlement Procedures in the OSCE – Genesis and Overview', in Michael Bothe, Natalino Ronzitti and Allan Rosas (eds.), *The OSCE in the Maintenance of Peace and Security: Conflict Prevention, Crisis Management and Peaceful Settlement of Disputes* (The Hague: Kluwer Law International, 1997), 343–56.

Odello, Marco, 'The Developing Legal Status of the Organisation for Security and Co-operation in Europe', *Anuario Espanol de Derecho Internacional* XXII (2006), 351–93.

'The Organization for Security and Co-operation in Europe and European Security Law', in Martin Trybus and Nigel White (eds.), *European Security Law* (Oxford: Oxford University Press, 2007), 295–328.

Martha, Rutsel, *The Legal Foundations of Interpol* (Oxford: Hart, 2010).

Peters, Anne, *Beyond Human Rights* (Cambridge: CUP 2016).

Peters, Ingo, 'Legitimacy and International Organizations – The Case of the OSCE', in Dominik Zaum (ed.), *Legitimating International Organizations* (Oxford: Oxford University Press, 2013), 196–220.

Portmann, Ronald, *Legal Personality in International Law* (Cambridge: Cambridge University Press, 2010).

Rama-Montaldo, Manuel, 'International Legal Personality and Implied Powers of International Organizations', *British Yearbook of International Law* 44 (1970), 111–55.

Ronzitti, Natalino, 'OSCE Peacekeeping', in Michael Bothe, Natalino Ronzitti and Allan Rosas (eds.), *The OSCE in the Maintenance of Peace and Security: Conflict Prevention, Crisis Management and Peaceful Settlement of Disputes* (The Hague: Kluwer Law International, 1997), 237–55.

Sands, Philippe and Klein, Pierre, *Bowett's Law of International Institutions* (London: Sweet and Maxwell, 2001).

Sapiro, Miriam, 'Changing the CSCE into the OSCE: Legal Aspects of a Political Transformation', *American Journal of International Law* 89 (1995), 631–7.

Schlager, Erika, 'A Hard Look at Compliance with "Soft" Law: The Case of the OSCE', in Dinah Shelton (ed.), *Commitment and Compliance* (Oxford: Oxford University Press, 2000), 346–72.

Schweisfurth, Theodor, 'Die juristische Mutation der KSZE: Eine internationale Organisation in statu nascendi', in Ulrich Beyerlin, Michael Bothe, Rainer Hofmann and Ernst-Ulrich. Petersmann (eds.), *Recht zwischen Umbruch und Bewahrung: Festschrift fűr Rudolf Bernhardt* (Berlin: Springer, 1995), 213–28.

Slaughter, Anne-Marie, *A New World Order* (Princeton: Princeton University Press, 2004).

Smouts, Marie, 'Les suites institutionnelles de la Conférence sur la Sécurité et la Coopération en Europe', *Revue Française de Science Politique* 24 (1974), 1230–6.

Stribis, Ioannis, 'Operational Update: Lack of Clarity of the Status of the OSCE: Impact on Project Implementation,' SEC.GAL/204/15, 15 July 2015.

Tabassi, Lisa, 'Operational Update: Legal Aspects of OSCE Peace Operations,' SEC.GAL/205/15, 5 October 2015.

'Operational Update: Legal Liability for Patrolling/Monitoring; Crisis Response; Tax Exemption', SEC.GAL/159/16, 19 October 2016.

'Update on the Operational Consequences of the Lack of a Clear Legal Status of the OSCE', SEC.GAL/26/17, 10 February 2017.

Tichy, Helmut and Quidenus, Catherine, 'Consolidating the International Legal Personality of the OSCE: A Headquarters Agreement with Austria', *International Organizations Law Review* 14 (2017).

Tomuschat, Christian, 'Ensuring the Survival of Mankind on the Eve of a New Century', *Recueil de Cours* 1999 281, Académie de Droit International de La Haye (The Hague, Boston, London: Martinus Nijhoff, 1999) 9–438.

White, Nigel, *The Law of International Organisations* (Manchester: Manchester University Press, 2005).

Wood, Michael, 'The Immunity of Official Visitors', in Armin von Bogdandy and Rüdiger Wolfrum (eds.), *Max Planck Yearbook of United Nations Law* 16 (Leiden, Boston: Martinus Nijhoff, 2012), 35–98.

'Do International Organizations Enjoy Immunity Under Customary International Law?', *International Organizations Law Review* 10 (2013), 287–318.

Zhun, Victoriya, 'Operational Aspects of Patrolling/Monitoring: A Legal Perspective', *OSCE Legal Digest* (2015–2016).

4

The Role of the Participating States in Reforming the Legal Framework of the OSCE: Past Developments, Status Quo and Future Ambitions

Helmut Tichy

1 INTRODUCTION

The present chapter aims to present my views on a subject I have been closely involved with for a long time: how to assist the OSCE to obtain recognised international legal personality. I admit that I find this subject intellectually stimulating, but as Legal Adviser to the Austrian Foreign Ministry I also have a strong professional interest in helping to ensure that this mainly Vienna-based organisation is able to exercise its important functions without being confronted on a daily basis with fundamental legal questions.

There is a risk in inviting somebody who has been involved for so long with this issue to analyse past developments, the present status quo and any future ambitions relating to the international legal personality of the OSCE: that such a figure describes past developments only from the perspective that 'everything has been tried already', that the status quo is 'unsatisfactory, as we all know' and that, as all these brilliant ideas have failed, there are 'no more ambitions for the future'. I shall endeavour to avoid such an approach.

As a starting point, I think we have to accept that there were good reasons for the former Conference on Security and Co-operation in Europe (CSCE) to be conceived in 1975 as a political, legally non-binding cooperation based on consensus, and that this concept has led to the great success of the CSCE and its contribution to the transformation of parts of central Europe and the partial transformation of eastern Europe towards democracy.[1] It is doubtful whether a more formal organisation would have had this success. Even today, the

[1] Georgiev, 'The Collapse of Totalitarian Regimes in Eastern Europe and the International Rule of Law', 329–44; von Grünigen and Renk, 'Forty Years of the Helsinki Final Act – A Cause for Celebration?', 41–52; for a comparative study see Schimmelfennig, Engert and Knobel, *International Socialization in Europe*.

political, legally non-binding commitments adopted in the OSCE context are able to play an important role in maintaining peace and security in Europe, as most OSCE participating States would recognise, whereas it is regrettable that efforts to restrict the consensus principle have largely failed.[2]

The new situation for the CSCE since the Charter of Paris for a New Europe of 1990, with the creation of permanent institutions and field missions in many countries, led to new challenges and made it impossible to remain fully outside the scope of the law. This was recognised by the CSCE Rome Decision of 1993, which committed the participating States politically – subject to their constitutional, legislative and related requirements – to confer legal capacity on CSCE institutions as well as privileges and immunities.[3] However, this 'national law approach' was only partly successful: only a certain number of participating States, including Austria as the host state, have adopted national laws for that purpose.[4] Because the approach relies only on national laws, it is unable to provide the same status and protection for the Organization, its components and its staff members in all participating States.[5]

The renaming of the Conference (CSCE) to the Organization for Security and Co-operation in Europe (OSCE) by the Budapest Decision of 1994, effective as of 1 January 1995, was intended to give a new political impetus, but changed neither the legal status of the conference nor the political nature of its commitments.[6]

2 THE PAST ATTEMPTS

In 2000, during the Austrian chairmanship of the OSCE, there were numerous discussions as to whether the incomplete implementation of the Rome Decision posed a problem for the Organization and whether the national law approach was sufficient to afford the Organization the necessary legal capacity and protection.[7] The OSCE Secretariat ably demonstrated in a paper referred

[2] Helsinki Commission, 'Consensus Denied? Challenges for OSCE Decision-Making in 2017', 27 March 2017, available at: www.csce.gov/sites/helsinkicommission.house.gov/files/Report%20-%20Challenges%20in%20the%20OSCE%20-%20Design%20V1.pdf., 2.

[3] Commission on Security and Co-operation in Europe, 'CSCE and the New Europe – Our Security Is Indivisible. Decisions of the Rome Council Meeting', 1 December 1993, CSCE/4 C/Dec.2.

[4] Austria, Federal Law on the Legal Status of the OSCE Institutions in Austria, Federal Law Gazette No. 511/1993 as amended.

[5] See also Pingel, 'Privileges and Immunities of the OSCE', Chapter 9 in this Volume.

[6] See CSCE, 'Budapest Document 1994: Towards a Genuine Partnership in a New Era', 1994, available at: www.osce.org/mc/39554?download=true.

[7] For further details on the discussions between 2000 and 2007 relating to the legal personality of the OSCE, see Tichy and Köhler, 'Legal Personality or Not' 2008, 455–78.

to as the 'Difficulties Paper',[8] which has been the basis for further elaborations ever since, that the OSCE faces serious difficulties by not having internationally recognised legal personality and the same privileges and immunities in all participating States.[9] It took a while to convince all participating States, in particular the USA, that this claim was well-founded, but now the problem seems to have been acknowledged as such. Concrete 'difficulties' discussed in this context relate to the inability of the OSCE to conclude treaties governed by international law, like headquarters, mission and cooperation agreements, to its lacking perception as an international organisation, to its lack of legal capacity under the national laws of certain participating States, to problems of legal standing before national (and possibly international) courts and to issues of responsibility and liability.[10]

Since 2000, legal experts in various configurations – such as OSCE working groups, panels of eminent persons, expert groups and consultations with selected states – have examined various approaches to establish the legal status of the OSCE under international law. These efforts have been primarily focused on the drafting of a convention that would confer international legal personality and privileges and immunities to the OSCE without, however, changing the mere politically binding nature of comprehensive OSCE commitments. A first draft convention was prepared by an open-ended working group in 2000–1 under my chairmanship.[11] One reason why it was not possible to adopt the draft convention at that time was the opposition of the USA to any legally binding text on the status of the OSCE.[12]

After many discussions this opposition was abandoned in 2006 and drafting of the convention resumed. In 2007, an informal working group, chaired by Ambassador van Veldhuizen-Rothenbücher of the Netherlands, whom I had the honour to serve as a vice-chairman, finalised the text of the Draft Convention on International Legal Personality, Legal Capacity and Privileges and Immunities of the OSCE.[13]

8 OSCE, Permanent Council, 'OSCE Legal Capacity and Privileges and Immunities: Report of the Permanent Council to the Ministerial Council', PC.DEC/383, 26 November 2000, Attachment 1 to Annex; OSCE, OSCE Secretariat, 'Legal Capacity and Privileges and Immunities', SEC.GAL/20/00, 6 March 2000.

9 Oberschmidt and Zellner, 'OSCE at the Crossroads', 11–12.

10 OSCE, OSCE Secretariat, 'Legal Capacity and Privileges and Immunities', SEC.GAL/20/00, 6 March 2000 (n. 8), 5, 9, 11.

11 See also Brander, 'Making a Credible Case', 20.

12 Simonet and Lüber, 'The OSCE and Its Legal Status', 287.

13 See the text in OSCE, Ministerial Council, 'Fifteenth Meeting of the Ministerial Council: 29 and 30 November 2007', MC.15EW72, 30 November 2007, Perception Papers by the Chairmanship.

However, the Draft Convention could not be adopted as Russia and Belarus insisted on inserting three footnotes in the text that refer to their request, expressed before and during the meetings of the working group, for a legally binding OSCE founding treaty – a 'Charter' – as a precondition for the adoption of the Convention. For this reason the Draft Convention was not adopted in 2007 nor any time since, notwithstanding the efforts of many succeeding OSCE chairmanships.[14] Nevertheless, apart from the Charter footnote problem, the Draft Convention now enjoys the support, at least in principle, of all OSCE participating States, with a common understanding arrived at in Madrid in 2007 that the text ought not to be re-opened.[15]

The proposal to draft an OSCE Charter is, however, heavily disputed. Russia and some other states base their request for a Charter on the claim that their constitution prevents them from signing and ratifying a convention that would confer privileges and immunities to an entity not based on a founding treaty. While, of course, it is the right of Russia to interpret its own constitution, an examination of the Russian constitution does not easily lead to the conclusion that it contains such a prohibition, the Russian constitution's provisions on international treaties being similar to those of other constitutions.[16]

The USA, on the other hand, is not prepared to go beyond its 2006 concession of accepting a limited convention on legal personality and privileges and immunities, and is not prepared to cooperate in the drafting of a Charter.[17] The EU member states, conversely, after some discussion signalled an openness towards embarking on the drafting of a document that would serve the purpose of a founding treaty of the OSCE, provided that the existing structures of the OSCE would not be changed as a result of such a treaty.[18]

Attempting to find a way forward out of this stalemate, a small Austrian–Netherlands OSCE Secretariat working group met in 2011 and elaborated, as a basis for further discussions and avoiding the expression 'Charter', a *non-*

14 See Simonet and Lüber, 'The OSCE and Its Legal Status' (n. 12) 289–90.

15 Brander, 'Making a Credible Case' (n. 11) 21; van Veldhuizen-Rothenbücher, 'Legal Personality of the OSCE', 23.

16 See also Bogush, 'Domestic Implications of the OSCE's Legal Personality under Russian Constitutional Law', Chapter 6 in this Volume.

17 See Baer, 'Bolstering the OSCE's Conflict Cycle Toolbox. Statement by Ambassador Daniel Baer at the 2016 OSCE Annual Security Review Conference', 30 June 2016, available at: https://osce.usmission.gov/bolstering-osces-conflict-cycle-toolbox-statement-2016-asrc/.

18 For example, OSCE, 'Statement by the Chairman-in-Office of the OSCE at the Closing Session of the Fifteenth Meeting of the Ministerial Council', MC.DEL/67/07, 30 November 2007, 3. The Chairman-in-Office at the time was Mr Miguel Angel Moratinos, Spanish Minister of Foreign Affairs and Co-operation.

paper on a draft 'constituent document' for the OSCE.[19] This non-paper sketched out elements for a constituent document that would codify existing OSCE principles, structures and rules, with the intention of illustrating that drafting a constituent document is not necessarily dangerous as long as it is restricted to a codification of existing politically binding provisions and their transformation into treaty provisions. Like the Draft Convention of 2007, this non-paper made it clear that its provisions did not affect the politically binding character of the OSCE commitments of participating States.

The document was circulated then slightly revised and is now known as the 'Irish Paper', in light of the Irish Chairmanship of 2012.[20] While it has met with some sympathy, it has not led to any progress on the issue of legal personality, as it has not helped the USA to overcome its political hesitations around drafting such a codifying constituent document.

3 THE PRESENT STATUS QUO

That was the past. As far as the status quo is concerned, several OSCE working group discussions on legal personality, frustrating by their repetitiveness, have taken place with long intervening periods during the last couple of years. The 'difficulties' resulting from the lack of international legal personality and non-existing or diverging privileges and immunities continue to pose problems, in particular when the OSCE is mandated to perform high-risk tasks, involving serious questions of responsibility and liability.[21] The professional and inventive legal services of the OSCE have managed to solve many of these problems pragmatically – or simply have had the good luck that potential dangers did not in reality materialise.[22]

Presently, there are four main options on the table for a solution of the legal personality dilemma under discussion.[23] First, the adoption of the 2007 Draft Convention,[24] which, as explained above, has been rejected by Russia and

19 Tichy, Schusterschitz and Bittner, 'Recent Austrian Practice in the Field of International Law', 180.

20 OSCE, 'Chairmanship Food-for-Thought-Paper: Strengthening the Legal Framework of the OSCE', CIO.GAL/63/12 of 18 May 2012; OSCE, Chairmanship Non-Paper, 'Draft Constituent Document, circulated by the Irish Chairmanship', CIO.GAL/68/12, 12 June 2012.

21 Simonet and Lüber, 'The OSCE and Its Legal Status' (n. 12) 300.

22 See also Tabassi, 'The Role of the Organisation in Asserting Legal Personality: The Position of the OSCE Secretariat on the OSCE's Legal Status', Chapter 3 in this Volume.

23 See OSCE, Ministerial Council, 'Report to the Ministerial Council on Strengthening the Legal Framework of the OSCE in 2015', MC.GAL/4/15, 1 December 2015.

24 'Draft Convention on the International Legal Personality, Legal Capacity, and Privileges and Immunities of the OSCE', CIO.GAL/48/07/Rev.6, 23 October 2007.

others; second, a parallel or consecutive adoption of a constituent document and the 2007 Draft Convention,[25] which, as explained above, has been rejected by the USA; third, the 'Convention Plus',[26] the proposal to enrich the 2007 Draft Convention with a couple of provisions of a statutory or constitutional character, which has been rejected by both Russia and the USA as insufficient or as going beyond the 2007 draft; and fourth, a ratification of the 2007 Draft Convention, without its formal adoption by the OSCE, by only those participating States that would be interested in implementing in this manner their political commitments under the 1993 Rome Decision.[27]

There is, however, yet another viable option that was proposed by the OSCE Secretary General Zannier and which would consist of a network of bilateral agreements concluded between the OSCE and its participating States that would grant international legal personality and privileges and immunities to the OSCE.[28]

Austria, like most OSCE participating States, would be able to support all of these options, even the option involving action outside the decision-making process of the OSCE. However, this option could only lead to a clarification of the OSCE's legal status if a significant number of participating States pursued this path, in particular those states that are hosts of OSCE institutions and field operations. Moreover, the opinions of these states should be assessed thoroughly before further work in pursuit of this option occurs.

These are all reasonable proposals that could provide a solution for the present status quo, but as is sometimes the case in International Relations the lack of political will by the key players to solve a contested issue makes achieving progress impossible. This is certainly not due to any lack of creative thinking by those interested in reaching a solution. Without of course being able to present a full list, let me just mention a few further ideas, in addition to the main options outlined above, that have been discussed at the expert level or negotiated at the political level in the last fifteen years.

25 Republic of Armenia, Republic of Belarus, Kyrgyz Republic, Russian Federation, Republic of Tajikistan, Republic of Uzbekistan, 'Food-for-Thought-Paper on the Legal Status of the OSCE', PC.DEL/252/10/Corr.3, 8 June 2010.

26 'Chairmanship Non-Paper on a possible "Convention Plus or OSCE Statute"', attached to CIO.GAL/173/14, 2 October 2014.

27 Ibid., see also OSCE, Permanent Council, 'Legal Capacity and Privileges and Immunities: Report of the Permanent Council to the Ministerial Council', Annex to PC.DD/50/00, 23 November 2000, para. 6.

28 OSCE, Secretary General, 'Model Standing Arrangement', SEC.GAL/135/16, 8 September 2016.

In 2000–1, one of the most discussed proposals was an explicit recognition of specific treaty-making powers of the OSCE and thereby implicit recognition of its legal personality – following the example of the EU after the Amsterdam Treaty, which provided for specific treaty-making powers of the EU Council, implying legal personality of the EU in addition to the existing legal personality of the European Community. Much attention centred also on the proposal to elaborate a document that would contain identical political and legal obligations concerning legal personality and privileges and immunities, legal only for those participating States that would be prepared to ratify the document as a treaty.[29]

Further proposals included: first, the adoption of a convention granting the OSCE only privileges and immunities, leaving the issue of legal personality to a separate convention or to a decision of the OSCE; second, the adoption of a decision by the OSCE that the OSCE is to be regarded as an international organisation and that, therefore, it can conclude agreements binding under international law; third, a declaratory decision of the OSCE that, in view of its development, the Organization has already acquired the status of an international organisation and that, therefore, it can conclude agreements binding under international law; fourth, a decision of the OSCE not only recommending the OSCE be granted legal capacity and privileges and immunities under national law, as agreed by the Rome Decision of 1993, but also recommending international legal personality and legal capacity be granted, as well as the privileges and immunities of the OSCE under international law; fifth, an OSCE model law on the international legal personality, legal capacity and privileges and immunities of the OSCE; and sixth, a model bilateral agreement between the OSCE and mission-receiving countries.[30] The wealth of proposals and ideas clearly demonstrates that lawyers trying to find a solution to the present status quo have not been inactive and that the constant requests of the annual OSCE chairmanships to come up with new ideas have been promptly heeded.

However, the OSCE is a consensus-based organisation. Decisions to be taken by participating States need the approval of all.[31] CSCE mechanisms providing for 'consensus minus one'[32] or 'consensus minus two' decisions have remained rarely used exceptions. Most solutions to the issue of legal

29 Simonet and Lüber, 'The OSCE and Its Legal Status' (n. 12) 287.

30 See also Tichy and Köhler, 'Legal Personality or Not' (n. 7) 468–70.

31 OSCE, 'Employee Spotlights: Madina Jaburossynova', 2017, available at: www.osce.org/node/142631.

32 CSCE, 'Prague Document on Further Development of CSCE Institutions and Structures', 1992, 16, available at: www.osce.org/mc/40270?download=true.

personality and privileges and immunities discussed so far would require consensus. Under the prevailing political circumstances in international affairs, it is therefore unlikely that consensus can be achieved on this important and disputed issue. Although the issue might give the impression of being technical in nature – and for some even a playground for lawyers – in reality it is one of power politics: of control over the Organization, of control over the freedom of action of its various components ('executive structures').[33]

Under the present system, which has evolved in a pragmatic way over the last decades, highly motivated individuals and institutions – I mention here only the OSCE Office for Democratic Institutions and Human Rights (ODIHR) in Warsaw – have been able to act independently and raise, if necessary, their critical voices. Any attempt to change this system – be it only to address the problems of legal personality and privileges and immunities which, as is now generally admitted, pose serious difficulties for the Organization – meets with suspicion that a reform, a new legal instrument, could be used to restrict this independence and to silence these critical voices. Arguments such as 'international organisations normally have founding treaties' may sound technical, but none of the proposals for OSCE decisions in the field of legal personality and privileges and immunities circulated so far has convinced all participating States that the status quo should be altered, or that it could be altered without negative consequences.

4 THE OUTLOOK: AN EMERGING CUSTOMARY INTERNATIONAL LAW?

What are the current ambitions an OSCE Chairmanship can possibly have in this situation? The most obvious is to keep the discussion going. We are confronted with an objectively existing dilemma, and we have prepared viable solutions. The only element missing is the right moment allowing us to act, the moment the ancient Greeks referred to as Καιρός. Such favourable moments have indeed occurred in the past; we have to wait.

But reflections also have to be pursued, and are being pursued, regarding the possibility of taking action outside the OSCE decision-making bodies by which the OSCE could gain international legal personality. One avenue to be explored in this context is the development of the practice of participating States treating the OSCE as a fully fledged international organisation. That could also include the conclusion of a network of bilateral agreements

33 On this political dimension, see also Hafner, 'The Legal Personality of International Organizations', 81–100.

between the OSCE and particular participating States, as suggested by the OSCE Secretary General Zannier.[34] It was in that spirit that Austria, in a formal letter of 29 May 2007, expressed its readiness 'to conclude a headquarters agreement under international law with the OSCE along the lines of existing headquarters agreements between Austria and International Organizations, if the OSCE is in a position to do so'.[35]

Any development trying to improve the situation of the OSCE by relying on state practice and the possibility of the OSCE gaining international legal personality by basing it on customary international law has to face the fact that important participating States would be persistent objectors to such a development. That, however, raises the question – relevant also in terms of general international law – whether persistent objectors, important as they may be, can prevent in perpetuity the emergence of an international legal personality of the OSCE based on customary international law? If that is not the case, further questions arise. For example, to what extent could international legal personality based on customary international law be considered satisfactory if it could not be invoked against persistent objectors, in particular if it is under their jurisdiction that the OSCE would most need such status and protection. Another question worth considering would be whether such a customary law approach could in any way affect the consensus rule within the OSCE or set a precedent for future decision-making within the OSCE. Still, these and similar concerns should not stand in the way of a more general consideration of the role that persistent objectors can have in the formation of customary international law.

It was, therefore, with the future of the OSCE in mind that Austria stated on 4 November 2015 in the 6th Committee of the UN General Assembly, during the discussion of the sub-item 'identification of customary international law', that it welcomed the fact that the draft conclusions on this sub-item addressed the difficult issue of persistent objectors and that it 'welcomed the explicit restriction of the effect of persistent objections to the opposing state, which, therefore, is not in a position to prevent the creation of a rule of customary international law'.[36] The same point was raised again in Austria's 6th

[34] OSCE, Secretary General, 'Model Standing Arrangement', SEC.GAL/135/16, 8 September 2016.

[35] Letter of the Legal Adviser of the Austrian Foreign Ministry, Ambassador Ferdinand Trauttmansdorff, 29 May 2007, reprinted in Hafner, 'Austrian Diplomatic and Parliamentary Practice in International Law'.

[36] Permanent Mission of Austria to the United Nations in New York, 'Statement by the Austrian Representative on the Report of the International Law Commission on the Work of Its 67th Session', 4 November 2015, 2–3, available at: http://statements.unmeetings.org/media2/7654746/austria.pdf.

Committee statement of 25 October 2016.[37] Persistent objectors should not be considered to be in a position to prevent the creation of a rule of customary international law and to prevent an organisation from obtaining international legal personality.

During the discussions at the conference on Strengthening the Legal Framework of the OSCE in Berlin-Dahlem,[38] in fact while I presented the Austrian position on a persistent objector doctrine, the legal adviser of the OSCE indicated that the Organization would now be prepared to accept Austria's proposal made in 2007 to negotiate a bilateral headquarters agreement.[39] This acceptance has to be seen in the context of the OSCE Secretary General's initiative, mentioned above, to try to conclude a network of bilateral agreements between the OSCE and its participating States relating to the international legal personality and privileges and immunities of the OSCE.[40]

While a headquarters agreement with Austria would not imply any material change relating to the legal situation of the OSCE in Austria – its legal personality and privileges and immunities are well established under Austrian law[41] – such an agreement could be interpreted as a clear recognition by Austria that it considers the OSCE to have obtained international legal personality on the basis of far-reaching, although not general, state practice accepted as law, that is, on the basis of customary international law. By concluding such an agreement during its 2017 OSCE Chairmanship, Austria could encourage other states to take similar steps and thus contribute to the recognition of the OSCE as a fully fledged international organisation.

37 The relevant part of the statement is as follows: 'Already last year, we welcomed the elaboration of draft conclusion 15 relating to "persistent objectors" and advised that the conclusion should also be interpreted to mean that a single state is not in a position to prevent the creation of a rule of customary international law. We thus welcome the formulation now found in paragraph 2 of the commentary to draft conclusion 15, distinguishing individual persistent objections from "a situation where the objection of a substantial number of States to the formation of a new rule of customary international law prevents its crystallization altogether".' Statement by the Austrian Representative on the Report of the International Law Commission on the work of its 68th session, 25 October 2016, available at: http://webtv.un.org/meetings-events/general-assembly/main-committees/6th-committee/watch/sixth-committee-21st-meeting-71st-general-assembly/5184781041001.

38 International conference 'Between Aspirations and Realities: Strengthening the Legal Framework of the OSCE' organised by the Max Planck Institute for Comparative Public Law and International Law in the Harnack-Haus of the Max Planck Society on 13 July 2016.

39 Ibid., a conference presentation by Lisa Tabassi, 'Taking Stock: The Current Legal Status of the OSCE'; see also Tabassi, 'The Role of the Organisation in Asserting Legal Personality: The Position of the OSCE Secretariat on the OSCE's Legal Status', Chapter 3 in this Volume.

40 See Section 3 of this Chapter.

41 Federal Law on the Legal Status of the OSCE Institutions in Austria, 1993 (n. 4).

Consequently, Austrian Foreign Minister Kurz applied for full powers for a delegation to negotiate a headquarters agreement with the OSCE. On the basis of his submission,[42] the Austrian federal government decided on 25 October 2016 to propose to the acting federal presidency to grant such full powers. Notably, the minister justified the need to act with full powers by stating:

> At the moment, there is no headquarters agreement between Austria and the OSCE. The rules on the privileges and immunities of the CSCE, as it then was, the present OSCE, were established in 1993 by an Austrian statute,[43] which extends the application of provisions of the seat agreement with the United Nations to the OSCE. At that time it was not possible to conclude a headquarters agreement, as the CSCE was no international organisation as defined by international law.[44]

Full powers for the negotiation were granted by the then Austrian collective federal presidency on 11 November 2016, and the negotiations were initiated on the basis of an Austrian draft. They were concluded in June 2017 and, on the Austrian side with new full powers for signature issued by the Federal President, the new 'Agreement between the Republic of Austria and the Organization for Security and Co-Operation in Europe (OSCE) regarding the Headquarters of the Organization for Security and Co-Operation in Europe' was signed by the secretaries-general of the Austrian Foreign Ministry and the OSCE on 14 June 2017.

The new OSCE Headquarters Agreement follows to a large extent the model of the Seat Agreement between Austria and the UN. However, Section 2 of the Agreement explicitly states that 'The Republic of Austria recognizes the legal capacity of the OSCE as an international organization.'

[42] Austrian Foreign Minister, Submission to the 'Council of Ministers' (*Ministerratsvortrag*), '*Abkommen zwischen der Republik Österreich und der Organisation für Sicherheit und Zusammenarbeit in Europa über den Amtssitz der Organisation für Sicherheit und Zusammenarbeit in Europa; Verhandlungen*', BMEIA-O1.8.19.12/0007-I.2/2016, 19 October 2016, available at: http://archiv.bundeskanzleramt.at/DocView.axd?CobId=64114. I would like to thank my colleague Catherine Quidenus for preparing the draft of that submission.

[43] Federal Law on the Legal Status of the OSCE Institutions in Austria (n. 4).

[44] Translation from German by the author.

5 CONCLUSION

Although the CSCE–OSCE is not based on an international treaty, the OSCE now has the option – following the creation and further development of an institutional structure, including permanent institutions, at and since the Paris Summit of 1990 – to take decisions that are separate from those of its participating States, and to conclude legally binding agreements with participating States,[45] which shows that the OSCE is increasingly regarded as a subject of international law and increasingly accepted as such by participating States. Also from the Austrian perspective it can be assumed that the OSCE possesses international legal personality.

In view of these developments, Austria had already in 2007 proposed to the OSCE to conclude a headquarters agreement, as noted above. At that time the offer was not acted upon; however, following the conference on the legal framework of the OSCE in Berlin-Dahlem,[46] the OSCE took up the Austrian offer in a letter by OSCE Secretary-General Lamberto Zannier of 22 July 2016, which resulted in the conclusion of the 2017 OSCE Headquarters Agreement,[47] replacing the domestic OSCE Law.

The conclusion of such a headquarters agreement with the OSCE is an important contribution of Austria towards the consolidation of the Organization.[48] It may now be a future ambition that other states will also conclude treaties recognising the international legal personality of the OSCE, either bilaterally or multilaterally. The signing of the host agreement between Poland and the OSCE on 28 June 2017 has already been a very important step in that direction.[49]

45 Such agreements include seat agreements with OSCE institutions and mission agreements ratified by the parliaments of the mission receiving states; see also the contribution of Boisson de Chazournes and Gadkowski, 'The External Relations of the OSCE', Chapter 10 in this Volume.

46 International conference 'Between Aspirations and Realities: Strengthening the Legal Framework of the OSCE' (n. 38).

47 Agreement between the Republic of Austria and the Organization for Security and Co-operation in Europe (OSCE) regarding the Headquarters of the Organization for Security and Co-operation in Europe, 14 June 2017, available at: http://archiv.bundeskanzleramt.at/DocView.axd?CobId=66211.

48 The Austrian negotiators forwarded a discussion paper to the OSCE in early December 2016 with first drafting suggestions for a headquarters agreement.

49 OSCE, 'OSCE/ODIHR and Polish Foreign Ministry Sign Host Country Agreement', Press statement, 28 June 2017, available at: www.osce.org/odihr/326711.

REFERENCES

Brander, Sonya, 'Making a Credible Case for a Legal Personality for the OSCE', *OSCE Magazine* (March–April 2009), 18–22.

Georgiev, Dencho, 'The Collapse of Totalitarian Regimes in Eastern Europe and the International Rule of Law', in Martin Krygiwer and Adam Czarnota (eds.), *The Rule of Law after Communism: Problems and Prospects in East-Central Europe* (Aldershot: Dartmouth Publishing Co., 1999), 329–44.

Grünigen, Marianne von and Renk, Hans-Jörg, 'Forty Years of the Helsinki Final Act – A Cause for Celebration?', in Institute for Peace Research and Security Policy at the University of Hamburg (ed.), *OSCE Yearbook* 2014 (Baden-Baden: Nomos Verlagsgesellschaft, 2015), 41–52.

Hafner, Gerhard, 'The Legal Personality of International Organizations', in August Reinisch and Ursula Kriebaum (eds.), *The Law of International Relations, Liber Amicorum Hanspeter Neuhold* (Utrecht: Eleven International Publishing, 2007), 81–100.

Novak, Gregor, Hafner, Gerhard and Prantner, Helmut, 'Austrian Diplomatic and Parliamentary Practice in International Law', *Austrian Review of International and European Law* 12 (2007), 293–436.

Oberschmidt, Randolf and Zellner, Wolfgang, 'OSCE at the Crossroads, Working Paper 2', in WP Core Working Papers (Hamburg: Centre for OSCE Research, Institute for Peace Research and Security Policy at the University of Hamburg, 2000).

Simonet, Loïc and Lüber, Hans Georg, 'The OSCE and Its Legal Status: Revising the Myth of Sisyphus', in Institute for Peace Research and Security Policy at the University of Hamburg (eds), *OSCE Yearbook* 2016 (Baden-Baden: Nomos Verlagsgesellschaft, 2017), 277–314.

Schimmelfennig, Frank, Engert, Stefan and Knobel, Heiko, *International Socialization in Europe, European Organizations, Political Conditionality and Democratic Change* (Basingstoke: Palgrave Macmillan, 2006).

Tichy, Helmut, Schusterschitz, Gregor and Bittner, Philip, 'Recent Austrian Practice in the Field of International Law: Report for 2011', *Zeitschrift für öffentliches Recht* 67 (2012), 157–99.

Tichy, Helmut and Köhler, Ulrike 'Legal Personality or Not – The Recent Attempts to Improve the Status of the OSCE', in James Crawford, Allain Pellet, Isabelle Buffard and Stefan Wittich (eds.), *International Law Between Universalism and Fragmentation – Festschrift in Honour of Gerhard Hafner* (Leiden, Boston: Martinus Nijhoff, 2008), 455–78.

Van Veldhuizen-Rothenbücher, Ida, 'Legal personality of the OSCE: Quo vadis?', *OSCE Magazine* (March–April 2009), 23.

5

'It's Politics, Stupid': an International Relations Perspective on Strengthening the Legal Framework of the OSCE

Tanja A. Börzel and Ingo Peters

1 INTRODUCTION*

The Organization for Security and Co-operation in Europe (OSCE) has attracted significant academic and political attention due to its increased visibility in the Ukraine Crisis since 2014.[1] In this context, a lively political and academic debate has (re-)emerged concerning the strengthening of both the Organization's legal status and its operational capacities as a way to equip it for a more effective role in the European security order. Reform proposals centre on transforming the OSCE into an organisation under international law and granting it legal personality.

The effectiveness and legitimacy of the OSCE have been questioned since the mid 2000s. Numerous public statements, books and journal articles – by political actors as much as by OSCE experts from academia and the think tank community – refer to the Organization as standing 'at the crossroads' between political significance and irrelevance; others explicitly speak of the Organization's 'crisis'.[2] The crisis discourse rests, first, on doubts about the effectiveness of the OSCE. After all, since the 1990s Europe experienced a return to warfare, first in the Balkans and later in post-Soviet Chechnya (1994–6, 1999–2009), Georgia (2008) and Ukraine (2014). Second, some OSCE field operations have been deprived of their ability to do their job by host governments, and some have even been expelled by participating States, apparently

* The authors gratefully acknowledge the research and editorial assistance of Helene Schmutzler.

1 Schweizerische Eidgenossenschaften, 'Factsheet Ukraine: OSCE Special Monitoring Mission to Ukraine Deployment of Swiss Experts Bern', 2015, available at: www.eda.admin.ch/dam/eda/en/documents/aktuell/dossiers/ams-factsheet-ukraine-SEF_EN.pdf.

2 For details see, e.g., I. Peters, 'Legitimacy and International Organizations', 196–8; Ghébali, 'Growing Pains at the OSCE'; Zellner, 'Managing Change in Europe'.

rendering the Organization helpless in the face of traditional power games and ethnic conflicts. Third, since the end of the Cold War the OSCE has not emerged as the overall 'clearing house' for European security as was foreseen in the OSCE Security Charter of 1999.[3] Instead, the OSCE has operated in a 'niche of common and cooperative security'.[4] While in absolute terms the OSCE might still perform vital work within this niche, it has largely become marginalised compared to other major European security organisations: the EU and NATO. Fourth, and most importantly, from the mid 1990s onwards Russia in particular has harshly criticised the OSCE for its ineffectiveness in guaranteeing security for all and preventing war. Moscow has complained about double standards and unfair practices related to what it considers 'interferences in the domestic affairs' of participating States and about some OSCE agencies claiming unwarranted political autonomy at the expense of political control by the participating States and governments.

Suggesting a comprehensive framework of reform as a possible remedy, Russia proposed the negotiating of a legally binding European Security Treaty (EST), encompassing an upgrading of the legal status of the Organization, as well as a revision of some principles contained in the Helsinki accord (Final Act) of 1975 and the Charter of Paris and related documents of the early 1990s.[5]

Proposals for strengthening the operational and political effectiveness of the OSCE by enhancing its legal status are not new. They date back to the negotiations of the Helsinki Final Act in 1975 establishing the Conference on Security and Co-operation in Europe (CSCE), later renamed the OSCE.[6] Reform proposals were also part of the 2005 report of the Panel of Eminent Persons.[7] Western states were open to some adjustments around procedural issues, as well as improving the OSCE's legal status – though to a different degree. They rejected, however, the drive for fundamental reform, especially regarding basic principles. Instead, the USA and its European allies have

3 OSCE, Charter for European Security, November 1999, available at: www.osce.org/mc/17502?download=true.

4 See I. Peters, 'The OSCE, NATO and the EU within the "Network of Interlocking European Security Institutions"'.

5 CSCE, Helsinki Final Act, 1 August 1975, available at: www.osce.org/helsinki-final-act?download=true; CSCE, Charter of Paris for a New Europe, November 1990, available at: https://www.osce.org/mc/39516?download=true.

6 See Wenig, 'The Status of the OSCE under International Law', 5; Sapiro, 'Changing the CSCE into the OSCE', 2.

7 See Ghébali, 'Growing Pains at the OSCE' (n. 2); Dunay, 'The OSCE in Crisis'; Tichy and Köhler, 'Legal Personality or Not'; Tillikainen, 'Reviving Co-operative Security in Europe through the OSCE'; Tomuschat, 'Legalization of the OSCE?'.

generally favoured the status quo, which the participating States – including the Soviet Union and later Russia – had negotiated at the end of the Cold War (1989–91). The 1990 Charter of Paris and its related documents defined, along the lines of liberal cultural traditions and political values and norms, a declaratory common political denominator in terms of democracy, human rights and the rule of law as the fundamental values supposedly governing the future practice of international relations in Europe.[8] For western states, the OSCE continues to promote these liberal values. In their eyes, the reforms advocated by Russia and the states belonging to the Commonwealth of Independent States (CIS),[9] especially the EST proposal, could easily devalue the OSCE's role in European security governance.

Recurring debates continue to neglect the argument, both academic and political, that a legal reform of the OSCE per se is unlikely to improve its performance beyond some operational nitty-gritties. On the contrary, renegotiating the Charter of Paris carries the danger of further undermining the political significance of the OSCE for European security governance. The thrust of the Russian proposals for an EST comes with the suggestion to enhance the OSCE's legal status. At the same time, however, Moscow's proposal demands renegotiating the normative foundations of the OSCE: most significantly, the abolishment of the right of every participating State to make a domestic incident in one participating State a matter of legitimate concern for others, as set out in the Charter and related documents. Accepting the Russian EST proposal would imply abandoning these liberal norms in favour of a formal and legally binding agreement, as part of the new statute would encompass the traditional international law provision of non-interference with domestic affairs. Thus, the EST proposal is not only unlikely to improve the performance of the OSCE, it could be perceived as a political carrot for dragging a Trojan horse into the reform negotiations that will harm the OSCE's significance in providing and protecting the normative backbone of Europe's security order.

In order to develop this argument, this chapter proceeds in three steps. We start by contending that the key problem of the OSCE's weakening governance performance lies in a lack of consensus on fundamental principles among its participating States rather than in the weak legal status of its governance framework. Disagreement on organisational principles has not

8 See Flynn and Farell, 'The CSCE and the "Construction" of Security in Post-Cold War Europe'; CSCE, Charter of Paris (n. 5).

9 See Lavrov, 'Speech by Russian Minister of Foreign Affairs at the 16th Meeting of the OSCE Ministerial Council', 5 December 2008, available at: www.mid.ru/en/vistupleniya_ministra/-/asset_publisher/MCZ7HQuMdqBY/content/id/302982.

only undermined the OSCE's effectiveness and legitimacy, it also renders any agreement on future legal reforms unlikely. The second part draws on academic and political debates to claim that strengthening the legal framework of the OSCE would be unlikely to do the trick anyway. Research on international relations shows that higher levels of formalisation and legalisation do not necessarily translate into the increased effectiveness and legitimacy of international institutions. In fact, it has been precisely the weakness of its legal status that has given the OSCE a comparative advantage over other international institutions in promoting peace and security in Europe. Finally, in the third part we discuss the perils that lie in a legal reform of the OSCE. Strengthening its legal framework could easily become a slippery slope towards a major political setback if it comes at the price of compromising those liberal foundations of the European security order the OSCE has been tasked to protect.

2 THE END OF THE POST-COLD WAR CONSENSUS

The CSCE, which emerged in the early 1970s as part of the East–West *détente* policy, was originally the brainchild of the Soviet Union. The Soviets sought western political recognition of its sphere of influence and of Europe's de facto borders. The negotiation process in the early 1970s resulted in the Helsinki Final Act of 1975. It established the CSCE as the European security organisation with the widest coverage both in terms of participants – the number of participating States in the CSCE–OSCE rose in stages from thirty-five in the first half of the 1990s to fifty-seven by 2016 – and geographical reach: 'from Vancouver to Vladivostok'. The CSCE–OSCE embedded traditional policy areas in a comprehensive concept of security. The three 'baskets' – politics and security (Basket I: containing the fundamental principles of relations between states as well as a set of military confidence- and security-building measures), economic relations (Basket II) and humanitarian matters and human rights issues (Basket III) – remained the Organization's domain after the end of the Cold War.

While academics and policy makers alike credit the CSCE with having a substantial role in the reunification of Europe in general and Germany in particular, they have increasingly questioned its effectiveness in protecting the post-Cold War European security order. Democratic transition in several participating States has stalled, with some showing signs even of democratic backsliding.[10] The biggest challenge, however, is Russia's violation of OSCE

[10] See Börzel and Schimmelfennig, 'Coming Together or Drifting Apart?'.

principles, particularly the principle of non-violation of European borders. The OSCE was unable to prevent the war in Georgia in 2008 or redress the annexation of Crimea in 2014 and bring the ensuing military conflict in Ukraine to a close.[11] These failures notwithstanding, western states continue to praise the Organization for facilitating security and cooperation in Europe. Referring to the war in Georgia, the then German Foreign Minister, Frank-Walter Steinmeier, emphasised the positive role of the Organization as a vehicle for dialogue, referring explicitly to the dangers of a revival of political truculence. He stressed that 'in times when new mistrust and occasional old, confrontational ways of thinking are becoming noticeable – in Europe as well', the OSCE is 'absolutely essential' for defining a new order: '[b]y strengthening democracy and the rule of law, and through its commitment to human rights and basic freedoms, the organisation affords Europe with greater security, deeper trust, but also better mutual understanding'.[12] In 2015, Steinmeier restated his reasoning with regard to the Ukraine crisis:

> Facilitating dialogue is one of the main purposes of the OSCE, particularly in stormy times. The variety of platforms the organization provides to that end is one of its main assets. The OSCE has developed proven fora in all its dimensions over the past decades: we will rely on these well-established dialogue formats.[13]

Russia's stance towards the OSCE is more ambiguous. On the one hand Moscow has continued to emphasise the importance of the OSCE for Europe's security architecture. On the other hand it has increasingly voiced concerns about the scope of the OSCE's operations for protecting and promoting free and fair elections and the rule of law in participating States. The Russian government considers such ambitions and actions as interferences in domestic affairs, violations of national sovereignty and a threat to security and peace in Europe, all of which is undermining political stability and infringing upon Russia's legitimate sphere of influence.[14]

11 Beyond the violation of OSCE principles, the legal qualification of Russia's actions, especially in Crimea, is disputed. See, for instance, the contributions in *ZaöRV/Heidelberg Journal of International Law* 75 (2015), Marxsen, 'Territorial Integrity in International Law'.

12 Steinmeier, 'Rede von Bundesaußenminister Frank-Walter Steinmeier beim OSZE-Ministerrat in Helsinki', 4 December 2008, available at: https://www.auswaertiges-amt.de/en/newsroom/news/081204-bm-rede-osze-dt/232820.

13 Steinmeier, 'Interview with the OSCE Chairperson-in-Office'.

14 Lavrov, 'Speech by Russian Minister of Foreign Affairs at the 17th OSCE Ministerial Council Meeting', 1 December 2009, available at: www.mid.ru/en/web/guest/foreign_policy/rso/osce/-/asset_publisher/bzhxR3zkq2H5/content/id/271322.

For Russia, the main vocation of the OSCE is not to promote and protect the rule of law, human rights and democracy but rather 'to provide equal and indivisible security for all' – a core principle of the Helsinki Final Act and the Paris Charter – and to prevent wars such as in 1999 the '78-day bombing of Yugoslavia, or the military attack on South Ossetia'.[15] '[N]egative tendencies in the evolution of the OSCE are seen as leading towards a 'fragmentation of the pan-European space' and possibly towards the collapse of Europe's security architecture.[16] The lack of legitimacy and effectiveness of the OSCE, according to Moscow, has been 'strongly affected by its incomplete institutionalization'.[17]

NATO and the EU, according to Moscow, undermine the authority of the OSCE: 'Unfortunately, the OSCE both as a real instrument for ensuring security and as a forum for dialogue and a search for mutually acceptable solutions continues to remain out of the mainstream of events.'[18] Overall, the European security architecture 'still bears the stamp of an ideology inherited from the past'[19], as the Russian President Medvedev stated. He specified that:

> [a]n organisation such as the OSCE could, it would seem, embody European civilization's newfound unity, but it is prevented from doing so, prevented from becoming a full-fledged general regional organisation. The problem is not just in the organisation's own incomplete institutional development but also in the obstruction created by other groups intent on continuing the old line of bloc politics.[20]

Next to lamenting the OSCE's political insignificance due to its informal foundations, Moscow has criticised a double standard regarding the equality of OSCE participating States – one of the ten principles laid down in the Helsinki Final Act and reiterated in many OSCE documents adopted after 1990. A case in point was Kazakhstan's offer, supported by all CIS states, to take on the OSCE Chair in 2009. Some participating States opposed the offer because they doubted Kazakhstan's suitability, a judgement that upset Russia's

[15] Lavrov, 'Speech by Russian Minister of Foreign Affairs at the 16th Meeting of the OSCE Ministerial Council', 5 December 2008 (n. 9).

[16] Lavrov, 'Speech by Russian Minister of Foreign Affairs at the 15th OSCE Ministerial Council Meeting', Madrid, 29 November 2007, available at: www.mid.ru/en/vistupleniya_ministra/-/asset_publisher/MCZ7HQuMdqBY/content/id/355906.

[17] Lavrov, 'Speech by Russian Minister of Foreign Affairs at the 16th Meeting of the OSCE Ministerial Council', 5 December 2008 (n. 9).

[18] Lavrov, 'Speech by Russian Minister of Foreign Affairs at the 15th OSCE Ministerial Council Meeting', 29 November 2007 (n. 16).

[19] Medvedev, 'Speech at Meeting with German Political, Parliamentary, and Civic Leaders', 5 June 2008, available at: http://en.kremlin.ru/events/president/transcripts/320.

[20] Ibid.

foreign minister at the time, Sergei Lavrov.[21] In reiterating the premise 'that any Chair of the OSCE must be in substantial compliance with all OSCE commitments', the US State Department left no doubt that this bid was unacceptable unless Kazakhstan substantially implemented its OSCE commitments, especially those on human rights and democratisation.[22] Germany expressed similar concerns but was more conciliatory, supporting in principle Kazakhstan's application for OSCE Chairmanship, which it took up in January 2010.[23]

To ensure the principle of equality, Moscow directly linked its proposal for a reform of the overall structure of the OSCE, and especially for a legally binding treaty, to the demand that all participants 'reaffirm their commitment to fundamental principles of the [*sic*] international law, such as the non-use of force and peaceful settlement of disputes, sovereignty, territorial integrity and non-interference in internal affairs as well as the inadmissibility of strengthening one's own security by infringing upon the security of others'.[24]

Russia has pushed for the transformation of the OSCE from a political institution into a 'fully-fledged regional organisation' founded on a new OSCE charter or statute.[25] According to then President Dmitry Medvedev's initiative of May 2008 and the draft statute, Russia proposed – together with the CIS – that a pan-European summit should decide on a kind of 'Helsinki 2'.[26] The heads of state were to advance a legally binding EST establishing an all-European collective security system: 'a truly indivisible space of equal security of all states in the Euro-Atlantic area'.[27] The

[21] Lavrov, 'Speech by Russian Minister of Foreign Affairs at the 15th OSCE Ministerial Council Meeting', 29 November 2007 (n. 16).

[22] Smith, 'Kazakhstan's Candidacy for OSCE Chairmanship' available at: https://www.congress.gov/congressional-record/2006/6/29/extensions-of-remarks-section/article/e1348-1?q=%7B%22search%22%3A%22OSCE+Chairmanship%22%7D&s=1&r=1.

[23] See Erler, 'Speech by the Minister of State in the Federal Foreign Office at the OSCE Ministerial Council in Brussels' MC.DEL/22/06, 4 December 2006.

[24] Lavrov, 'Speech by Russian Minister of Foreign Affairs at the 15th OSCE Ministerial Council Meeting', 29 November 2007 (n. 16).

[25] Ibid.

[26] President of Russia, 'The Draft of the European Security Treaty', 29 November 2009, available at: http://en.kremlin.ru/events/president/news/6152; see also Lavrov, 'Speech by Russian Minister of Foreign Affairs at the 16th Meeting of the OSCE Ministerial Council', 5 December 2008 (n. 9); Medvedev, 'Speech at Meeting with German Political, Parliamentary, and Civic Leaders', 5 June 2008 (n. 19); OSCE, 'Draft Decision On The Charter Of The OSCE' 2007; Klein, 'Russia's Plan for a New Pan-European Security Regime', 6–9.

[27] Lavrov, 'Speech by Russian Minister of Foreign Affairs at the 15th OSCE Ministerial Council Meeting', 29 November 2007 (n. 16).

OSCE Secretariat and the Parliamentary Assembly have favoured the endowment of the OSCE with legal personality and legal capacity, and participating States per se have not rejected the idea. However, Russia and its CIS partners linked the issue of an EST and legal personality to their demands for a formal treaty establishing a new European security organisation. Nordic and eastern European participating States in particular have resisted Russia's efforts to promote the OSCE as the prime European security organisation under international law. They do not want to compromise the role of other European security organisations, especially NATO and the EU. The USA and western European countries have also opposed the proposal of giving the OSCE's legal status by turning it into a formal security organisation because they see it as intrinsically linked to Russia's attempts to revise the principles of the Paris Charter.

In sum, the ongoing debate on the Organization's reforms is framed by the fact that 'the consensus between participating States of the early post-Cold War years has eroded'.[28] The lack of consensus on the liberal foundations of the European security order agreed in 1990 undermines the effectiveness and the legitimacy of the OSCE. Western countries see strengthening the effectiveness of the OSCE's role in promoting and protecting the rule of law, democracy and minority rights at the domestic level as the best method of conflict prevention and post-conflict rehabilitation. For Russia and its allies, it is precisely such interferences in domestic affairs that threaten security and peace in Europe. Moreover, while Russia wants the OSCE to become the dominant European security organisation, western countries continue to rely on NATO and, increasingly, the EU.

Even if both sides saw legal reforms as a means of only strengthening the role of the OSCE, they would still have very different ideas on what the institution's role should be and specifically whether this should go hand in hand with a revision of OSCE principles.[29] As long as the USA and Russia with their respective allies disagree on the 'main vocation' of the OSCE, any legal reform of the OSCE remains unlikely. And even if participating States agreed on a strengthening of the OSCE's legal framework, this would not solve the internal disputes on the 'overrepresentation of Western values' and the role of NATO and the EU as alternative European security organisations.[30]

28 Brichambaut, 'The OSCE and the 21st Century'.

29 On the evolution of the debate on the OSCE's legal status, see Brander, 'Making a Credible Case for a Legal Personality for the OSCE'.

30 I. Peters, 'Legitimacy and International Organizations', 209.

3 THE FALSE PROMISE OF LEGAL REFORM

With the end of the conflict between East and West, participating States including the Soviet Union – and Russia after the breakup of the Soviet Union – negotiated and accepted the Charter of Paris for a New Europe and its related documents. In 1990, a declaratory common political denominator was defined, comprising democracy, human rights and the rule of law as the fundamental values governing the future practice of international relations in Europe.[31] New institutions and structures, including the instruments the OSCE used in order to perform its nascent functions, were largely in place by 1995 when the CSCE became the OSCE.[32] Though its new name suggested otherwise, the OSCE was not established as a formal organisation under international law and based on an international treaty (normally deposited at the United Nations).

Debates on giving the OSCE's legal status are not new.[33] With the end of the Cold War on the one hand, and the challenges posed by German reunification on the other, Europe was experiencing a time of great transition, and the unusual levels of uncertainty and feelings of insecurity that this period produced were putting the existing security structures of the time under sustained pressure. This transition was not just a transformation *within* but actually one *of* the structures of the international system.[34] This was the heyday for all kinds of proposals coming from various 'security architects', among them some who considered that the imminent challenges required an international law treaty as the basis for what was then still the CSCE.

As part of this expert debate, proponents of a broad and comprehensive understanding of legal status sought to transform the OSCE from a political to a formal international organisation under international law.[35] Others have favoured a much narrower approach in providing the OSCE with legal personality,[36] or legal capacity,[37] to overcome obstacles affecting the everyday

31 See Flynn and Farell, (n. 8).

32 For an earlier systematic comparison of the institution pre- and post-1989–90, see I. Peters, 'From the CSCE to the OSCE'.

33 Brander, Making a Credible Case for a Legal Personality for the OSCE, *OSCE Magazine* March-April, 18–22; see also Ryngaert, 'The OSCE's Domestic Legal Status: An Exploration of Relevant International Law Sources', Chapter 8 in this Volume.

34 See Waltz, *Theory of International Politics*, 67–77; Gilpin, *War and Change in World Politics*, 40–3.

35 See Bahr, *Sicherheit für und vor Deutschland*.

36 Tichy and Köhler, n. 7, 9–11.

37 See ibid., 7.

work of the OSCE in its different operational assignments.[38] The benefits of awarding the OSCE legal personality were identified as follows:[39] (1) solving administrative and bureaucratic obstacles, especially regarding the status of OSCE staff who would gain diplomatic privileges and immunities;[40] (2) allowing the OSCE to conclude treaties at the international level and act as a person under private law;[41] (3) making cooperation with other subjects of international law advantageous;[42] and (4) improving the implementation of OSCE commitments and allowing the incorporation of external auditors and expertise from international organisations with a strong legal framework.[43] Furthermore, it would (5) 'enhance its effectiveness and ensure uniform treatment on the territories of its participating States and its equality in comparison to other international organisations'.[44]

These advantages regained traction following deployment of the field operation to Ukraine, as the problems around the OSCE's weak legal status and the lack of an international legal personality became evident. For example, the requirements of extensive inter-agency consultations or parliamentary approval for deploying a mission have been criticised by some as time consuming and rendering the OSCE field operation 'another victim of lack of legal status'.[45] Moreover, the Ukraine field operation is taken as a further example of non-existing security guarantees by the host state resulting in the OSCE's de facto neglect of its staff.[46] In view of such anticipated advantages, the proposal for appointing a Special Advisor of the Chairperson-in-Office on the Legal Framework follows suit.[47] Albeit, overall '[i]t seems that the OSCE would not do much more with legal personality – but it would do the same things with greater legal certainty and relieved from the necessity to work around its basic defect all the time'.[48]

38 See Ghébali, 'The Reform Process of the OSCE since the 2001 Bucharest Ministerial Decisions', 7; Ghébali, 'Growing Pains at the OSCE', 18, 26.

39 See Tichy and Köhler, n. 7, 9–11; Brander and Estébanez, 'The OSCE Matures', 3; Brander, n. 29, 21.

40 See Tomuschat, n. 7; Tabassi, 'The Question of Legal Status for the OSCE and Implications for Ukraine', 27 April 2015, available at: www.oscepa.org/documents/alldocuments/helsinki-40/seminar-4-diis/2919-presentation-by-lisa-tabassifor-helsinki-40-seminar-27-april-2015/file, 2.

41 See Tomuschat, n. 7.

42 See Wenig, 'The Status of the OSCE under International Law', 17.

43 See Tillikainen, 'Reviving Co-operative Security in Europe through the OSCE', 15–16.

44 Tichy and Köhler, n. 7, 9–11.

45 Tabassi, n. 40, 3–4.

46 See OSCE, 'Lessons Learned for the OSCE from Its Engagement in Ukraine', Interim Report and Recommendations of the Panel of Eminent Persons on European Security as a Common Project, 2015, available at: www.osce.org/networks/164561?download=true; ibid., 1.

47 See Brander, n. 29, 22.

48 Ley, 'Legal Personality for the OSCE?'.

Sceptics, however, question whether an enhanced legal status could have prevented the Ukraine crisis from happening.[49] After all, representatives of the OSCE themselves argue that 'even if perfect legal arrangements were agreed and in force, it does not guarantee perfect implementation'.[50] The unanimously agreed Special Monitoring Mission in eastern Ukraine is still facing obstructions to its work on the ground.[51] Moreover, it is often much easier to agree on political than legal obligations.[52] Finally, despite not being a legal entity under international law, the OSCE has used recommendations and guidelines from the High Commissioner for National Minorities and the OSCE's Office for Democratic Institutions and Human Rights (ODIHR) legal advisory instruments – for example, in Croatia.[53] Moreover, the OSCE has not been prevented from drafting legal treaties,[54] which – once agreed – have been formally located outside the OSCE framework.[55]

Political arguments in favour of strengthening the legal framework of the OSCE can draw support from liberal theories of international cooperation. Those authors pleading for the Organization's legalisation, for instance, argue that international institutions are more effective when they have the authority to issue legally binding rules, when these rules are precise and when they can rely on an independent dispute settlement body for their enforcement.[56] Although form (in terms of competencies, instruments and decision-making modes) is significant in relation to the possible performance of an institution, higher degrees of formalisation and legalisation do not necessarily translate into better performance. Rather, performance depends on the 'scope conditions' under which institutional options are actually translated into political practice.[57] The respective 'problem structure' (or type of cooperation problem) – that is the specific mix of converging and diverging interest of involved actors in a given political situation – defines a necessary (but not sufficient) precondition for international cooperation; political actors need to share an

49 See Bogush, 'OSCE: Do We Really Need an International Legal Personality and Why?'.

50 Tabassi, n. 40, 6.

51 See Kahlweit, 'Zwischen den Zeilen des Minsker Abkommens'.

52 See Tichy and Köhler, n. 7, 456–8.

53 See Zanotti, 'Post-Structuralism Soft Power as Governmentality', 101–2.

54 There are only documents emanating from the OSCE that have acquired the status of an international treaty, namely the Convention on Conciliation and Arbitration (1992) and the Treaty on Conventional Armed Forces (1990). However, neither of them is considered an OSCE document. See Fastenrath and Weigelt, 'Organization for Security and Cooperation in Europe (OSCE)', para. 35.

55 See Manton, 'The OSCE Human Dimension and Customary International Law Formation', 4.

56 See Kahler, 'The Causes and Consequences of Legalization'; Tallberg, 'Paths to Compliance'; Helfer and Slaughter, 'Toward a Theory of Effective Supranational Adjudication'.

57 See Keohane, 'Neoliberal Institutionalism'; Abbott *et al.*, 'The Concept of Legalization'.

interest in cooperation and compromise due to a given and perceived 'problem interdependence', rendering both cooperation and compromise valuable to all actors involved.[58] In the case of Crimea, Russia shares no such interest with the western participating States.[59] As a result, the OSCE's mandate has been confined to eastern Ukraine, while Russia claims authority over Crimea and has excluded the Organization's mandate covering other parts of Ukraine.

Governance research, which is less state-centred and gives equal weight to formal and informal institutions, challenges the assumption that the legal framework of an institution matters for its effectiveness and legitimacy.[60] Quite the contrary, voluntariness, flexibility and multi-stakeholder participation facilitate both consent on and compliance with international decisions.[61] Moreover, mirroring Bahr's dictum that '[s]oft power can in fact be harder than hard power',[62] 'soft law' may provide socialising effects, which sooner or later lead to 'hard' international law. As Fastenrath suggested, the CSCE–OSCE documents 'express an opinio juris which, together with the ensuing practice, could provide the starting point for new regional international customary law'.[63] After all, '[t]he non-legal agreements or decisions of international organizations can, finally, have the effect of legitimating the norms of international law or depriving them of legitimacy by either confirming existing legal rules or undermining them with substantial deviations or by calling them completely into question'.[64]

While different approaches give rise to competing theoretical expectations, there is not much empirical evidence demonstrating that the performance of international institutions depends on their legal status and legal capacity. In fact, the OSCE is used in the international relations literature as an example of an international institution that has been effective precisely because of its less formalised nature, allowing the organisation to be more flexible, prompt and inclusive in dealing with international conflicts and crises when it comes to crisis consultations. Moreover, some of the more 'invasive' instruments,

58 See Martin, 'The Rational State Choice of Multilateralism'; Zürn, *Interessen und Institutionen in der internationalen Politik*.

59 See Marxsen, n. 11.

60 See, on the governance aspects of the OSCE, Krahmann, 'Conceptualizing Security Governance'; Kirchner and Dominguez, *The Security Governance of Regional Organizations*.

61 See Sabel and Zeitlin, *Experimentalist Governance in the European Union*; Héritier and Rhodes, *New Modes of Governance in Europe*.

62 Bahr, 'Germany's Ostpolitik and the Road to Helsinki', 6.

63 Fastenrath, 'The Legal Significance of CSCE/OSCE Documents', 13–14; see also Shelton, 'Soft Law'.

64 Fastenrath, n. 63, 14.

including on-site inspection in the case of suspected human rights violations, could only be agreed because these were 'merely' political obligations.[65]

Finally, the only codified element of the OSCE – namely the Court of Conciliation and Arbitration – is itself not working. The Court of Conciliation and Arbitration, established in 1992, has still to be called upon.[66] Its non-use is another illustration of the claim that higher degrees of institutionalisation (here legalisation) do not directly translate into greater effectiveness.[67]

Participating States have been largely content to consolidate existing institutions and their operational activities. This has generally been a matter of making minor organisational changes in light of practical experience.[68] Still, this existence in the 'niche of cooperative security' has not prevented but actually enabled the CSCE–OSCE to play a core role as a political forum and clearing house for controversial security issues.[69] This had been its chief role during the breakdown of arms-control negotiations in the wake of the Intermediate Nuclear Forces (INF) controversy and the imposition of martial law in Poland in the early 1980s, and it became obvious once again most recently during the 2014 Ukraine crisis.

The weakness of its legal framework notwithstanding, the OSCE has continuously been involved in conflict prevention and the promotion of its values and norms. The ODIHR, frequently in cooperation with the Council of Europe, has trained members of the executive, judicial and legislative branches of government in the new democracies of central and eastern Europe. Its fact-finding and monitoring missions have served to examine standards in political life and have formed the basis for institutional recommendations. The OSCE High Commissioner on National Minorities (HCNM) has played a key role in pursuing these goals and has received considerable recognition for doing so. Long-term OSCE field operations have attempted to head off potential crisis situations and to eliminate deficits in the application of OSCE principles and norms. For example, in 2001 OSCE field operations were present in seventeen countries (and employed some 4,000 people) as compared to 2012, when twenty operations were in place, while fifteen others were already terminated – despite the political controversies elaborated below. The mandates of OSCE field operations

65 See I. Peters, 'From the CSCE to the OSCE', 112–22.

66 See OSCE, 'Convention on Conciliation and Arbitration within the OSCE', 15 December 1992, available at: www.osce.org/cca/111409.

67 Tomuschat, n. 7.

68 For details of the institutional development, see I. Peters, 'The OSCE, NATO and the EU within the "Network of Interlocking European Security Institutions"'.

69 I. Peters, 'Von der KSZE zur OSZE'.

have ranged across concrete conflict-management efforts, election monitoring and the monitoring of ceasefires and peacekeeping forces.[70]

4 THE PERILS OF LEGAL REFORM

Moreover, OSCE standards have become part and parcel of international law by incorporating a reference to these standards in bilateral international treaties, such as Germany's treaties with its eastern neighbours on partnership and cooperation.[71] 'It has become clear that the political norms of the CSCE/OSCE have often been more effective than legally binding provisions.'[72] Not having legal character, OSCE norms come with 'the advantages of acting innovatively and flexibly to fill existing gaps'.[73] In fact, flexibility is to be maintained also in the eyes of proponents (working for the OSCE) of an upgrading of the legal status of the Organization, stating that 'while a clear legal status would not necessarily hamper the flexibility and operational advantages of the OSCE, its lack comes clearly at a cost'.[74]

The difference between a legally and politically binding status for the overall institution, as much as for the documents or acts agreed upon in this framework, may be less important than the academic and political discourse suggests. After all, international law itself was 'created from political processes', as Manton argues.[75] By strengthening its legal framework, the OSCE could lose its competitive advantage over other security organisations in Europe as 'a venue for regular discussion, reportedly very frank, closed-doors debates between participant states' diplomats and ministers'.[76] Its legal personality 'may come at the cost of losing the most precious function of the OSCE, the one of being a place for open debate between Russia and the West'.[77] One may question whether having legal quality per se infringes upon the OSCE's capacity to be a forum for controversial debates. At the same time, the OSCE is unlikely to gain much in terms of effectiveness and legitimacy

70 See OSCE, 'Annual Report 2001 on Interaction between Organizations and Institutions in the OSCE Area', 2001, 27–88, available at: www.osce.org/secretariat/14521; OSCE, 'Survey of OSCE Field Operations', SEC.GAL/27/16, 18 February 2016.

71 See Fastenrath, n. 63, 7.

72 Heintze, 'Double or Treble Human Rights Protection?', 12.

73 Ibid.

74 Tabassi, n. 40, 7; see also Brander, n. 29, Dominguez, *The OSCE. Soft Security for a Hard World*, 17; Dunay, 'The OSCE in Crisis', 89.

75 Manton, 'The OSCE Human Dimension and Customary International Law Formation', 5.

76 Ley, n. 48.

77 Ibid.

since the real issue is the internal disputes over those 'western values' that form the foundation of the post-Cold War security order in Europe, values that the OSCE is supposed to protect. It is this liberal *acquis* that might be the biggest price of a legal reform, if the Russian position would take effect in the above-mentioned EST as the new statute for the OSCE.

Beside the debate on the causal relationship between legal framework and performance, a legal upgrade of the OSCE raises more fundamental considerations. Granting legal personality may have 'a paradoxical effect in strengthening the confrontational element in Europe, the division of Europe into spheres of influence and geopolitical battle between "East" and "West"'.[78] By compromising its founding principles, the OSCE may in fact contribute to the general setback. As we have seen in the first section of this chapter, debates about the effectiveness and legitimacy of the OSCE are marked by the increasingly incompatible political stances of Russia (and its CIS partners) on the one hand, and the EU and NATO participating States on the other. While the former argues in favour of a revision of the OSCE's foundations, the latter defend the status quo, encompassing Russia's formal acceptance that liberal values govern the work of the OSCE. After all, the unique quality of the political principles of the OSCE allow, contrary to the usual standards of international law, 'that appropriate action may be taken by the Council or the Committee of Senior Officials, if necessary in the absence of the consent of the State concerned, in cases of clear, gross and uncorrected violations of relevant CSCE commitments'.[79]

Negotiating a new de jure status for the Organization, as well as reinvigorating the traditional provisions of international law, could mean enhancing the OSCE's legal status at the expense of its political role – based on its transformative governance principles – resulting in an 'OSCE-minus', that is, an organisation deprived of its politically most innovative regulations.

Since the run-up to the Budapest Summit in 1994, Russia and its CIS partners have pushed for rendering the OSCE's de jure status along the lines of an international organisation, similar to the one enjoyed by NATO and the UN.[80] What at first glance looks like a merely legal issue constitutes a severe challenge to the main features of the OSCE, and has been a bone of political contention among participating States and governments concerning the form and functions (and thus the legitimacy and effectiveness) of the Organization.

78 Bogush, n. 49.
79 OSCE, n. 66.
80 See CSCE, 'Budapest Document 1994: Towards a Genuine Partnership in a New Era', 1994, available at: www.osce.org/mc/39554?download=true.

In the mid 1990s, Moscow had finally accepted that the informal foundations of the Organization would remain unchanged. But the issue (re-) emerged with the renewed reform debate in 2004–5, not least because of the recommendation made in the report by the Panel of Eminent Persons that participating States 'devise a concise statute or charter of the OSCE containing its basic goals, principles and commitments, as well as the structure of its main decision-making bodies'.[81] The panel also suggested that participating States 'agree on a convention recognizing the OSCE's legal capacity and granting privileges and immunities to the OSCE and its officials'.[82]

As we have argued above, the Russian Federation's prompting for a return to the traditional principle of non-interference undermines any chances for an agreement on any legal reform of the OSCE. Moreover, Russian revisionism is arguably the most significant challenge to the Organization's effectiveness and legitimacy, by weakening the commitments of the signatory states to allow political interventions of other participating States on behalf of democratic standards, human rights and the rule of law.

Western states have made efforts to accommodate Russia and discuss problems of election monitoring, as well as to actively promote election monitoring on their own territories. At the same time, they have generally rejected Russia's revisionist moves by making references to the OSCE's fundamental character of following a 'comprehensive concept of security',[83] legitimising the concerns of OSCE states about the domestic affairs of fellow participating States and their implementation of OSCE principles, norms and rules. Criticising those participating States, including Russia, that have been trying to undo what they had initially signed up to in core OSCE documents, including the Moscow Document of 1991, Washington argued:

> Not surprisingly, it is from those participating States where fundamental freedoms are most challenged by government actions, and where democratic safeguards are the weakest, that we tend to hear the most criticism by state officials of the way the OSCE and its institutions and field missions

[81] OSCE, 'Common Purpose, Towards a More Effective OSCE, Final Report and Recommendations of the Panel of Eminent Persons On Strengthening the Effectiveness of the OSCE', 2005, available at: https://www.osce.org/cio/15805?download=true.

[82] Ibid.

[83] Crisis Management Initiative, Rintakoski, Autti. *Comprehensive Approach. Trends, Challenges and Possibilities for Cooperation in Crisis Prevention and Management, Comprehensive Approach Seminar 17 June 2008 Helsinki* Helsinki: Ministry of Defence, Finland, available at: https://www.defmin.fi/files/1316/Comprehensive_Approach_-_Trends_Challenges_and_Possibilities_for_Cooperation_in_Crisis_Prevention_and_Management.pdf.

conduct their work. It is precisely where the distance between commitment and conduct is greatest that the OSCE must continue to concentrate its efforts.[84]

The German government spoke out for a dialogue on what traditionally were considered states' domestic affairs.[85] However, most EU and NATO states participating in the OSCE feared that Russian reform proposals, and specifically an OSCE statute, 'may undermine the commitments of member states that have been built up within the OSCE', a critique rejected by Russia as groundless.[86] Western states have acknowledged Russian and CIS countries' concerns, and broader discussions on the role of the OSCE within the wider European security architecture have continued since 2009 under the umbrella of the 'Corfu process'. Yet, the USA and Germany have continuously resisted Russian proposals for institutional reforms, which has also spared them the trouble of agreeing on which institutional reforms they would be willing to support if they were not linked to a revision of the OSCE's liberal values.

Washington has always stressed that the OSCE as it is now structured, as viewed from the US, does excellent work, and that reforms should strengthen what the OSCE does best without reshuffling the whole organization. Their baseline has been that 'new procedures must not come at the expense of principles', and 'any institutional reforms should be geared to strengthening OSCE's ability to produce results on the ground, particularly through its field missions'.[87] Consequently, the US government has remained opposed to 'any effort that – either in its intent or its effect – would diminish OSCE's credibility, dilute the commitments of signatory states, divert OSCE's attention from tough human dimension issues or undermine OSCE's effectiveness on the ground'.[88] Originally, Washington had resisted any treaty or charter establishing the OSCE as an international organisation with legal personality, since it asserted that such a formal treaty would 'misdirect our energies and

84 Ibid.

85 See Steinmeier, 'Rede des Bundesministers des Auswärtigen, Dr. Frank-Walter Steinmeier, vor dem Ständigen Rat der OSZE am 18. Januar 2007 in Wien', 2007, available at: www.bundesregierung.de/Content/DE/Bulletin/2001_2007/2007/01/04-4-aa-osze.html.

86 Lavrov, 'Speech by Russian Minister of Foreign Affairs at the 15th OSCE Ministerial Council Meeting', 29 November 2007 (n. 16).

87 Rice, 'Rice Urges European Parliamentarians to Think Boldly, Globally', 2005, available at: https://2001-2009.state.gov/secretary/rm/2005/48912.htm; Burns, 'United States Intervention to the 2008 OSCE Ministerial Council', United States Mission to the OSCE, MC.DEL/28/08, 4 December 2008, available at: https://www.osce.org/mc/35359?download=true.

88 Ibid. For a pointed treatment of Lavrov's main points (i.e., non-interference with internal affairs principle, imbalance of baskets, unfair standards in the human dimension and election monitoring), see Pryor, 'Criticism of OSCE by Nine CIS Countries Draws the Response', 28 July 2004, available at: www.brama.com/news/press/2004/07/040729csce.html.

political capital away from the OSCE's substantive work'.[89] Rather, they suggested that 'the Helsinki Document and the OSCE's *acquis* of agreements and decisions speak for themselves'.[90] However, over time, the US government increasingly considered the proposals as distinct issues that did not necessarily have to go together, and ultimately 'firmly supported' the adoption of the legal convention granting the OSCE legal personality but no formal treaty foundation.[91]

Germany, ever since the debate's revival in the mid 2000s, has also considered an OSCE charter and a convention on its legal personality as distinct issues, favouring only the latter.[92] Its baseline concerning institutional reforms has been that 'a dynamic organisation needs change and renewal'.[93] In support of the US position, Berlin has also emphasised that 'it is therefore very important ... that there is no move to encroach upon the OSCE's basic values, values which we all share and which make up the organization's strength'.[94] Efficiency and transparency of the OSCE's work should be improved on the basis of reform and consensus, partnership, common responsibility and enhanced geographic balance.[95]

In response to Medvedev's 2009 proposal for negotiating a new all-European security treaty, German and US officials repeatedly emphasised the OSCE's indispensability for establishing a new political order in Europe. They adjured the need for open dialogue in order to 'restore the consensus and the comprehensive operability of the OSCE', as the lack of which had become apparent by the fact that since 2002 no Declaration of Ministers had been adopted at the Organization's annual Council meetings.[96] Holding the OSCE Chair in 2016, the German government underlined its support for providing the OSCE with legal personality, but remained firm in its position that the

89 Volker, 'State's Volker Outlines, Vision of Reformed but Flexible OSCE'.

90 Ibid.

91 Finley, 'Response to Russian Foreign Minister Lavrov', 23 May 2007, available at: https://www.osce.org/fsc/25335?download=true: 'Recalling the 2006 Ministerial Decision, we do not believe that a "Charter" should not be negotiated, nor is it necessary, to give the OSCE the same legal status as other organisations.' See also Finley, 'Looking Ahead to OSCE Ministerial', 14 November 2008, PC.DEL/997/08, available at: https://www.osce.org/pc/34977?download=true.

92 Steinmeier, (n. 85).

93 Ibid.

94 Erler (n. 23).

95 Steinmeier, 'Rede des Bundesministers des Auswärtigen, Dr. Frank-Walter Steinmeier, beim Ministerrat der OSZE am 5. Dezember 2005 in Ljubljana 2005, available at: www.bundesregierung.de/Content/DE/Bulletin/2001%5F2007/2005/12/97-1_Steinmeier.html.

96 Ibid. In fact, the first substantial Ministerial Document since 2002 was adopted in December 2009.

basis of reform should occur on the report of the Panel of Eminent Persons and must not lead to the watering down or renegotiating of the OSCE *acquis*.[97]

In sum, the divisions underlying the political debates on reforming the OSCE have remained largely unresolved. These issues concern OSCE principles, the autonomy of the ODIHR, the norms and rules directly or indirectly pertaining to the OSCE legal (and political) framework, operational activities (OSCE field operations) and the role of civil society actors within the OSCE.[98] After sullen toleration during the first years following the breakdown of communism, Russia, and to different degrees also the CIS states, is resurgent and attempting to re-reform the OSCE at the level of operational practices towards the status quo ante and in effect dismissing formerly agreed standards of democratic order, human rights and the rule of law. NATO and EU member states not surprisingly have favoured maintaining those established rules, procedures and operational activities of the OSCE that were built on liberal values.

5 *CUI BONO*: SECURITY AND COOPERATION FOR WHICH EUROPE?

We have argued that strengthening its legal framework in general, and giving it legal personality in particular, is no panacea for the effectiveness and legitimacy problems affecting the OSCE. In fact, engaging in legal reforms could give away what used to be the core – and arguably the strength – of the Organization. If the Trojan horse of the Russian EST proposal, which links legal status reforms to revisions of fundamental principles, should successfully disperse its hidden cargo among EU and NATO member states, the OSCE would lose its trademark as a flexible political platform for political dialogue (especially) in times of severe conflict and crisis among its participating States. It could also be deprived of its liberal values, upon which the very foundations of the European security order at the end of the Cold War rested.

97 See Steinmeier, 'Rede von Außenminister Frank-Walter Steinmeier beim 21. OSZE-Ministerrat in Basel', 4 December 2014, available at: https://www.auswaertiges-amt.de/en/newsroom/news/141204-bm-ministerrat-osze/267434; Deutscher Bundestag, 'Initiativen für Abrüstung, Rüstungskontrolle und vertrauensbildende Maßnahmen unter dem OSZE-Vorsitz Deutschlands', 10.

98 For a detailed account of the diverging lines of argument, see I. Peters, 'Legitimacy and International Organizations' 2013, 207–218.

The OSCE is facing today contesting views on its legitimacy and, as a result, on the need and direction of institutional reforms. The vast majority of western states – despite varying positions regarding the specifics of legal reforms – want to preserve the Organization's principles and functions relating to human rights, democracy and the rule of law, and regard them as essential to the OSCE's legitimacy. Russia – at least since Vladimir Putin first became president in 1999 and the policies emanating from Moscow grew more assertive – has taken the position of a 'revisionist power', arguing that OSCE interventions in its participating States undermine the Organization's legitimacy. Accordingly, Russia – supported by some CIS governments as much as by experts – has tried to push institutional reforms that would advance more traditional understandings of sovereignty and non-interference with domestic affairs.

Western governments consider Russia's proposals not so much as an attempt at a 'progressive' process of institutionalised cooperation and regional integration, but rather an effort to roll back the scope of the OSCE's activities when it comes to protecting liberal values. It is not only that the incompatibility of ideas and interests regarding the role and the fundamental principles of the OSCE render any prospects for legal reform unlikely, but that the contesting views of participating States – rather than the weak legalisation or formalisation of the current governance framework – undermine the overall effectiveness of the Organization. This is not to say that awarding the OSCE legal personality and legal capacity could not facilitate operational safety and effectiveness for OSCE personnel. However, as long as such legal reforms are linked to a formal legal treaty foundation for the OSCE, they stand little chance of becoming reality.

REFERENCES

Abbott, Kenneth, Keohane, Robert, Moravcsik, Andrew, Slaughter, Anne-Marie and Snidal, Duncan, 'The Concept of Legalization', *International Organization* 54 (3) (2000), 385–99.

Bahr, Egon, *Sicherheit für und vor Deutschland* (Munich, Vienna: Carl Hanser Verlag GmbH & Co. KG, 1991).

'Germany's Ostpolitik and the Road to Helsinki', in Institute for Peace Research and Security Policy at the University of Hamburg (eds.), *OSCE Yearbook* 2005 (Baden-Baden: Nomos Verlagsgesellschaft, 2005).

Bogush, Gleb, 'OSCE: Do We Really Need an International Legal Personality and Why?', *Völkerrechtsblog* 15 August 2016, available at: http://voelker

rechtsblog.org/osce-do-we-really-need-an-international-legal-personality-and-why/.

Börzel, Tanja and Schimmelfennig, Frank, 'Coming Together or Drifting Apart? The EU's Political Integration Capacity in Eastern Europe', *Journal of European Public Policy* 24 (2) (2017), 278–96.

Brander, Sonya, 'Making a Credible Case for a Legal Personality for the OSCE', *OSCE Magazine* (March–April 2009), 18–22.

Brander, Sonya and Estébanez, María Martín, 'The OSCE Matures: Time for Legal Status', *Helsinki Monitor* 18 (1) (2007), 2–5.

Brichambaut, Marc Perrin de, 'The OSCE and the 21st Century', *Helsinki Monitor: Security and Human Rights* 18 (3) (2007), 180–91.

Deutscher Bundestag, 'Initiativen für Abrüstung, Rüstungskontrolle und vertrauensbildende Maßnahmen unter dem OSZE-Vorsitz Deutschlands, Antwort der Bundesregierung auf die kleine Anfrage der Abgeordneten Katrin Kunert, Wolfgang Ehrcke, Christine Buchholz, weiterer Abgeordneter und der Franktion DIE LINKE', Bundestag Drucksache 18/9795, 2016.

Dominguez, Roberto (ed.), *The OSCE. Soft Security for a Hard World: Competing Theories for Understanding the* OSCE (Brussels: P. I. E. Peter Lang, 2014).

Dunay, Pál, 'The OSCE in Crisis', in EU Institute for Security Studies, Chaillot Paper No. 88 (Paris: 2006).

Erler, Gernot, 'Speech by the Minister of State in the Federal Foreign Office at the OSCE Ministerial Council in Brussels', MC.DEL/22/06, 4 December 2006.

Fastenrath, Ulrich, 'The Legal Significance of CSCE/OSCE Documents', in Institute for Peace Research and Security Policy at University of Hamburg (eds.), *OSCE Yearbook* 1996 (Baden-Baden: Nomos Verlagsgesellschaft 1996).

Fastenrath, Ulrich and Weigelt, Katja, 'Organization for Security and Cooperation in Europe (OSCE)', in Rüdiger Wolfrum (ed.), *Max Planck Encyclopedia of Public International Law*, vol. VII (Oxford: Oxford University Press, 2012).

Flynn, Gregory and Farell, Henry, 'The CSCE and the "Construction" of Security in Post-Cold War Europe', *International Organization* 53 (3) (1999), 505–35.

Ghébali, Victor-Yves, 'The Reform Process of the OSCE since the 2001 Bucharest Ministerial Decisions', in Institute for Peace Research and Security Policy at University of Hamburg (eds.), *OSCE Yearbook 2002* (Baden-Baden: Nomos Verlagsgesellschaft, 2002), 329–36.

'Growing Pains at the OSCE: The Rise and Fall of Russia's Pan-European Expectations', *Cambridge Review of International Affairs* 18 (3) (2005), 375–88.

Gilpin, Robert, *War and Change in World Politics* (Cambridge: Cambridge University Press, 1981).

Heintze, Hans-Joachim, 'Double or Treble Human Rights Protection? The Interplay of OSCE Standards with Other Systems of Norms', in Institute for Peace Research and Security Policy at University of Hamburg (eds.), *OSCE Yearbook* 2006 (Baden-Baden: Nomos Verlagsgesellschaft, 2006), 237–49.

Helfer, Laurence and Slaughter, Anne-Marie, 'Toward a Theory of Effective Supranational Adjudication', *Yale Law Journal* 107 (2) (1997), 273–391.

Héritier, Adrienne and Rhodes, Martin (eds.), *New Modes of Governance in Europe, Governing in the Shadow of Hierarchy* (Houndmills: Palgrave Macmillan, 2010).

Kahler, Miles, 'Conclusion: The Causes and Consequences of Legalization', *International Organization* 54 (3) (2000), 661–83.

Kahlweit, Cathrin, 'Zwischen den Zeilen des Minsker Abkommens', *Sueddeutsche Zeitung* (12 February 2015).

Keohane, Robert, 'Neoliberal Institutionalism: A Perspective on World Politics', in Robert Keohane (ed.), *International Institutions and State Power: Essays in International Relations Theory* (Boulder: Westview Press, 1989), 1–20.

Kirchner, Emil and Dominguez, Roberto, *The Security Governance of Regional Organizations*. vol. 58 (Milton Park, Abingdon: Routledge, 2013).

Klein, Margarete, 'Russia's Plan for a New Pan-European Security Regime: A Serious Proposal or an Attempt at Division?', *Russian Analytical Digest* 55 (2009), 6–9.

Krahmann, Elke, 'Conceptualizing Security Governance', *Cooperation and Conflict* 38 (1) (2009), 5–26.

Ley, Isabelle, 'Legal Personality for the OSCE? Some Observations at the Occasion of the Recent Conference on the Legal Status of the OSCE', *Völkerrechtsblog*, 8 August 2016, available at: http://voelkerrechtsblog.org/legal-personality-for-the-osce/.

Manton, Eric, 'The OSCE Human Dimension and Customary International Law Formation', in Institute for Peace Research and Security Policy at the University of Hamburg (eds.), *OSCE Yearbook* 2005 (Baden-Baden: Nomos Verlagsgesellschaft, 2004), 1–20.

Martin, Lisa, 'The Rational State Choice of Multilateralism', in John Gerard Ruggie (ed.), *Multilateralism Matters: The Theory and Praxis of an Institutional Form* (New York: Columbia University Press, 1993), 91–121.

Marxsen, Christian, 'Territorial Integrity in International Law – Its Concept and Implications for Crimea', *Zeitschrift für ausländisches öfentliches*

Recht und Völkerrecht (Heidelberg Journal of International Law) 75 (1) (2015), 7–26.

'International Law in Crisis: Russia's Struggle for Recognition', Max Planck Institute for Comparative Public Law and International Law (ed.), MPIL Research Paper Series No. 2016–05 (Heidelberg, 2016), available at: https://ssrn.com/abstract=2771293.

OSCE, 'Draft Decision on the Charter of the OSCE: Submitted by Armenia, Belarus, Kazakhstan, Kyrgyzstan, Uzbekistan, Russian Federation, Tajikistan', PC.DEL/897/07, 18 September 2007.

Peters, Ingo, 'From the CSCE to the OSCE – Institutional Quality and Political Meaning', in Ingo Peters (ed.), *New Security Challenges: The Adaptation of International Institutions. Reforming the UN, NATO, EU and CSCE since* 1989 (Münster, New York: Lit Verlag, St. Martin's Press, 1996), 85–122.

'Von der KSZE zur OSZE: Überleben in der Nische kooperativer Sicherheit', in Helga Haftendorn and Otto Keck (eds.), *Kooperation jenseits von Hegemonie und Bedrohung, Sicherheitsinstitutionen in den internationalen Beziehungen* (Baden-Baden: Nomos Verlagsgesellschaft, 1997), 57–100.

'The OSCE, NATO and the EU within the "Network of Interlocking European Security Institutions": Hierarchization, Flexibilization, Marginalization', in Institute for Peace Research and Security Policy at the University of Hamburg (eds.), *OSCE Yearbook* 2003 (Baden-Baden: Nomos Verlagsgesellschaft, 2004), 381–402.

'Legitimacy and International Organizations: The Case of the OSCE', in Dominik Zaum (ed.), *Legitimacy and International Organizations* (Oxford, New York: Oxford University Press, 2013), 196–220.

Sabel, Charles and Zeitlin, Jonathan (eds.), *Experimentalist Governance in the European Union: Towards a New Architecture* (Oxford: Oxford University Press, 2010).

Sapiro, Miriam, 'Changing the CSCE into the OSCE: Legal Aspects of a Political Transformation', *American Journal of International Law* 89 (3) (1995), 631–7.

Shelton, Dinah, 'Soft Law', in David Armstrong (ed.), *Routledge Handbook of International Law* (Abingdon: Routledge Press, 2009), 68–81.

Smith, Christopher, 'Kazakhstan's Candidacy for OSCE Chairmanship', US House of Representatives: Proceedings of the 109th Congress, 2nd Session, Congressional Record 152 (2006), 29 June 2006, 87.

Steinmeier, Frank-Walter, 'Interview with the OSCE Chairperson-in-Office, German Federal Minister for Foreign Affairs', *Security Community, OSCE Magazine* (2015), 3–4.

Tabassi, Lisa, 'The Question of Legal Status for the OSCE and Implications for Ukraine', 27 April 2015, available at: www.oscepa.org/documents/all

-documents/helsinki-40/seminar-4-diis/2919-presentation-by-lisa-tabassi-for-helsinki-40-seminar-27-april-2015/file.

Tallberg, Jonas, 'Paths to Compliance. Enforcement, Management, and the European Union', *International Organization* 56 (3) (2002), 609–43.

Tichy, Helmut and Köhler, Ulrike, 'Legal Personality or Not – The Recent Attempts to Improve the Status of the OSCE', in Isabelle Buffard, James Crawford, Alain Pellet and Stephan Wittich (eds.), *International Law Between Universalism and Fragmentation: Festschrift in Honour of Gerhard Hafner* (Leiden, Boston: Martinus Nijhoff Publishers, 2008), 455–78.

Tillikainen, Teija, 'Reviving Co-operative Security in Europe through the OSCE', *Contribution of the OSCE Network of Think Tanks and Academic Institutions to the Panel of Eminent Persons* (2015), available at: www.fiia.fi/assets/news/Reviving%20Co-operative%20Security%20in%20Europe%20through%20the%20OSCE.pdf.

Tomuschat, Christian, 'Legalization of the OSCE?', *Völkerrechtsblog*, 1 August 2016, available at: http://voelkerrechtsblog.org/legalization-of-the-osce/.

Waltz, Kenneth, *Theory of International Politics* (Massachusetts: Addison-Wesley Publishing Company, 1979).

Wenig, Marcus, 'The Status of the OSCE Under International Law – Current Status and Outlook, III. Organizational Aspects', in Institute for Peace Research and Security Policy at University of Hamburg (eds.), *OSCE Yearbook 1997* (Baden-Baden: Nomos Verlagsgesellschaft, 1997), 367–83.

Zanotti, Laura, 'Post-Structuralism: Soft Power as Governmentality and Normalization in the OSCE's Role in Croatia', in Roberto Dominguez (ed.), *The OSCE Soft Security for a Hard World: Competing Theories for Understanding the OSCE* (Brussels: P. I. E. Peter Lang, 2014), 93–110.

Zellner, Wolfgang, 'Managing Change in Europe. Evaluating the OSCE and Its Future Role: Competencies, Capabilities, and Missions', Working Paper 13, in WP Core Working Papers (Hamburg: Centre for OSCE Research, Institute for Peace Research and Security Policy at the University of Hamburg, 2005).

Zürn, Michael, *Interessen und Institutionen in der internationalen Politik: Grundlegung und Anwendung des situationsstrukturellen Ansatzes* (Opladen: Leske+Budrich, 1992).

6

Domestic Implications of the OSCE's Legal Personality under Russian Constitutional Law

Gleb Bogush

1 THE POLITICAL CONTEXT: RUSSIA AND THE OSCE'S INTERNATIONAL LEGAL PERSONALITY

The Organization for Security and Co-operation in Europe (OSCE) remains one of the key priorities of Russian foreign policy. Russia treats the Organization as a fundamental part of Europe's security architecture and an important tool for advancing Russian interests throughout the OSCE region, including Russia's growing opposition to NATO and the Euro-Atlantic community more generally.[1] An integral part of Russian strategy towards the OSCE is in promoting its transformation into a fully fledged international organisation by the drafting and subsequent adoption of the Organization's binding constituent instrument in the form of an international treaty.[2]

The new Russian Foreign Policy Concept, approved by President Vladimir Putin on 30 November 2016, proclaims that 'Russia views the OSCE as an important mechanism for building an equitable and indivisible system of pan-European security, and is interested in strengthening its role and authority. Setting clear priorities, primarily regarding countering transnational challenges and threats, as well as drafting the OSCE Charter and reforming its executive bodies with a view to ensuring appropriate prerogatives of the collective intergovernmental bodies, are the prerequisites for making the OSCE even more relevant.'[3]

[1] See the article by the Russian foreign minister, Sergei Lavrov:, 'The Euro-Atlantic Region: Equal Security for All' (2010), available at: http://eng.globalaffairs.ru/number/The_Euro-Atlantic_Region:_Equal_Security_for_All-14888.

[2] Tichy and Köhler, 'Legal Personality or Not', 468–9.

[3] President of the Russian Federation, 'Foreign Policy Concept of the Russian Federation', 30 November 2016, available at: http://www.mid.ru/en/foreign_policy/official_documents/-/asset_publisher/CptICkB6BZ29/content/id/122186.

It is notable that official Russian foreign policy objectives include a reference to the need for the 'legalisation' of the OSCE by adopting a charter for the Organization. As one of the proponents of establishing international legal personality for the OSCE, Russia categorically insists on the adoption of a legally binding constituent instrument – an OSCE Charter – as a necessary reform for the Organization. In the framework of the fourteenth meeting of the OSCE Ministerial Council in Brussels, Russian Foreign Minister Sergei Lavrov said that 'without the development of a single constituent document, the OSCE cannot be viewed as a fully-fledged international organisation'.[4] Most recently, Russia's representative at the OSCE, Alexander Lukashevich, in the course of welcoming the Austrian chairmanship, said 'We support the spirit of the Austrian chairmanship in strengthening the institutional foundations of the OSCE. Russia, as you may know, has long been promoting the idea of drafting a charter/constituent document of the OSCE.'[5]

Apparently, the adoption of the constituent document as the *conditio sine qua non* for recognising the international legal personality of the OSCE is Russia's principal position, adopted at the highest level. This may also explain the fact that Russia failed to adopt any national legislation on the privileges and immunities of OSCE institutions or on cooperation with the OSCE in general. Russia is well aware that the political consequence of adopting such a charter would be that the OSCE should come to resemble other international organisations, and to some extent becoming a counterpart to the UN within Europe. The central pillar of the Russian proposal is the incorporation of the consensus principle at the heart of OSCE decision-making.[6]

At the same time, Russia rejects any compromises aimed at providing the OSCE with only some of the individual elements of international legal personality, including the adoption of a special Convention on the international legal personality and privileges and immunities of the OSCE.[7]

4 Speech by Russian Minister of Foreign Affairs Sergei Lavrov at the fourteenth OSCE Ministerial Council Meeting, Brussels, 4 December 2006, unofficial translation from Russian available at: www.mid.ru/en/vistupleniya_ministra/-/asset_publisher/MCZ7HQuMdqBY/content/id/385980.

5 Lukashevich, Alexander, 'Statement of the Permanent Representative of the Russian Federation, at the meeting of the OSCE Permanent Council of 12 January 2017' (translated from Russian by the author) 12 January 2017, available at: www.mid.ru/foreign_policy/news/-/asset_publisher/cKNonkJE02Bw/content/id/2592601.

6 See, e.g., a good analysis of Russia's objectives: Zagorskiy and Entin, 'Zachem ukhodit iz OBSE?' ('Why leave the OSCE?'), *Rossiya v global'noy politike*, (July – August 2008).

7 Draft Convention on the International Legal Personality, Legal Capacity, and Privileges and Immunities of the OSCE, CIO.GAL/48/07/Rev.6, 23 October 2007.

In Russia's view, accession to such a Convention is impossible without the adoption of the constituent agreement of the Organization. Russia also argues that it faces difficulties with its own constitutional order, which requires a legal constitutive Act as a precondition to Russia's recognition of the OSCE's international legal personality. For that purpose, Article 79 of the Russian Constitution, which serves as a constitutional basis for Russia's relations with interstate associations, is invoked.[8]

The aforementioned argument, based on the Russian constitutional law, is the subject matter of this chapter. Russia's position on the international legal personality of the OSCE will be analysed in terms of Russia's current Constitution (section 2), as well as the case law of the Russian Constitutional Court (section 3) and the Russian international and constitutional law scholarship to which Russia refers in order to justify its position with regard to the international personality of the OSCE (section 4). The analysis seeks to answer the question of whether the political position of the Russian Federation really stands on the firm legal ground of Russian constitutional law and on doctrinal foundations (section 5).

2 THE CONSTITUTIONAL LEGAL FRAMEWORK: RUSSIA'S CONSTITUTION AND INTERNATIONAL ORGANISATIONS

The Russian Constitution of 1993 is one of the 'friendliest' towards international law among modern European constitutions.[9] Adopted at the peak of the political and legal reforms of the 1990s that followed the collapse of the Soviet Union, the basic law was designed by its drafters to inaugurate Russia's 'return' to Europe and the international community. In its preamble the Constitution proclaims that Russia 'recognizes itself as part of the international community'. According to Article 15(4), universally recognised principles and norms of international law, as well as international treaties entered into by Russia, are 'a part of the Russian legal system'. The same provision also grants priority to treaty rules in the event of a conflict with national legislation. This provision reflects a rather monist view of international rules as an integral part of the national legal system.[10]

8 For the official Russian position pursued within the OSCE, see Tichy and Köhler, 'Legal Personality or Not', 468.

9 The English version is available on the website of the European Commission for Democracy through Law, 'Constitution of the Russian Federation, adopted by Popular Vote on 12 December 1993', 23 February 2003, available at: www.venice.coe.int/webforms/documents/default.aspx?pdffile=CDL(2003)018-e.

10 The progressive monist wording of Article 15 of the Constitution contrasts with practice and conservative international law scholarship. As Lauri Mälksoo rightly noted, the 'constitution may be monist but conservative scholars continue to interpret the position of international law

Article 15(4) has been interpreted and applied on several occasions by the Russian Constitutional Court and has generated controversy among scholars. The Constitution is silent on the position of international law vis-à-vis the Constitution itself. The Russian Constitutional Court, however, in its more recent jurisprudence, ascribes to the Constitution absolute primacy in the Russian legal order, which therefore prevails also over the rules of international law. On this basis the Court has reached its conclusion on the 'non-enforceability' of the judgments of the European Court of Human Rights (ECtHR) in the event that they contradict the Constitution, and therefore a conclusion that is in clear contradiction with Article 46 of the European Convention on Human Rights (ECHR).[11] Thus the Constitution, against its initial mission and the will of its drafters, has gradually become a shield for resisting international legal obligations and justifying non-compliance with international law.

The core provision of the Constitution dealing with Russia's participation in international organisations is Article 79, which states: 'The Russian Federation may participate in interstate associations and transfer to them part of its powers according to international treaties and agreements, if this does not involve the limitation of the rights and freedoms of man and citizen and does not contradict the principles of the constitutional system of the Russian Federation.'

Article 79 has not received broad discussion in legal scholarship or in the case law of the Russian Constitutional Court. It could be argued that the Article provides for two basic principles. The first of them enables Russia's participation in international organisations as a manifestation of Russia's external sovereignty as an independent state. The second principle sets up limitations to such participation that are related to constitutional human rights and the observance of fundamental constitutional principles.

in Russia in a dualist fashion', Mälksoo, *Russian Approaches to International Law*, 121; see also Danilenko, 'Implementation of International Law in CIS States', 51–69.

11 Constitutional Court of the Russian Federation, 'Case concerning the review of constitutionality of the provisions of Article 1 of the Federal Law "On Ratification of the Convention for the Protection of Human Rights and Fundamental Freedoms and Protocols thereto", Items 1 and 2 of Article 32 of the Federal Law "On International Treaties of the Russian Federation", Sections 1 and 4 of Article 11, Item 4 of Section 4 of Article 392 of the Civil Procedure Code of the Russian Federation, Sections 1 and 4 of Article 13, Item 4 of Section 3 of Article 311 of the Arbitration Procedure Code of the Russian Federation, Sections 1 and 4 of Article 15, Item 4 of Section 1 of Article 350 of the Administrative Judicial Proceedings Code of the Russian Federation and Item 2 of Section 4 of Article 413 of the Criminal Procedure Code of the Russian Federation in connection with the request of a group of deputies of the State Duma', Judgment of 14 July 2015, No. 21-П/2015.

See, on this judgment and new mechanism, Mälksoo, 'Russia's Constitutional Court Defies the European Court of Human Rights', 377–95.

Some commentators, familiar with the Constitution's drafting history, have noted that the norm was drafted in order to protect Russian sovereignty, and informed largely by Russia's limited participation in foreign affairs while being a part of the Soviet Union. Many participants in the Constitutional Conference of 1993 considered this provision to be a guarantee of Russia's future sovereign development.[12] Thus, Article 79 was conceived as a kind of 'guarantee' against a loss of sovereignty that would result from Russia's absorption by a supranational body.

This provision supplements other provisions of the Constitution that uphold the principle of Russian sovereignty, as well as a clear orientation towards international integration. Commentators also point to another feature of this Article: it emphasises that in International Relations, including its participation in international associations, the Russian Federation acts as a single entity.[13] It is noteworthy that the Article is placed in the Constitution's section on federalism.

Like other provisions of the Russian Constitution, the norm in question is of a rather abstract nature and needs additional interpretation, paying particular attention to the specific terms used. In this regard, it is important that the Constitution uses the term 'interstate association' and not 'international organisation', without defining the criteria that such an interstate association must meet.

Commentators espouse different approaches to the interpretation of this provision. For example, the commentary to the Constitution edited by Valery Zorkin, the current chairman of the Russian Constitutional Court, says that the Article deals with 'interstate (intergovernmental) associations, i.e. organisations of states established on the basis of an international treaty to achieve common goals with permanent bodies and acting in the interests of their member states with respect to their sovereignty (UN, CoE etc.)'.[14] This definition is similar to the one given by Russian scholarship to the term 'international organisation'.

In the same commentary, however, it is stressed that 'participation' may be of a closer character (for example, a confederation).[15] The term 'interstate association' as used in the Constitution can therefore mean a union that is closer than 'just' an international organisation. Thus, while the term 'interstate association' could possibly be used as a synonym for international (intergovernmental) organisations, it seems more plausible to conclude that an

12 Lazarev, *Kommentariy k Konstitutsii Rossiyskoy Federatsii*, 278.

13 Ibid., 279.

14 Zor'kin, *Kommentariy k Konstitutsii Rossiyskoy Federatsii*, 356 (translation by the author).

15 Ibid., 357 (translation by the author).

interstate association, in terms of Russia's Constitution, is to be understood as having supranational features, such as the one created on the basis of the Treaty between the Russian Federation and the Republic of Belarus on the Establishment of a Union State on 8 December 1999, which the parties consider to be 'a stage in the procedure for the unification of the peoples of the two countries in the union democratic state', or arguably the Eurasian Economic Union.[16]

Importantly, the Article in question does not limit Russia's participation in any type of interstate association. It also follows from the wording of the Article that the Constitution distinguishes between organisations to which no powers from Russia need to be transferred and organisations that do require such a transfer and thereby acquire a supranational character in a certain sense. However, in this latter case, the relevant international treaties providing for the transfer of part of the powers of the Russian Federation or establishing treaty bodies competent to issue decisions binding upon the Russian Federation are subject to ratification in accordance with Article 15 (D) of the Law on International Treaties of the Russian Federation. It may also be argued that the strict requirement of subjecting an international treaty to national ratification and in some cases to constitutional control concerns accessions to international organisations of the second category (those based on the transfer of state powers). In other words, participation in the OSCE, as long as it does not involve the acceptance of binding decisions of its organs or an establishment of a treaty regime, does not fall within constitutional restrictions.

Another important and yet unresolved issue is what constitutes a 'transfer of sovereign rights' of the state to an international organisation in the sense of the Russian Constitution. There is little doubt that acceptance of the binding decisions of the organs of international organisations falls within this notion. For instance, Article 46(3) of the Constitution grants everyone the right to 'appeal, in accordance with international treaties of the Russian Federation, to international bodies for the protection of human rights and freedoms, if all the existing internal means of legal protection have been exhausted'.

In the OSCE context it is essential to determine whether granting privileges and immunities to an international organisation could be considered such a transfer. While the grant of privileges and immunities before domestic courts could hardly be considered a transfer of powers on the organs of an international organisation in the narrow sense of the term, such a grant by definition obliges the state to renounce its jurisdiction in the matters concerned.

16 Treaty on the Eurasian Economic Union, 29 May 2014, UNTS Registration Number I-52764, translation available at: www.un.org/en/ha/sixth/70/docs/treaty_on_eeu.pdf.

There are few differences between the conferral of immunities and privileges to foreign states and to international organisations, including the legal basis on which these immunities are granted. While international organisations are granted privileges and immunities on the basis of treaty law, states enjoy immunities on the basis of customary international law.[17] For instance, Russia recognises immunities of heads of state under customary international law, and the Russian Penal Code establishes that the question of the responsibility of persons enjoying immunity (Article 11) is to be 'resolved in accordance with international law'.

3 THE JURISPRUDENCE OF THE RUSSIAN CONSTITUTIONAL COURT

Article 79 has not received much attention in the case law of the Russian Constitutional Court. The Court has addressed this provision a few times, and only briefly, never giving it a full interpretation or explaining terms such as the notion of an interstate association. In this respect, the authority of the Constitutional Court to review the constitutionality of international treaties that have not yet entered into force is of particular importance. According to the Law of the Constitutional Court,[18] such a constitutional review may only be preliminary in character (before the entry into force of the respective international treaty), and cannot be carried out by the Court *proprio motu*.[19]

Given the sheer number of international treaties and Russia's post-Soviet integration projects, it is rather surprising that the Court has so far passed only two judgments within the framework of this review procedure. The more recent was a ruling of March 2014 on the treaty with the so-called 'Republic of Crimea' – a sham one-day state – domestically 'legitimizing' the subsequent

[17] See also the UN, General Assembly, United Nations Convention on Jurisdictional Immunities of States and Their Property, 2 December 2004, available at: http://legal.un.org/ilc/texts/instruments/english/conventions/4_1_2004.pdf. The convention is not in force yet.

[18] The English version of the law is available at the website of the Constitutional Court: Russian Federation, Federal Constitutional Law on the Constitutional Court of the Russian Federation, 21 July 1994, translation available at: www.ksrf.ru/en/Info/LegalBases/FCL/Documents/Law.pdf.

[19] According to the Constitutional Law on the Constitutional Court of the Russian Federation, 1994 (n. 18), Article 88, 'the right to petition the Constitutional Court of the Russian Federation with an request to verify the constitutionality of the international treaty of the Russian Federation pending its entry into force shall be vested in the President of the Russian Federation, the Federation Council, the State Duma, one fifth of the number of the members (deputies) of the Federation Council or of the deputies of the State Duma, the Government of the Russian Federation, the Supreme Court of the Russian Federation, bodies of legislative and executive power of the constituent entities of the Russian Federation'.

Russian annexation of the Crimean Peninsula.[20] The judgment in the so-called 'Crimea case' was issued overnight, *ex camera*. The Court clearly avoided all issues related to international law, including the need for examination of the more than dubious international legal personality of the other party to the treaty. The judgment well illustrates the general unwillingness of the Constitutional Court to take into account international legal personality considering the 'constitutionality' of an international treaty.

Another more noteworthy case was considered by the Constitutional Court in 2012. It dealt with the constitutionality of the Protocol on Russia's Accession to the Marrakesh Agreement on the Establishment of the World Trade Organization (WTO).[21] Despite the obvious difference between the OSCE and the WTO (the latter being based on a constituent treaty), the Constitutional Court ruled that the Protocol fully complied with the letter and spirit of Article 79 of the Constitution, thereby giving this constitutional provision its only official interpretation.[22]

In the 'WTO case', the applicants pointed out that the status of the WTO (either an intergovernmental or an interstate organisation) was uncertain. In response to that argument the Court noted that it was the Protocol on WTO Accession, and not the Marrakesh Agreement as such, that was a subject for constitutional review. Referring to the provisions of the federal law 'On International Treaties of the Russian Federation',[23] the Constitutional Court found that Russia may conclude international treaties with 'foreign

[20] Constitutional Court of the Russian Federation, 'Case concerning the review of constitutionality of the International Treaty Between the Russian Federation and the Republic of Crimea on Admission of the Republic of Crimea into the Russian Federation and Creation of New Subjects in the Composition of the Russian Federation, pending its entry into force, in connection with the request of the President of the Russian Federation', Judgment of 19 March 2014, Number 6-II/2014.' For a résumé see: Constitutional Court of the Russian Federation, 'Resume of Judgment of 19th March, 2014, No. 6-П/2014 the Constitutional Court', 2014, available at: www.ksrf.ru/en/Decision/Judgments/Documents/Resume19032014.pdf.

See Nuzov, 'National Ratification of an Internationally Wrongful Act', 353–76.

[21] Protocol on the Accession of the Russian Federation to the Marrakesh Agreement Establishing the World Trade Organization, 16 December 2011, 2874 UNTS, Registration Number A-31874, available at: http://economy.gov.ru/wps/wcm/connect/6a8797004983acf68844aa5f9eae86bc/russia_protocol.pdf?MOD=AJPERES&CACHEID=6a8797004983acf68844aa5f9eae86bc.

[22] Constitutional Court of the Russian Federation, 'Case concerning the review of constitutionality of an international treaty of the Russian Federation pending its entry into force – the Protocol on Accession of the Russian Federation to the Marrakesh Agreement Establishing the World Trade Organization', Judgment of 9 July 2012, No. 17-П/2012, available at: www.ksrf.ru/en/Decision/Judgments/Documents/2012%20July%209%2017-P.pdf.

[23] Federal Law no. 101-fz of 15 July 1995 'On the International Treaties of the Russian Federation'. An English version is available at: https://www.wto.org/english/thewto_e/acc_e/rus_e/WTACCRUS48_LEG_56.pdf.

states, as well as with international organisations and other entities'[24]. The Court further observed that from the perspective of the Russian legal system, a possible characterisation of the WTO as an intergovernmental or interstate organisation is irrelevant for determining the legality of domestic procedures to formalise Russian accession to the Marrakesh Agreement and, accordingly, its membership of the WTO.

It seems that in this case the Constitutional Court has developed its basic approach to assessing the compliance of the international treaty with the requirements of Article 79 of the Constitution. The decisive criterion for the Constitutional Court in reviewing the constitutionality of an international treaty has thereby not been the name of the organisation, the form of its creation, its acting bodies or indeed its international legal personality, but its possible restrictions upon human rights and freedoms and infringements of constitutional principles that might arise as a consequence of the accession to the treaty. In particular, when deciding on the constitutionality of accession to the WTO, the Court noted that the dispute settlement mechanism provided by the WTO could not as such be regarded as affecting the rights and freedoms of individuals and in any way diminishing Russian sovereignty.[25]

It is notable that in both instances of resorting to the review procedure, the Constitutional Court avoided reviewing the legal personality of the other treaty party in accordance with international law. It is rather difficult to predict the argumentation of the Court, should the possible Convention on the OSCE's international legal personality be submitted to constitutional review. Given the general flexibility of the constitutional framework and the Court's predisposition to the teleological interpretation of the Constitution,[26] the likely outcome might, however, be in favour of the constitutionality of such

[24] Constitutional Court of the Russian Federation, 'Case concerning the review of constitutionality of an international treaty of the Russian Federation pending its entry into force – the Protocol on Accession of the Russian Federation to the Marrakesh Agreement Establishing the World Trade Organization', Judgment of 9 July 2012, No. 17-П/2012, para. 3.2.

[25] 'Neither the Marrakesh Agreement itself, nor the 14 Protocol contemplate entrance of restrictions of rights and freedoms of the citizens of the Russian Federation and reconsideration of the fundamentals of its constitutional order.' Constitutional Court of the Russian Federation, 'Case concerning the review of constitutionality of an international treaty of the Russian Federation pending its entry into force – the Protocol on Accession of the Russian Federation to the Marrakesh Agreement Establishing the World Trade Organization', Judgment of 9 July 2012, No. 17-П/2012, para. 3.

[26] Belov, 'Tsennostnoe obosnovanie reshenii kak proyavlenie sudebnogo aktivizma Konstitutsionnogo Suda Rossiiskoi Federatsii' ('The Value-based Approach to the Argumentation as a Form of Judicial Activism of the Russian Constitutional Court'), 140–50.

a convention on international legal personality, especially if the review were requested by the government.

4 RUSSIAN LEGAL SCHOLARSHIP AND THE 'CHARTER ARGUMENT'

In the absence of an authoritative interpretation of Article 79 of the Constitution and the silence of Russian constitutional lawyers on the matter, it cannot be ruled out that to a certain extent Russian international legal scholarship, which has traditionally adhered to rather conservative positions, could have inspired the official Russian position on conditioning the granting of international legal personality to the OSCE with the adoption of an OSCE Charter.

Soviet and Russian legal scholars share the view that an international organisation should be founded on a constitutive treaty.[27] When discussing the criteria for a constitutive treaty, however, the scholarly approach is more nuanced. According to the prevailing view, such a treaty should be a constituent instrument for the respective international organisation. Scholars insist that a constituent treaty, usually a charter, is a necessary legal condition for the creation and functioning of an international organisation and for its acquisition of legal personality. In one of the monographs specifically dedicated to the OSCE, the authors state that the OSCE could be granted international legal personality by the adoption of a constitutive Act of the OSCE as a single document.[28]

Interestingly, the authors put forward a political argument, stating that 'there are some Western States that oppose the adoption of the OSCE Charter, as they do not want a strong OSCE opposing NATO'.[29] It is worth noting, however, that it is most unlikely that these same 'Western States' (presumably NATO members) would support opposition to NATO.[30] On the other hand, it is also argued that such a constitutive legal basis may consist of a set of documents serving as a constituent instrument, as is the case

[27] See, e.g.: Shibaeva, *Pravo mezhdunarodnykh organizatsii (Law of International Organizations)*, 75; Lukashuk, *Mezhdunarodnoe pravo. Osobennaya chast International Law. Special Part)* , 29.

[28] Kurdyukov and Makarova, *Rol' organizatsii po bezopasnosti i sotrudnichestvu v Yevrope (OBSE/SBSE) v razvitii mirovogo politicheskogo protsessa na rubezhe XXI veka* (*The Role of the Organization for Security and Co-operation in Europe in the Development of the World Political Process at the Turn of the XXI Century*), 15 (translation by the author).

[29] Ibid., 17 (translation by the author).

[30] See Börzel and I. Peters, '"It's Politics, Stupid": An International Relations Perspective on Strengthening the Legal Framework of the OSCE', Chapter 5 in this Volume.

with the OSCE.[31] For example, Gennady Ignatenko and Oleg Tiunov believe that the OSCE does 'not yet have a constituent act', but that at the same time the role of a constituent Act 'is provisionally played by the documents of the Paris (1990), Helsinki (1992) and Budapest (1994) meetings'.[32]

Interestingly, in many Russian scholarly sources, even those that consider a constituent treaty as an obligatory requirement for an international organisation to be granted international legal personality, the OSCE is referred to as an example of a regional international organisation, without any reservations, notwithstanding its lack of legal personality.

In general, the issue of the (international) legal personality of the OSCE is not well studied in contemporary Russian legal scholarship. Most scholars consider the OSCE an international organisation, even though it lacks a legal constitutive Act. They agree, however, that without such an Act it cannot be granted legal personality. In a remarkable doctoral thesis, unique it its being specifically dedicated to the topic, Mestnikov argues that the OSCE in its current form is a de facto international organisation, whereby the Paris, Budapest and Helsinki documents are its constitutive instruments. But to become a de jure international organisation, the OSCE's participating States would need to adopt a charter (Statute).[33] Remarkably, no single Russian legal scholar has put forward the alleged constitutional obstacle and invoked Article 79 of the Constitution in the OSCE context.

5 CONCLUSION: THE LEGAL PERSONALITY OF THE OSCE IN LIGHT OF RUSSIAN CONSTITUTIONAL LAW

As the analysis in the present chapter demonstrates, Russia's argument that the Constitution in general and Article 79 in particular require adoption of a charter as the only method for obtaining international legal personality for the OSCE is far from tenable. In the author's view, this argument is based not on the wording of the Constitution and its textual interpretations, but on traditionally conservative and politically coloured scholarly positions.

Within a purely legal interpretation of the Russian constitutional framework, however, it could be argued that the adoption of the Convention on the legal personality and privileges and immunities of the OSCE could meet the requirements of Article 79 of the Constitution. With regard to the requirement

31 See Malinin *Izbrannoe Trudy* (Selected Works) 5.

32 Ignatenko, Tiunov and Bezborodov, *Mezhdunarodnoye pravo* (*International Law*), 339.

33 Mestnikov, 'Problemy statusa i deyatel'nosti Organizatsii po bezopasnosti i sotrudnichestvu v Yevrope (OBSE)'. Dissertatsiya na soiskaniye uchonoy stepeni kandidata yuridicheskikh nauk, 12.

of the Constitution that 'participation in interstate associations should be in accordance with an international treaty', the Convention on international legal personality could possibly serve as the legal basis for such a participation, including for delegation of sovereign powers. As mentioned above, it is also unclear whether the OSCE attains the level of interstate association, even if endowed with international legal personality. In any event, it should be up to the Russian Constitutional Court to rule on the constitutionality of such a Convention, and such a review would be the most competent forum in which the Charter argument of Russian legal scholarship could be ultimately tested.

REFERENCES

Belov, Sergey, 'Tsennostnoe obosnovanie reshenii kak proyavlenie sudebnogo aktivizma Konstitutsionnogo Suda Rossiiskoi Federatsii' ('The Value-based Approach to the Argumentation as a Form of Judicial Activism of the Russian Constitutional Court'), *Sravnitel'noe Konstitutsionnoe Obozreniye* 2 (2012), 140–50.

Danilenko, Gennady, 'Implementation of International Law in CIS States: Theory and Practice', *European Journal of International Law* 10 (1999), 51–69.

Ignatenko, Gennadij, Tiunov, Oleg and Bezborodov, Jiurij, *Mezhdunarodnoe pravo (International Law)*(Moscow: Norma, 2014).

Kurdyukov, Gennady and Makarova, Galina, *Rol' organizatsii po bezopasnosti i sotrudnichestvu v Yevrope (OBSE/SBSE) v razvitii mirovogo politicheskogo protsessa na rubezhe XXI veka (The Role of the Organization for Security and Co-operation in Europe in the Development of the World Political Process at the Turn of XXI Century)* (Kazan, 2008).

Lazarev, Valerij (ed.), *Kommentariy k Konstitutsii Rossiyskoy Federatsii (Commentary to the Constitution of the Russian Federation)* 3rd edn (Moscow: Prospekt, 2008).

Lukashuk, Igor, *Mezhdunarodnoe pravo Osobennaya chast (International Law: Special Part)*, 3rd edn (Moscow: Wolters Kluwer, 2008).

Mälksoo, Lauri, 'Russia's Constitutional Court Defies the European Court of Human Rights: Constitutional Court of the Russian Federation Judgment of 14 July 2015, No 21-П/2015', *European Constitutional Law Review* 12 (2) (2016), 377–95.

Russian Approaches to International Law (Oxford: Oxford University Press, 2015).

Malinin, Sergei, 'Izbrannoe' (Selected Works) (Saint Petersburg: Yuridicheskiy Tsentr Press, 2003).

Mestnikov, Viktor, 'Problemy statusa i deyatel'nosti Organizatsii po bezopasnosti i sotrudnichestvu v Yevrope (OBSE)', Dissertatsiya na soiskaniye uchonoy stepeni kandidata yuridicheskikh nauk ('Problems of Status and Activity of the Organization for Security and Co-operation in Europe'), unpublished PhD thesis, 2005.

Nuzov, Ilya, 'National Ratification of an Internationally Wrongful Act: The Decision Validating and Russia's Incorporation of Crimea: Constitutional Court of the Russian Federation, Decision of 19 March 2014, No. 6-P', *European Constitutional Law Review* 12 (2) (2016), 353–76.

Shibaeva, Elena, *Pravo mezhdunarodnykh organizatsii* (*Law of International Organizations*) (Moscow: Mezhdunarodnye otnosheniya, 1986).

Tichy, Helmut and Köhler, Ulrike, 'Legal Personality or Not – The Recent Attempts to Improve the Status of the OSCE', in Isabelle Buffard, James Crawford, Alain Pellet and Stephan Wittich (eds.), *International Law between Universalism and Fragmentation: Festschrift in Honour of Gerhard Hafner* (Leiden, Boston: Martinus Nijhoff, 2008), 455–78.

Zagorskiy, Andrei and Entin, Mark, 'Zachem ukhodit iz OBSE?' (Why leave the OSCE?), *Rossiya v global'noy politike* 4 (July–August 2008).

Zorkin, Valerij (ed.), *Kommentariy k Konstitutsii Rossiyskoy Federatsii (Commentary to the Constitution of the Russian Federation)* (Moscow: Norma, 2013).

PART III

MANIFESTATIONS OF THE LEGAL POSITION UNDER INTERNATIONAL LAW

7

Revisiting Questions of Organisationhood, Legal Personality and Membership in the OSCE: the Interplay Between Law, Politics and Practice

Niels M. Blokker and Ramses A. Wessel

1 INTRODUCTION: THE OSCE'S CURRENT LEGAL STATUS*

More than forty years after the 1975 Helsinki Final Act was adopted by the Conference on Security and Co-operation in Europe (CSCE), and more than twenty years after transforming this conference system into the Organization for Security and Co-operation in Europe (OSCE), the OSCE still struggles with its legal status. Indeed, since the adoption of the so-called Budapest Declaration in 1994, there is no disagreement as to the fact that the OSCE is an international organisation (IO). In that Budapest Declaration, the participating States agreed to the following:

> The new era of security and co-operation in Europe has led to a fundamental change in the CSCE and to a dramatic growth in its role in shaping our common security area. To reflect this the CSCE will henceforth be known as the Organization for Security and Co-operation in Europe (OSCE). The change in name will be effective on 1 January 1995. As of this date, all references to the CSCE will henceforth be considered as references to the OSCE.[1]

This decision was a logical consequence of an institutionalisation process that had already resulted in the creation of permanent organs.[2] As of 1995 these

* Many thanks to Lisa Tabassi and to the editors of this Volume for their useful comments and suggestions.

[1] CSCE, *Towards a Genuine Partnership in a New Era*, Budapest Decisions attached to the Budapest Document, 21 December 1994, available at: www.osce.org/mc/39554?download=true.

[2] For more on this process, see, for instance, the introduction by Bloed, 'Two Decades of the CSCE Process', 1–117; Odello, 'The Developing Legal Status of the Organisation for Security and Co-operation in Europe', 351–93; Schlager, 'The Procedural Framework of the CSCE', 221–37; Szafarz, 'CSCE: An International Organization in Statu Nacsendi?', 15–21; Berger, 'OSCE and International Law', 37–47.

organs replaced the former institutional structure of the CSCE, which currently consists of: Summits (occasional meetings of Heads of State or Government of the fifty-seven OSCE participating States that set priorities at the highest political level); a Ministerial Council (convened, as a rule, to review OSCE activities and to make appropriate decisions in the years when no Summit takes place); a Permanent Council (the day-to-day decision-making body, convening on a weekly basis in Vienna). The OSCE structures furthermore include a Forum for Security Co-operation (to increase military security and stability in Europe: it covers some of the most fundamental politico-military agreements of the OSCE participating States); and a Secretariat (to provide operational support to the Organization under the direction of the Secretary General: it is based in Vienna and assisted by the Office in Prague). Finally, there is the OSCE Parliamentary Assembly (an autonomous OSCE institution comprised of 323 parliamentarians headquartered in Copenhagen with its own Secretary General and International Secretariat; it provides a forum for parliamentary diplomacy and debate, leads election observation missions and strengthens international cooperation to uphold commitments on political, security, economic, environmental and human rights issues).

Furthermore, three special bodies ('institutions' or 'executive structures', in OSCE parlance) work in the area of human rights: the High Commissioner on National Minorities (HCNM) in The Hague, the OSCE Office for Democratic Institutions and Human Rights (ODIHR) in Warsaw and the OSCE Representative on Freedom of the Media in Vienna. Despite its name, the OSCE Court of Conciliation and Arbitration is not formally part of the OSCE's institutional structure but based on a separate Convention.[3] The Court is a non-permanent body and creates conciliation commissions and arbitral tribunals on an ad hoc basis. In addition, a number of OSCE-related bodies are linked to the Organization.[4] The institutional structure of the OSCE is thus quite similar to other IOs: it has policy-making organs and a Secretariat (which forms the backbone of most IOs), as well as a number of other organs and bodies. The OSCE Chairmanship is held for one calendar year by the OSCE participating State designated as such by a decision of the Ministerial Council. The function of the Chairperson-in-Office (CiO) is exercised by the Minister of Foreign Affairs of that State.

[3] Convention on Conciliation and Arbitration within the OSCE, adopted by the Council of Ministers at its meeting held on 15 December 1992 in Stockholm, as part of the Decision on Peaceful Settlement of Disputes, 15 December 1992, available at: www.osce.org/cca/111409?download=true.

[4] See OSCE, OSCE-related bodies, 2019, available at: www.osce.org/who/108304.

However, while legal personality has been conferred on nearly all IOs, either explicitly or implicitly, this is not the case for the OSCE. The 1994 Budapest Document was categorical: 'The change in name from CSCE to OSCE alters neither the character of our CSCE commitments nor the status of the CSCE and its institutions.'[5] This sentence was particularly important since no consensus could be reached on expressly granting international legal personality to the OSCE. In the 1993 Rome Decision, Ministers merely recommended that participating States grant (and harmonise) *national* legal capacities and privileges and immunities to particular institutions but not to the OSCE as such.[6] And fourteen years later, in 2007, a Convention drafted to regulate the *international* legal personality, legal capacity and privileges and immunities of the OSCE still proved a bridge too far.[7] When the Swiss Chairmanship revisited the issue in 2014, they noted the following:

> While the general agreement on the contents of the 2007 Draft Convention has never been challenged, the Convention has not been adopted because of three footnotes, inserted by some participating States, predicating the adoption of the draft on the conclusion of an OSCE Constituent Document. Since then it has become clear that for a number of participating States the adoption of the 2007 Draft Convention was linked to the issue of an OSCE Constituent Document, while the start of discussion on such an OSCE Constituent Document could not attain consensus.[8]

On the basis of a number of meetings of the so-called Informal Working Group on Strengthening the Legal Framework of the OSCE (IWG), the Swiss Chairmanship concluded that 'the strengthening of the legal framework of the OSCE is a common goal shared by all participating States but divergences exist as to the way to achieve this goal'.[9] The main controversy (related to the footnotes referred to in the Swiss statement) centres around a disagreement between the Russian Federation and the United States of America.[10] The Russian Federation takes the view that the 2007 Draft Convention can only be adopted if the OSCE is

5 See CSCE, Budapest Decision, 1994 (n. 1), point 29.

6 See CSCE, Fourth Meeting of the Council, CSCE and the New Europe – Our Security Is Indivisible, Decisions of the Rome Council Meeting, no. CSCE/4-C/Dec.2, 1 December 1993.

7 OSCE, Fifteenth Meeting of the Ministerial Council, 2007 Draft Convention on the international legal personality, legal capacity, and privileges and immunities of the OSCE, Annex to MC.DD/28/07, 29 November 2007, 65–77.

8 OSCE, Report to the Ministerial Council on Strengthening the Legal Framework of the OSCE in 2014, OSCE Doc. MC.GAL/5/14, 2 December 2014, para. 1.

9 Ibid., para. 14.

10 For a more extensive discussion on the views of the participating States on the Organization's legal status, see Tichy, 'The Role of the Participating States in Reforming the Legal Framework of the OSCE – Past Developments, Status Quo and Future Ambitions',

given a treaty basis – something the 1975 Helsinki Final Act was not meant to be. Or, as the opinion is referred to informally: *'no convention without a charter'*.[11] The Russian proposal is unacceptable to the USA, which was originally against the idea of elaborating a convention. In 2006, Washington finally accepted this idea but remains unwilling to go further and adopt more than just the 2007 Draft Convention. By concluding a charter, as a constituent instrument of the OSCE, the USA fears that the Organization would lose its flexibility, which is regarded as the OSCE's main strength.[12]

This leaves us with an international entity whose creators deliberately chose to move from a 'conference' to an 'organisation' but still cannot reach agreement on the Organization's international legal status and continue to emphasise their being participating States of the OSCE and not member states. These participating States have agreed to give the OSCE legal capacities in their domestic legal orders but not at the international level. So far they have been unwilling to endow the OSCE with the attributes normally associated with IOs and thereby deny it the benefits of what is sometimes termed 'organisationhood'.[13]

An underlying question in the present chapter is to what extent the OSCE and its participating States can escape the application of international rules by simply using different terms (participating States, non-binding decisions[14])

Chapter 4 in this Volume; Tichy and Köhler, 'Legal Personality or Not – The Recent Attempts to Improve the Status of the OSCE', 455–78.

11 Cf. Delegation of the Russian Federation to the OSCE, 'Interpretative statement under Paragraph IV.1(A)6 of the OSCE Rules of Procedure to the Ministerial Council Decision No. 16/06 of December 2006' (The decision established the informal working group that subsequently prepared the 2007 Draft Convention), 5 December 2006, Attachment: 'While it has joined the consensus on the Ministerial Council decision on the legal status and privileges and immunities of the OSCE, the Russian delegation continues to insist that the only way of settling this matter in accordance with the norms of international law is to devise a founding OSCE document in the form of a charter or statute. Without a charter, the OSCE cannot be regarded as a fully-fledged international organization. We believe it is necessary to proceed from the recommendation made in that connection in the report of the Panel of Eminent Persons, pursuant to which the participating States should devise a concise statute or charter of the OSCE containing its basic goals and principles along with reference to existing commitments and the structure of its main decision-making bodies. In any case, the entry into force of a convention on privileges and immunities, if and when there is agreement on a draft, will be possible only in conjunction with the entry into force of a statute or charter of the OSCE.' Available at: www.osce.org/mc/23203?download=true.

12 See, e.g., US Secretary of State Clinton, 'Comment at the OSCE Ministerial Council First Plenary Session', 6 December 2012, available at: https://osce.usmission.gov/dec_6_12_dublin_mc1/.

13 See, e.g., Klabbers, *An Introduction to International Organizations Law*, 12.

14 Cf. ICJ, *Case Concerning Maritime Delimitation and Territorial Questions between Qatar and Bahrain (Qatar* v. *Bahrain)*, Jurisdiction and Admissibility, Judgment of 15 February 1995, ICJ Reports 1995, 6.

and by denying the international legal existence of the Organization. Or, to put it bluntly: to what extent is the OSCE living in a fantasy world where using a certain terminology has become more important than facing legal realities? As we will see, part of the answer is found in the interplay between law, politics and practice. In this interplay, 'law' stands for a number of rules that simply cannot be ignored in the relations between the Organization and its founders, as well as with third states; 'politics' represents the policy choices related to what the majority of the participating States prefer the role of the OSCE to be; and 'practice' corresponds to the extent to which pragmatic choices sometimes have to be found to overcome those legal or political hurdles that prevent the Organization from functioning day-to-day.

The EU experienced something similar. While the legal personality of its predecessors, the European Communities, had never been an issue, in both the 1992 Maastricht and the 1997 Amsterdam Treaties member states could not reach an agreement on an express reference to the legal status of the EU. Yet, with time the EU was recognised by third states as a legal partner and simply began concluding international agreements.[15] Indeed, nothing negative came of it, which in turn paved the way for an acknowledgement of the Union's legal personality in the 2007 Lisbon Treaty.[16]

As that Treaty also resulted in a full succession of the European Community by the EU, there was no way to escape the international legal personality of the EU. This is not to say that certain member states (the UK in particular) were not still nervous about this process, which resulted in the adoption of Declaration No. 24 (annexed to the Treaty of Lisbon): 'The Conference confirms that the fact that the European Union has a legal personality will not in any way authorise the Union to legislate or to act beyond the competences conferred upon it by the Member States in the Treaties.'[17] While, legally, this Declaration adds nothing new to the existing provisions, it was politically important to underline that the acknowledgement of legal personality does not allow the EU to act beyond what the members had agreed on.[18] For the other member states this was a small price to pay.

[15] Wessel, 'The International Legal Status of the European Union', 109–29; Wessel, 'Revisiting the International Legal Status of the EU', 507–37.

[16] See Art. 47 Treaty on European Union 7 February 1992, 1759 UNTS 3: 'The Union shall have legal personality.'

[17] Declaration concerning the legal personality of the European Union (No. 24), Annexed to The Final Act of the Intergovernmental Conference which adopted the Treaty of Lisbon, signed on 13 December 2007.

[18] See in particular Art. 5(2) Treaty on the Functioning of the European Union 13 December 2007, OJ C 202: 'Under the principle of conferral, the Union shall act only

While explicit references to the international legal status of an IO in its constituent document are not necessary (the UN being a prime example), the acceptance of legal personality by the member states does make sense from both a conceptual and a practical perspective. Moreover, it is the practical functioning of an organisation that can suffer from a lack of legal clarity. As other chapters in this Volume address these issues more extensively, suffice it to say that uncertainty in the legal status of the OSCE is hindering its effectiveness and efficiency, damaging efforts to fulfil its mandates, generating uncertainty in relation to its international responsibility and leading to additional expenditures and legal risk.[19]

The purpose of the present chapter is to revisit a number of the classical aspects of 'organisationhood', and to assess the extent to which the institutionalisation of international cooperation in the case of the OSCE has led to the creation of an international entity that should be understood as being distinct from the states participating in it.[20] In addition, it will point to the (often decisive) interplay between law, politics and practice in this context.

2 CRITERIA FOR 'ORGANISATIONHOOD'

2.1 *The Constitutive Act*

Whether the OSCE really is an IO depends, of course, on one's definition. An authoritative definition of 'international organisation' comes from the UN International Law Commission's (ILC) 2011 Draft Articles on the Responsibility of International Organizations (ARIO): an IO is 'an organisation established by a treaty or other instrument governed by international law

within the limits of the competences conferred upon it by the Member States in the Treaties to attain the objectives set out therein. Competences not conferred upon the Union in the Treaties remain with the Member States.' To make sure no one would miss this, an additional Declaration (No. 18) was adopted, which simply repeated it: 'The Conference underlines that, in accordance with the system of division of competences between the Union and the Member States as provided for in the Treaty on European Union and the Treaty on the Functioning of the European Union, competences not conferred upon the Union in the Treaties remain with the Member States.'

[19] See, in particular, the chapters by Tabassi, 'The Role of the Organisation in Asserting Legal Personality: The Position of the OSCE Secretariat on the OSCE's Legal Status', Chapter 3 in this Volume; Gasbarri, 'The International Legal Responsibility of the OSCE', Chapter 11 in this Volume and Moser, 'Conceptualising Accountability in the Legal and Institutional Framework of the OSCE', Chapter 13 in this Volume.

[20] For those with knowledge of Dutch, see Dekker and Wessel, 'Van CVSE naar OVSE' 2002, 425–38.

and possessing its own international legal personality'.[21] Under this definition, the OSCE would not be an IO.[22] It was not established by a treaty or other instrument governed by international law, and there has been no agreement on its international legal personality (for the examination of this second criterion, see further below, Section 2.2). However, this ILC definition was only given for the purpose of ARIO and does not claim to have any broader scope.

Leaving the ILC definition aside, doctrine generally regards the OSCE as an IO. One textbook even states: 'the OSCE now qualifies as a fully-fledged international organisation'.[23] While other textbooks also seem to regard the OSCE as an IO, some question whether it qualifies as a *fully-fledged* organisation because it lacks a treaty basis and international legal personality. This is illustrated by the following references to the OSCE:

> Organizations such as the Organization for Security and Co-operation in Europe (OSCE), Asia-Pacific Economic Cooperation (APEC), the Arctic Council and the Wassenaar Arrangement are based on some kind of document, but it remains unclear whether they are all to be regarded as full-blown organizations.[24]
>
> The OSCE 'n'est pas encore, dans son ensemble, personnifiée ou est fictivement tenue pour un sujet de droit international.[25]

[21] United Nations International Law Commission, Draft Articles on the Responsibility of International Organizations, A/66/10, 9 November 2011, para. 87. See also the special Forum on this topic in *International Organizations Law Review* 9 (2012), 1 *et seq.*, as well as several other contributions to other issues of this journal.

[22] It is interesting to note that the OSCE objected to the reference made to the OSCE in the initial ILC comments on the definition of an IO (see United Nations General Assembly, Responsibility of International Organizations: Comments and observations received from international organizations A/CN.4/637 14 February 2011, 18: 'the Commission appears to consider that OSCE, though not established by treaty, fulfils the two criteria provided for in draft article 2, subparagraph (a), defining international organizations. For the time being, there is no consensus among the OSCE participating States that OSCE should fulfil either of the two listed conditions: whether OSCE possesses its own legal personality, or whether the founding documents of OSCE (in the first place the Helsinki Final Act and the Charter of Paris for a New Europe) are governed by international law. These issues are currently under discussion by the deliberative and decision-making bodies of OSCE, and the OSCE Secretariat stands ready to inform the International Law Commission on the progress or finalization of these deliberations.' The reference to the OSCE was removed in the final text of the ARIO, 9 November 2011 (n. 21), paras. 74–5.

[23] Sands and Klein, *Bowett's Law of International Institutions*, 203.

[24] Klabbers, *An Introduction to International Organizations Law*, 12 (footnotes omitted).

[25] Lagrange and Sorel, *Droit des organisations internationales*, 55. Translation by the authors: The OSCE 'is not yet, as a whole, personified or is fictitiously held for a subject of international law'.

[W]ithout a treaty, establishing clearly the organisation's legal autonomy from member States, it is difficult to ascribe to it international legal personality.[26]

Irrespective of this complex institutional structure, which, in fact, resembles very much that of traditional International Organisations, the OSCE is still considered to lack international legal personality because it is not based on a legally binding international treaty. However, it is not inconceivable that the OSCE could acquire international legal personality if it acts in its own name and is respected as an independent actor by the international community.[27]

Internationale Organisation aufgrund von soft law.[28]

An international organisation 'dont l'acte constitutive n'est pas un traité'.[29]

In practice also the OSCE is generally seen as an IO, or indeed something very close to it. For all practical purposes, wherever the OSCE is present, states and IOs have usually been able to work out arrangements similar to those in place for other IOs. Examples include: a law adopted in the Netherlands in 2002 concerning the OSCE's High Commissioner on National Minorities (based in The Hague): 'For the purpose of this law, the OSCE is regarded as equal to a public international organisation of which the High Commissioner is a part. The privileges and immunities included in this law will be applied in the same way as those given to other IOs based in the Netherlands.'[30] The substance of this law is similar to the substance of headquarters agreements concluded with the more than thirty IOs based in the Netherlands. A number of IOs, such as the UN, the EU and the Council of Europe cooperate closely with the OSCE. The features of such cooperation are similar to those governing cooperation with other IOs.[31]

The question then is to what extent the OSCE remains unique. Indeed, there have been several other cases in which a transformation took place from a conference, or some other framework for cooperation, to an IO (with legal personality). A well-known example is the General Agreement on Tariffs and

26 White, *The Law of International Organisations*, 53.

27 Ruffert and Walter, *Institutionalised International Law*, 217.

28 Seidl-Hohenveldern, 'Internationale Organisationen aufgrund von soft law', 229–39. Translation by the authors: an 'international organisation on the basis of soft law'.

29 David, *Droit des Organisations Internationales*, 30. Translation by the authors: 'An international organisation, despite the fact that the constitutive act is not a treaty.'

30 Netherlands, Wet van 31 oktober 2002, houdende bepalingen inzake rechtspersoonlijkheid, privileges en immuniteiten van de Hoge Commissaris inzake Nationale Minderheden (Wet HCNM) (translated from the original), 31 October 2002, Art. 2.2, available at: http://wetten.overheid.nl/BWBR0014169/2003-01-01.

31 See also Boisson de Chazournes and Gadkowski, 'The External Relations of the OSCE', Chapter 10 in this Volume.

Trade (GATT). Created in 1947 as an executive agreement, the GATT went through a long process of institutionalisation. The question of it being an IO with legal personality was not deemed very important in practice. One of the former directors of the GATT's legal affairs division once observed: 'jurists may differ on the question whether the GATT is also an IO in a formal legal sense. The administrators of that institution are as fascinated by that issue as birds are by ornithology. The fact that counts for them is that the GATT has been acting consistently as an entity legally separate from its contracting parties and has been treated as having legal capacity.'[32] This will no doubt sound familiar to OSCE staff members who, regardless of legal academic debates, have no choice but to solve emerging legal issues on a pragmatic basis.[33] Nevertheless, in the 1990s it was deemed necessary to provide the GATT with an explicit legal footing and so it was transformed by a treaty into the World Trade Organization (WTO).[34]

A more recent and less well-known example relates to the International Commission on Missing Persons (ICMP), created in 1996 on the initiative of the USA to assist families in locating and identifying the many missing persons as a result of the war in the former Yugoslavia.[35] The ICMP was not at that time created as an IO. However, in practice, a gradual process of institutionalisation took place. In 1998, the ICMP concluded a Headquarters Agreement with Bosnia and Herzegovina, which refers to the Commission as something 'comparable to an international organisation'. Soon the ICMP's expertise, for instance on DNA, was also needed in other parts of the world when mass graves were unearthed or corpses had to be identified, as was the case in countries like Iraq and Libya, or in South East Asia after the December 2004 tsunami. But outside the region for which it was originally created, the ICMP experienced practical difficulties due to its lack of legal status. It could not open bank accounts and its staff could not get adequate legal protection. It took years of consultations to overcome resistance to reorganise it into a formal IO. In 2014, the Commission was finally transformed by an agreement into a formal organisation having legal personality.[36]

32 Roessler, 'The Agreement Establishing the World Trade Organization', 69.

33 See also Tabassi, 'The Role of the Organisation in Asserting Legal Personality: The Position of the OSCE Secretariat on the OSCE's Legal Status', Chapter 3 in this Volume.

34 See Jackson, *Restructuring the GATT System*; and Marrakesh Agreement Establishing the World Trade Organization, 15 April 1994, 1867 UNTS, 154.

35 What follows relating to the ICMP is largely reproduced from Schermers and Blokker, *International Institutional Law*, 34.

36 Agreement on the status and functions of the International Commission on Missing Persons, 15 December 2014, Tractatenblad (Dutch Treaty Series) 2014, No. 219.

One may argue that in comparison to these and other examples, the OSCE is indeed unique in that it has so far not been possible to reach a consensus on its legal status. However, in other cases in which similar institutionalisation processes were discussed, it was deliberately decided that a particular conference or framework should not be transformed into an IO having legal personality. For example, a few years ago a discussion took place within the G20 about the creation of a permanent G20 Secretariat. This proposal was rejected in 2011. It was concluded that the G20 is 'a Leader-led and informal group and it should remain so'.[37] A slightly different example is the Arctic Council. The idea to set it up as an IO was rejected in the 1990s. It is seen, instead, as a 'Forum'. However, in recent years it has undergone a degree of institutionalisation: a permanent Secretariat has been created, based in Tromsø (Norway), and a Headquarters Agreement has been concluded between Norway and said Secretariat (2013).[38] Indeed, in the case of the OSCE, the situation has been largely left open. While the term 'Organization' became the formal denomination for the entity and though legal capacities and privileges and immunities have been regulated in many of the domestic legal orders of the participating States, the 2007 Draft Convention is still awaiting adoption.

2.2 *International Legal Personality and the OSCE*

2.2.1 A Demystification of Legal Personality

As the express acknowledgement of legal personality seems to be the main obstacle in furthering the process within the OSCE to accept its separate legal status, this section will shortly revisit its key characteristics and perhaps 'demystify' the notion somewhat.[39] Does the acknowledgement of legal personality really lead to what has been termed the 'Frankenstein problem'?[40] It is a truism that legal personality is a key notion in international institutional law and has

[37] G20 Information Centre, 'Cannes Summit Final Declaration', 2011, available at: www.g20.utoronto.ca/2011/2011-cannes-declaration-111104-en.html, para. 91.

[38] See Takei, 'The Role of the Arctic Council from an International Law Perspective', 353–5; Takei, 'Are the Polar Regions Converging?', 363–78. For more in general about governance in the Arctic, see Jakobson and Melvin (eds.), *The New Arctic Governance*.

[39] This section is largely reproduced from Wessel, 'Reparation for Injuries Suffered in the Service of the United Nations', 11–18.

[40] Guzman, 'International Organizations and the Frankenstein Problem', 999–1025; the Frankenstein metaphor was previously used by others, in particular Klabbers, *An Introduction to International Organizations Law*, and Alvarez, *International Organizations as Law-makers*, 585.

been addressed abundantly in the relevant academic literature. The main purpose of the present section, therefore, is to remind us of its key characteristics.[41]

In an international legal system that was set up around states, it is unsurprising that the question of the international legal status of IOs persists, both in legal doctrinal debates and in judicial proceedings. The question of the legal status of IOs is connected to their coming of age as autonomous legal subjects. After all, it is only by accepting the distinction between the organisation and its members that the rights and duties of IOs emerge.

At the same time, it is the very tension between the organisation and its members that seems to underlie most of the debates in international institutional law, and textbooks often refer to the Janus-faced nature of IOs: they are created by and composed of states, while at the same time require a certain autonomy.[42] In order for states to become *members*, there needs to be something for them to join; states make the rules from which IOs draw their competences, though in turn IOs may be created to make rules to limit the freedom of the self-same states. IOs, therefore, are both creations and creators. For some IOs it is true that they have found their place in global governance, and are even considered 'autonomous actors', following an agenda that is no longer fully defined by their member states (hence, the Frankenstein problem).[43] There should be no doubt that these elements play a role in – particularly US – hesitance to accept a separate legal status of the OSCE under international law.

Yet, the legal status question concerns an organisation's subjectivity under international law. It has to do with the entity's legal *existence* and does not necessarily define its concrete *legal capacities* or *political powers*. Once legal existence can be established, one may say that an IO enjoys legal personality: it can have legal rights and duties (or at least one right or duty) of its own. Literature on the legal personality of IOs is abundant and the classic debates never seem to reach a fully unified conclusion. Can IOs exist without legal personality, or is legal personality a (or perhaps *the*) feature that distinguishes them from a more loosely organised international conference? Can IOs have a 'partial' legal personality, or is their partiality related only to their competences? Perhaps the most pragmatic solution would be to follow Klabbers'

41 For some examples, see the subsequent references in this section. See also Ryngaert, 'The OSCE's Domestic Legal Status: An Exploration of Relevant International Law Sources', Chapter 8 in this Volume.

42 On the autonomy of international organisations, see Steinbrück Platise, 'Legitimate Governance as a Privilege and Price for the Autonomy of International Organisations', Chapter 14 in this Volume.

43 White and Collins (eds.), *International Organizations and the Idea of Autonomy*.

(somewhat circular) notion that 'as soon as an organisation performs an act which can only be explained on the basis of international legal personality, such an organisation will be presumed to be in possession of international legal personality'.[44]

Indeed, accepting a separate legal status of IOs is a logical consequence of the fact that IOs were established as separate entities. In that sense legal personality is, indeed, an element of 'organisationhood'. The states that created these organisations became members of these new entities and in that capacity willingly subjected themselves to their rules. The moment they take their 'seat' in the organs and bodies of the organisation they are in fact part of its institutional structure. Yet, both in a practical and a conceptual sense it is difficult to deny the fact that member states remain sovereign states. Allowing them to hide behind an institutional veil would not only imply a denial of their individual international legal responsibilities but also of political realities.

This was recognised already in the famous *Reparation for Injuries* Advisory Opinion.[45] Ever since the International Court of Justice (ICJ) delivered its opinion in 1949, the case has featured in most introductory lectures and leading textbooks on the law of IOs. Indeed, the relevance of the case can hardly be overestimated as it deals with the recognition of IOs (in this case the UN) as entities enjoying a legal position in the international legal order separate from their member states. The question of the legal status of IOs recurred in later opinions and judgments, but the ground rules were clearly laid down in the *Reparation* Advisory Opinion.[46] It underlines the idea that international personality is seen as a characteristic of IOs – something that was later confirmed by the ICJ in the *WHO–Egypt* case.[47] In this view it only makes sense to talk about an IO when it occupies a distinctive legal position vis-à-vis its founders, and it is this distinct legal position that is often equated with the possession of legal personality, or what amounts to the same thing: being a legal person. It is the latter narrative that seems to be dominant these days and the autonomy of IOs (and the related constitutional questions) have sparked new debates.[48] This reveals that legal personality is not just about the

[44] Klabbers, *An Introduction to International Organizations Law*, 49; and more extensively Klabbers, 'Presumptive Personality: The European Union in International Law', 231–53.

[45] ICJ, *Reparation for Injuries Suffered in the Service of the United Nations*, Advisory Opinion of 11 April 1949, ICJ Reports 1949, 174; for a recent analysis, see Wessel, 'Reparation for Injuries Suffered in the Service of the United Nations'.

[46] Ibid., the Part on 'Legal Status (Personality)'.

[47] ICJ, *Interpretation of the Agreement of 25 March 1951 between the WHO and Egypt*, Advisory Opinion of 6 June 1980, ICJ Reports 1980, 73.

[48] Cf. White and Collins (eds.), *International Organizations and the Idea of Autonomy*.

capacity to bring claims or to engage in other legal actions: it is part of the defining nature of IOs.

Since international legal personality was not explicitly mentioned by the founders of the UN in the UN Charter, it was instead derived from the organisation's (perceived) objectives ('it could not carry out the intentions of its founders if it was devoid of international personality'[49]) and from subsequent practice ('It is difficult to see how such a [concluded] convention could operate except upon the international plane and as between parties possessing international personality'[50]). The idea of legal personality as a threshold (the organisation cannot act legally when it is devoid of legal personality, so we first have to establish or construct it) has been contested ever since.[51]

The main point of criticism seems to be that IOs do indeed act and that these actions can, or should have, legal consequences irrespective of whether the legal personality problem has been solved. In a way, the approach of the ICJ in the *Reparation* case (let's look at what the organisation is supposed to do and what it is actually doing and derive legal personality from that) has become quite common in legal doctrinal approaches to the question of legal personality. In the case of the UN, any reference to legal personality in the Charter was also omitted. It was held that the international personality of the UN 'will be determined implicitly from the provisions of the Charter taken as a whole'.[52]

All in all, we maintain that the concept of legal personality is first and foremost relevant to settling the separate status of the international entities within the international legal order. As a pragmatic solution, the OSCE's participating States have agreed to give the OSCE legal capacities in their respective domestic legal orders without giving it international legal personality. While this seems to work in practice, it is problematic from a more conceptual perspective. We would argue that legal personality concerns a *quality*, whereas legal capacity is an *asset*.[53] Where legal personality means not much more than being a subject of a certain legal order, capacity is

49 ICJ, *Reparation for Injuries* (n. 45), 174.

50 Ibid.

51 See, e.g., Klabbers, 'The Concept of Legal Personality', 35–66; for another conceptual approach to the different theories on legal personality, see Gazzini, 'Personality of International Organizations', 33–55.

52 United Nations Conference on International Organizations, Report on Article 104 of the UN Charter, 13 U.N.C.I.O. Doc. 803, IV/2/A/7, 1945, 817. See further Reinisch and Bachmayer (eds.), *The Conventions on the Privileges and Immunities of the United Nations and the Specialized Agencies*, 49–56.

53 For more on this distinction, see Bekker, *The Legal Position of Intergovernmental Organizations*.

concerned with what the entity is potentially entitled to do (and where *implied powers* may come in). What is possible, however, is that an entity is recognised as a legal person in one legal order but not in another.

It follows from this approach that there is also not much sense in speaking of a 'partial legal personality' of IOs. Neither are we in favour of saying that a particular international entity possesses legal personality 'to some extent'. The possession of legal personality ('being a legal person') is a binary phenomenon: you either have it or you do not.[54] Competences (and capacities based on them), on the other hand, seem to depend on what was attributed to the organisation, although a case could be made for the existence of competences inherent to the enjoyment of legal personality, such as the conclusion of certain international agreements or (at least in the eyes of the ICJ) bringing an international claim.

With a view to our aim of demystifying the notion of legal personality, it is thus important to highlight that it is not so much the acknowledgement of legal personality that would cause inflexibility or allow an organisation to turn against its creators (to come back to the Frankenstein metaphor), but rather the capacities. And, in fact, these capacities can be of a very practical nature, allowing an organisation to act legally within the boundaries set by the participating States. At the present moment, the fear of granting the OSCE international legal personality seems to stand in the way of allowing it to facilitate its participating States in taking care of a number of practical tasks.

2.2.2 International Legal Personality and the Power of Practice

Yet, legal and political arguments are often intertwined and in that sense a more general development in international law and International Relations does not seem to make it easier for the proponents of a clearer legal status for the OSCE. In the last two decades, a prevailing idea (or zeitgeist) has taken hold in which there is a certain reluctance to create new IOs enjoying legal personality. This is also reflected in a shift from formal to more informal forms of international cooperation that has been widely noticed in the academic literature.[55] Whereas during and after the Second

[54] See also Steinbrück-Platise, 'Legitimate Governance as a Privilege and Price for the Autonomy of International Organisations', Chapter 14 in this Volume. We acknowledge the different view of the ICJ presented in the ICJ *Reparation for Injuries* case (n. 45) in this respect when it refers to the fact that the UN must have 'a large measure of legal personality'.

[55] For further references, see, e.g., Pauwelyn, Wessel and Wouters, 'When Structures Become Shackles', 733–63; and Pauwelyn, Wessel and Wouters (eds.), *Informal International Lawmaking*.

World War many IOs were created almost automatically as soon as some new international problem was identified, almost the opposite is true today, as was experienced, for example, during the abovementioned transformation of the ICMP into a formal IO.

This zeitgeist is part of the context in which discussions of the OSCE's legal personality take place. But there are also more specific contextual elements. Thus, discussions on the international legal personality of IOs are generally influenced by what we may safely call 'the politics of international legal personality'. The question of granting legal personality to an IO is often not only seen as a more or less technical, legal question but also (and perhaps above all) a sensitive political issue. The two most famous examples are the UN and the EU.

Regarding the UN, legal personality was certainly discussed during the 1945 San Francisco Conference establishing the UN Charter. Yet, the final agreement only contains an explicit provision in the Charter (Article 104) on the legal personality of the UN in the national legal orders of the member states. No provision on international legal personality was included. The reason for this omission can perhaps be found in the report by the US delegation prepared after the San Francisco Conference, which states: 'the Committee which discussed the matter was anxious to avoid any implication that the UN will be in any sense a "superstate"'.[56]

A few years later, in a more legal context, the ICJ considered it important to get back to this idea: 'the Court has come to the conclusion that the Organisation is an international person. That is not the same thing as saying that it is a state, which it certainly is not, or that its legal personality and rights and duties are the same as those of a state. Still less is it the same thing as saying that it is "a superstate", whatever that expression may mean.'[57] Indeed, political arguments do not always make sense to judges, though such arguments often define the outcome.

The second example relates to the EU. As we have seen, the 1992 Maastricht Treaty created the EU but did not contain any provision on its legal status. In the years after the Treaty was signed, negotiations on this issue began but no agreement was reached. The issue became a *Chefsache* and was put on the table of the European Council meeting that took place in Amsterdam on 17 June 1997. Again, no agreement was reached because the issue was a red line for the UK. Like in 1945 in San Francisco, providing international legal

[56] Department of State Publication 349, Conference Series 71 (quoted by Jenks, 'The Legal Personality of International Organizations' 1945, 269–270).

[57] ICJ, *Reparation for Injuries* (n. 45), 179.

personality to the EU was associated with the creation of a superstate. The day after the European Council meeting, on 18 June, upon his return to the UK, Prime Minister Tony Blair proudly stated before the House of Commons: 'others wanted to give the EU explicit legal personality across all pillars. At our insistence, this was removed.'[58]

The decades-long debate within the OSCE reveals that it is indeed not so much the legal issues that form the obstacles but that legal choices are perceived as having undesirable political side-effects: while fears of an OSCE superstate are perhaps less relevant, an independent legal status is seen as potentially affecting the influence that participating States have over the Organization's activities (indeed, the Frankenstein problem again). Furthermore, the idea that the OSCE is merely a centre 'for harmonizing the actions of nations in the attainment of ... common ends' (to again use a quote from *Reparation*) remains dominant.[59]

However, it is not only 'the politics of international legal personality' that is interesting. Perhaps even more fascinating (and to a certain extent reassuring) is the fact that no matter how politically loaded the question of international legal personality might be, practice has sometimes proved more powerful than politics. This is the story of the UN after 1945 and the EU after the 1997 European Council meeting. In practice, it was generally agreed that these organisations needed to perform certain functions in their own name (for example, claiming reparations and concluding treaties), which could only be done if they were considered as international legal persons. The practical need to perform these functions outweighed the political reluctance to explicitly give them international legal personality.

Even though in 1945 there was a reluctance to view the UN as an international legal person, practice simply forced the UN to act as such in order to perform its functions. From the outset, agreements were concluded, such as the UN–US Headquarters Agreement. Furthermore, the UN needed to have the capacity to bring a claim against Israel after its mediator Count Bernadotte was killed there (see the 1949 *Reparation* Advisory Opinion referred to above). Less than four years after the founders of the UN had been unwilling to regulate the UN's legal personality in the Charter, they had to accept that practice gave them no other choice.

As we have seen, something similar happened to the EU in the years following the 1997 European Council meeting in Amsterdam. Not too long

58 Hansard, HC 'column 314', 18 June 1997, available at: www.publications.parliament.uk/pa/cm199798/cmhansrd/vo970618/debtext/70618-22.htm#70618-22_spmin6.

59 ICJ, *Reparation for Injuries* (n. 45), 178.

after Prime Minister Blair gave his victory speech to the House of Commons, practice revealed that the EU simply could not live up to the wishes of its members to remain legally inactive vis-à-vis third parties. In 2001, the EU concluded an agreement with Serbia as if Tony Blair had in fact lost his battle in Amsterdam.[60] As Council members, the member states took the decision that this agreement would be concluded by the EU and not by the member states. The only legal underpinning of the conclusion of this agreement by the EU was that it was within the EU's *implied* powers to conclude agreements, in line with the (good old) *Reparation* Advisory Opinion. The EU has since concluded many more agreements. Subsequently, the 2007 inclusion of a specific provision on legal personality in the Treaty on European Union was largely a formality, as it was confirming existing practice. The UK resisted no longer.

Hence, while 'the politics of international legal personality' may at first have been the main reason for the difficulty to expressly acknowledge the international legal status of the UN and the EU, these examples equally underline that practice can be more powerful than politics. It was clear that these organisations would simply not be able to perform their functions if they were devoid of legal status under international law. Admittedly, a comparison with the UN is flawed on many points. To start with, the UN has a constituent instrument, the UN Charter, from which the ICJ could derive international legal personality. In addition, while the ICJ could partly rely on the existing practice of the UN, such practice is largely absent in the OSCE. Finally, the OSCE lacks a court that could do for it what the ICJ did for the UN in 1949.

Yet, parallels exist. It is largely for political reasons that no agreement has been reached thus far on the OSCE's international legal status. The lesson learnt from the UN and the EU suggests that perhaps practice has not, or not yet, been sufficiently powerful to overcome the political hurdles. This is not to say that there is no practice. Other chapters in this Volume testify to the existence of the international legal activities of the OSCE and we may also point to the example of the 1998 Agreement on the OSCE Kosovo Verification Mission,

60 Agreement concluded between the EU and Yugoslavia concerning the activities of the EU Monitoring Mission in Yugoslavia, OJ 2001, L 125/1. For a more extensive look (and for many references) on the conclusion of international agreements by the EU, see Wessel, 'The European Union as a Party to International Agreements: Shared Competences, Mixed Responsibilities', 145–80; and Wessel and Arribas, 'EU Agreements with Third Countries: Constitutional Reservations by Member States', 291–308. For possible earlier indications of the EU's legal personality, see Wessel, 'Revisiting the International Legal Status of the EU', 507–37.

which was concluded between the CiO, on behalf of the OSCE, and the Foreign Minister of the Federal Republic of Yugoslavia.[61] The Chairmanship also represents the Organization in relations with third states and other IOs. The most recent examples are two treaties concluded with the OSCE in June 2017: the OSCE Headquarters Agreement with the Republic of Austria and the Arrangement between the OSCE and the Republic of Poland on the Status of the OSCE in the Republic of Poland.[62]

So far, however, too many statements by the Organization and its participating States indicate an unwillingness to accept the OSCE's international legal personality. And as far as written law is concerned, the 2007 Draft Convention on the international legal status of the OSCE is still a sleeping beauty waiting for the political prince to kiss it awake. As briefly mentioned above, it would make sense to not wait too long. Not only because the fears of a separate legal personality of IOs have so far not proved realistic, but also because in its daily activities the Organization struggles with its unclear legal situation.

As an international legal person, the OSCE would be able to achieve more effectively and more efficiently what many participating States consider necessary, as successive OSCE legal advisers have emphasised. But perhaps most importantly, as illustrated by the Special Monitoring Mission in Ukraine, it is irresponsible if the OSCE and its staff, in the offices as well as in the field, are unable to perform their functions without having a reliable legal status that is normally in place for similar functions performed by other IOs and their staff. Currently, legal protection can only be given to OSCE personnel by their own national governments. This is fundamentally wrong and highly impractical since the people concerned do not perform tasks for their home country but for the OSCE, and because it is ineffective and inefficient if only indirect and fragmented legal protection can be offered.

The adoption of the 2007 Draft Convention would make it much easier for the OSCE to arrange its legal status whenever missions are carried out, as is currently the case in East Ukraine. It would allow the OSCE to be responsible for what it is doing and offer the necessary protection to individuals who carry out its work in offices and in the field. To quote from the *Reparation* Opinion once more, to allow an individual working for the OSCE to 'perform his duties satisfactorily, he must feel that this protection is assured to him by the Organisation, and that he may count on it'.[63] Finally, acknowledging the

61 Agreement on the OSCE Kosovo Verification Missions, 16 October 1998, CIO.GAL/65/98/Corr.1.

62 On these two agreements, see Tichy and Quidenus, 'Consolidating the International Legal Personality of the OSCE'; Arsić-Đapo, 'Another Brick in the Wall'.

63 ICJ, *Reparation for Injuries* (n. 45), 183.

legal status of the OSCE would bring an end to the ad hoc solutions currently required to deal with political resistance, even though to a certain extent the Organization 'is in fact exercising and enjoying functions and rights which can only be explained on the basis of the possession of a large measure of international personality and the capacity to operate upon an international plane'.[64]

Against this background, it is important to underline that there are no legal impediments to the adoption of the 2007 Draft Convention. The objections by the two most powerful participating States are largely of a political nature. The Russian resistance ('no convention without a charter') does not seem to relate to any insurmountable international legal problem, despite the fact that one of their arguments is of a domestic constitutional nature.[65] From an international legal point of view, it would be perfectly possible to grant international legal personality to the OSCE without embedding this in a general constituent instrument, given the fact that the objectives and tasks of the Organization and its bodies are laid down in various constitutive documents and have been further developed in practice. This view was supported by all participants in the negotiations on the 2007 Draft Convention, except the Russian Federation and Belarus.

In addition, practice has revealed cases in which legal personality was expressly granted to an IO on the basis of a separate agreement. Thus, in 1999 an agreement was concluded for the sole purpose of bestowing international legal personality upon the International Potato Center, as was the case in 2009 regarding PEMSEA, a sustainable development partnership in East Asia.[66] Obviously, it would be difficult to accept certain legal capacities and privileges and immunities when the mandate and competences of an IO is unclear, but, as the various chapters in this Volume emphasise, over the many decades of its existence the OSCE has been active in taking decisions and engaging in activities on the basis of clear mandates.

Likewise, while the political argument of the USA may be clear ('the OSCE would lose its flexibility if it were given a constituent instrument'), from a legal point of view there is no reason why a charter would affect the flexible nature of cooperation within the OSCE. After all, a charter can be restricted to a few

64 ICJ, *Reparation for Injuries* (n. 45), 179.

65 See Bogush, 'Domestic Implications of the OSCE's Legal Personality under the Russian Constitutional Law', Chapter 6 in this Volume.

66 Agreement for the Recognition of the International Legal Personality of the International Potato Center (CIP), 26 November 1999, Tractatenblad (Dutch Treaty Series) 2001 No. 32). For PEMSEA, which previously existed as a project-based arrangement without such status, see Art. I.1 of the Agreement recognizing the International Legal Personality of the Partnerships in Environmental Management for the Seas of East Asia, 1 November 2009, available at:http://pemsea.org/sites/default/files/pemsea-legal-personality.pdf.

basic issues and does not have to be long – the constituent instrument of NATO, for example, contains only fourteen articles. In addition, the provisions could be inspired by those used in the 1994 Budapest Document when the CSCE was transformed into the OSCE (e.g., 'The change in legal status of the OSCE does not alter the nature of cooperation within the Organization. In its organisational development, the CSCE will remain flexible and dynamic.').[67] This way, a charter could simply be limited to codifying the existing institutional practice of the OSCE. Yet, political objections by the Russian Federation and the USA have so far outweighed the practical benefits that the OSCE and its participating States would reap by adopting the 2007 Draft Convention. Apparently, the need to give international legal personality to the OSCE – on which there is a consensus – has not yet become sufficiently persuasive to overcome the stalemate created by the political objections of the two most powerful participating States.

3 PARTICIPATION OR MEMBERSHIP?

3.1 *The Difference between Participation and Membership*

Part and parcel of the debates within the OSCE is the choice to use the term 'participating States' rather than 'member states'. Indeed, a certain unease may be detected within OSCE circles when the term member states is used accidentally. In international institutional law the notion of membership forms a central element, which is one reason why it features in the title of this chapter. Thus, one of the key questions flowing from recent debates on the responsibility of IOs and their member states is how to distinguish the one from the other. The question of the allocation of responsibilities is gaining in importance, also in the light of recent case law on the responsibility of states for acts performed in the framework of or by IOs. As underlined by one of the present authors: 'The issue is the responsibility of States in their capacity as member states of international organizations. In this sentence, the word member is fundamental.'[68]

Although important from a practical perspective, the question of international responsibility is just one element in the debate on membership, which is more conceptual in nature. As with legal personality, the issue of membership within the OSCE seems to be surrounded by political considerations that

[67] See CSCE, Budapest Decision, 1994 (n. 1), point 29.

[68] Blokker, 'Member State Responsibility for Wrongdoings of International Organizations', 319–32.

from a legal perspective make little sense. Academic literature points to the fact that states do not lose their identity as states when they become a member state. It remains difficult to neglect the Janus-faced nature of IOs and it has been duly noted by Ryngaert and Freitas de Barros, for instance, that '[a]lthough the separate personality of an international organisation "establishes the will of the organization as a whole", this does not mean that the various "member state wills" that led to it lose their relevance'.[69]

More generally, lawyers tend to point to the rules of the game that must be followed, and stress the fact that even plenary bodies are organs of an IO in which states function as member states once they occupy a seat. Indeed, the existence of elements such as an 'organ', 'membership' or a 'decision' all imply a distinction between the participating States and the international entity. In fact, there is a strong interlinkage between these elements. Organs act on behalf of the international entity, and are not to be equated with the (collectivity of) states, in which case the term conference would be more appropriate.

The notion of membership (in contrast to participation) underlines a similar distinctiveness of the international entity. This seems to allow for the well-known view in international institutional law that for an international entity to be regarded as existing separately from its member states, the entity must have a decision-making organ that is able to produce a 'corporate' will, as opposed to a mere 'aggregate' of the wills of its member states.[70] The outcomes of collective decision-making processes must be ascribable to an international organ rather than to the collectivity of the participants (something that becomes particularly relevant in the context of establishing international responsibility in cases of wrongdoing).[71]

All in all, the notion of participation would fit the idea of a conference, whereas in the case of an IO the states would be members. Apart from this distinction, it is important to note that even as members of an organisation, states have different identities.[72] Therefore, as with legal personality, insistence on using the term 'participating States' rather than 'members' – even

69 Barros and Ryngaert, 'The Position of Member States in (Autonomous) Institutional Decision-Making: Implications for the Establishment of Responsibility'. See also Blokker, 'International Organizations and Their Members', 139–61.

70 Cf. also Brölman, *The Institutional Veil in Public International Law*.

71 Cf. Klabbers, 'Presumptive Personality: The European Union in International Law', 243; an older quote is also relevant in this context: 'It is the existence of organs which makes it possible to distinguish international organizations from other looser associations of States like, for example, the British Commonwealth', Rama-Montaldo, 'International Legal Personality', 145. For a more extensive look at the distinction between states and member states, see Wessel, 'Revisiting the International Legal Status of the EU', 507–37.

72 See further Dekker and Wessel, 'Identities of States in International Organizations', 293–318.

though the decision was taken to transform what was originally a conference into an IO – is largely explained by political considerations. Possible legal consequences would relate to the fact that the identity of the state would indeed be different: as outlined above, rather than a participant, the state would become a member, and hence a part of an organisation. Member states allow an organisation to take decisions rather than being contractual partners to agreements themselves.

At the same time, the continued use of the term 'participating States' is mainly a *conceptual* problem, whereas acceptance of the OSCE's legal personality is needed to solve a number of *practical* problems. Thus, while it makes sense for conceptual reasons, there is no practical legal need to change 'participating States' into 'member states' and neither is this change suggested in the 2007 Draft Convention. However, and again mainly for reasons of conceptual sanity, we would advise accepting the role of states as members as this seems to be an inherent consequence of turning a conference into an organisation.

3.2 *Decision-Making and Monitoring Mechanisms in the OSCE*

Indeed, like many international institutions, the role of the OSCE seems to have developed beyond a 'centre for harmonizing the actions of nations' and underlines its separate existence. For IOs, decision-making takes place not only on the basis of well-defined procedures that involve institutional actors other than states but also on the basis of a sometimes dynamic interpretation of the original mandate of the organisation.[73] The outcome comes closer to decision-making *by* rather than *through* an IO.[74] As indicated in the Introduction to this chapter, the OSCE has organs, with the Permanent Council acting as the daily decision-making body.[75] The outcome of the decision-making process is indeed a 'Decision' – of which the Permanent Council has so far taken a total of 1273 (as of November 2017) – adopted at Meetings of the Heads of

[73] 'It is possible … that the treaty provisions pertaining to the law-making powers of the organization will be construed in a different way than was originally intended by the drafting nations, as it proves very difficult to draft an instrument in such a manner as to effectively preclude any other possible interpretation', Wouters and De Man, 'International Organizations as Law-Makers', 192.

[74] Wessel, 'Institutional Law-Making: The Emergence of a Global Normative Web', 179–99.

[75] See OSCE, Documents by the OSCE Decision-making bodies, available at: www.osce.org/resources/documents/decision-making-bodies. The Summit, the Ministerial Council, the Forum for Security Co-Operation and the Chairperson-in-Office, but not the Permanent Council, are considered as 'decision-making bodies'.

State or Government (Summit), the Ministerial Council and the Forum for Security Co-operation.[76] The various decisions often contain commitments that are to be followed up by the participating States.

Rules of procedure underline the institutionalisation of the decision-making process.[77] Decisions are taken by consensus, just like in other IOs, including NATO and the WTO. Consensus 'shall be understood to mean the absence of any objection expressed by a representative and submitted by him as constituting an obstacle to the taking of the decision in question'.[78] In order to introduce a degree of flexibility into the consensus rule, 'consensus minus one' was introduced, whereby 'appropriate action may be taken by the Council or Committee of Senior Officials, if necessary in the absence of the consent of the State concerned, in cases of clear, gross and uncorrected violations of relevant CSCE commitments'.[79]

In addition, there is the possibility of a decision being taken in accordance with the rule of 'consensus minus two' with regard to the peaceful settlement of disputes. Thus, 'the Council or the Committee of Senior Officials of the CSCE (now the OSCE Permanent Council) may direct any two participating States to seek conciliation to assist them in resolving a dispute that they have not been able to settle within a reasonable period of time'.[80] Finally, a tacit (or silent) approval procedure makes it possible for a decision to be adopted within a specific timeframe, provided no objection is raised.[81] This procedure

76 See, e.g., OSCE, Permanent Council, Deployment of an OSCE Special Monitoring Mission to Ukraine, Decision No. 1117, PC.DEC/1117, 21 March 2014, in which the Permanent Council inter alia 'Decides. . . .to deploy a special OSCE monitoring mission of international observers to Ukraine', OSCE: Index of Permanent Council Decisions (Nos. 1–1236), available at: www.osce.org/pc/70160.

77 See OSCE, Ministerial Council, 'Rules of Procedure of the Organization for Security and Co-operation in Europe', MC.DOC/1/06, 1 November 2006. Credits are due to www.cvce.eu, a research body located at the University of Luxembourg, for collecting the different existing procedures. CVCE, 'The procedures and mechanisms of the OSCE', 8 July 2016, available at: www.cvce.eu/content/publication/2006/2/16/32a78695-6b86-46d0-98cc-e6db63fd4037/publishable_en.pdf.

78 Rule II(A) 2 of the OSCE Rules of Procedure (n. 77).

79 This was introduced by the OSCE, Final Document of the Second Meeting of the CSCE Council of Ministers, Prague, 30–31 January 1992, 31 January 1992, available at: www.osce.org/mc/40270.

80 CSCE, Third Meeting of the Council Summary of Conclusions Decision on Peaceful Settlement of Disputes Stockholm 1992, 1992, available at: www.osce.org/mc/40342?download=true.

81 This procedure has developed since the adoption of the CSCE, Charter of Paris for a New Europe, November 1990. Para. 14 of the Procedures and Modalities concerning CSCE Institutions stipulates that it be used for the appointment of the first Director of each institution, available at: www.oscepa.org/documents/all-documents/documents-1/historical-documents-1/673-1990-charter-of-paris-for-a-new-europe/file.

may also be used for the setting up of an ad hoc steering group on a proposal from the CiO.[82]

These relatively settled decision-making procedures even allow for an occasional (albeit largely theoretical) breaking of the consensus rule, indicating that decision-making within the OSCE consists not merely of deciding *through* but also *by* the OSCE. Furthermore, the OSCE has developed several mechanisms to monitor and control the implementation of OSCE commitments regarding both the human and the politico-military dimension. They are based principally on diplomatic consultations, exchanges of information, good offices and mediation, as well as the sending of observers and the drafting of reports. They demonstrate that, over the decades, the OSCE has been more than a forum for cooperation and has always been able to discuss and develop mechanisms to monitor commitments.

While it goes beyond the scope of this chapter to analyse in detail the OSCE mechanisms in relation to the so-called human dimension of the OSCE, they are relevant with respect to the monitoring competences. They include the *Vienna mechanism* (which allows for requests for information and bilateral meetings); the *Moscow mechanism* (which consolidated and further developed the Vienna mechanism in regard to time limits and introduced the possibility of using expert missions and rapporteurs); and *the possibility to send observers* to participating States in case of elections or when proceedings are brought before the courts.[83] In relation to the so-called politico-military dimension, we have seen the development of *risk-reduction mechanisms* (in relation to confidence- and security-building measures (CSBMs)); *emergency mechanisms* (including the so-called *Berlin mechanism* on a consultation and cooperation procedure concerning emergency situations that may arise from a violation of the OSCE principles or as a result of major disruptions endangering peace, security or stability); and *early warning and preventive measures* (to enable the participating States to be rapidly alerted in cases where, within the OSCE area, situations have the potential to develop into crises, including armed conflicts). Finally, the *Valletta mechanism* and the *Convention on Conciliation and Arbitration* relate specifically to the peaceful settlement of disputes.

While the many mechanisms differ substantially in their objectives and functioning, they were all established to overcome the problem of having to

[82] Ibid., Chapter I, para. 18.

[83] See, for more details, the OSCE, Handbook, 3 December 2015, available at: www.osce.org/files/documents/b/3/22624.pdf, as well as CVCE, 'The procedures and mechanisms of the OSCE', 8 July 2016 (n. 77), and Bloed, 'Two Decades of the CSCE Process' 1993.

decide on crisis situations or to monitor compliance (for instance through the sending of OSCE experts and rapporteurs) on the basis of a consensus among the fifty-seven participating States.[84] The OSCE decision-making thus not only results in decisions with concrete rules that commit the participating States to act accordingly and, for instance, allow for the establishment of missions, but over the past decades the Organization has also developed several mechanisms to monitor and control the implementation of the agreed principles and adopted decisions. All of this supports the idea that the OSCE is indeed more than 'a centre for harmonizing the actions of nations in the attainment of common ends' and occupies a distinct position in relation to its participating States.

4 CONCLUSION

The lack of consensus among OSCE participating States has so far led the Organization to deny its international legal personality – despite the fact that certain OSCE organs, such as the Secretariat, seem to find workarounds leading to situations of de facto legal personality – and to this very day using the term 'member states' in the context of the OSCE continues to raise eyebrows. There is no doubt that, by now, OSCE legal advisors must experience some fatigue with academic debates and resort in practice to pragmatic solutions to combine political preferences and legal realities. Indeed, there is only so much lawyers can do when the politics of international legal personality prevails and legal arguments prove unable to reassure certain participating States.

In the meantime, OSCE practice – although perhaps not yet strong enough to create a new legal reality – seems close to how many other IOs function. Decisions are taken by decision-making bodies and participating States have their seats in the organs, which in turn function on the basis of detailed procedural rules and mechanisms developed to monitor compliance.

The various chapters in this present Volume underline that the discussion is still as vivid today as it was twenty years ago. Not many new arguments have been developed and everything seems to have been said. In this situation our role as lawyers may indeed be to continue to highlight the importance of legal clarity – not just for states but also for individuals who have been confronted with OSCE activities – and at the same time to have solutions ready when the two most powerful participating States become more willing to water down

[84] See, for details, Bloed, 'Two Decades of the CSCE Process', as well as the OSCE Handbook (n. 79).

their political wine and find a compromise. Or when the time comes that practice proves stronger than politics. First steps in this direction have been made in June 2017, when the OSCE concluded a Headquarters Agreement with Austria and an agreement on its status in Poland with that country (see above, Section 2.2.2.).

Outsiders would probably almost always see the OSCE as an IO. According to the 'duck test' (if it looks like a duck, swims like a duck, and quacks like a duck, it probably is a duck) this seems fully justified. While the OSCE started as a conference and at that time most probably could not qualify as an IO, its participating States gradually and deliberately developed it into an organisation and in 1994 also chose to name it as such. The OSCE is in almost every aspect similar to other IOs (especially regarding its institutional structure), bringing participating States together to perform a wide variety of functions in their common interest, taking decisions and performing monitoring tasks. Its headquarters and offices have also been given a status similar to that of other IOs.

As we have seen in Section 2, insiders also almost always regarded the OSCE as an IO. At the same time, they are aware of the issue surrounding the OSCE's legal personality, which has something pertinacious about it. Following the decision in 1994 to change the conference into an organisation without international legal personality, this issue has remained. Finally, the 2007 negotiations succeeded in bridging the long-standing differences of opinion and produced a Draft Convention. These days, opposition to granting the OSCE international legal personality seems to have disappeared. However, the conditions imposed by the Russian Federation and the USA stand in the way of taking this final step. The only reason the 2007 Draft Convention is still awaiting adoption is the difficulty of combining the Russian 'no convention without a charter' requirement with the American 'convention only' approach. Hence, the issue seems no longer centred around a disagreement on whether to grant the OSCE international legal personality but whether it is necessary to conclude a constituent instrument for the Organization.

In our view, breaking the current deadlock is essential. We have pointed to a number of not only conceptual but also practical problems – for instance, related to the privileges and immunities of the OSCE's missions staff. For the time being, in the absence of a formal agreement on the OSCE's international legal personality, there is no alternative but to rely on 'implied powers', following the reasoning in *Reparation*, whenever this is necessary.

However, this does not really provide the necessary solutions, as we have seen, because a comparison with the UN is flawed on many points: the

UN has a clear treaty basis and, not unimportant, a court to interpret it. Therefore, it is for the participating States themselves to break the impasse and for the Russian Federation and the USA to soften their prerequisites for the acceptance of the 2007 Draft Convention. Practice may help in bringing politics more in line with legal realities, and – to return to our main question – as practice further develops it will be increasingly difficult for the OSCE to escape the application of international rules by simply using different terms (participating States, non-binding decisions) and by denying the international legal existence of the Organization. The OSCE does not operate in an international legal vacuum and pragmatic solutions and workarounds create legal effects and expectations by third parties. Other examples have revealed that at a certain moment the need for an organisation to function in practice and to achieve its objectives triggers an acceptance of its international legal status. And, perhaps more importantly, the same examples show that this has so far not at all been detrimental to an IO or to its member states.

REFERENCES

Alvarez, José, *International Organizations as Law-makers* (Oxford: Oxford University Press, 2005).

Arsić-Đapo, Jasna, 'Another Brick in the Wall: Building Up the OSCE as an International Organization One Agreement at a Time', *International Organizations Law Review* 14 (2017), 414–29.

Barros, Ana Sofia and Ryngaert, Cedric, 'The Position of Member States in (Autonomous) Institutional Decision-Making: Implications for the Establishment of Responsibility', *International Organizations Law Review* 11 (2014), 53–82.

Bekker, Pieter, *The Legal Position of Intergovernmental Organizations: A Functional Necessity Analysis of Their Legal Status and Immunities* (Dordrecht: Martinus Nijhoff Publishers, 1994).

Berger, Christian, 'OSCE and International Law', *International Journal of Legal Information* 24 (1996), 37–47.

Bloed, Arie, 'Two Decades of the CSCE Process: From Confrontation to Co-operation, An Introduction', in Arie Bloed (ed.), *The Conference on Security and Co-operation in Europe: Analysis and Basic Documents, 1972–1993* (Dordrecht: Kluwer Academic Publishers, 1993), 1–117.

Blokker, Niels, 'International Organizations and Their Members', *International Organizations Law Review* 1 (2004), 139–61.

'Member State Responsibility for Wrongdoings of International Organizations: Beacon of Hope or Delusion?', *International Organizations Law Review* No. 2 (2015), 319–32.

Brölmann, Catherine, *The Institutional Veil in Public International Law: International Organisations and the Law of Treaties* (Oxford: Hart Publishing, 2007).

David, Eric, *Droit des organisations internationales* (Brussel: Bruylant, 2016).

Dekker, Ige and Wessel, Ramses, 'Identities of States in International Organizations', *International Organizations Law Review* 12 (2015), 293–318.

'Van CVSE naar OVSE. De sluipende institutionalisering en onvermijdelijke juridisering van een internationale conferentie', *Vrede en Veiligheid* 4 (2002), 425–38.

Gazzini, Tarcisio, 'Personality of International Organizations', in Jan Klabbers and Åsa Wallendahl (eds.), *Research Handbook on the Law of International Organizations* (Cheltenham, Northampton: Edward Elgar, 2011), 33–55.

Guzman, Andrew, 'International Organizations and the Frankenstein Problem', *European Journal of International Law* 24 (2013), 999–1025.

Jackson, John, *Restructuring the GATT System* (London: The Royal Institute of International Studies, 1990).

Jakobson, Linda and Melvin, Neil (eds.), *The New Arctic Governance*, SIPRI Research Report No. 25 (Oxford: Oxford University Press, 2016).

Jenks, Clarence Wilfred, 'The Legal Personality of International Organizations', *British Yearbook of International Law* 22 (1945), 267–75.

Klabbers, Jan, *An Introduction to International Organizations Law* 3rd edn (Cambridge: Cambridge University Press, 2015).

'Presumptive Personality: The European Union in International Law', in Martti Koskenniemi (ed.), *International law Aspects of the European Union* (The Hague: Kluwer Law International, 1998), 231–53.

'The Concept of Legal Personality', *Ius Gentium* 11 (2005), 35–66.

Lagrange, Evelyn and Sorel, Jean-Marc, *Droit des organisations internationales* (Paris: Librairie générale de droit et de jurisprudence, 2013).

Odello, Marco, 'The Developing Legal Status of the Organisation for Security and Co-operation in Europe', *Anuario de derecho internacional* XXII (2006), 351–93.

Pauwelyn, Joost, Wessel, Ramses and Wouters, Jan (eds.), *Informal International Lawmaking* (Oxford: Oxford University Press, 2012).

Pauwelyn, Joost, Wessel, Ramses and Wouters, Jan, 'When Structures Become Shackles: Stagnation and Dynamics in International Lawmaking', *European Journal of International Law* 25 (2014),733–63.

Rama-Montaldo, Manuel, 'International Legal Personality and Implied Powers of International Organisations', *British Yearbook of International Law* 44 (1970), 111–55.

Reinisch, August and Bachmayer, Peter (eds.), *The Conventions on the Privileges and Immunities of the United Nations and the Specialized Agencies – A Commentary* (Oxford: Oxford University Press, 2016).

Roessler, Frieder, 'The Agreement Establishing the World Trade Organization', in Jacques Bourgeois, Frederique Berrod and Eric Gippini Fournier (eds.), *The Uruguay Round Results – A European Lawyers' Perspective* (Brussels: European Interuniversity Press, 1995), 67–85.

Ruffert, Matthias and Walter, Christian, *Institutionalised International Law* (Baden-Baden, Portland: Nomos and Hart Publishers, 2015).

Sands, Phillipe and Klein, Pierre, *Bowett's Law of International Institutions* 6th edn (London: Sweet & Maxwell, 2009).

Schermers, Henry and Blokker, Niels, *International Institutional Law* 5th edn (Leiden: Brill, 2011).

Schlager, Erika, 'The Procedural Framework of the CSCE: From Helsinki Consultations to the Paris Charter, 1972–1990', *Human Rights Law Journal* 12 (1991), 221–37.

Seidl-Hohenveldern, Ignaz, 'Internationale Organisationen aufgrund von soft law', in Ulrich Beyerlin *et al.* (eds.), *Recht zwischen Umbruch und Bewahrung – Völkerrecht, Europarecht, Staatsrecht: Festschrift für Rudolf Bernhardt* (Berlin, Heidelberg: Springer, 1995), 229–39.

Szafarz, Renata, 'CSCE: An International Organization in Statu Nacsendi?', in Arie Bloed and Wilco de Jonge (eds.), *Legal Aspects of a New European Infrastructure* (Utrecht: Europa Instituut: Nederlands Helsinki Comité, 1992), 15–21.

Takei, Yoshinobu, 'Are the Polar Regions Converging? A Study of the Evolution of the International Regime Governing the Arctic Region Compared to the Antarctic Treaty System', in Mariano Aznar and Mary Footer (eds.), *Select Proceedings of the European Society of International Law*, vol. 4 (Oxford: Hart Publishers, 2012), 363–78.

'The Role of the Arctic Council from an International Law Perspective: Past, Present and Future', *The Yearbook of Polar Law VI* (2015), 349–74.

Tichy, Helmut and Quidenus, Catherine, 'Consolidating the International Legal Personality of the OSCE: A Headquarters Agreement with Austria', *International Organisations Law Review* 14 (2017).

Tichy, Helmut and Köhler, Ulrike, 'Legal Personality or Not – The Recent Attempts to Improve the Status of the OSCE', in Isabelle Buffard, James Crawford, Alain Pellet and Stefan Wittich (eds.), *International Law between Universalism and Fragmentation. Festschrift in Honour of Gerhard Hafner* (Leiden, Boston: Martinus Nijhoff Publishers, 2008), 455–78.

Wessel, Ramses, 'Institutional Law-Making: The Emergence of a Global Normative Web', in Catherine Brölmann and Yannick Radi (eds.),

Handbook on the Theory and Practice of International Law-Making (Cheltenham, Northampton: Edward Elgar Publishing, 2016), 179–99.

'Reparation for Injuries Suffered in the Service of the United Nations', in Cedric Ryngaert, Ige Dekker, Ramses Wessel and Jan Wouters (eds.), *Judicial Decisions on the Law of International Organizations* (Oxford: Oxford University Press, 2016), 11–18.

'Revisiting the International Legal Status of the EU', *European Foreign Affairs Review* 5 (2000), 507–37.

'The European Union as a Party to International Agreements: Shared Competences, Mixed Responsibilities', in Alan Dashwood and Marc Maresceau (eds.), *Law and Practice of EU External Relations – Salient Features of a Changing Landscape* (Cambridge: Cambridge University Press, 2008), 145–80.

'The International Legal Status of the European Union', *European Foreign Affairs Review* 2 (1997), 109–29.

Wessel, Ramses and Arribas, Gloria Fernandez, 'EU Agreements with Third Countries: Constitutional Reservations by Member States', in Steven Blockmans (ed.), *The European Union and International Crisis Management: Legal and Policy Aspects* (The Hague: T.M.C. Asser Press, 2008), 291–308.

White, Nigel, *The Law of International Organisations* 2nd edn (Manchester: Manchester University Press, 2005).

White, Nigel and Collins, Richard (eds.), *International Organizations and the Idea of Autonomy: Institutional Independence in the International Legal Order* (Routledge: Taylor and Francis Group, 2011).

Wouters, Jan and Man, Philip De 'International Organizations as Law-Makers', in Jan Klabbers and Åsa Wallendahl (eds.), *Research Handbook on the Law of International Organization* (Cheltenham, Northampton: Edward Elgar, 2011), 190–225.

8

The OSCE's Domestic Legal Status: an Exploration of Relevant International Law Sources

Cedric Ryngaert

1 INTRODUCTION[*]

The dispatching of the OSCE Special Monitoring Mission (SMM) to Ukraine in 2014 has (again) brought to the fore the importance of an appropriate legal status for the OSCE and its staff. While before the Ukraine crisis the OSCE may have lain relatively dormant, the events in Ukraine have allowed the Organization to reclaim its position as a pan-European security forum. However, in the absence of a clear legal status under the domestic laws of the OSCE's participating States, it was not self-evident whether or how the OSCE SMM would be deployed in Ukraine. A precious ten weeks were lost before a Memorandum of Understanding (MOU) between the OSCE and Ukraine, which pertained to the field mission's legal status, was signed and ratified and all arrangements for the SMM were in place.[1] During this period, eight OSCE monitors were abducted and held incommunicado, and the SMM was unable to 'open bank accounts, enter into contracts, issue vehicle number plates or import equipment – some of it vital for security'.[2] In light of

[*] The author acknowledges the financial support from the European Research Council (Proposal 336230 – UNIJURIS) and the Dutch Organisation for Scientific Research (VIDI Proposal No. 016.135.322).

[1] OSCE, Ministerial Council, 'Report to the Ministerial Council on Strengthening the Legal Framework of the OSCE in 2014', 2 December 2014, MC.GAL/5/14, 1. It was observed that 'it might not be possible to replicate such a short timeframe in every instance', OSCE, Ministerial Council, 'Report to the Ministerial Council on Strengthening the Legal Framework of the OSCE in 2015', 1 December 2015, MC.GAL/4/15, 4.

[2] OSCE, Panel of Eminent Persons on European Security as a Common Project, 'Interim Report and Recommendations of the Panel of Eminent Persons on European Security as a Common Project: Lessons Learned for the OSCE from Its Engagement in Ukraine', 11 June 2015, available at: http://www.osce.org/networks/ 164561?download=true. The OSCE Panel of Eminent Persons, established in the wake of the OSCE's deployment in Ukraine, was highly critical of this situation. As the Panel noted, even after the ratification of the MOU, 'other OSCE staff travelling to Ukraine have no official status, privileges, immunities or security guarantees there'.

these limitations, the Panel of Eminent Persons in 2015 strongly urged the participating States to confer on the OSCE international legal personality and legal status under their domestic laws.[3]

Concerns that the absence of legal status hampers the implementation of the OSCE's mandate are hardly new. However, neither are efforts to grant such legal status. As early as 1993, the then Conference on Security and Co-operation in Europe (CSCE) Council, at its Rome meeting, adopted a Decision on Legal Capacity and Privileges and Immunities (1993 Rome Decision; non-binding, like all OSCE decisions), which called on participating States to confer such status unilaterally under their domestic law.[4] Unfortunately, this Decision was not fully implemented by the participating States, partly owing – somewhat ironically perhaps – to the absence of formal legal personality of the OSCE under international law.[5] After 1993, the Permanent Council and the Secretariat continued their initiatives to strengthen the OSCE's legal status,[6] but it was mainly after a damning report by the Panel of Eminent Persons in 2005 that the OSCE's legal status moved up the political agenda.[7] In the aftermath of the 2005 report, an expert group agreed on a draft Convention on International Legal Personality, Legal Capacity and Privileges and Immunities of the OSCE in 2007 (the 2007 Draft Convention),[8] although, for apparently political reasons, efforts to draft and agree on an OSCE constitutional instrument (Charter)

3 OSCE, Panel of Eminent Persons on European Security as a Common Project, 'Interim Report', 2015 (n. 2), 11. The four other lessons to be learnt from the Ukraine crisis pertained to the failure of prevention, the importance of leadership, the primacy of politics, and capacity and cooperation.

4 Commission on Security and Cooperation in Europe, 'CSCE and the New Europe – Our Security Is Indivisible: Decisions of the Rome Council Meeting', 1 December 1993, CSCE/4 C/Dec.2.

5 See, for a complete overview of the OSCE's legal status as of 2000, OSCE, Permanent Council, 'Decision No. 383: Report on OSCE Legal Capacity and on Privileges and Immunities to the Ministerial Council', 26 November 2000, PC.DEC/383, 1–11. See, for an overview of implementing measures taken by national parliaments: International Secretariat of the OSCE, Parliamentary Assembly/OSCE, Secretariat for Legal Services, 'Helsinki +40 Project Food-for-Thought Paper: The OSCE's Lack of an Agreed Legal Status – Challenges in Crisis Situations', April 2015, 8–10, available at: www.oscepa.org/documents/all-documents/helsinki-40/seminar-4-diis/2814-helsinki-40-food-for-thought-paper-the-osce-s-lack-of-an-agreed-legal-status-challenges-in-crisis-situations/file.

6 See, for an overview, OSCE, Permanent Council, 'Report on OSCE Legal Capacity and on Privileges and Immunities to the Ministerial Council', 2000 (n. 5).

7 OSCE, Panel of Eminent Persons on European Security as a Common Project, 'Final Report and Recommendations of the Panel of Eminent Persons on Strengthening the Effectiveness of the OSCE', 27 June 2005, available at: www.osce.org/cio/15805?download=true.

8 OSCE, Ministerial Council, 'Draft Convention on the International Legal Personality, Legal Capacity, and Privileges and Immunities of the OSCE', 29 November 2007, MC.DD/28/07, Annex.

stumbled.[9] Since – at least for some participating States – the adoption of both instruments should be linked, the adoption of the 2007 Draft Convention on legal status has also become uncertain. As a way out of the impasse, an open-ended Informal Working Group on Strengthening the Legal Framework of the OSCE (IWG) was subsequently established in 2009.

In this chapter the options identified by the IWG as to how to take the 2007 Draft Convention forward are briefly sketched (Section 2). Subsequently, assuming that the 2007 Draft Convention is *not* adopted or implemented, I examine whether the OSCE could possibly claim legal status on the basis of unwritten international law. It is ascertained whether such status applicable to international organisations (IOs) could exist under general customary international law (Section 3), or, alternatively, on the basis of an institutional duty of loyalty of OSCE participating States vis-à-vis the Organization (Section 4) – in fact, a norm of intra-institutional customary law, or a general principle of law.

This enquiry is not devoid of practical significance, as one can well imagine that the conventional avenue remains foreclosed for the time being, since the normative seriousness that goes with formal treaties may, in the OSCE context, be politically unpalatable. Alternative normative sources of legal status thus remain to be explored. The gist of the argument developed here relates to the legal status of the OSCE in the domestic legal order of its participating States. Such a domestic legal status has several dimensions. It covers (1) the OSCE's 'legal capacity' as is necessary for the exercise of its functions, including the capacity to contract, acquire and dispose of movable and immovable property, and to institute and participate in legal proceedings;[10] (2) the inviolability of its premises, property, assets and archives;[11] (3) its immunity from jurisdiction and execution;[12] (4) tax exemptions and customs privileges;[13] (5) financial controls;[14] and (6) facilities with respect to communication.[15] It includes the legal status of the Organization itself, as well as members of OSCE institutions and field operations, and representatives of participating

9 But see Swiss chairmanship non-paper, OSCE, Ministerial Council, 'Draft "Convention Plus" [Statute] for the Organization for Security and Co-Operation in Europe Convention on the International Legal Personality, Legal Capacity, and its Privileges and Immunities of the OSCE', 1 December 2015, MC.GAL/4/15, Annex B.

10 OSCE, Ministerial Council, 'Draft Convention' 2007 (n. 9), Art. 4.

11 OSCE, Ministerial Council, 'Draft Convention' 2007 (n. 9), Arts. 5–6.

12 OSCE, Ministerial Council, 'Draft Convention' 2007 (n. 9), Art. 7.

13 OSCE, Ministerial Council, 'Draft Convention' 2007 (n. 9), Arts. 8–9.

14 OSCE, Ministerial Council, 'Draft Convention' 2007 (n. 9), Art. 10.

15 OSCE, Ministerial Council, 'Draft Convention' 2007 (n. 9), Art. 11.

States taking part in the work of the OSCE.[16] In essence, the OSCE's legal status is mainly concerned with its capacity to act in a domestic setting, as well as with the privileges and immunities that the Organization and its representatives enjoy in the domestic legal order of the participating States.[17] What is considered as legal status in this chapter is only *domestic* legal status. However, the legal *source* of this status need not be domestic. In fact, I argue that this source could well be *international*.

This chapter does not address the distinct question of *international* legal personality. International legal personality is understood here as being based on, or entailing, an organisation's capacity to file claims for damages at the international level,[18] or to be held responsible for violations of international law.[19] This is obviously not to gainsay the importance of international legal personality for the OSCE. In fact, the 2007 Draft Convention addresses the OSCE's international legal personality *before* its legal status. Nonetheless, this chapter's focus lies on the legal arrangements that are directly relevant to the OSCE's operations and functioning in domestic settings.

2 STRENGTHENING THE OSCE'S LEGAL FRAMEWORK: OPTIONS ON THE BASIS OF THE 2007 DRAFT CONVENTION

As of 2015, the IWG had tabled four options to strengthen the OSCE's legal framework in the short run, all of which are based on the 2007 Draft Convention: (1) formal adoption of the 2007 Draft Convention; (2) parallel or consecutive adoption of a constituent treaty for the OSCE and the 2007 Draft Convention; (3) a 'Convention Plus' or 'OSCE Statute' – an option that would supplement the Draft Convention with some constitutional provisions; and (4) implementation of the 1993 Rome Decision through signature and ratification of the 2007 Draft Convention by interested participating States.[20]

16 OSCE, Ministerial Council, 'Draft Convention' 2007 (n. 9), Arts. 14–16.

17 Compare article 104 of the UN Charter, 'The Organization shall enjoy in the territory of each of its Members such legal capacity as may be necessary for the exercise of its functions and the fulfilment of its purposes', Charter of the United Nations, 24 October 1945, 1 UNTS XVI.

18 This was the question addressed by the International Court of Justice in the famous *Reparation* case: ICJ, *Reparation for Injuries Suffered in the Service of the United Nations*, Advisory Opinion of 11 April, ICJ Reports 1949, 174.

19 United Nations, International Law Commission, 'Draft Articles on the Responsibility of International Organizations, with Commentaries', UN Doc. A/66/10, 26 April to 3 June and 4 July to 12 August 2011. For the distinction between domestic and international legal personality, see further Steinbrück Platise, 'Legitimate Governance as a Privilege and Price for the Authority of International Organisations, Chapter 14, Section 3, in this Volume.

20 OSCE, Ministerial Council, '2015 Report' (n. 1), 1–3.

Given the current tensions between East and West, it is doubtful whether there is sufficient political momentum to adopt a constituent document of the OSCE forty-one years after the Helsinki Final Act. Even during the period that the CSCE became the OSCE in 1995 – which surely constituted a major constitutional transformation – it was already considered, at least by the USA, that a constituent treaty was, given that the Organization had moved beyond its formative stage, no longer 'a reasonable option for an entity with important ongoing activities and responsibilities, and with more than fifty participants with different political structures'.[21]

While a constituent treaty is from the *international* legal perspective not entirely necessary for the granting of *domestic* legal status to the OSCE, unambiguous recognition of the international legal personality of the OSCE in a constituent treaty may, at least in some participating States, overcome domestic legal obstacles to the strengthening of the Organization's legal status.[22] Thus, ideally, both a constituent treaty and a convention on legal status – or a combination of both – would be adopted, even in a version only containing basic provisions on personality and status. However, as some states continue to make adoption of the 2007 Draft Convention dependent on adoption of a constituent treaty, this option is unlikely to be taken in the foreseeable future.[23]

[21] Sapiro, 'Changing the CSCE into the OSCE', 634.

[22] OSCE, Ministerial Council, '2015 Report', 2015 (n. 1), 6: stating that national impediments to the conclusion of an agreement with the OSCE might not be overcome just with political willingness. Along the same lines, the United Kingdom considered that, as a result of its lack of international legal personality, the OSCE was not an 'organisation' in the terms of the International Organisations Act 1968, under which legal capacity and privileges and immunities are given to a number of international organisations. The UK stated, however, that it has a political commitment dating to the 1993 Rome Decision to confer legal capacity and privileges and immunities on the OSCE. On that basis, it decided to treat the OSCE as 'an international organisation of which the UK is a member for the purposes of s. 1 of the International Organisations Act 1968', United Kingdom, House of Commons Library, 'International Organisations Act', Research Paper 05/31, 6 April 2005, 11–12, available at http://researchbriefings.files.parliament.uk/documents/RP05-31/RP05-31.pdf.

[23] This concerns in particular the Russian Federation. The stance of the Russian Federation was enunciated in an attachment to OSCE, Ministerial Council, 'Decision No. 16/06, Legal Status and Privileges and Immunities of the OSCE, Interpretative Statement Under Paragraph IV.1(A)6 of the OSCE Rules of Procedure', 5 December 2006, MC.DEC/16/06: 'While it has joined the consensus on the Ministerial Council decision on the legal status and privileges and immunities of the OSCE, the Russian delegation continues to insist that the only way of settling this matter in accordance with the norms of international law is to devise a founding OSCE document in the form of a charter or statute. Without a charter, the OSCE cannot be regarded as a fully fledged international organisation. We believe it is necessary to proceed from the recommendation made in that connection in the report of the Panel of

Accordingly, the most effective route appears to be the aforementioned fourth option identified by the IWG: that is, implementation of the 1993 Rome decision by a formal adoption, signature and ratification by interested OSCE participating States.[24] This option does not require that *all* OSCE participating States give their consent, nor does it require that the Convention formally enters into force in order for (parts of) the Convention to apply in the domestic legal order of the states parties to it. While (current) Article 22(3) of the 2007 Draft Convention provides that the Convention 'shall enter into force sixty days after the date of deposit of the instruments of ratification, acceptance, approval or accession by two-thirds of the participating States', Article 23 provides that a 'participating State may declare at any time that it will apply the present Convention provisionally until it enters into force for it in accordance with [paragraph 3] of Article 22'.

This well-known technique of provisional treaty application ensures that signing and ratifying states are under an immediate legal obligation to grant the necessary legal status to the OSCE and its officials and are no longer subject to a mere political commitment to implement the outdated 1993 Rome Decision.[25] Unlike the Decision, the 2007 Draft Convention unambiguously addresses the legal status of the OSCE itself,[26] exemption from income tax for OSCE officials,[27] and the international legal personality of the OSCE.[28]

Eminent Persons, pursuant to which the participating States should devise a concise statute or charter of the OSCE containing its basic goals and principles along with reference to existing commitments and the structure of its main decision-making bodies. In any case, the entry into force of a convention on privileges and immunities, if and when there is agreement on a draft, will be possible only in conjunction with the entry into force of a statute or charter of the OSCE.'

24 See also OSCE, Panel of Eminent Persons on European Security as a Common Project, 'Interim Report' (n. 2), 11.

25 A treaty provisionally applied is binding and enforceable. See Dörr and Schmalenbach, *Vienna Convention on the Law of Treaties*, 420; see also Lefeber, 'The Provisional Application of Treaties'. Obviously, the domestic consequences of legal treaty commitments depend on the participating State's constitutional tradition of giving effect to international law in its domestic legal order. Thus, in monist states, the Convention will *ipso facto* be incorporated in the domestic legal order, and the OSCE can directly invoke the Convention's provisions on legal status; whereas in dualist states, these provisions will need to be transformed into national legislation before the OSCE can rely on them.

26 OSCE, Ministerial Council, 'Draft Convention' 2007 (n. 8), Art. 4.

27 OSCE, Ministerial Council, 'Draft Convention' 2007 (n. 8), Arts. 15(1)(c), 16(1)(d).

28 OSCE, Ministerial Council, 'Draft Convention' 2007 (n. 8), Arts. 3.

3 THE OSCE'S DOMESTIC LEGAL STATUS UNDER CUSTOMARY INTERNATIONAL LAW

It is not certain that any of the options suggested by the IWG will prove successful. After all, the implementation of all of them is a function of political willingness, which in the past has been lacking. Accordingly, it could be that everything stays the same: no formal legal framework governing the OSCE's domestic legal status will be devised, and there will be a continued reliance on ad hoc or de facto arrangements. However, a third course, separate from the adoption of a formal legal framework and reliance on the current patchwork of arrangements, could possibly be charted: that the Organization is entitled to domestic legal status, including privileges and immunities, under customary international law.

This is in fact the default position adopted by the OSCE Secretariat, which has informed the IWG 'that in the absence of any firmer arrangement to address operational needs, the Secretariat asserts the objective legal personality of the OSCE and functional privileges and immunities as a matter of custom, in particular when faced with the special exigencies of a legal framework for the OSCE in case of rapid deployment'.[29] A customary norm would, like a fully ratified Convention, be of general application and would do away with the prevailing legal uncertainty and potential for arbitrariness – although obviously, from a legal certainty perspective, a convention would be preferable. The customary law argument is certainly not fanciful, as it has been argued in scholarship that member states, and in particular host states, are customarily obliged to grant domestic legal status to IOs in the absence of a provision in the relevant instruments.[30] In essence it draws on the theory of functional necessity, pursuant to which an IO is entitled to legal status under domestic law insofar as this is necessary to fulfil the mandate assigned to the IO.

[29] OSCE, Ministerial Council, '2014 Report', 2014 (n. 1), 2. See, for more on the OSCE Secretariat's position, Tabassi, 'The Role of the Organisation in Asserting Legal Personality: The Position of the OSCE Secretariat on the OSCE's Legal Status', Chapter 3 in this Volume. A similar position has also been taken by the Serbian OSCE Chairmanship which stated at a Helsinki +40 seminar in Copenhagen in 2015: 'Recognition of the OSCE as a legal entity and the granting of functional privileges is nothing more and nothing less than what is *customarily and routinely granted* to other international organisations established under public international law' (emphasis added), OSCE, Parliamentary Assembly, 'Time to tackle the OSCE's lack of legal status, say participants at Helsinki +40 seminar', 28 April 2015, available at www.oscepa.org/news-a-media/press-releases/ 2015/2197-time-to-tackle-the-osce-s-lack-of-legal-status-say-participants-at-helsinki-40-seminar#sthash.U62x1 Mfb.dpuf.

[30] Gazzini, 'Personality of International Organizations', 46.

However, there are three potential problems with the customary law argument. Firstly, it is debatable whether functional necessity, as a sociological category, could independently provide a legal basis for the legal status of an IO. Secondly, stating that an IO has legal status does not say anything about the exact content and scope of this legal status; put differently, the functional necessity theory may be too abstract to determine concrete rights and obligations. Thirdly, and most importantly, the position that the OSCE has a legal status may run counter to the very wishes of the OSCE membership. After all, in order to claim the existence of a customary law rule regarding OSCE's legal status, proof of sufficient state practice and *opinio juris* has to be offered.

3.1 *Implied Legal Status Based on Functional Necessity*

As to the first concern, there is admittedly little doubt that an IO's legal status is normally based on considerations of functional necessity. Thus, Article 104 of the United Nations Charter provides that '[t]he [United Nations] Organization shall enjoy in the territory of each of its Members such legal capacity as may be necessary for the exercise of its functions and the fulfilment of its purposes'. It is similarly accepted that the immunities of IOs are claimed on the basis of functional necessity.[31]

However, this only means that functional necessity is the policy rationale or the material source of an IO's capacity and privileges and immunities, which have formally been laid down in constituent documents, headquarters agreements or other legal arrangements. It does not mean that in the absence of such arrangements the functional necessity of an IO's legal status has *necessarily been implied* by the member states.[32] It is debatable indeed that functional necessity as an argumentative tool can, in an unmediated fashion, give rise to a legal status for IOs and their officials as a matter of customary international law.

In fact, most domestic courts have rejected arguments which based an IO's immunities directly on customary law, or general principles of law for that

[31] Ryngaert, 'The Immunity of International Organisations Before Domestic Courts'.

[32] It is of note that the ICJ in the *Reparation* case based the UN's international legal personality (although not its legal status) on functional necessity. However, it did not just derive functional necessity from sociological realities, but linked it to member states' *intentions*, holding that the UN 'could not carry out the intentions of its founders if it was devoid of international personality. It must be acknowledged that its Members, by entrusting certain functions to it, with the attendant duties and responsibilities, have clothed it with the competence required to enable those functions to be effectively discharged', ICJ, *Reparations for Injuries* (n. 18), 17.

matter. Instead they have required a treaty basis.[33] True, proponents of customary OSCE's legal status may perhaps find solace in some 1980s (and not yet formally overruled) case law from the Netherlands, Italy and the USA.[34] Still, Sir Michael Wood, after conducting a survey of relevant practice, has recently observed that '[w]hile one still comes across assertions, by writers, governments or courts, that international organisations enjoy immunity under customary international law, the authorities relied upon are largely unconvincing'.[35]

Another concern over functional necessity as an argument in favour of the customary character of the OSCE's legal status is that domestic courts may have difficulties establishing the purposes, mandate and powers of the OSCE in the first place. After all, the OSCE does not have at its disposal a constituent treaty setting out what it is supposed to do. How can courts then assess whether a legal status is necessary for the OSCE to fulfil its purposes? This concern may, however, be somewhat exaggerated insofar as the Organization's role is indeed set out in a number of key documents, namely the Helsinki Final Act (1975), the Charter of Paris for a New Europe (1990), the Istanbul Charter for European Security (1999) and the Astana Commemorative Declaration (2010).[36]

Moreover, where legal status is needed in case of deployment of an OSCE special field mission – the occurrence where the issue typically arises – the

[33] Reinisch, 'Transnational Judicial Conversations on the Personality, Privileges, and Immunities of International Organisations', 5–7. See, for IOs, e.g., Belgian Court of Cassation, *League of Arab Nations*, Judgment of 12 March 2001, ILDC 42 and, notably, Supreme Court New York, *Nafissatou Diallo* v. *Dominique Strauss-Kahn*, 11 June 2012, Index No 307065/11. The decision is quoted in *United Nations Juridical Yearbook* (2012), 537–44: holding that the IMF Managing Director does not enjoy immunity under customary international law. Obviously, IOs and their officials could theoretically enjoy privileges and immunities under customary international law, but then proof of near-universal and virtually uniform state practice and *opinio juris* needs to be offered.

[34] Netherlands Supreme Court, *Spaans* v. *Iran–US Claims Tribunal*, Judgment of 20 December 1985 (1987) 18 NYIL 357; Italian Court of Cassation, *Cristiani* v. *Istituto italo-latino-americano*, Judgement of 23 November 1985, (1986) 69 Rivista di diritto internazionale 146–52; US Court of Appeals for the District of Columbia Circuit, *Mendaro* v. *The World Bank*, Judgment of 27 September 1983, 717 F.2d 610.

[35] Wood, 'Do International Organisations Enjoy Immunity Under Customary International Law?', 316–17.

[36] These are the key documents identified by the OSCE itself: CSCE, Helsinki Final Act, 1 August 1975, available at: www.osce.org/helsinki-final-act?download=true; CSCE, Charter of Paris for a New Europe, November 1990, available at: www.oscepa.org/documents/all-documents/documents-1/historical-documents-1/673-1990-charter-of-paris-for-a-new-europe/file; OSCE, Charter for European Security, November 1999, available at: www.osce.org/mc/17502?download=true; OSCE, Astana Commemorative Declaration, 3 December 2010, available at: www.osce.org/mc/74985?download=true.

mission's mandate can easily be found in the OSCE Permanent Council's decision deploying the field mission. Thus, the OSCE's decision on the deployment of a SMM to Ukraine (2014) sets out in detail the aims and tasks of the field mission.[37] Courts could consult this decision to determine whether it would be functionally necessary for the OSCE and its staff to have legal status in the state of operation.

3.2 *The Normative Content of Legal Status*

As to the second concern, even assuming, *arguendo*, that the OSCE *is* entitled to legal status under customary international law, it is one thing to state such an entitlement but quite another to outline its exact normative scope and content. Just like the notion of international legal personality, the notion of domestic legal status is in fact an empty box, an *ex post* descriptive category that bundles together a variety of privileges, rights and possible obligations, the extent of which is the outcome of political negotiations between the IO and the (member) state(s).

One could argue that the immunity of the IO is one of the most important rights commonly granted to IOs that enjoy legal status under domestic law. However, when it comes to more detailed arrangements regarding the immunities of different categories of officials, and *a fortiori* regarding the privileges of IOs and their officials, the customary law route may fail to deliver concrete solutions. While templates of multilateral agreements and bilateral headquarters agreements regarding privileges may obviously exist, even across organisations, such privileges ultimately differ per agreement. Even if a survey of the relevant practice yields a list of common principles, it is questionable whether this list is accompanied by the *opinio juris* of states and IOs required for the crystallisation of customary law norms.

Against this, one may perhaps argue that some MOU concluded between the OSCE and a number of participating States make reference to the 1961 Vienna Convention on Diplomatic Relations,[38] and thus the relatively specific norms contained in this Convention could inform the content of the OSCE's customary international law status. This argument is not convincing, however, as the 1961 Convention is only included in the MOU by *renvoi*, and thus the normative basis of the (legally or politically) binding character of the

37 OSCE, Permanent Council, Decision No. 1117: Deployment of an OSCE Special Monitoring Mission to Ukraine, PC/DEC/1117, 21 March 2014, 2–3.

38 See, e.g., Memorandum of Understanding between the Government of Ukraine and the Organization for Security and Co-operation in Europe (OSCE) concerning the Creation of a New Form of Cooperation, 13 July 1999, Art. 6(1).

arrangements between the OSCE and its participating states is the MOU itself. Were it not for the MOU being a relatively formal act, the norms of the 1961 Convention would not have been applicable; after all, the 1961 Convention only governs the relations between states and not between states and IOs. Moreover, even if the Convention were to apply *mutatis mutandis* to the OSCE, it does not address all aspects relevant to the OSCE: it does not cover the question of the immunity of the Organization nor the status of staff without diplomatic status.[39]

3.3 *The Missing Evidence of Customary International Law OSCE's Legal Status*

A third, even more serious concern is that the OSCE Secretariat's position on the legal status of the Organization under customary international law may be at loggerheads with the very wishes of the participating States. It is glaring indeed that, in the framework of the OSCE, the OSCE participating States have not made far-reaching arrangements for the legal status of the Organization. After all, the 1993 Rome Decision left it to states to take the necessary implementation measures regarding the OSCE's legal status.

The light touch approach to the issue of OSCE's legal status is in fact a conscious choice, at least on the part of a number of states (the USA in particular) that did/do not want to overly institutionalise the Organization lest it become too rigid. Purportedly, the flexibility of the Organization may make it more amenable to informal influence-peddling by more powerful (western) states, even if the uncertain domestic legal status may actually undermine its very effectiveness.[40] Where it is clear that – in spite of explicit decades-old initiatives on legal status and the ongoing work of the IWG – the 2007 Draft

39 Note that the question of state immunity is also governed by another convention, namely the UN Convention on Jurisdictional Immunities of States and their Properties, 17 January 2005, Doc. A/59/508 (not yet entered into force).

40 The informal structure of the OSCE, and the lack of centralised oversight of the Organization's activities has mainly been criticised by the Russian Federation, which sees itself marginalised within the Organization, since powerful and richer participating States second personnel and make voluntary contributions to the Chairman-in-Office, the Heads of Mission and the heads of OSCE institutions, which have considerable political room for autonomous action. See Oberschmidt/Zellner, 'OSCE at the Crossroads', 6, available at: https://ifsh.de/file-CORE/documents/16_working_paper_2.PDF. See on reviewing the powers, role and functions of the OSCE Chairperson-in-Office and Secretary General: Zagorski Andrei, 'Strengthening the OSCE: Building a Common Space for Economic and Humanitarian Cooperation, an Indivisible Security Community from the Atlantic to the Pacific', 23, available at: www.oscepa.org/documents/all-documents/helsinki-40/riac/2660-report-strengthening-the-osce-av-zagorski/file.

Convention has only been adopted at the expert level and not at the political level, one is left to wonder whether the OSCE Secretariat has the internal competence to overrule the political masters of the OSCE, acting through the OSCE Council, and argue for a legal status under customary law.

These contradictory tendencies within the OSCE itself will not be lost on the states within whose domestic legal order the OSCE claims legal status. In fact, they may provide fodder to contest the customary law character of the OSCE's legal status on the grounds of a lack of internal uniformity or consistency. As to the uniformity of state practice, the International Law Association's Committee on the Formation of Customary (General) International Law has opined in respect of internal uniformity that '[f]or State practice to create a rule of customary law, it must be virtually uniform, both internally and collectively', with internal uniformity meaning 'that each State whose behaviour is being considered should have acted in the same way on virtually all of the occasions on which it engaged in the practice in question'.[41] Consequently, and *mutatis mutandis*,[42] an IO that internally does not speak with one voice is an easy prey for states contesting the customary law argument made by one of the organisation's organs.

However, the OSCE Secretariat could argue that the internal uncertainties and contradictions are more apparent than real. After all, the OSCE 'hold-out' participating States may not as such be against granting the OSCE domestic legal status, but rather wish to make the granting of legal status conditional on the adoption of an OSCE Charter that would govern a number of constitutional questions. No state has questioned the suitability, or even the necessity, of the arrangements laid down in the 2007 Draft Convention.[43] Only a small group of participating States appended three footnotes to the text of the Convention requiring a linkage between the 2007 Draft Convention and a future OSCE Charter in order for the former to be signed and ratified.[44] It would go too far, however, to consider these states as persistent objectors to

[41] International Law Association, Committee on Formation of Customary (General) International Law, 'Final Report of the Committee: Statement of Principles Applicable to the Formation of General Customary International Law', 2000, 21.

[42] The ILA Committee has held that '[t]he practice of intergovernmental organisations in their own right is a form of 'State practice', International Law Association, Committee on Formation of Customary (General) International Law, 'Final Report' (n. 41), 19.

[43] The USA, while possibly opposing the institutionalisation of the OSCE, has also supported a grant of domestic legal status, although its initial position was that legal status was to be 'limited to what was essential to carrying out [at the time] CSCE functions and responsibilities'; Sapiro, 'Changing the CSCE into the OSCE', 634.

[44] OSCE, Ministerial Council, 'Report to the Ministerial Council on Strengthening the Legal Framework of the OSCE in 2014', 5 December 2013, MC.GAL/6/13, 3.

the formation of a customary international law norm on the OSCE's legal status: what they object to is not the OSCE's legal status but rather the failure to constitutionalise the OSCE. Thus, as the Secretariats of the OSCE and the OSCE Parliamentary Assembly have recently pointed out, the 2007 Draft Convention 'continues to enjoy very broad support among participating States'.[45]

However, even if within the OSCE there is broad agreement regarding the suitability of legal status for itself, it is clear that the OSCE cannot just assert the existence of a norm of customary international law pertaining to the Organization's legal status. Instead, such a norm, which may require the application of privileges and immunities by the authorities and courts of states, can obviously not come into being without the practice of these very states.[46]

Put differently, sufficient collective consistency of practice among states and IOs is required. Virtually uniform international practice regarding the legal status of IOs is required for the OSCE to make a convincing customary law showing vis-à-vis host states. As an IO's legal status is often governed by treaty law, there may be little actual practice to draw on, and – as is known – one cannot just rely on treaty arrangements as evidence of practice for customary international law purposes.[47]

Admittedly, national authorities may sometimes accommodate the Organization's legal status on the basis of domestic law and practice. There is evidence that a number of states – but definitely not all – have done so in

45 International Secretariat of the OSCE, Parliamentary Assembly/OSCE Secretariat for Legal Services, 'Food-for-Thought Paper', April 2015 (n. 5), 5. In light of this reality of relative uniformity at the internal level, the OSCE Secretariat may want to rely on the *dictum* of the International Court of Justice in the *Fisheries* case, in which the Court, examining the opposability of the Norwegian system of straight base-lines for the delimitation of the territorial sea, considered 'that too much importance need not be attached to the few uncertainties or contradictions, real or apparent, which the United Kingdom Government claims to have discovered in Norwegian practice', ICJ, *Fisheries Case (United Kingdom* v. *Norway)*, Judgment of 18 December 1951, ICJ Reports 1951, 116 & 138; also ICJ, *Asylum case (Colombia* v. *Peru)*, Judgment of 20 November 1950, ICJ Reports 1951, 266 & 278.

46 This is not to say that the practice of IOs regarding the formation of customary international law is irrelevant. See United Nations, International Law Commission, 'Report of the International Law Commission, Sixty-seventh session (4 May to 5 June & 6 July to 7 August 2015) Chapter VI: Identification of customary international law', UN Doc. A/CN.4/L.869, 14 July 2015, draft conclusion 4[5].2: 'In certain cases, the practice of international organisations also contributes to the formation, or expression, of rules of customary international law.'

47 See International Law Association, Committee on Formation of Customary (General) International Law, 'Final Report' (n. 41), Principle 25: 'There is no presumption that a succession of similar treaty provisions gives rise to a new customary rule with the same content.' See also Supreme Court New York, *Nafissatou Diallo* v. *Dominique Strauss-Kahn* (n. 33).

respect of the OSCE; some of them have even domestically implemented the 1993 Rome Council Decision.[48] However, this practice varies significantly, and accordingly does not necessarily yield a coherent set of regulations on legal status. Moreover, it is unclear to what extent this practice is accompanied by an *opinio juris* on the part of states. To conclude, the OSCE faces the uphill battle of finding proof of near-universal and virtually uniform state practice and *opinio juris* as to its entitlement to legal status.[49] The argument that it is mere common sense that the Organization is entitled to domestic legal status in every (participating) state may, legally speaking, be unconvincing.

4 GRANTING LEGAL STATUS AS AN ASPECT OF THE PRINCIPLE OF COOPERATION

In the previous section, it was argued that the customary international law argument regarding the OSCE's legal status is a difficult one to make. In this section, I suggest that, in the continued absence of formal arrangements governing the legal status of the OSCE, granting domestic legal status could be viewed as an aspect of the principle of loyal cooperation. By virtue of this principle, member states and the IO they have established – in the case at hand the OSCE – should assist each other in carrying out the tasks assigned to them, and in particular to the IO, by its constitutive documents.

This principle of cooperation is best known in its EU iteration: the principle of 'sincere cooperation' between the EU and EU member states, codified in Article 4 of the Treaty on European Union (TEU).[50] However, it also exists in the relationship between the UN Security Council and member states, and

48 See, for an overview, International Secretariat of the OSCE, Parliamentary Assembly/OSCE Secretariat for Legal Services, 'Food-for-Thought Paper', April 2015 (n. 5), 5. Seven states have passed parliamentary legislation for the implementation of the 1993 Rome Council Decision. In four states the executive branch has adopted measures for the implementation of the 1993 Rome Decision. In five states, national laws have ratified host country agreements or memoranda of understanding.

49 Compare the UN Specialised Agencies, Barros and Ryngaert, 'Officials'.

50 See Article 4.3 of the Treaty on European Union, stating that pursuant to the principle of sincere cooperation, the Union and the Member States shall, in full mutual respect, assist each other in carrying out tasks that flow from the Treaties, and that the Member States shall take any appropriate measure, general or particular, to ensure fulfilment of the obligations arising out of the Treaties or resulting from the acts of the institutions of the Union. The Member States shall facilitate the achievement of the Union's tasks and refrain from any measure that could jeopardise the attainment of the Union's objectives. Consolidated Version of the Treaty on European Union, 7 February 1992, Official Journal of the European Union, C 326/13.

the relationship between UN specialised agencies and their member states.[51] As far as the latter is concerned, one should recall that the ICJ held in its *WHO Egypt* Advisory Opinion (1980), as to the relationship between the WHO and the host state of a WHO regional office (Egypt), that '[t]he very fact of Egypt's membership of the Organisation entails certain mutual obligations of co-operation and good faith incumbent upon Egypt and upon the Organisation', and that 'the legal relationship between Egypt and the Organisation became, and now is, that of a host state and an international organisation, the very essence of which is a body of mutual obligations of co-operation and good faith'.[52]

Applying these insights to the OSCE, as participating states have tasked the OSCE with carrying out a mandate to comprehensively realise security in the pan-European area,[53] they arguably owe it to the Organization to endow it with the necessary domestic legal status in order to enable it to *effectively* carry out this mandate (for example, when the OSCE authorises the deployment of monitoring field missions in the territory of a participating State).[54] The *dictum* in *WHO Egypt* demonstrates that the principle of OSCE–participating State cooperation need not explicitly be laid out in a constitutive document of the OSCE.

A complicating factor is obviously that commitments within the OSCE context are meant to be political in nature only, so that a commitment to cooperate loyally, therefore, also must only be political. An additional complication is that the character of the OSCE as an organisation separate from its participating States may be placed in doubt, as a result of which the question of state–organisation loyalty may become moot. Indeed, in the absence of unambiguous legal personality of the OSCE, it may well be submitted that all OSCE action in fact amounts to joint action by the aggregated OSCE participating States, who simply use the OSCE as a transparent vehicle to pursue their aims. In such a constellation, in which the Organization

51 UN Charter, 1945 (n. 17), Art. 25: 'The Members of the United Nations agree to accept and carry out the decisions of the Security Council in accordance with the present Charter.'

52 ICJ, *Interpretation of the Agreement of 25 March 1951 between the WHO and Egypt*, Advisory Opinion of 20 December 1980, ICJ Reports 1980, 73 & 93.

53 CSCE, Helsinki Final Act, 1975 (n. 36).

54 Compare the relationship between the International Committee of the Red Cross (ICRC) and states, for purposes of domestic legal status: Debuf, 'Tools to do the Job', 344: 'Granting privileges and immunities to the ICRC is not a matter of courtesy, but is rather a concrete manner in which States reaffirm their commitment to the ICRC's humanitarian mandate and role and give the ICRC the tools that are indispensable for its efforts to alleviate as much as possible the human suffering caused by armed conflicts and other situations of violence.'

disappears from view as an independent entity, the duty of loyalty may well not be applicable.

As far as the latter argument is concerned, one may have to bear in mind that the questions of international legal personality and domestic legal status are distinct,[55] which means that an organisation that cannot avail itself of the former can still be entitled to the latter. These concepts speak to different rights and obligations: international legal personality is mainly concerned with questions of responsibility (the right to bring and receive international claims against and from other international legal subjects, though states in particular),[56] whereas legal status mainly pertains to privileges and immunities in the domestic legal order of states. Thus, even when lacking international legal personality, the OSCE can still claim domestic legal status. Absent a binding international agreement, the conferral of this status has so far been dependent on OSCE participating States' domestic law.

It is argued here, however, that the OSCE's domestic legal status also follows from the international institutional principle of loyal cooperation between member or participating States and the IO, as, for example, laid down in Article 4 of the TEU and confirmed by the ICJ in the *WHO Egypt* Advisory Opinion. Admittedly, a duty to grant legal status does not as a matter of course flow from the principle of cooperation, but a proper argument in this sense can surely be made. As it is a core function of the OSCE to send field missions to the territories of its participating States, a failure on the part of participating States to facilitate these missions by not granting legal status may hamper the overall effectiveness of the Organization in fulfilling its mandate, and hence conflict with the principle of cooperation.

What specific privileges and immunities this legal status entails will ultimately be a function of organisational/field operation effectiveness, balanced against the legitimate interests of states. This tension between institutional and national considerations is normally resolved through negotiations resulting in bilateral or multilateral agreements, or unilateral commitments. Obviously, we are back to square one: the need to have a detailed arrangement on the OSCE's legal status in force, such as the 2007 Draft Convention. However, as the 2007 Draft Convention has been drawn up within the OSCE itself and no

55 Gazzini, 'Personality of international organizations', 43: 'a state may certainly grant immunity to an international organisation not possessing international legal personality by treating the organisation as a collectivity of states and its organs as common organs through which member states perform jointly certain acts'.

56 In the *Reparations* Advisory Opinion, the question of the international legal personality of the United Nations was closely tied up with the question of whether the UN could bring a claim for damages against a state, ICJ, *Reparations for Injuries* (n. 18), 174.

principled opposition against the content of its norms has emerged, one may submit that it elaborates on, and arguably further substantiates, a pre-existing general duty of cooperation between participating States and the OSCE.

It could even be argued that, irrespective of the 2007 Draft Convention's formal adoption and entry into force, compliance with the principles of the 2007 Draft Convention is already an obligation, based on the principle of loyal cooperation resting on the participating States. This argument may be a stretch insofar as the binding effect of this duty of cooperation bypasses the more direct consent-based treaty process. But at the very least, when called on to draw the more precise contours of the OSCE's legal status in their legal systems, domestic authorities should look at the 2007 Draft Convention for guidance: the 2007 Draft Convention is after all a more detailed iteration of the duty of loyalty. Ultimately, however, the problem of under-determination of legal status absent a specific conventional or other written regime remains difficult to overcome, whether in respect of the OSCE's legal status under customary international law or under the principle of loyal cooperation.

5 CONCLUDING OBSERVATIONS

The 2007 OSCE Draft Convention adequately addresses the pertinent issues regarding the OSCE's legal status, understood mainly as the Organization's legal capacity and privileges and immunities in the domestic legal order of its participating States. It is hoped that this convention will one day be formally adopted. It remains possible, however, that this will not happen. This has prompted my enquiry into international law sources other than the 2007 Draft Convention, bearing in mind that a proper legal status for the OSCE and its staff is sorely needed, especially in the conflict areas to which the Organization dispatches special field missions.

Advocates of OSCE's legal status, including the OSCE Secretariat, have so far relied mainly on customary international law as a default option. The argument that granting legal status is compelled by customary international law is not fully convincing, however. Instead, I suggest that granting legal status may be required pursuant to the concept of an institutional principle of loyal cooperation between the OSCE and the participating States. In order for the OSCE to effectively carry out the mandate that participating States have given it, the latter are arguably under an obligation to grant the Organization an adequate legal status. The 2007 Draft Convention could thereby offer inspiration to domestic authorities as a more specific embodiment of the duty of cooperation.

However, one cannot expect them to merely apply a document that has not formally entered into force. Absent binding legal acts of international or domestic origin that articulate the OSCE's legal status, it will therefore remain a challenge to derive specific status-based rights from a general duty of the participating States to cooperate with the OSCE.

REFERENCES

Barros, Ana Sofia and Ryngaert, Cedric, 'Officials (Art. VI Sections 18–250, Specialized Agencies Convention)', in August Reinisch (ed.), *The Conventions on the Privileges and Immunities of the United Nations and Its Specialized Agencies: A Commentary* (Oxford: Oxford University Press, 2016), 395–436.

Debuf, Els, 'Tools to do the Job: The ICRC's Legal Status, Privileges and Immunities', *International Review of the Red Cross* 97 (2016), 319–44.

Dörr, Oliver and Schmalenbach, Kirsten, *Vienna Convention on the Law of Treaties – A Commentary* (Berlin, Heidelberg: Springer-Verlag, 2011).

Gazzini, Tarcisio, 'Personality of International Organizations', in Jan Klabbers and Asa Wallendahl (eds.), *Research Handbook on the Law of International Organisations* (Cheltenham: Edward Edgar Publishing, 2011), 33–55.

Lefeber, René, 'The Provisional Application of Treaties', in Jan Klabbers and René Lefeber (eds.), *Essays on the Law of Treaties: A Collection of Essays in Honour of Bert Vierdag* (The Hague: Martinus Nijhoff Publishers, 1998), 81–96.

Oberschmidt, Randolf and Zellner, Wolfgang, 'OSCE at the Crossroads, Working Paper 2', in WP Core Working Papers (Hamburg: Centre for OSCE Research, Institute for Peace Research and Security Policy at the University of Hamburg 2000).

Reinisch, August, 'Transnational Judicial Conversations on the Personality, Privileges, and Immunities of International Organisations: An Introduction', in August Reinisch (ed.), *The Privileges and Immunities of International Organisations in Domestic Courts* (Oxford: Oxford University Press, 2013), 1–16.

Ryngaert, Cedric, 'The Immunity of International Organisations Before Domestic Courts: Recent Trends', *International Organizations Law Review* 7 (2010), 121–48.

Sapiro, Miriam, 'Changing the CSCE into the OSCE: Legal Aspects of a Political Transformation', *The American Journal of International Law* 89 (3) (1995), 631–7.

Wood, Michael, 'Do International Organisations Enjoy Immunity Under Customary International Law?', *International Organizations Law Review* 10 (2013), 287–318.

9

Privileges and Immunities of the OSCE

Isabelle Pingel

1 INTRODUCTION*

On 3 July 1973, the world powers took advantage of relatively peaceful relations between western Europe and the communist bloc in order to meet and discuss ways in which they would cooperate. The international conference that was held in Finland for this purpose led to the signing of the Helsinki Final Act of 1 August 1975. The Final Act defined the three 'baskets' (nowadays called 'dimensions') around which the Conference on Security and Co-operation in Europe (CSCE) would be structured, covering issues of (i) security in Europe; (ii) cooperation in the areas of economics, science and technology and the environment; and (iii) cooperation in humanitarian and other fields.[1] Institutionally, the structure agreed upon was particularly flexible: as a 'low-profile diplomatic process' it amounted to no more than a 'follow-up' to the conference as provided for by the last chapter of the Final Act.[2] Ever since its adoption, the text left open the question of its legal nature. While it certainly is not an international treaty, 'we remain in the dark as to its scope'.[3] Being both a declaration and a programme, the very nature of the Final Act remains unclear.

The Charter of Paris for a New Europe, signed on 21 November 1990, did not clarify the legal basis of the CSCE's institutional structure.[4] Following the

* The author wishes to thank Mohamed Mahayni (Solicitor of England & Wales, admissible to register before the Versailles Bar) for his help and useful suggestions to the English version of this chapter.

[1] CSCE, Helsinki Final Act, 1 August 1975, available at www.osce.org/helsinki-final-act?download=true.

[2] See Manton, 'The OSCE Human Dimension Process', 197 and references cited.

[3] Prévost, 'Observations', 130.

[4] CSCE, Charter of Paris for a New Europe, 21 November 1990, available at www.osce.org/mc/39516?download=true.

fall of the Berlin Wall in 1989, the Charter opened up a new era in East–West relations and laid the foundations for the institutionalisation of the CSCE. That process included, in particular, the establishment of permanent institutions such as the Conflict Prevention Centre in Vienna and the Office for Free Elections (today known as the Office for Democratic Institutions and Human Rights, ODIHR) in Warsaw.[5] The Charter, however, limits the commitments given by the states hosting these permanent institutions, providing simply that they shall 'enable the institutions to function fully and enter into contractual and financial obligations'.[6] Its final part expressly states that it 'is not eligible for registration under Article 102 of the Charter of the United Nations'. Therefore, it is not a treaty creating an international organisation but, to put it in the language of sociology, a partnership that uses conflict(s) 'to rearrange the situation in a dynamic of never-ending negotiation'.[7]

In the years following the Charter's adoption, the Conference – as a 'baroque' organisation[8] – continued to gradually change. At the 1992 Helsinki Summit, an agreement was reached among the participating States to consider the CSCE a 'regional arrangement' within the meaning of Chapter VIII of the UN Charter.[9] Soon after, at the 1994 Budapest Summit, the CSCE changed its name to the Organization for Security and Co-operation in Europe (OSCE). Contrary to its previous name (i.e., 'Conference'), this new name has been noted as being a 'more accurate' description of the actions conducted by the OSCE and the form it takes to do so.[10] In fact, nobody denies that the institutional structure of the OSCE is fairly similar to other international organisations, having policy-making entities, a Secretariat and a number of other organs and related bodies.[11] However, as paragraph 29 of the Budapest Declaration expressly states, '[t]he change in name from CSCE to OSCE alters neither the character of our CSCE commitments nor the status of the CSCE and its institutions. In its organisational development the CSCE will remain flexible and dynamic.'[12]

5 CSCE, Charter of Paris, 1990 (n. 4), chapter on New Structures and Institutions of the CSCE Process.

6 CSCE, Charter of Paris, 1990 (n. 4), supplementary document to give effect to certain provisions contained in the Charter of Paris for a New Europe, H 11.

7 Mérini, 'Le partenariat', 25.

8 To use the expression of Dupuy and Kerbrat, *Droit international public*, para. 146.

9 See CSCE, Helsinki Document 1992: The Challenges of Change, Helsinki Summit Declaration, 10–11 July 1992, available at: www.osce.org/mc/39530?download=true, para. 25.

10 See Sapiro, 'Changing the CSCE into the OSCE', 632.

11 See Dailler, Forteau and Pellet, *Droit international public*, para. 378 *et seq.* The authors highlight 'a particularly remarkable institutionalisation of the CSCE' ('une institutionnalisation assez spectaculaire de l'OSCE').

12 Budapest decision, I. Strengthening the CSCE, available at: www.osce.org/mc/39554?download=true.

This status quo has prevailed until today, and questions surrounding the Organization's status and the strengthening of its legal framework continue to prompt debate.[13] States such as Russia and France[14] are in favour of establishing a more structured organisation to offset the influence of NATO and are in opposition to those states – essentially the USA – which on the contrary prefer a flexible, cooperative structure.[15] Discussions continue without any tangible progress.[16]

Nevertheless, the permanent OSCE institutions and various field operations, and the range of their activities, make the Organization an undisputed player in the international legal order to the extent that it equates to a de facto international organisation.[17] To pick up on Michel Virally's classic analysis, the OSCE operates as 'a centre for decision-making and action that is capable of taking initiatives, for its own purposes'.[18] Therefore, the OSCE is seeking to obtain an international status comparable to that of other international organisations on the basis that it assumes similar functions and wishes to put an end to the 'perpetual motion' that it has experienced since its establishment.[19] For the same reasons, the OSCE is calling for a uniform regime of privileges and immunities, which is the focus of the present chapter.

Such a regime should bear two characteristics. First, it should be founded on an international convention rather than national laws. This would make it more predictable and uniform throughout participating States and would therefore avoid the current divergences between their domestic laws. Second, the regime should address as thoroughly as possible the question of privileges and immunities. In particular, it should encompass the status of entities, namely (i) permanent OSCE institutions (i.e., Secretariat, ODIHR,

13 For a comprehensive analysis of this question, see Tichy and Köhler, 'Legal Personality or Not', 455–78; Ryngaert, 'Basing the Legal Status of the OSCE on Participating States' Duty of Loyalty', 3 August 2016, available at: http://voelkerrechtsblog.org/basing-the-legal-status-of-the-osce-on-participating-states-duty-of-loyalty/, 1–5; Simonet and Lüber, 'The OSCE and Its Legal Status', 277–316.

14 See Ghébali, *Le rôle de l'OSCE en Eurasie*, 57.

15 See, e.g., Oberschmidt and Zellner, 'OSCE at the Crossroads', 12.

16 See especially, International Secretariat of the OSCE, Parliamentary Assembly/OSCE, Secretariat for Legal Services, 'Helsinki +40 Project. Food-for-thought Paper: The OSCE's Lack of an Agreed Legal Status – Challenges in Crisis Situations', April 2015, available at: www.oscepa.org/documents/all-documents/helsinki-40/seminar-4-diis/2814-helsinki-40-food-for-thought-paper-the-osce-s-lack-of-an-agreed-legal-status-challenges-in-crisis-situations/file.

17 According to Dupuy/Kerbrat, *Droit international public*, para. 146, and, as the authors point out, despite the fact that the OSCE cannot 'properly speaking rely on the existence of any particular constitutive legal instrument'. See also Bertrand, 'La nature juridique', 365–406.

18 Virally, 'Le rôle des organisations internationales', 534–5.

19 See Decaux, 'La CSCE au lendemain du Conseil de Rome', 269.

etc.), (ii) permanent missions of participating States to the OSCE (iii) OSCE field operations; and, as far as individuals are concerned, (iv) representatives of participating States and (v) OSCE staff members (both at headquarters and the diverse field operations).

For the time being, however, no such regime exists. Consequently, the privileges and immunities of the OSCE and its staff vary from one participating State to another and from one legislative act to another, if there even is an act. This situation has proved problematic. As has been correctly pointed out, '[f]or the OSCE, work would be much easier if it enjoyed a clearly defined status'.[20] This chapter therefore examines first the current situation of the OSCE regarding the topic of its privileges and immunities (Section 2). It subsequently highlights the difficulties that arise from the lack of a single regime and discusses how the conclusion of an international treaty on the subject could improve the day-to-day work of the OSCE (Section 3).

2 THE OSCE PRIVILEGES AND IMMUNITIES: *DE LEGE LATA*

Although the CSCE was formed in 1975, it was the 1990 Charter of Paris that first briefly addressed the question of privileges and immunities. In a supplementary document appended to the Charter, the text provides under the chapter on 'Institutional Arrangements' that the states hosting the permanent institutions shall accord them 'appropriate diplomatic status' and their staff 'will be accredited by the seconding State to the host country where they will enjoy full diplomatic status'.[21]

However, it soon became clear that those provisions were inadequate to ensure equal treatment for all staff. In order to remedy these inconsistencies and to secure a safe and stable environment for both the CSCE and its employees, including local officials, discussions began pursuant to the 1992 Helsinki Summit decision to 'consider the relevance of an agreement granting an internationally recognized status' to the CSCE institutional structures.[22] On the basis of an expert group report, the Rome Council Decision on legal capacity and on privileges and immunities was adopted

[20] Tomuschat, 'International Law', 148.

[21] CSCE, Charter of Paris, 1990 (n. 4), supplementary document to give effect to certain provisions contained in the Charter of Paris for a New Europe, I H, paras. 11 and 9.

[22] See CSCE, Helsinki Document 1992: The Challenges of Change, Helsinki Summit Declaration (n. 9), point I, para. 25. For a short history of the negotiations, see Ghébali, *L'OSCE dans l'Europe post-communiste*, 71–3.

on 1 December 1993.[23] The Rome Decision recommended that states should aim to harmonise the rules to be applied 'subject to their constitutional and related requirements'.[24]

The regime set out in the Rome Decision is comparable to those contained in other international instruments on privileges and immunities (e.g., the Convention on the Privileges and Immunities of the United Nations, adopted by the UN General Assembly on 13 February 1946).[25] First, it provides for privileges and immunities to be granted 'to the CSCE institutions in the interests of those institutions'.[26] These include that permanent institutions enjoy for their property and assets 'the same immunity from legal process as is enjoyed by foreign States',[27] inviolability of premises and archives,[28] and exemption from all direct taxes.[29] The Rome Decision then provides for privileges and immunities to be granted to individuals, specifying that the privileges and immunities are given 'not for the personal benefit of the individuals concerned, but in order to safeguard the independent exercise of their functions'.[30]

As is usual in international organisations, the scope of these immunities varies in accordance with the category of staff involved.[31] The Rome Decision provides that participating States in whose territory permanent missions to the CSCE are located will accord to the members of their missions 'diplomatic privileges and immunities in conformity with the Vienna Convention on Diplomatic Relations of 1961'.[32] As a result, the members of permanent missions to the CSCE are afforded maximum protection. There are three other categories of staff covered by the provisions of the Rome Decision, namely the representatives of participating States involved in the Organization's work,[33] CSCE officials,[34] and members of CSCE missions

23 CSCE, Rome Council, CSCE and the New Europe – Our Security is Indivisible, CSCE/4-C/Dec.2, 1 December 1993; for the text, see OSCE, Permanent Council, Decision No. 383, Report on OSCE legal capacity and on privileges and immunities to the Ministerial Council, PC.DEC/383, 26 November 2000, Attachment 1 to Annex, Annex 1 to Annex A.

24 See CSCE, Rome Council, Rome Decision, 1993 (n. 23), para. 8.

25 Convention on the Privileges and Immunities of the United Nations, 13 February 1946, 1 UNTS 15/90 UNTS 327 (corrigendum to vol. 1).

26 See CSCE, Rome Council, Rome Decision, 1993 (n. 23), para. 2.

27 Ibid., para. 4.

28 Ibid., paras. 5, 6.

29 Ibid., para. 8(a).

30 Ibid., para. 3, ss. 2.

31 For an overview, see Pingel, 'Les privilèges et immunités', 648–54.

32 See CSCE, Rome Council, Rome Decision, 1993 (n. 23), para. 11.

33 Ibid., para. 12.

34 Ibid., para. 13.

(i.e., field operations).[35] These categories benefit from fewer privileges and immunities than those of members of permanent missions of participating States. That said, all three categories of staff are attributed immunity from legal process for acts performed in their official capacity and facilities in matters of immigration and foreign exchange.[36]

However, it was observed at the Istanbul Summit in November 1999 that 'a large number of OSCE participating States' had been unable to implement the Rome Decision and the reason for such 'difficulties [could] arise from the absence of a legal capacity of the Organization'.[37] In order to improve the situation, new talks were conducted on the basis of the proposals of an 'informal open-ended working group', the creation of which was provided for by the Istanbul Declaration.[38] These negotiations failed at that time due to a lack of consensus among the participating States.[39]

Eventually, a Draft Convention on the international legal personality, legal capacity and privileges and immunities of the OSCE was presented by the Informal Working Group in 2007.[40] The draft was largely inspired by the Rome Decision but nevertheless differs significantly from it. Whereas the Decision merely aims to achieve uniformity between the regimes of privileges and immunities granted under domestic legal systems, the draft, if adopted, would lead to the implementation of a single international regime to the benefit of the OSCE.

However, the draft has yet to be adopted. This can be explained as follows: Three footnotes have been inserted into the text by some participating States, tying the draft's adoption to the conclusion of an OSCE constituent treaty (Charter). Since then, it has become clear that a number of participating States require the adoption of a constituent treaty as a precondition for approving the terms of a convention on privileges and immunities.

35 Ibid., para. 14.

36 Ibid., para. 12, (a), (c), (d); para. 13, (a), (c), (d); para. 14 (b), (e), (f).

37 See OSCE, 'Charter for European Security', November 1999, available at: www.osce.org/mc/17502?download=true, point 18.

38 See ibid., Declaration of Istanbul, point 34.

39 For a summary of the discussions, see Ghébali, *Le rôle de l'OSCE en Eurasie*, 57–60. The author attributes the deadlock in talks to 'the negative attitude of a single country: the United States', 59; see also Tichy, 'The Role of the Participating States in Reforming the Legal Framework of the OSCE – Past Developments, Status Quo and Future Ambitions', Chapter 4 in this Volume.

40 See the text in OSCE, Ministerial Council, Fifteenth Meeting of the Ministerial Council 29 and 30 November 2007, MC15EW72, 30 November 2007, Perception Papers by the Chairmanship.

Unfortunately, discussions on this issue did not yield a consensus.[41] Although talks continue to this day within a new open-ended Informal Working Group, they have yet to achieve any significant progress.[42]

Deadlock in negotiations perpetuates the patchwork of different regimes on legal capacity and privileges and immunities that have been granted to OSCE institutions and their staff members under the domestic legal orders of particular participating States – if they have been granted at all. The position of permanent OSCE institutions in the host states is generally regulated by legislative means,[43] as is the case in Austria (the headquarters of the OSCE Secretariat[44]) or the Netherlands (where the High Commissioner on National Minorities is based[45]). Although the texts of the legislative acts adopted are similar, they are not identical; in particular the fiscal treatment of the relevant OSCE institution and its staff seems to vary from one country to another.[46] The situation in countries that host field operations is even less uniform, since legal capacity and privileges and immunities always need to be agreed on an ad hoc basis by the conclusion of memoranda of understanding (MOU) that may vary substantially.[47]

Lastly, the practice in other participating States – those not hosting any OSCE permanent institutions or field operations – is likewise diverse.[48] While some of them, such as Italy[49] and the USA[50], have passed legislation implementing the Rome Decision, most countries have not done so. In Belgium, for

41 See OSCE, Ministerial Council, Report to the Ministerial Council on strengthening the legal framework of the OSCE in 2014, MC.GAL/514, 2 December 2014, para. 1. See also OSCE, Ministerial Council, Decision No. 16/06 Legal Status and Privileges and Immunities of the OSCE, MC.DEC/16/06, 5 December 2006, Attachment: Interpretative Statement under Paragraph IV.1(A)6 of the OSCE Rules of Procedure, by which Russia emphasises that the only possible way to settle the matter 'is to devise a founding OSCE document in the form of a charter or statute'.

42 See OSCE Ministerial Council, Report to the Ministerial Council, 2014 (n. 41), paras. 14–15.

43 For an overview, see Cogen, *An Introduction to European Intergovernmental Organizations*, 148–9; OSCE Parliamentary Assembly, 'Helsinki + 40' (n. 16), 8–10.

44 See Austria, Bundesgesetz über die Rechtsstellung von Einrichtungen der OSZE in Österreich, 30 July 1993 (as amended in 1995 and 2002), BGBl. Nr. 511/1993.

45 See the High Commissioner on National Minorities, 'Act of 31 October 2002', 31 October 2002, available at: https://archive.icann.org/en/psc/annex15.pdf.

46 OSCE Permanent Council, Decision No. 383 (n. 23), Attachment 1 to Annex, SEC.GAL/20/00, 6, para. 22.

47 Ibid., para. 23. On the resulting difficulties, see below.

48 See OSCE Permanent Council, Decision No. 383 (n. 23), 7, para. 29.

49 See Italy, Disposizioni concernenti la capacità giuridica delle istituzioni dell'Organizzazione per la sicurezza e la cooperazione in Europa (OSCE) ed i relativi privilegi ed immunità, 30 July 1998, Act No. 301.

50 See US, Foreign Relations Authorization Act Fiscal Year 1994 and 1995, 30 April 1994, Public Law 103–236, Sect. 422.

example, the adoption of such a law has proved difficult 'since it could not be based on the signature of a treaty [on OSCE privileges and immunities]'.[51] In Finland, the authorities consider that 'the absence of such regulations seems to have caused no major problems in the practical cooperation with the OSCE institutions'.[52] However, several difficulties remain. For instance, OSCE operations frequently involve contracting and procurement. In the event of a dispute with the co-contractor, the absence of any rule on the subject of immunity before domestic courts might prove prejudicial to the OSCE.[53] The OSCE therefore continues to call for the adoption of a uniform, conventional regime.

3 THE OSCE PRIVILEGES AND IMMUNITIES: *DE LEGE FERENDA*

As emphasised above, the legal framework of the OSCE is not entirely safe. An OSCE official observed that, '[a]lthough we appear to be a house with a roof and some windows, we have no foundation'.[54] In particular, the question of the OSCE's legal status and privileges and immunities continues to be debated in the absence of any uniform regime. OSCE officials strive for the adoption of a Convention that would settle the OSCE's legal status at the international level. These efforts have essentially been based on three central arguments.

First, it is argued that a multilateral convention would spare the OSCE the need to negotiate bilateral agreements on legal status and privileges and immunities necessary for the establishment of new OSCE field operations. Such agreements are rarely identical. As a result, OSCE field operations are not subject to the same legal regime in each of the host states,[55] which allegedly makes it more difficult for the OSCE to find partners. This is because IOs frequently need to conclude contracts with private parties (e.g., suppliers for the provision of goods or services) for whom the predictability of their rights and obligations is a key factor in deciding whether or not to enter into contractual and commercial relationships with the organisations.

51 OSCE Permanent Council, Decision No. 383 (n. 23), para. 31.

52 Ibid., para. 31.

53 Ibid., para. 32.

54 See Brander, 'Making a Credible Case', 19.

55 The annual loss arising from this position has been put at 1 per cent of the OSCE's total budget, see OSCE, Ministerial Council, Report to the Ministerial Council on strengthening the legal framework of the OSCE in 2012, MC.GAL/15/12, 7 December 2012, para. 2.

It has also been rightly emphasised that, despite the lack of any clear legal status, the OSCE could incur international responsibility in the event of unlawful acts. If, for instance, an official of the OSCE committed a crime during a field operation, the state whose citizen is the victim could certainly raise a claim against the Organization. To the ordinary lawyer, what matters in this case is the effectiveness of the OSCE, which operates – at least in some areas – as 'an integrated whole'.[56] As a result, 'the participating States may prevent the Organization from assuming the role of an active player in international relations; they could not, however, prevent third states from identifying their Organization as the author of wrongful acts'.[57] This might result in 'adverse consequences' if, at the same time, the OSCE is still 'unable to enjoy rights such as privileges and immunities'.[58] Such privileges and immunities are intended to ensure the independence of international institutions and, in particular, to prevent the proliferation of lawsuits in national courts.[59]

At the same time, the OSCE's entitlement to immunities before domestic courts may discourage potential partners from entering into contractual relations with the OSCE. This is nothing new. It occurred in 1876 in a ruling by the civil court of Antwerp on state immunity (which in the nineteenth century was commonly considered absolute). As the court then indicated, a foreign government cannot escape the obligations it has entered into with a private person 'without at the same time foregoing its consideration and credit'.[60] That reasoning is still valid today. If private parties cannot rely on the judicial protection of their contractual claims against a state, they may hesitate to enter into contractual relations with it. The same conclusion stands by analogy for international organisations. If private parties cannot have access to justice when required, they may be reluctant to enter into contractual relationships with such organisations in the first place.

Another argument put forward in favour of the adoption of a convention on privileges and immunities is that it would facilitate the work of the OSCE and the recruitment of staff. For the time being, the regime varies depending on

56 See Tomuschat, 'International Law', 148. See however Steinbrück Platise, 'Legitimate Governance as a Privilege and Price for the Autonomy of International Organisations', Chapter 14, Section 4, in this Volume; for competitive scenarios see also Gasbarri, 'The International Legal Responsibility of the OSCE', Chapter 11 in this Volume.

57 Ibid.

58 See OSCE Ministerial Council, Report to the Ministerial Council 2014 (n. 41), para. 3.

59 See Pingel, 'Les privilèges et immunités' (n. 30), 633–4.

60 Civil Court of Antwerp, De la compétence des tribunaux nationaux á l'égard des Gouvernements et des Souverains étrangers, 1876, *Journal du Droit International* 340, 342. For details, see Pingel, *Les immunités des Etats*, 53, para. 38.

the country where the OSCE carries out its activities. The most controversial issue in this respect is that of tax exemption. The rule of exemption from taxation – offset for employees by taxation levied on the organisation[61] – is widely recognised.[62] It is based on two premises.

First, tax exemption ensures equal pay among civil servants of the same grade within an international institution. As pointed out by the Administrative Tribunal of the International Labour Organisation in the Settino case on 11 December 1980, '[t]he employees of international organisations are of course of many different nationalities. Consequently, if their salaries were diminished by taxation under their own national laws, there would be inequalities in the amounts of their net earnings. This is thought by all the international organisations to be undesirable.'[63] Moreover, the institution's ability to attract staff may be impaired. This was the case for the OSCE field operation in Uzbekistan, where the local members were not entitled to any tax exemption, unlike those of the United Nations (UN).[64] The UN therefore enjoyed a competitive advantage in recruiting local members of staff.

Second, tax exemption ensures that contributions paid by member states to international organisations are not diverted back to the benefit of host countries through the taxation system.[65] The risk is not merely theoretical. For example, the OSCE calculated that the amounts received in 2011 by the host states of six field operations through income tax on local staff amounted to EUR 374,900, which is as much as the budget for the OSCE field operation in Minsk.[66] In this light, tax exemption serves the important purpose of achieving equity among member states.

Nevertheless, its rationale is increasingly questioned in scholarship and case law. For example, one author highlights the fact that 'the argument based on

61 See, e.g., European Union, Consolidated Version of the Treaty on the Functioning of the European Union, Protocol No. 7 on the Privileges and Immunities of the European Union, Official Journal of the European Union, C 202/1, 7.6.2016, Art. 12. 1.

62 See, e.g., United Nations General Assembly ('UNGA'), Convention on the Privileges and Immunities of the United Nations, 13 February 1946, 13 Feb 1946, 1 UNTS 15a, Art. V, sect. 18 (b); European Union, Protocol No. 7 to the Treaty on the Functioning of the European Union, 2016, Art. 12.2 and, for a full explanation, Martha, *Tax Treatment*.

63 ILO Administrative Tribunal, '*In re* Settino, Judgment No. 426', 11 December 1980, available at: www.ilo.org/dyn/triblex/triblexmain.fullText?p_lang=en&p_judgment_no=426&p_language_code=EN, Consideration 1.

64 See Cadet, *Le statut juridique de l'OSCE*, 527.

65 See, e.g., France, French Senate, Report No. 169 of the French Senate of 27 January 1999 on the bill authorising the French Republic to adhere to the Convention on the Privileges and Immunities of the Specialized Agencies, of 21 November 1947, pt. I, A para. 1.

66 See OSCE, Advisory Committee on Management and Finance, Concept Paper, PC/ACMF/27/11, 11 March 2011, cited in Cadet, *Le statut juridique de l'OSCE*, 528.

equity among Members falls short in cases where the country relies on indirect taxes for its revenues rather than on direct taxes'.[67] The same is true whenever an organisation is funded with the proceeds of commercial activities. This is the case, for example, for the International Telecommunications Satellite Organization (INTELSAT). The entity operates for the most part as a commercial enterprise even though it was set up on the basis of a treaty in 1964. As a result, 'it does not deserve to be treated differently than other commercial enterprises'.[68]

In addition, it is important to keep in mind that tax exemption – like all other privileges and immunities and as stated in the 1993 Rome Decision – is not granted for the 'personal benefit' of the individuals concerned but 'in order to safeguard the independent exercise of their functions'.[69] This gives rise to an obligation on international civil servants not to invoke them abusively and to a corresponding obligation on the organisation to waive the immunity whenever granting it 'would impede the course of justice and [when it] can be waived without prejudice to the interests of the [organisation]'.[70] The question of whether this is always the case is open to debate.[71]

The last and probably strongest argument in favour of adopting a convention implementing a uniform regime of privileges and immunities for the OSCE relates to the protection of field staff, especially those working in crisis areas.[72] The number of field operations in crisis areas has significantly increased since 1992, when the first CSCE long-term field operation was sent to Kosovo. Consequently, the 1993 Rome Decision acknowledged that participating States should provide 'appropriate treatment' to individuals

67 See Martha, *Tax Treatment*, 37.

68 See De Vries, *Belastingheffing bij internationale ambtenaren vanuit Nederlands perspectief (deel 2)*, *Fiskaal* 1999/2, 19, cited in Martha, *Tax Treatment*, 38.

69 OSCE Permanent Council, Decision No. 383 (n. 23), Attachment 1 to Annex, Annex 1 to Annex A, para. 3, ss. 2.

70 See, e.g., UNGA, Convention on the Privileges and Immunities, 1946 (n. 62), Art. V, section 20.

71 In litigation with the landlord of his apartment over expulsion for non-payment of rent, the Austrian trial court granted immunity to a German senior civil servant who claimed to be acting as a special envoy of the OSCE Parliamentary Assembly and claimed the benefit of the 1961 Vienna Convention (Austria, Landgericht für Zivilrechtssachen Wien, GZ 38 R 300/04f-23, 2 February 2005); the Supreme Court adopted a less clear-cut position, in a decision of 1 December 2005, questioning both the scope of immunity on this point, the defendant's status and the position of Germany (Austria, OGH, 6Ob150/05k, 1 December 2005, available at: www.ris.bka.gv.at/Dokumente/Justiz/JJT_20051201_OGH0002_0060OB00150_05K0000_000/JJT_20051201_OGH0002_0060OB00150_05K0000_000.pdf, paras. 8, 9); for a summary of the case and the court's decision in English, see Wittich, 'Austrian Judicial Decisions', 197–203; for a commentary, see Schmalenbach, 'Austrian Courts', 460–1.

72 See Brander, 'Making a credible case', 18.

concerned.[73] The Decision therefore decided to grant such individuals – without distinguishing between expatriates and local staff – immunity from arrest or detention, criminal immunity for acts performed in the exercise of their functions and inviolability for all papers and documents.[74] Because no state hosting a field operation has implemented the Decision, in practice the situation of members of OSCE field operations is regulated by memoranda of understanding (MOU) between the OSCE and the host countries.

However, the use of MOU to that end is unsatisfactory for several reasons. One reason is that negotiating a MOU is a lengthy and complex process, especially because every new activity within the framework of a field operation requires the negotiation and conclusion of a new memorandum.[75] This is particularly problematic when rapid deployment is required.[76] Even assuming that negotiations can be concluded swiftly, they require at least a few weeks. During that time, members of the field operation are not covered by the privileges and immunities, as was the case in Ukraine in 2015. Likewise, due to the lack of legal capacity, it is also not possible for field operations to open bank accounts, enter into procurement contracts or import equipment.[77] Such situations are worrying and even dangerous in crisis areas.

Another reason why MOU are an unsatisfactory solution is that more often than not memoranda refer to the application of the 1961 Vienna Convention on Diplomatic Relations. This is a 'valuable' reference because – in principle – it ensures a high standard of protection for field operations in the absence of any other legal instrument governing OSCE privileges and immunities.[78] However, it is not without difficulties, for two main reasons. The first relates to the duty of accreditation of the OSCE's staff in the host country since the staff of field operations can only be granted privileges and immunities by the MOU once the process of accreditation has been completed. This formality caused difficulties to field operations in Belarus and Uzbekistan and delayed operations for several months.[79]

[73] OSCE Permanent Council, Decision No. 383 (n. 23), Attachment 1 to Annex, Annex 1 to Annex A, para. 4.

[74] Ibid., para. 15 (a), (b), (c).

[75] See Tabassi, 'The Question of Legal Status', 3, para. 5, 3.

[76] Notably, the deployment of a field operation to Kyrgyzstan, decided on 22 July 2010, was delayed by the negotiation of a memorandum between the OSCE and the host country. See OSCE, Secretariat, Update Information on the Police Advisory Group to Kyrgyzstan, SEC. GAL/150/10, 1 September 2010.

[77] See Tabassi, 'The Question of Legal Status', 4, para. 5, 8.

[78] See OSCE Permanent Council, Decision No. 383 (n. 23), Attachment 1 to Annex, SEC.GAL/20/00, 6, para. 24.

[79] See Cadet, *Le statut juridique de l'OSCE*, 510.

The second and even more pressing reason is that, under the 1961 Convention, local staff benefit from privileges and immunities only to the extent granted to them by the accrediting state.[80] This lack of protection may prove particularly severe. For example, local staff may risk prosecution if they fail to appear as witnesses before domestic courts in matters concerning the OSCE. Worse yet, local staff can risk arrest or detention for acts performed as part of their official functions. This was notably the case for a member of the field operation to Bosnia and Herzegovina who was arrested in Croatia and sentenced to more than ten years' imprisonment, and for a member of the former Kosovo Verification Mission who was sentenced to fourteen years' imprisonment on espionage charges.[81] Similarly in 2014, members of the OSCE field operation to Ukraine were abducted and detained for periods ranging from twenty-six to thirty-one days.[82] The risks involved are real and consequential.

The most suitable way of minimising these risks would probably be to agree upon a uniform regime of privileges and immunities for all members of field operations, and in particular for those recruited locally. Article 16 of the 2007 Draft Convention could be used to this end. Largely inspired by the 1993 Rome Decision,[83] Article 16 paragraph 1 states that members of field operations shall enjoy (a) immunity from arrest or detention and (b) immunity from legal process in respect of acts performed in their official capacity, as well as various privileges including tax exemption, exemption from national service, facilities concerning currency and exchange and repatriation facilities.[84]

Article 16 paragraph 2 makes it clear that states parties shall not be obliged to accord their own nationals or permanent residents the privileges and immunities referred to in the first paragraph 'except those granted under items (a) and (b) for acts performed in their official capacity'.[85] This means that *all* members of field operations regardless of their nationality or place of residence should enjoy immunity from arrest or detention and immunity from legal process for acts performed in their official capacity. In other words, protection must be granted to those whose mission it is to protect. However, such a rule is only acceptable under the condition that individuals who have

80 See Vienna Convention on Diplomatic Relations, 18 April 1961, 500 UNTS 95, Art. 38(2).

81 See OSCE Permanent Council, Decision No. 383(n. 23), Attachment 3 to Annex, p. 4, point 3.

82 Tabassi, 'The Question of Legal Status' 2015, 5, para. 6, 2.

83 See OSCE Permanent Council, Decision No. 383(n. 23), Attachment 1 to Annex, Annex 1 to Annex A, para. 15.

84 See CSCE, Rome Council, Rome Decision 1993 (n. 23), Art. 16, (d), (f), (i), (j).

85 Ibid., Art. 16(2) further provides that 'States Parties which do not grant exemption from taxation under their national law shall consider concluding an agreement with the OSCE for the reimbursement of national income tax paid to them by Members of Field Operations'.

claims vis-à-vis the OSCE can, when necessary, also assert their own rights in an appropriate forum: 'justice requires balance'.[86]

In fact, the scope of international organisations' immunities has evolved during the last sixty years. In the 1950s, these immunities needed to be absolute in order to protect new and growing organisations and allow them to operate efficiently.[87] Today, limitations to privileges and immunities are admitted in light of the increasing influence and power of organisations in the exercise of their functions; their independence is resilient against the threat – or actual commencement – of claims against them.[88] While limitations to privileges are justified in that light, immunity must nevertheless be preserved in certain circumstances. In particular, such immunity should be granted to staff members of international organisations when they put their lives at risk defending peace in field operations throughout the world. Yet again: 'justice requires balance'.

REFERENCES

Bertrand, Christine, 'La nature juridique de l'Organisation pour la sécurité et la coopération en Europe (OSCE)', *Revue générale de droit international public* 102 (1998), 365–406.

Brander, Sonya, 'Making a Credible Case for a Legal Personality for the OSCE', *OSCE Magazine* (March–April 2009), 18–22.

Cadet, Hélène, 'Le statut juridique de l'OSCE', PhD thesis, Université Paris 1 (2012).

Cogen, Marc, *An Introduction to European Intergovernmental Organizations* (Farnham: Ashgate, 2015).

Dailler, Patrick, Forteau, Mathias and Pellet, Alain, *Droit international public* (Paris: L. G. D. J., 2009).

Decaux, Emmanuel, 'La CSCE au lendemain du Conseil de Rome: un bilan de la transition institutionnelle', *European Journal of International Law* 5 (1994), 267–84.

Dupuy, Pierre-Marie and Kerbrat, Yann, *Droit international public* 14th edn (Paris: Dalloz, 2018).

Gaillard, Emmanuel and Pingel, Isabelle, 'International Organisations and Immunity from Jurisdiction: To Restrict or to Bypass', *International & Comparative Law Quarterly* 51 (2002), 1–15.

Ghébali, Victor-Yves, *L'OSCE dans l'Europe post-communiste 1990–1996* (Brussels: Bruylant, 1996).

86 See Gaillard and Pingel, 'International Organisations and Immunity from Jurisdiction', 15.
87 See Jenks, *International Immunities*, 40.
88 See, for a comprehensive survey, Steinbrück Platise, 'The Development of the Immunities'.

Le rôle de l'OSCE en Eurasie, du sommet de Lisbonne au Conseil ministériel de Maastricht (1996–2003) (Brussels: Bruylant, 2014).
Jenks, Clarence, *International Immunities* (London: Stevens and Sons, 1961).
Manton, Eric, 'The OSCE Human Dimension Process and the Process of Customary International Law Formation', in Institute for Peace Research and Security Policy at University of Hamburg (ed.), *OSCE Yearbook 2005* (Baden-Baden: Nomos Verlagsgesellschaft, 2006), 195–214.
Martha, Rutsel, *Tax Treatment of International Civil Servants* (Leiden, Boston: Martinus Nijhoff, 2010).
Mérini, Corinne, 'Le partenariat: Instrument juridique et/ou politique, le cas de l'OSCE', *Revue Québecoise De Droit international* 9 (1995), 21–34.
Oberschmidt, Randolf and Zellner, Wolfgang, 'OSCE at the Crossroads', Working Paper 2, in WP Core Working Papers (Hamburg: Centre for OSCE Research, Institute for Peace Research and Security Policy at the University of Hamburg 2000).
Pingel, Isabelle, *Les immunités des Etats en droit international* (Brussels: Bruylant, 1997).
'Les privilèges et immunités de l'organisation internationale', in Evelyne Lagrange and Jean-Marc Sorel (eds.), *Droit des organisations internationales* (Paris: L. G. D. J., 2013), 626–56.
Prévost, Jean-François, 'Observations sur la nature juridique de l'Acte final de la Conférence sur la sécurité et la coopération en Europe', *Annuaire Français de Droit International* 21 (1975), 129–53.
Ryngaert, Cedric, 'Basing the Legal Status of the OSCE on Participating States' Duty of Loyalty', Völkerrechtsblog (3 August 2016), https://voelkerrechtsblog.org/basing-the-legal-status-of-the-osce-on-participating-states-duty-of-loyalty/.
Sapiro, Miriam 'Changing the CSCE into the OSCE: Legal Aspects of a Political Transformation', *American Journal of International Law* 89 (1995), 631–7.
Schmalenbach, Kirsten, 'Austrian Courts and the Immunity of International Organizations', *International Organizations Law Review* 10 (2013), 446–63.
Simonet, Loïc and Lüber, Hans Georg, 'The OSCE and Its Legal Status: Revisiting the Myth of Sisyphus', in Institute for Peace Research and Security Policy at University of Hamburg (ed.), *OSCE Yearbook 2016* (Baden-Baden: Nomos Verlagsgesellschaft, 2017), 277–316.
Steinbrück Platise, Mateja, 'The Development of the Immunities of International Organisations in Response to Domestic Contestations', in Machiko Kanetake and André Nollkaemper (eds.), *The Rule of Law at the National and International Levels* (Oxford, Portland: Hart Publishing, 2016).

Tabassi, Lisa, 'The Question of Legal Status for the OSCE and Implications for Ukraine', 27 April 2015, www.oscepa.org/documents/all-documents/helsinki-40/seminar-4-diis/2919-presentation-by-lisa-tabassi-for-helsinki-40-seminar-27-april-2015/file.

Tichy, Helmut and Köhler, Ulrike, 'Legal Personality or Not – The Recent Attempts to Improve the Status of the OSCE', in Isabelle Buffard, James Crawford, Alain Pellet and Stephan Wittich (eds.), *International Law between Universalism and Fragmentation: Festschrift in Honour of Gerhard Hafner* (Leiden, Boston: Martinus Nijhoff, 2008), 455–78.

Tomuschat, Christian, 'International Law: Ensuring the Survival of Mankind on the Eve of a New Century: General Course on Public International Law', *Recueil des Cours de l'Académie de Droit International de la Haye* 281 (The Hague, Boston, London: Martinus Nijhoff Publishing, 2013), 9–438.

Virally, Michel, 'Le rôle des organisations internationales dans l'atténuation et le règlement des crises internationales', *Politique étrangère* 6 (1976), 529–62.

10

The External Relations of the OSCE

Laurence Boisson de Chazournes and Andrzej Gadkowski

1 INTRODUCTION

International organisations (IOs) are numerous, reflecting the ever-increasing need to conduct activities at the international level. Various types of relationships between IOs have been devised: they may exchange information or participate in their respective fora of discussion; they can establish institutional arrangements to implement a given activity and provide a framework for common purposes; and, for operational purposes, they can also receive logistical, material or financial aid from each other.

In the context of this chapter, emphasis will be placed on the external relations of the Organisation for Security and Co-operation in Europe (OSCE) with other international organisations and institutions, states, and non-state actors. Although the OSCE does not have a clear international legal status, it is nevertheless an active actor on the international plane, entertaining various diplomatic as well as operational relationships with states and other international organisations and institutions.

2 COOPERATIVE ARRANGEMENTS AND ACTIVITIES: A VARIETY OF VEHICLES FOR COOPERATION

The relationships that exist among IOs have developed around the need to effectively pursue a wide range of activities and objectives.[1] Multiple stakeholders can be involved and *new methods of cooperation* have emerged since the establishment of the Organization. This is the case with multi-sectoral cooperation. The embodiment of such relationships are structured around a division of labour – in which each institution's expertise and resulting

[1] Boisson de Chazournes, *Interactions Between Regional and Universal Organizations*, 384; Boisson de Chazournes, 'Relations with other International Organizations', 691–711.

comparative advantages are considered – but in a coordinated framework based on specific and identified purposes. Multi-sectoral cooperation is therefore carried out primarily through a specific approach of agreed goals. Activities recognised as being essential to achieving the identified goals are subsequently distributed among the various concerned actors with a view to making their coordinated pooling effective.[2] The OSCE is involved in a sophisticated web of cooperative arrangements of this type.

A good example of such cooperation exists between the OSCE and the United Nations (UN) in the management of the Kosovo crisis. Based on UN Security Council Resolution 1244, adopted on 10 June 1999, the OSCE Mission in Kosovo was established as a distinct component within the overall framework of the UN Interim Administration Mission in Kosovo (UNMIK). UNMIK initially brought together four pillars under the overall leadership of the UN: (1) humanitarian assistance led by the United Nations High Commissioner for Refugees (UNHCR), (2) a civil administration led by the UN itself, (3) reconstruction and economic development led by the European Union (EU) and (4) democratisation and institution building led by the OSCE. Each of the four components was placed under the authority of the Special Representative of the UN Secretary-General. In order to contribute to the implementation of Resolution 1244, the OSCE Permanent Council adopted Decision No. 305 on 1 July 1999, according to which: '[t]he OSCE Mission in Kosovo will, within this overall framework, take the lead role in matters relating to institution- and democracy-building and human rights. It will *cooperate closely with other relevant organisations* – intergovernmental and, as appropriate, non-governmental – in the planning and implementation of its tasks.'[3] Decision No. 305 also specified the fields and institutions with which this cooperation was to be carried out, for example, with the Council of Europe in the field of human resources capacity building or with the Office of the United Nations High Commissioner for Human Rights (OHCHR) in the area of protection monitoring and human rights promotion.[4]

The four-pillar structure of UNMIK – administered either directly by the UN or together with the regional organisations involved, including the OSCE – raises questions in terms of the accountability and responsibility issues between the various organisations. In 2000, UNMIK ensured immunities for its personnel by issuing Regulation No. 2000/47: On the Status,

[2] For a detailed analysis of various methods of coordination, see De Pooter, *Le droit international face aux pandémies*, 247–68.

[3] OSCE, Permanent Council, Decision No. 305, PC.DEC/305, 1 July 1999 (emphasis added).

[4] Ibid., points 1 and 4.

Privileges and Immunities of KFOR and UNMIK.[5] The granting of immunity by UNMIK 'set off alarm bells in Kosovo',[6] as it was said that such a move made the accountability of the actors involved in the UNMIK Mission difficult and almost impossible for individuals to defend their rights against these international authorities.[7] To remedy this situation, the Kosovo Human Rights Advisory Panel was created by UNMIK Regulation No. 2006/12 to render the activities of UNMIK accountable through the lens of possible human rights violations by UNMIK.[8] OSCE representatives took part in discussions on the status and competences of the Panel, which stated clearly that: 'the establishment of a quasi-judicial institution which cannot issue binding decisions is contrary to the principles of the rule of law which states that no one, especially a governmental authority (UNMIK), is above the law. This would clearly send the wrong message to the people and institutions of Kosovo.'[9] This call for accountability, highlighting the need to abide by the rule of law, was made to all the institutions that were part of UNMIK, including the OSCE. The OSCE was reminded, like the other institutions, that it should be legally accountable.

IOs can include a breakdown of their activities within the framework of *cooperation agreements*. Agreements between organisations and other actors

5 Section 3 of the Regulations provides that 'UNMIK, its property, funds and assets shall be immune from any legal process ... UNMIK personnel shall be immune from legal process in respect of words spoken and all acts performed by them in their official capacity ... UNMIK personnel shall be immune from any form of arrest or detention'; see UNMIK, Regulation No. 2000/47 on the Status, Privileges and Immunities of KFOR and UNMIK and their Personnel in Kosovo, UNMIK/REG/2000/47, 18 August 2000; KFOR is a NATO-led peacekeeping operation in Kosovo established under the authority of the United Nations (UN Security Council Resolution 1244).

6 Kosovo Human Rights Advisory Panel, 'The Final Report. History and Legacy. Kosovo, 2007–2016', 30 June 2016, available at: http://www.unmikonline.org/PublishingImages/2016/HRAP%20Final%20Report/HRAP%20Final%20Report%20(final%20version%2030%20June%202016).pdf, 29.

7 See Pacquée and Dewulf, 'International Territorial Administrations and the Rule of Law: The Case of Kosovo', 1–14. In the same vein, the Ombudsperson in Kosovo noted that UNMIK Regulation No. 2000/47 was incompatible with recognised international human rights standards: see Ombudsperson Institution in Kosovo, Special Report No. 1, 26 April 2001.

8 UNMIK, Regulation No. 2006/12 on the Establishment of the Human Rights Advisory Panel, UNMIK /REG/2006/12, 23 March 2016. On this mechanism, see Klein, 'Panels, médiateurs et mécanismes informels de contrôle des activités des organisations internationales', 217–28.

9 Kosovo Human Rights Advisory Panel, 'The Final Report' (n. 6), 8. Moreover, as indicated in the Final Report, the representatives of the mission of the OSCE in Kosovo 'thought that the UNMIK Regulation establishing the Panel should explicitly state what types of decisions the Panel would be authorized to issue. In this respect, the OMiK (Mission of the OSCE in Kosovo) deemed that the Panel's decisions should include the power to award a specific amount in just compensation to victim(s), including restitution'.

can contain a list of the responsibilities of each organisation, as well as the activities that involve joint action. The OSCE is part of such cooperative agreements. As an example, on 2 February 2012 the OSCE, the United Nations Development Programme (UNDP) and the Serbian Ministry of Defence officially launched a joint Capacity Development Programme for Conventional Ammunition Stockpile Management for the Republic of Serbia (CASM).[10] Within CASM, the OSCE and UNDP were to assist the Serbian Ministry of Defence in the demilitarisation and disposal of ammunition, the development of infrastructure for ammunition storage areas and the improvement of infrastructure of existing demilitarization facilities. More recently, on 6 March 2016, the Heads of the United Nations Office on Drugs and Crime (UNODC) and the OSCE signed a new Joint Plan of Action for further cooperation on key thematic issues, such as terrorism prevention, human trafficking, migrant smuggling and illicit drugs trafficking.[11]

The OSCE also concludes *Memoranda of Understanding* (MOU) to elaborate specific collaborative projects with international organisations and institutions, a good example being the 2011 MOU concluded with UNHCR, or that of 2014 concluded with INTERPOL.[12] The nature of these cooperative agreements can differ: some are legally binding, others not.[13] The OSCE resorts to these instruments to ensure that it is not faced with the elementary question of its legal personality, as they enable the Organization to conclude

[10] The CASM programme, launched on 2 February 2012 and originally scheduled to last until 31 December 2015, was extended by two years to the end of 2017. For more information on CASM, see Capacity Development Programme for Conventional Ammunition Stockpile Management for the Republic of Serbia (CASM), 'Ensuring Community Security through Safer Ammunition Management', 2017, available at: www.seesac.org/CASM-1/Capacity-Development-Programme-for-Conventional-Ammunition-StockpileManagement-for-the-Republic-of-Serbia-CASM/.

[11] See United Nations, Office on Drugs and Crime, 'UNODC/OSCE Agree New Joint Action Plan', 9 March 2016, available at: www.unodc.org/unodc/en/frontpage/2016/March/unodc-osce-agree-new-joint-action-plan.html.

[12] MOU between the OSCE Office for Democratic Institutions and Human Rights and the Office of the United Nations High Commissioner for Refugees, signed on 22 June 2011, available at: www.unhcr.org/partners/partners/4e0839166/memorandum-understanding-osce-office-democratic-institutions-human-rights.html. MOU between the General Secretariat of the ICPO–INTERPOL and the Secretariat of the OSCE in the area of Law Enforcement, Capacity Building and Training, signed on 27 May 2014, available at: www.osce.org/secretariat/119194.

[13] As noted by Anthony Aust, each MOU must be evaluated on a case-by-case basis, since its legal character depends primarily on the intention of the parties 'which must also be determined on the basis of factors other than (its) name, especially (its) wording', Aust, 'The Theory and Practice of Informal International Instruments', 800; see also Aust, 'Alternatives to Treaty-Making: MOUs as Political Commitments', 46–72; Klabbers, *The Concept of Treaty in International Law*.

arrangements and agreements without having to demonstrate their legal nature. This is possible as, in practice, many cooperation activities do not need to be implemented through international agreements. Instruments like MOU serve to advance internationally agreed goals. The use of these more flexible forms of cooperation has a further advantage as, contrary to the rather slow conventional process, they allow for a prompt response to the fast-paced developments faced by the Organization.[14]

Cooperative activities can take place within *joint initiatives*, such as the Environment and Security Initiative (ENVSEC Initiative). Established in 2003, the ENVSEC Initiative is a partnership of organisations – UNDP, the United Nations Economic Commission for Europe (UNECE), the United Nations Environment Programme (UNEP), the Regional Centre for Central and Eastern Europe (REC) and the OSCE – aimed at providing integrated responses to environmental and security challenges. Within this platform for cooperation, participating organisations bring their specialised mandate and know-how to strengthen cooperation on environmental issues in south-eastern Europe, eastern Europe, and the south Caucasus and central Asia regions.[15]

The OSCE also maintains a relationship with its Partners for Co-operation, consisting of five Asian and six Mediterranean countries, through ongoing dialogue and joint initiatives.[16] Asian and Mediterranean Partners of Co-operation are regularly invited as observers to attend meetings of the OSCE Ministerial Council, Permanent Council meetings and Forum for Security Co-operation meetings. Following a decision of the Permanent Council, the Contact Group with Asian Partners for Co-operation was launched in 2003.[17] The Partners for Co-operation also contribute to extra-budgetary projects implemented by the OSCE.[18]

[14] For a detailed analysis of more flexible forms of cooperation, see Gadkowski, Treaty-Making Powers of International Organizations, 39–57 and 245–292.

[15] Environment and Security Initiative, 'Transforming Risks into Cooperation', 2003–2017, available at: www.envsec.org/.

[16] Mediterranean Partners for Co-operation include Algeria, Egypt, Israel, Jordan, Morocco and Tunisia while Asian Partners for Co-operation include Afghanistan, Australia, Japan, the Republic of Korea and Thailand. See OSCE, 'Partners for Cooperation', 2017, available at: www.osce.org/partners-for-cooperation.

[17] OSCE, Permanent Council, Recommendations Concerning Future Applications for Partnership, PC.DEC/430, 19 July 2001.

[18] A good example of such an agreement is a three-year grant agreement signed by Australia and the OSCE on 21 February 2012 in support of the OSCE effort to combat the effects of human trafficking in central Asia, see Australian Embassy and Permanent Mission to the United Nations, Austria, 'Australia to support the OSCE's anti-human trafficking work in Central

Finally, cooperative arrangements between organisations may include a financial assistance component. The OSCE's lack of an explicitly recognised international legal personality does not seem to have hindered its entering into such cooperative arrangements and partnerships and, in practice, states and IOs have shown a willingness to engage in cooperation with the OSCE. When conducting activities with other IOs, the OSCE concludes cost-sharing agreements, a good example being the 2014 third-party cost-sharing agreement between the OSCE and UNDP within the ENVSEC Initiative Trust Fund.[19] When it receives funds from states to conduct an activity, the OSCE concludes a *grant agreement*. In practice, this category of agreements is governed by international law.

3 THE GRANTING OF OBSERVER STATUS

The practice of granting observer status counts as another meaningful facet of the possible external relations available to an institutional actor. It is indeed the most widespread and direct way of establishing institutional relations. The granting of observer status is important because it allows the organisations concerned to exchange information and coordinate their respective policies with one another. In addition, with respect to the OSCE, it constitutes an acknowledgment by other entities of the international profile of the organisation, it facilitates the establishment of official relationships with other IOs and helps to ascertain its autonomous status at the international level. It also increases transparency between organisations, as well as a greater harmonisation and coherence in their activities.[20]

In May 1993, the OSCE (at that time called the Conference on Security and Cooperation in Europe; CSCE) and the UN agreed upon a Framework for Co-operation and Co-ordination. The OSCE was qualified by its participating States as 'a regional arrangement in the sense of Chapter VIII of the United Nations'.[21] In addition, upon its request, the Organization was granted in 1993 observer status based on the UN General Assembly Resolution 48/5, in which

Asia', 21 February 2012, available at: https://austria.embassy.gov.au/vien/OSCEMediaRelease OSCEMediaRelease.html.

[19] Third-party Cost-sharing Agreement between the Organization for Security and Co-operation in Europe, represented by its Secretariat (OSCE) and the United Nations Development Program (UNDP), 26 June 2013, available at: https://info.undp.org/docs/pdc/Documents/MNE/CSA%20OSCE%20UNDP%20ADA%20%202013%20transfer%20EnvSec%20phase%20II.pdf.

[20] See Dupuy, 'Le droit des relations entre les organisations internationales', 457–589.

[21] CSCE, Helsinki Document, Challenges of Change, 9–10 July 1992, available at: www.osce.org/mc/39530?download=true, point 25. Framework for Co-operation and Co-

the General Assembly noted the desire of the OSCE to intensify its cooperation with the UN.[22] The two organisations have subsequently strengthened their inter-institutional cooperation. For example, the OSCE participates in UN Security Council meetings with regional organisations dedicated to thematic issues related to peace and security, held annually since 2003. There are also annual UN–OSCE staff-level meetings to exchange information and coordinate activities. Moreover, UN agencies and missions together with the OSCE cooperate closely within field operations. The best example of such cooperation is the OSCE Mission in Kosovo, which constitutes an integral part of the UN Mission in Kosovo.

Though the OSCE has established close relationships with numerous international organisations and institutions, it is yet to grant any of them permanent observer status; there is no agreement among the participating States on this issue. As a compromise, the OSCE has granted the Council of Europe (CoE) an observer seat, albeit on a weekly basis and it is unclear how long this arrangement will last. The EU, for its part, has a special status within the OSCE. In this context, the participation of EU institutions in OSCE proceedings are based on a longstanding practice formalised in 2006 with the adoption by the OSCE Ministers of the Organization's Rules of Procedure, which granted the European Commission a seat next to the participating State holding the rotating EU Presidency.[23] This was revised, however, in order to take into account the EU's new profile and the changes made to the governance of the EU's external relations introduced in 2009 by the Treaty of Lisbon. These changes include the establishment of the High Representative of the Union for Foreign Affairs and Security Policy, and the division of competences between the EU and its member states provided for in the Treaty, the latter resulting from the desire of EU member states to achieve a high degree

ordination between the United Nations Secretariat and the CSCE, exchange of letters between the Secretary General of the United Nations and the Chairman-in-Office of the Council of the Conference on Security and Cooperation in Europe, A/48/185, 26 May 1993, Annexes I and II.

22 United Nations, General Assembly, Observer Status for the Conference on Security and Cooperation in Europe in the General Assembly, A/RES/48/5, 22 October 1993. The OSCE is listed on the United Nations, General Assembly, List of non-Member States, entities and organisations having received a standing invitation to participate as observers in the sessions and the work of the General Assembly, A/INF/71/5, 12 January 2017, in its Part III 'Intergovernmental organizations having received a standing invitation to participate as observers in the sessions and the work of the General Assembly.'

23 OSCE, Ministerial Council, 'Rules of Procedure of the Organization for Security and Co-operation in Europe', MC.DOC/1/06, 1 November 2006, Art. IV.2 (B) 11 of the Rules provides that: 'At the meetings of the decision-making bodies, the European Commission shall have one seat next to the participating State holding the EU Presidency.'

of cooperation in foreign policy and defence.[24] The Treaty consolidated institutional evolution by providing for a merger into one organisation, the EU, with a single legal personality.[25] Since the entry into force of the Treaty of Lisbon on 1 December 2009, the EU Delegation to the International Organisations in Vienna is regarded as being part of the Delegation of the OSCE participating State holding the rotating Presidency of the Council of the EU. It participates in all proceedings except those concerning issues that fall outside the scope of the EU.

In practice, the international legal status of observers varies. That said, the granting of an observership allows for official relations to be established and contributes to greater visibility and autonomy at the international level.

4 A SPECIAL RELATIONSHIP WITH ORGANISATIONS IN EUROPE

The OSCE has a special relationship with several organisations based in or linked to Europe. As previously mentioned, the relationship with the EU is distinct in many respects from other organisations. All member states of the EU are participating States of the OSCE, which results in a special relationship between the two institutions, and over the years cooperation between both entities has developed significantly. Interestingly, the Treaty of Lisbon refers expressly to cooperation between the two. Article 220 of the Treaty on the Functioning of the European Union (TFEU) provides that: 'The Union shall establish all appropriate forms of cooperation with the organs of the United Nations and its specialized agencies, the Council of Europe, the Organization for Security and Co-operation in Europe and the Organization for Economic Cooperation and Development.' Both the EU and the OSCE share similar interests and pursue common objectives. This is reflected in Article 21 (2)(c) of the Treaty on European Union (TEU), which states:

> The Union shall define and pursue common policies and actions, and shall work for a high degree of cooperation in all fields of international relations, in order to preserve peace, prevent conflicts and strengthen international security, in accordance with the purposes and principles of the United Nations

24 Consolidated Versions of the Treaty on European Union and Treaty on the Functioning of the European Union, 9 May 2008, Official Journal of the EU 2008/C 115/01, Art. 1(3); see also Kuijper, 'Superpower Frustrated?', 10.

25 Treaty of Lisbon amending the Treaty on European Union and the Treaty establishing the European Community, 13 December 2007, Official Journal of the EU 2007/C 306/01.

Charter, with the principles of the Helsinki Final Act and with the aims of the Charter of Paris, including those relating to external borders.

OSCE–EU cooperation is both political and operational. They pursue a permanent dialogue, for example, via cross-representation at meetings, contacts between the Secretary General of the OSCE and the High Representative of the Union for Foreign Affairs and Security Policy, and consultations between the OSCE Troika and EU officials. Moreover, the Heads of OSCE field operations cooperate and coordinate with EU representatives in host countries.

The EU's active support of OSCE initiatives and the strong ties between them are also reflected in financial contributions. The OSCE is funded by contributions from its fifty-seven participating States. In 2015 the contributions of EU member states to the OSCE's unified budget amounted to roughly EUR 100 million, which is more than two-thirds of the OSCE's main budget.[26] Moreover, the EU itself and its member states contribute to the funding of a number of extra-budgetary projects. A recent example is the EU's support for the OSCE Special Monitoring Mission to Ukraine (SMM). The contributions from the EU and its member states amounted to around two-thirds of the SMM budget.[27]

In addition to its special relationship with the EU, the OSCE cooperates closely with other IOs, and most importantly with the Council of Europe and the North Atlantic Treaty Organization (NATO). The need for cooperation with these organisations is essential, particularly given the overlaps in their respective mandates, agendas and, to a great extent, their memberships.

Cooperation between the OSCE and the Council of Europe, based as it is on the common values of democracy, human rights and the rule of law, resulted in the 2000 Common Catalogue of Co-operation Modalities compiled by the Secretariats of both organisations.[28] This document aimed at 'guaranteeing the institutional memory and ensuring that existing good practice (was) not forgotten or lost'.[29] In order to review cooperation and identify areas for enhanced cooperation, a Co-ordination Group between the OSCE and the CoE was established in 2004.[30] With the objective of enhancing

[26] OSCE, The OSCE Annual Report 2015, 13 May 2016, available at: https://www.osce.org/annual-report/2015.

[27] Ibid., 102–3.

[28] Council of Europe, Relations between the Council of Europe and the OSCE. Common Catalogue of Co-operation Modalities, Committee of Ministers Documents 2000/52, 25 April 2000.

[29] Ibid., Introduction.

[30] The Co-ordination Group meets on a bi-annual basis in Strasbourg and in Vienna.

collaboration between the organisations, the Permanent Council of the OSCE adopted in 2005 a Declaration on Co-operation between the CoE and the OSCE.[31] The OSCE and the CoE agreed in the document to explore various forms of cooperation 'as joint meetings and joint activities, with more active involvement of the member and participating States, in order to produce synergies and avoid unnecessary duplication, giving the fullest account however to the different nature and membership of the two organisations, and make best use of their comparative advantages'.

To favour synergies between the two organisations, four priority areas for enhanced cooperation have been identified. These are (1) the fight against terrorism, (2) the combatting of human trafficking, (3) the promotion of tolerance and non-discrimination, and (4) protecting the rights of persons belonging to national minorities.

Because of the OSCE and NATO's complementary roles in building security and maintaining stability, the two organisations cooperate closely at both the political and operational levels. This close cooperation is reflected in the wording of the Istanbul Summit Communiqué, which states: 'NATO and the OSCE have largely complementary responsibilities and common interests, both functionally and geographically. NATO will continue to further develop cooperation with the OSCE in areas such as conflict prevention, crisis management and post-conflict rehabilitation.'[32]

However, in contrast to the OSCE's cooperation with the UN or the EU, cooperation with NATO is not framed in an overarching political document.[33] Relations between the two organisations at the political level are maintained through activities like addresses by the NATO Secretary General to the OSCE Permanent Council, regular contact between the Secretaries General of both organisations, cross-representation at meetings, and annual staff-level talks on topical issues that are on the agenda of each organisation.[34]

5 OTHER TYPES OF PARTNERSHIPS

IOs increasingly interact and cooperate with a wide range of new actors to achieve common goals. In this context, assistance provided by non-state actors

[31] OSCE, Permanent Council, Decision on Co-operation between the Council of Europe and the Organization for Security and Co-operation in Europe, PC.DEC/670, 26 April 2005.

[32] NATO, Press Release 096, 28 June 2004, available at: www.nato.int/docu/pr/2004/p04-096e.htm.

[33] Zwarenburg, 'What's in a Word?', 112.

[34] On the political cooperation between the two organisations, see Trifunovska, *North Atlantic Treaty Organization (NATO)*, paras. 314–330A.

can be useful. Non-state actors – such as individuals, NGOs, foundations, scientific associations and the private sector more broadly – play an increasingly important role in the life of IOs. New tools have been put in place to allow for close collaboration with these actors.

In field operations, the Organization works closely with a range of governmental agencies and institutions, UN agencies, IOs and NGOs. For example, the OSCE Office in Yerevan (Armenia), in cooperation with UNDP, regional authorities and local communities helped rehabilitate an irrigation canal preventing land pollution. The Office, together with the Armenian Ministry of Justice and a national civil society coalition, brought together representatives from businesses, government and civil society to examine how risk assessment, codes of ethics and corporate social responsibility could help address challenges faced by the private sector.[35] The OSCE Mission to Montenegro along with the Ministry of the Interior and UNDP, and with support of the EU, the German Government and the NGO Centre for Democratic Transition, launched the public campaign 'Respect Life – Return Weapons' with the aim of raising awareness about the danger posed by small arms and light weapons as well as facilitating the collection of unwanted weapons.[36]

Moreover, the OSCE cooperates and develops operational relations with institutions involved in economic and environmental activities. The development of such cooperation is coordinated by the Office of the Co-ordinator of OSCE Economic and Environmental Activities (OCEEA). The primary objective of OCEEA is to assist OSCE participating States in strengthening security and stability in the OSCE area by promoting cooperation on economic and environmental issues. The OCEEA provides a platform for dialogue between civil society representatives and government counterparts on a variety of good governance and anti-corruption issues. It also supports capacity building and anti-corruption training programmes for civil society. The activities of the OCEEA, for example, stretch from anti-money laundering, migration and water management, to developing more efficient border and customs policies. A good example of such activities is the OCEEA's continuous support for the operation and networking of the Aarhus Centres operating in fourteen countries throughout the OSCE area and aimed at the promotion and implementation of the Convention on Access to Information, Public Participation in Decision-Making and Access to Justice in Environmental Matters (Aarhus Convention).[37]

[35] OSCE, OSCE Annual Report 2015 (n. 25), 78.

[36] Ibid., 61.

[37] Ibid., 38. During the 2015 Annual Aarhus Centres Meeting, Aarhus Centres from Albania, Bosnia and Herzegovina, Montenegro and Serbia signed a Joint Declaration for Co-operation,

6 RELATIONSHIPS WITH OTHER IOS IN THE AREA OF PEACE AND SECURITY AND THE RESPONSIBILITY TEST

The relationships between the UN Security Council and regional organisations have evolved in the area of the maintenance of international peace and security since the 1990s. The end of the Cold War was accompanied by a reactivation of the UN Security Council and a strengthening of the use of regional organisations. This was the case with the OSCE. Participating States of the OSCE declared their organization to be a UN Charter Chapter VIII arrangement in 1992.[38] Moreover, the lack of financial and military resources available to the UN Security Council for the implementation of the collective security system, as foreseen in the United Nations Charter, led the UN Security Council to turn more often to regional organisations to share the burden of this responsibility. This could lead one to think that there would be an increasing invocation of Chapter VIII of the UN Charter, which deals with regional arrangements. This, however, is not the case.[39] The practice of the UN Security Council varies in its reference to Chapter VII as well as to Chapter VIII for authorising the security operations of a regional organisation.[40] This shows that, in reality, discussions on the conditions for the invocation of Chapter VII or VIII are of little interest to the UN Security Council, with the UN body using different legal forms for its cooperation with regional organisations.[41] Pragmatism and flexibility appear to explain this situation.

The abovementioned situation has given rise to hybrid models of cooperation between the UN and regional organisations. This was the case with UNMIK: the magnitude, diversity and complexity of the responsibilities of the international civil presence in Kosovo led the United Nations Secretary General to develop new types of cooperation with regional organisations willing to participate in the administration of the territory in question.[42] Each UNMIK component was to be led by a Deputy Special Representative of the UN Secretary General, whose appointment is proposed by the

see OSCE, OSCE-supported Aarhus Centres in South-East Europe sign Joint Declaration, 3 June 2015, available at: www.osce.org/secretariat/161921.

38 CSCE, Helsinki Document, 1992 (n. 20), point 25.

39 See the observations of Sicilianos, 'Entre multilatéralisme et unilatéralisme', 267.

40 Daillier, 'L'Intervention des organisations internationales dans les conflits armés', 63; Gray, *International Law and the Use of Force*, 284.

41 Gaja, 'The Use of Force Made or Authorized by the United Nations', 53.

42 United Nations, Security Council, Resolution 1244 (1999) adopted by the Security Council at its 4011th meeting, 10 June 1999, s. 11.

organisation bearing primary responsibility for the respective domain but decided upon and implemented by the UN Secretary General.

Activities in the pillars in question form an integral part of the UN operation since they are placed under the authority and supervision of the Special Representative of the UN Secretary General.[43] Nevertheless, issues of command and control arise between the UN, which leads the operation, and the EU and OSCE, which have responsibility in a specific pillar. An open question is whether the pillar structure impacts upon the allocation of international responsibility between different organisations.[44]

In the context of cooperation, the OSCE's lack of an explicitly acknowledged legal personality makes legal and operational relationships with other IOs more complex. A direct reference to the issue of international legal personality in the UN International Law Commission's Draft Articles on the Responsibility of International Organizations appears to be of material significance, since an IO having no legal personality cannot, in general, be held responsible for its acts; responsibility would instead be bestowed on its members.[45] In the context of IOs, personality is a precondition of responsibility. There are still many questions about whether the OSCE is or is not a subject of international law, and if it can incur international responsibility for its acts despite the lack of a clear legal status.[46] The strengthening of the legal framework of the OSCE would lead to a more effective and efficient functioning of the Organization.

More generally, the uncertainty as to the legal status of the OSCE may result in a reluctance of other organisations and institutions to establish relations with it. To use the expression referred to in the Report to the Ministerial Council on Strengthening the Legal Framework of the OSCE in 2012, 'the lack of legal personality causes reputational damage, since other regional or international organisations may fail to take the OSCE seriously as

43 United Nations, Secretary General, Report of the Secretary-General on the United Nations Interim Administration Mission in Kosovo, S/1999/779, 12 July 1999, s. 43. Friedrich, 'UNMIK in Kosovo', 237; Hofmann, 'International Protection of Human Rights and International Territorial Administration', 128.

44 Hoffmeister, 'Inter-pillar Coherence in the European Union's Civilian Crisis Management', 155 *et seq*.

45 United Nations, International Law Commission, Report of the ILC to the General Assembly for the Year 2009, 64th Session, Supplement No. 10, UN Doc. A/64/10, 4 February 2010, 86; see also Steinbrück Platise, 'Legitimate Governance as a Privilege and Price for the Autonomy of International Organisations', Chapter 14, Section 4, in this Volume.

46 See Blokker and Wessel, 'Revisiting Questions of Organisationhood, Legal Personality and Membership in the OSCE: The Interplay between Law, Politics and Practice', Chapter 7 in this Volume.

a proper organisation or, in some cases, may be unable to deal with the OSCE as a partner'.[47]

The question of responsibility is even more apparent in relations between the OSCE and states in which the Organization operates, as national courts may engage the responsibility of either the Organization or the officials working on behalf of the Organization. In practice, the status of the OSCE and its officials varies significantly. In some participating States, both the Organization and its officials have legal status and enjoy privileges and immunities. These are mostly the countries that host OSCE offices and centres: Austria for the OSCE Secretariat, the Netherlands with respect to the OSCE High Commissioner on National Minorities, Switzerland in relation to the OSCE Court of Conciliation and Arbitration, and Denmark with respect to the OSCE Parliamentary Assembly. In other participating States, the OSCE has legal status and enjoys privileges and immunities in accordance with MOUs concluded between the Organization and the respective countries. In other countries, no national measures addressing the status of the Organization nor the privileges and immunities for OSCE officials exist. The OSCE presence and legal status in Kosovo is particularly interesting in this context as the OSCE field operation enjoys legal status and privileges and immunities by virtue of UN Security Council Resolution 1244 (1999).[48]

7 CONCLUDING REMARKS

Undeniably, the lack of an explicitly recognised international legal personality does not prevent the OSCE from being an active player on the international plane. It has not reduced the willingness of states and IOs to engage in cooperative activities with the OSCE, and the Organization has developed a wide array of external relations with international institutions, states and non-state actors.

That said, uncertainty regarding legal status may limit and hinder the ability of the OSCE to act in the field where it is most needed, for instance, in solving crisis situations. Due to the extension of the scope of the activities of the Organization, the mandate of the OSCE often overlaps with the activities of

[47] OSCE, Ministerial Council, Report of the Ministerial Council on Strengthening the Legal Framework of the OSCE in 2012, MC.GAL/15/12, 7 December 2012, 2.

[48] The Special Representative of the Secretary-General, pursuant to its authority deriving from UN Security Council resolution 1244 (1999), has issued Regulation On the status, privileges and immunities of KFOR and UNMIK and their personnel in Kosovo, in which immunities have been granted also to the OSCE and its personnel Regulation No. 2000/47, 18 August 2000, available at: www.unmikonline.org/regulations/2000/reg47-00.htm.

other IOs. This has led the OSCE to favour synergies through more or less elaborated forms of cooperation. In this context, the OSCE is certainly not 'lost in transition', nor 'lost in translation', but is rather gaining a more established profile.

REFERENCES

Aust, Anthony, 'Alternatives to Treaty-Making: MOUs as Political Commitments', in Duncan Hollis (ed.), *The Oxford Guide to Treaties* (Oxford: Oxford University Press, 2012), 46–72.

'The Theory and Practice of Informal International Instruments', *International and Comparative Law Quarterly* 38 (1986), 787–812.

Boisson de Chazournes, Laurence, *Interactions Between Regional and Universal Organizations: A Legal Perspective* (Leiden, Boston: Brill Nijhoff, 2016).

'Relations with other International Organizations', in Jacob Katz Cogan, Ian Hurd and Ian Johnstone (eds.), *Oxford Handbook on International Organizations* (Oxford: Oxford University Press, 2016), 691–711.

Daillier, Patrick, 'L'Intervention des organisations internationales dans les conflits armés. Sécurité "collective" et sécurité régionale', in Madjid Benchikh (ed.), *Les Organisations internationales et les conflits armés* (Paris: L'Harmattan, 2002).

De Pooter, Hélène, *Le droit international face aux pandémies: vers un système de sécurité collective?* (Paris: Pedone, 2015), 247–68.

Dupuy, René-Jean, 'Le droit des relations entre les organisations internationales', in *Collected Courses of the Hague Academy of International Law* (Leiden, Boston: Martinus Nijhoff, 1960) vol. 100, 457–589.

Friedrich, Jürgen, 'UNMIK in Kosovo: Struggling with Uncertainty', *Max Planck Yearbook of United Nations Law* 9 (2005), 225–93.

Gadkowski, Andrzej, Treaty-Making Powers of International Organizations (Poznan: Adam Mickiewicz University Press, 2018).

Gaja, Giorgio, 'The Use of Force Made or Authorized by the United Nations', in Christian Tomuschat (ed.), *United Nations at Age Fifty: A Legal Perspective* (The Hague, Boston, London: Kluwer Law International, 1995).

Gray, Christine, *International Law and the Use of Force* 3rd edn (Oxford: Oxford University Press, 2008).

Hoffmeister, Frank, 'Inter-pillar Coherence in the European Union's Civilian Crisis Management', in Steven Blockmans (ed.), *The European Union and Crisis Management: Policy and Legal Aspects* (The Hague: TMS Asser Press, 2008), 157–80.

Hofmann, Rainer, 'International Protection of Human Rights and International Territorial Administration: A Legal Black Hole', in

Andreas Fischer-Lescano, Hans-Peter Gasser, Thilo Marauhn and Natalino Ronzitti (eds.), *Frieden in Freiheit–Peace in Liberty–Paix en liberté: Festschrift für Michael Bothe zum 70. Geburtstag* (Baden-Baden, Berlin: Nomos Verlagsgesellschaft, 2008), 123–41.

Klabbers, Jan, *The Concept of Treaty in International Law* (The Hague: Kluwer Law International, 1996).

Klein, Pierre, 'Panels, médiateurs et mécanismes informels de contrôle des activités des organisations internationales: entre accountability et responsibility', in *Actes du colloque de la Société européenne de droit international (Cambridge)* (Oxford: Hart Publishing, 2012), 217–28.

Kuijper, Pieter-Jan, 'Superpower Frustrated? The Costs of Non-Lisbon in EU External Affairs', *German Yearbook of International Law* 51 (2008), 9–37.

Pacquée, Didier and Dewulf, Stewen 'International Territorial Administrations and the Rule of Law: The Case of Kosovo', *Essex Human Rights Review* 4 (2007), 1–14.

Sicilianos, Linos-Alexandre, 'Entre multilatéralisme et unilatéralisme: l'autorisation par le Conseil de sécurité de recourir à la force', *Collected Courses of the Hague Academy of International Law* (Leiden, Boston: Martinus Nijhoff, 2008) vol. 339 9–436.

Stribis, Ioannis, 'La présidence ukrainienne de l'OSCE en 2013. Opportunités et défis', Annuaire français de relations internationales 13 (2012), 141–57.

Trifunovska, Snežana, *North Atlantic Treaty Organization (NATO)* 2nd edn (Alphen aan den Rijn: Kluwer Law International, 2012).

Zwarenburg, Marten, 'What's in a Word? NATO "Partnerships" between NATO and Other International Institutions and Some Issues of Shared Responsibility', *International Organizations Law Review* 13 (2016), 100–25.

11

The International Legal Responsibility of the OSCE

Lorenzo Gasbarri

1 INTRODUCTION

At the beginning of the decade that gave birth to the Draft Articles on the Responsibility of International Organizations (ARIO),[1] the UN International Law Commission (ILC) had no doubts that the project would apply also to the OSCE. As early as 2002, the first report of the ILC working group included the OSCE within the definition of an intergovernmental organisation, established by means of a treaty 'or, in exceptional cases (such as that of OSCE), without a treaty'.[2] The working group stressed this position, stating that '[i]t is to be assumed that international law endows these international organizations with legal personality, because otherwise their conduct would be attributed to their members and no question of an organization's responsibility under international law would arise'.[3]

One year later, the ILC presented Article 2 'Use of Terms', in which international organisations were defined as being 'established by a treaty or other instrument governed by international law'.[4] The commentary to the ARIO at that time included a reference to the OSCE and explicitly acknowledged the application of the projected provisions to an implicit international agreement establishing an international organisation.[5] Shortly after, the 2003

[1] UN, International Law Commission, Draft Articles on the Responsibility of International Organizations A/CN.4/L.778, 31 May 2011.

[2] UN, International Law Commission, Yearbook of the International Law Commission 2002, Volume II, Part Two, A/CN.4/SER.A/2002/Add.1, 2002, para. 469.

[3] Ibid.

[4] UN, General Assembly, Report of the International Law Commission, A/58/10, 2003, para. 54, Art. 2.

[5] Ibid., para. 4 of the commentary to Art. 2: 'although an implicit agreement may be held to exist, member States insisted that there was no treaty concluded to that effect, as for example in respect of the Organization for Security and Cooperation in Europe (OSCE)'.

ILC report to the UN General Assembly acknowledged the unresolved issue of the OSCE's international legal personality, in parallel with the distinction between the European Community and the EU, by taking the position that it was something that 'the members of the two entities would have to solve'.[6]

The position with respect to the applicability of the ARIO and the unresolved international legal personality of the OSCE was maintained throughout the work of the ILC, and the commentary to its Article 2 was left unmodified until the final draft.[7] However, in 2011 Austria and the OSCE reacted to the ILC approach by submitting comments and observations. They both maintained that, for the time being, the OSCE is not an international organisation under Article 2 ARIO, it does not possess legal personality and it is not governed by international law.[8] As a consequence, the final commentary to Article 2 ARIO makes no reference to the OSCE.

Following the approach adopted by the ILC, this chapter could end now: without a clear legal status under international law, the conduct of the OSCE is attributable to its participating States which would be responsible for any breaches of international law.[9] More conveniently, the chapter could instead focus on the extremely complicated interactions of participating States' joint conduct, leading to their shared responsibility in the absence of a clear rule on joint and several obligations.[10] However, doing so would mean circumventing the topic of the OSCE's international responsibility, and it would bring us back to the time when scholars defined international organisations as states' common organs.[11]

International responsibility and a related obligation thereof to make reparations are the consequences that international law attaches to violations of its

6 UN, General Assembly, Report of the International Law Commission on the Work of its Fifty-Fifth Session (2003), A/CN.4/537, 21 January 2004, para. 37; Schermers and Blokker, *International Institutional Law*, para. 1569.

7 See UN, International Law Commission, First Report on Responsibility of International Organizations, Giorgio Gaja, Special Rapporteur, A/CN.4/532, 2003, para. 14; UN, International Law Commission, Summary record of the 2753rd meeting, A/CN.4/SR.2753, 2003, para. 27.

8 UN, International Law Commission, Responsibility of International Organizations: Comments and Observations Received from Governments, A/CN.4/636, 14 February 2011, 9; UN, International Law Commission, Responsibility of International Organizations: Comments and Observations Received from International Organizations, A/CN.4/637, 14 February 2011, 18.

9 Ryngaert, 'Basing the Legal Status of the OSCE on Participating States' Duty of Loyalty', 3 August 2016, available at: http://voelkerrechtsblog.org/basing-the-legal-status-of-the-osce-on-participating-states-duty-of-loyalty/.

10 See, in general, Nollkaemper and Plakokefalos, *Principles of Shared Responsibility*.

11 Anzilotti, 'Gli organi comuni'.

rules.[12] In the context of international organisations, one of the main questions is whether their structure allows for an assumption of responsibility separate from their member states.[13] International responsibility is an attribute of autonomy, but the problem is that no organisation is truly independent from its member states. In the framework of this debate, the OSCE took an extreme position claiming that it cannot even be considered a proper international organisation.[14]

This chapter will start from the assumption that the existence of the OSCE depends neither on it being governed by international law nor on the presence or absence of legal personalities, which are conferred by the legal systems in which it acts. It will deal with the OSCE's international responsibility by distinguishing three different but correlated phenomena: (1) its capacity to develop a legal system; (2) its possession of legal personality, whether international or domestic, does not compromise the existence of the institution as such; and (3) how its international responsibility is dependent upon the fact that the OSCE is either considered as founded by an instrument of international law or by an act of creation not based on international law.

Too much attention has been dedicated to the importance of the legal personality of international organisations and too little to the study of their capacity to develop a legal system. Indeed, we can doubt the presence of legal personality, and we can doubt that the OSCE is governed by international law, but we cannot doubt the fact that the OSCE exists, performs its functions and has developed a normative system. For instance, the chapter will later describe how the OSCE's human dimension creates an internal normative system despite the Organization's unclear relation to international law.[15] Indeed, the use of the expression 'normative system' will not find opposition from those who consider the OSCE a source of political and not legal obligations. Every institution develops a system of norms that governs its internal functioning, whether we call them political or legal norms. It is a different and more pertinent issue to determine the relation that international organisations have with international law.

The nature of the legal system developed by an international organisation pivots around a dichotomy between 'original' and 'derivative'.[16] For example,

12 PCIJ, *Case Concerning the Factory at Chorzów (Claim for Indemnity) (Germany* v. *Poland)*, Judgment of 26 July 1927, Series A n. 9, 21.

13 Klabbers, *An Introduction to International Organizations Law*, 306.

14 ILC, Responsibility of International Organizations: Comments and Observations Received from Governments, 14 February 2011 (n. 8).

15 Barberini, *Sicurezza e cooperazione*, 165.

16 Cahier, 'L'ordre juridique interne'.

the EU can be considered an international organisation derived from international law and producing international law, or it can be understood as an institution that it is not based on international law and producing law which is internal in nature.[17] The latter conceptualisation produces a legal system that is 'original' in the sense of not being based on something that existed before. 'Originality' may take various forms: in the case of the EU it is represented by the claim of being 'exceptional', while in the case of the OSCE, it is represented by the claim that the Organization is political in nature. We will discuss this point in Section 3, as it is similar to the criticism of the concept of soft law (that is, a critique of the idea that obligations can be more or less binding).[18]

Thus, the chapter will focus on how the international responsibility of the OSCE is affected as much by the nature of its legal system as by the absence or presence of international legal personality. This choice follows the traditional distinction between the attribution of conduct and the violation of an obligation.[19] As we will see, the characteristics of the legal system developed by international organisations have fundamental consequences for the attribution of conduct.

This chapter does not define once and for all what the OSCE is and how its legal responsibility is to be assessed, but instead discusses the potential consequences that different legal conceptions would have on its responsibility. Section 2 further discusses the interaction between legal personality and the development of an 'original' or 'derivative' legal system. Section 3 then outlines four possibilities: (1) the OSCE possesses a derivative legal system and does not have international legal personality; (2) the OSCE possesses a derivative legal system and does have international legal personality; (3) the OSCE possesses an original legal system and does not have international legal personality; and (4) the OSCE possesses an original legal system and does have international legal personality.

2 LEGAL PERSONALITY AND THE DEVELOPMENT OF A LEGAL SYSTEM

Legal personality, the capacity to hold rights and obligations under a given legal system, is conferred by the legal system in which an entity performs its actions.[20] In its process of institutionalisation, the OSCE has been subjected to

[17] Compare, for instance, Pellet, 'Les fondements juridiques' with Ličková, 'European Exceptionalism'.

[18] Klabbers, *The Concept of Treaty*, 157.

[19] Stern, 'The Elements of an Internationally Wrongful Act'.

[20] Klabbers, *An Introduction to International Organizations Law*, 43.

different attempts at recognising its legal personality within different legal systems.[21] While in national legal systems the conferral of legal personality is governed by national law, the international system allows for an implicit mechanism that confers legal personality onto an organisation even against the will of the entity in question or of its founders.[22] Concerning the OSCE, there is a risk of misleading this finding, sustaining that legal personality flows directly from the existence of the entity.[23] The OSCE is commonly anthropomorphised, the logic being that the then Conference for Security and Cooperation in Europe (CSCE) matured with the passage of time, acquiring along the way the status of 'organisation' and, finally, international legal personality.[24] For example, scholars affiliated with the OSCE legal service have considered that 'at the 1994 Budapest Review Conference, the participating States agreed that the CSCE had become too mature to be called a "Conference"', and they called for final recognition of international legal personality.[25]

Conversely, the finding that international legal personality is something different from the development of a legal system has been acknowledged since studies on international organisations began. Already in 1938, Riccardo Monaco sustained that the internal functioning of an organisation does not depend on its possession of a plurality of legal personalities within multiple national or international regimes.[26] Eighty years later, this description resembles the status of the OSCE. In order to grant legal personality, different options based on different concepts of organisation have been suggested.[27] Some states suggest the adoption of a constitutive document, while others favour merely the adoption of a convention on legal personality. This controversy shows that the two elements are conceptually different.[28]

21 Starting from CSCE, Fourth Meeting of the Council CSCE and the New Europe – Our Security is Indivisible. Decisions of the Rome Council Meeting, 1993; Sapiro, 'Changing the CSCE into the OSCE'.

22 Brölmann, *The Institutional Veil*, 85.

23 Bertrand, 'La nature juridique'.

24 Brander and Martin Estebanez, 'The OSCE Matures'.

25 Ibid., 3.

26 Monaco, Riccardo, 'I regolamenti interni': 'sia che gli enti di cui si tratta si evolvano tanto da abbandonare la loro qualità di organi o di istituti per diventare persone giuridiche internazionali, sia che invece si muovano nell'ordinamento giuridico di più Stati senza divenire soggetti dell'ordinamento internazionale, la loro situazione nei confronti del loro funzionamento interno non muta'. More recently, a similar reasoning is considered in Amerasinghe, *Principles of the Institutional Law*, 67.

27 OSCE, Report to The Ministerial Council on Strengthening the Legal Framework of the OSCE in 2015, MC.GAL/4/15, 1 December 2015, para. 4.

28 Brander, 'Making a Credible Case'.

Different definitions picture the OSCE as a non-binding conference of states, as a soft law organisation providing for soft security or as a primitive international organisation.[29] These different theses have in common the unclear legal nature of the Organization's internal normative system.[30] The OSCE is not the only organisation affected by the absence of a clear understanding of its capacity to develop a legal system, even if the consequences are more pronounced due to its unclear relation with international law.

On the one hand, organisations can be perceived as having an 'original' legal system, under which their norms do not belong to international law.[31] On the other hand, organisations can be perceived as being derived from international law, under which the nature of their legal system comes from the will of member states, which are regarded as primary subjects of international law.[32] The uncertain legal nature of the rules of international organisations – as either 'derived' from international law or as 'original' – was recently discussed in the context of international responsibility.[33] The difference between original and derivative legal systems seems to depend on the interpretation of an organisation's constitutive instrument, which can be viewed as a constitution or as a contract.[34] Scholars have debated the issue since the 1960s, focusing mainly on the development of the EU's legal system by the European Court of Justice (ECJ),[35] but the concept has a famous ancestor in the work of Santi Romano.[36] Romano explains the relationships among legal systems with the concept of relevance/irrelevance, which is a legal relation based on the ways that legal systems interconnect independently from any de facto balance of power.[37] To use a contemporary example, the 'relevance' of UN Security Council Resolutions for the EU would be determined by the formal interaction of their legal systems and not by factual circumstances determined by relative distributions of political power. In particular, the two

29 Dominguez, *The OSCE*.

30 Prevost, 'Observations sur la nature juridique'.

31 Sereni, *Le organizzazioni*.

32 Decleva, *Il diritto interno*.

33 UN, International Law Commission, Draft Articles on the Responsibility of International Organizations with Commentaries, in Yearbook of the International Law Commission 2011, Volume II, Part Two, A/CN.4/SER.A/2011/Add.1, commentary to Art. 10.

34 Cahier, 'L'ordre juridique interne'; A. Peters, 'Das Gründungsdokument internationaler Organisationen als Verfassungsvertrag', *Zeitschrift für öffentliches Recht* 68 (2013), 1–57.

35 ECJ, *van Gend & Loos* v. *Nederlandse Administratie der Belastingen*, judgment of 5 February 1963, case 26/62; ECJ, *Costa v. ENEL* judgment of 15 July 1964, case 6/64.

36 Romano, *L'Ordinamento giuridico*.

37 Schultz, *Transnational Legality*, 86.

legal systems are independent of each other but they share the same relation to international law. Concrete consequences imply that UN Security Council Resolutions and EU Regulations have the same position in their relationship with international law, defying the contrast between 'internal' and 'international' that the ECJ had introduced.[38]

Among different criteria to determine the 'relevance' between legal systems, Santi Romano made a distinction between originality and derivation. Legal systems are original when they are not established by a legal instrument belonging to a different legal system (e.g. states). Conversely, legal systems are derivative when they are established by a legal instrument belonging to a different legal system (e.g. international organisations). This relation between existing and newly developed legal system is independent from the possession of legal personality in the latter. Obviously, a legal system cannot exist without its founder subjects, but the same subjects can create either an original or a derivative system.

The two faces of international organisations have long been discussed,[39] particularly in terms of the transparent quality of their institutional veil.[40] The expression 'transparency' was first used by René-Jean Dupuy in the context of the law of treaties. Dupuy considered that 'à l'ordre juridique unique et "intégré" de l'Etat s'oppose également l'opacité ou la transparence, selon le cas, des ordres juridiques propres à chaque Organisation internationale'.[41] The debates on the position of member states in the treaty concluded by the organisation reflect that they are neither parties nor third parties to the organisation, and the institutional veil of the organisation can be considered as either 'transparent' or 'opaque' in the following way: if conceived as original legal entities, organisations possess a closed ('opaque') structure in the same way in which states are opaque. This is how 'EU exceptionalism' is traditionally considered.[42] Conversely, if conceived as derivative legal entities, organisations possess an open ('transparent') structure based on the concept of a forum, under which the conduct of member states remains visible. This is how the North Atlantic Treaty Organization (NATO) is traditionally considered.[43] From this distinction derives the academic

38 ECJ, *Kadi and Al Barakaat International Foundation* v. *Council and Commission*, Judgment of 3 September 2008, C-402/05 P and C-415/05 P, para. 280.

39 Virally, *L'Organisation mondiale*.

40 Brölmann, *The Institutional Veil*.

41 'The single and "integrated" legal order of the state contrasts with the opacity or, depending on the context, transparency of the legal system of each international organisation.' Institut de Droit International, *Annuaire de l'Institut de Droit International*, 221.

42 White, *The Law of International Organisations*, 8.

43 Ibid., 76.

debate about the existence of either separate legal systems (original and opaque)[44] or the presence of constant permeability (derivative and transparent).[45] The former traces a clear distinction between the responsibility of an international organisation in the international system, in the internal system of the organisation and in national systems.[46] The latter was developed by the ILC, where Special Rapporteur Giorgio Gaja devoted a fundamental role to *lex specialis*, implying a permeability between the international legal system and an organisation's legal system.[47] For example, Article 64 ARIO states that the project does not apply where the internal rules of an organisation constitute *lex specialis*.[48] Only when an organisation's legal system is not separated from international law the *lex specialis/lex generalis* dynamic plays a role in relation to internal rules.

The OSCE is affected by the double nature of its legal system to a similar extent experienced by other organisations. In terms of international responsibility, the two faces of international organisation have outstanding implications concerning the relationship between member states and the organisation in question. Indeed, if an organisation is considered an original entity, member states tend to become internal organs; conversely, if an organisation is considered an entity derived from international law, member states tend to become third parties. In practice, even the same organisation is often considered to wear one or the other face, depending on circumstances and necessities of argument.[49] For example, the EU is traditionally considered as a closed autonomous entity before World Trade Organization panels, but as a vehicle for member states before the European Court of Human Rights.

The nature of the legal systems possessed by international organisations affects the essential question of whether it is possible to establish a general regime of responsibility, or whether every organisation is subject to a *sui generis* responsibility regime.[50] The perception of organisations as having

44 Focsanenau, 'Le droit interne'.

45 Balladore Pallieri, 'Le droit interne'.

46 Klein, *La responsabilité des organisations internationales*.

47 Forteau, 'Régime général'.

48 UN, International Law Commission, Draft Articles on the Responsibility of International Organizations with Commentaries 2011 (n. 33), Art. 64: 'These articles do not apply where and to the extent that the conditions for the existence of an internationally wrongful act or the content or implementation of the international responsibility of an international organization, or a State in connection with the conduct of an international organization, are governed by special rules of international law. Such special rules of international law may be contained in the rules of the organization applicable to the relations between an international organization and its members.'

49 Gaja, 'Note introductive'.

50 Wouters and Odermatt, 'Are All International Organizations Created Equal?'.

either original or derived legal systems makes general rules difficult to apply. It is not by chance that the OSCE proposed to move Article 64 on *lex specialis* to Part One of the ILC draft in order to reaffirm that exception is the rule.[51] In that respect, the OSCE's exceptionalism is no different from the EU's exceptionalism.[52] They both demand special treatment due to the unclear nature of their legal systems.

The EU requires that the conduct of its member states be considered as the EU's own conduct when the member states are performing actions under its exclusive competence.[53] It contends that its legal system is so autonomous that member states are transformed into quasi-organs of the organisation, not unlike in a federal state. In sum, it requires to be treated as an original legal system with international legal personality. Conversely, the OSCE's 'request' for exceptionalism requires that the organisation be treated as an original legal system without international legal personality.[54]

The OSCE, as much as every other international organisation, is constrained by a combination of two interacting elements: (1) the nature of its legal system, which can be perceived as either original or derivative; and (2) international legal personality, which it either possesses or it does not. If it is a derived entity without legal personality, only participating States can be internationally responsible (Section 3.1). If it is a derived entity with legal personality, the OSCE can incur legal responsibility and it is subject to the general regime envisaged by the ILC (Section 3.2). If it is an original entity without legal personality, the OSCE is subject only to its internal system of compliance (Section 3.3). Whereas if it is an original entity with legal personality, the OSCE is treated similar to a federal state and can therefore incur legal responsibility under international law (Section 3.4).

[51] ILC, Responsibility of International Organizations, Comments and Observations Received from International Organizations, 14 February 2011 (n. 8), 40.

[52] Decaux, 'L'institutionalisation de la CSCE'.

[53] UN, International Law Commission, Responsibility of International Organizations Comments and Observations Received from Governments, A/CN.4/545, 22 June 2004, 28; UN, International Law Commission, Responsibility of International Organizations Comments and Observations Received from Governments, A/CN.4/556, 12 May 2005, 31; UN, International Law Commission, Responsibility of International Organizations Comments and Observations Received from Governments, A/CN.4/568, 12 May 2006, 127; ILC, Responsibility of International Organizations Comments and Observations Received from International Organizations, 14 February 2011 (n. 8).

[54] ILC, Responsibility of International Organizations, Comments and Observations Received from International Organizations, 14 February 2011 (n. 8).

3 FOUR ALTERNATIVE LEGAL CONCEPTIONS

3.1 *The OSCE's Legal System Is Derived from International Law and Does not Possess International Legal Personality*

In the first scenario, the OSCE is totally dependent on the conduct of its member states. It cannot conclude international agreements and it cannot incur international legal responsibility. However, the law it produces, whether binding or non-binding, is international in character. Its functioning is not different from a conference of the parties of an environmental treaty, instituted with limited administrative capacity.[55] Indeed, this way of conceptualising international institutions is not different from the Conference of the Parties to the United Nations Framework Convention on Climate Change (UNFCCC), which 'shall keep under regular review the implementation of the Convention and any related legal instruments that the Conference of the Parties may adopt, and shall make, within its mandate, the decisions necessary to promote the effective implementation of the Convention'.[56] Its structure can be more or less permanent, its activities more or less invasive, but it is incapable of creating a community of states that could separate itself from international law.

At the 1992 Helsinki Summit, the OSCE was defined as 'a forum for dialogue, negotiation and co-operation, providing direction and giving impulse to the shaping of the new Europe'.[57] At the same time, participating States made the first step towards a process of formalisation, declaring their understanding that the then CSCE was a regional arrangement in the sense of Chapter VIII of the UN Charter.[58] Since the failure of the 2000 Vienna Ministerial Meeting, the OSCE has remained ambivalent between formal structure and flexibility, reflecting the two concepts of international organisation based either on the original or derivative nature of its legal system.[59]

This image is usually criticised by supporters of the need for legal personality, describing the negative consequences of this situation, as in the case of the Special Monitoring Mission to Ukraine.[60] Under this first legal

55 Dupuy and Viñuales, *International Environmental Law*, 27.

56 UN Framework Convention on Climate Change, 9 May 1992, 1771 UNTS 107, Art. 7(2).

57 CSCE, Helsinki Document 1992: The Challenges of Change, Helsinki Summit Declaration, 9/10 July 1992, para. 22.

58 Ibid., Chapter IV (2); Ferrari-Bravo, 'Difficultés et perspectives'; Abass, *Regional Organizations*, 149.

59 Oberschmidt and Zellner, 'OSCE at the Crossroads'.

60 Tabassi, 'The Question of Legal Status for the OSCE and Implications for Ukraine', Helsinki +40 Supplementary Seminar: The OSCE's Lack of Legal Status – Challenges in Crisis Situations, Copenhagen, 27 April 2015.

conceptualisation, the OSCE is not independent from its participating States and does not enjoy privileges and immunities under international law, but in order to be able to fulfil its mandate it signed a Memorandum of Understanding with Ukraine granting it legal status within Ukraine's national legal system. In sum, following this conceptualisation, at the international level the OSCE is merely a forum that sets 'standards for international behaviour',[61] 'a transparent vehicle' used by participating States.[62] Indeed, less formalisation means greater transparency of the institutional veil.[63] For example, in the context of the Special Monitoring Mission to Ukraine, the OSCE would not have the capacity to present an international claim. In the unfortunate circumstance of officials deployed under the auspices of the OSCE suffering injuries, such as being kidnapped, the Organization would not be able to take legal action for demanding reparations. At the same time, the OSCE would not be itself responsible for injuries caused by its officials, as in cases of human rights violations.

Consequently, if the OSCE does not possess international legal personality, only its participating States would be responsible should violations of international law occur in the fulfilment of the OSCE's mandate. There are no issues concerning the piercing of the institutional veil of the Organization, due to its perfect transparency.[64] Actually, envisaging the responsibility of participating States is used as one of the arguments in favour of establishing international legal personality for the OSCE.[65] Despite this intention, participating States do not disappear behind the legal personality of a derived entity, as we will see in the second conceptualisation (see Section 3.2).[66] In order to ascertain the responsibility of participating States, the Articles on State Responsibility elaborated by the ILC are applicable. Complex but not insurmountable problems may arise in the context of joint conduct by participating States.[67]

Different issues arise when OSCE commitments are violated. Once it is clear that the Organization derives from international law, there is no need to distinguish between legally binding and politically binding obligations. This controversial issue arises from the practice of the so-called soft law, under

61 Lehne, 'Reviving the OSCE: European Security and the Ukraine Crisis', 22 September 2015, available at: http://carnegieeurope.eu/2015/09/22/reviving-osce-european-security-and-ukraine-crisis-pub-61362.

62 Ryngaert, 'Basing the Legal Status of the OSCE on Participating States' Duty of Loyalty' (n. 9).

63 Zagorski, 'Make the OSCE Institutions Less Dependent'.

64 Brölmann, 'Member States and International Legal Responsibility'.

65 Tabassi, 'The Question of Legal Status for the OSCE and Implications for Ukraine' (n. 60).

66 UN, International Law Commission, Second Report on Responsibility of International Organizations, Giorgio Gaja, Special Rapporteur, A/CN.4/541, 2004, para. 6.

67 Dominicé, 'Attribution of Conduct to Multiple States'.

which the law should not be a binary phenomenon but rather a matter of degree.[68] We cannot enter here into an exhaustive discussion, but it is interesting to note that legality as a matter of degree is mistakenly applied in the context of the OSCE to separate legal obligations from political or morally binding obligations. Under the soft-law thesis '[s]tates can intentionally decide to make their agreements legally binding in varying degrees, while remaining within one and the same (international) legal order'.[69] Conversely, what states do in the context of the OSCE is to call political what they pretend to be a non-legal obligation. The distinction between legal and political is in reality a distinction between international and non-international, and it has consequences only in the conceptualisations based on original legal system.[70] The derivative legal system cannot acknowledge the distinction between legally binding and politically binding obligations within the same (international) legal system, because it does not acknowledge different degrees of bindingness, but only an either/or option.

Moreover, internal dispute settlement mechanisms of the OSCE apply by virtue of the *lex specialis* rule on state responsibility. There is however no need to refer to accountability of the OSCE in order to describe the internal functioning of the OSCE.

3.2 *The OSCE's Legal System Derives from International Law, and Possesses International Legal Personality*

The idea that the OSCE could be transformed from a conference to an organisation was discussed during the 1990s, in parallel with the institution of permanent organs entrusted with the 'responsibility' for the implementation of OSCE decisions.[71] Despite the lack of a constitutive treaty, the OSCE was renamed as an intergovernmental organisation whose legal status (above all, its legal personality) remained however an open issue.[72] Under this concept, 'the OSCE is a subject of international law in the sense that it can incur international responsibility for its acts, despite the lack of a clear internal legal status'.[73]

68 Robilant, 'Genealogy of Soft Law'.
69 Klabbers, *The Concept of Treaty*.
70 See Section 3.3 of this chapter.
71 CSCE, 'Fourth Meeting of the Council CSCE' 1993 (n. 21), 7.4.
72 OSCE, Decision No. 383: Report on OSCE Legal Capacity and on Privileges and Immunities to the Ministerial Council, PC.DEC/383, 26 November 2000, para. 5.
73 OSCE, Report to The Ministerial Council on Strengthening the Legal Framework of the OSCE in 2012, MC.GAL/15/12, 7 December 2012, para. 3.

Under this second conceptualisation, the OSCE is responsible for its own conduct and the ARIO apply to it. This does not however help clarify the nature of the legal systems developed by international organisations. The ILC does not provide a clear answer concerning the derived or original nature of the legal system of international organisations, neither does it ultimately determine the legal nature of the rules of international organisations.[74]

For example, the absence of a respective provision such as Article 3 of the Draft Articles on State Responsibility[75] in the text of the ARIO means that the OSCE may not be internationally responsible if the challenged act is characterised as lawful by an internal rule that is international in character.[76] Thus, Article 6(2) ARIO defines the 'rules' of an international organisation as the organisation's internal law, which determines, inter alia, the functions of the organ or agent.[77] However, Article 7 ARIO, which regulates the attribution of conduct to the organisation in case of effective control over the conduct of a member state, implicitly defines the relations between member states and the organisation as being subject to international law.[78] Article 10 ARIO therefore suggests that the OSCE can be internationally responsible for the violation of an internal rule only if that rule is international in nature.[79] Moreover, the ILC project is not applicable to the OSCE if the Organization's internal rules are *lex specialis* in relation to the conditions, the content or the implementation of international responsibility, as envisaged in Article 64 ARIO.[80]

74 Ahlborn, 'The Rules of International Organizations'.

75 'The characterization of an act of a State as internationally wrongful is governed by international law. Such characterization is not affected by the characterization of the same act as lawful by internal law.'

76 UN, International Law Commission, Draft Articles on the Responsibility of International Organizations with Commentaries 2011 (n. 33), para. 2 of the commentary to Art. 5.

77 Art. 6: '1. The conduct of an organ or agent of an international organization in the performance of functions of that organ or agent shall be considered an act of that organization under international law, whatever position the organ or agent holds in respect of the organization. 2. The rules of the organization apply in the determination of the functions of its organs and agents.'

78 Art. 7: 'The conduct of an organ of a State or an organ or agent of an international organization that is placed at the disposal of another international organization shall be considered under international law an act of the latter organization if the organization exercises effective control over that conduct.'

79 Art. 10: '1. There is a breach of an *international obligation* by an international organization when an act of that international organization is not in conformity with what is required of it by that obligation, regardless of the origin or character of the obligation concerned. 2. Paragraph 1 includes the breach of any international obligation that may arise for an international organization towards its members under the *rules of the organization*' (emphasis added).

80 Art. 64: 'These draft articles do not apply where and to the extent that the conditions for the existence of an internationally wrongful act or the content or implementation of the

These are only some consequences of the unclear (original or derived) nature of organisations' legal systems, but others could be discussed, as for example those relating to countermeasures and shared responsibility.[81] Indeed, if the OSCE is considered an entity derived from international law, its legal system will produce law that is international in character.

In that case, participating States do not hide behind the institutional veil of the Organization when a conduct is taken within the OSCE framework. The transparent nature of its institutional veil is owed to the fact that the relationship between participating States and the Organization is founded on international law.

In the hypothetical circumstance that the OSCE were to violate a human rights obligation during its field activity, the participating State(s) involved could therefore be held responsible in addition to the Organization. For example, in the fulfilment of the OSCE's mandate, officials seconded by participating States could incur responsibility for alleged violations such as destruction of private property, personal injuries or restriction of the freedom of movement. In case that the participating State is a member of the European Convention on Human Rights, the European Court of Human Rights will probably attribute the conduct to the participating State, refusing to attribute it to the OSCE only.[82] Indeed, in *Al-Dulimi* v. *Switzerland* both the Chamber and the Grand Chamber followed the precedent set by *Nada* v. *Switzerland* and *Al-Jedda* v. *UK*[83] in piercing the institutional veil and considering that conduct is not exclusively imputable to the organisation (in that case the UN).

3.3 *The OSCE's Legal System Is Original, and Does Not Possess International Legal Personality*

This scenario renders the implementation of international responsibility, both of the OSCE and of its participating States, most difficult. Under this conception, the OSCE cannot conclude international agreements, cannot incur international responsibility and it is not governed by

international responsibility of an international organization, or of a State in connection with the conduct of an international organization, are governed by special rules of international law. Such special rules of international law may be contained in the rules of the organization applicable to the relations between an international organization and its members.'

81 Ahlborn, 'The Rules of International Organizations'.

82 See, e.g., ECHR, *Al-Dulimi and Montana Management Inc.* v. *Switzerland* [GC], Judgment of 21 June 2016, no. 5809/08 and ECHR, *Al-Dulimi and Montana Management Inc.* v. *Switzerland*, Judgment of 26 November 2013, No. 5809/08.

83 ECHR, *Nada* v. *Switzerland* [GC], decision of 12 September 2012, No. 10593/08; ECHR, *Al-Jedda* v. *the United Kingdom* [GC], decision of 7 July 2011, No. 27021/08.

international law. In sum, it constitutes an independent legal system, in the way that national legal systems are independent from international law, but without being a subject of international law. Indeed, following this approach the OSCE's status (under international law) resembles the status of multinational corporations: institutional networks not founded by the law of any individual legal system, but 'originally' created by subjects of national law.[84]

This image of the OSCE is proposed by those who support the distinction between legally binding and politically binding obligations.[85] Indeed, the thesis that participating States are politically obliged to respect OSCE commitments finds its origin in the will to disconnect the Organization from international law. The 2006 report on strengthening the effectiveness of the OSCE, named 'Common Responsibilities', implies this conceptualisation when it states that '[t]he OSCE is referred to as a community of values. These values are expressed in a number of commitments that are not formally legal, but nevertheless binding, obligations.'[86]

Under this conception, the activities of the Organization are governed only by its internal legal system, providing for a system of compliance, which is parallel to and not influenced by international law. In this context, the distinction between legally binding and politically binding obligations may have a justification, reaffirming the idea that OSCE commitments are not governed by international law at all, but belong to a different, and totally separate legal system. In this context, theories arise that depict the OSCE as an organisation that provides 'soft security'.[87] One may contend that from 'soft security' derives 'soft responsibility', and indeed this is how internal forms of accountability and the OSCE legitimacy more generally have been described.[88]

Within an original legal system, internal systems of compliance are based on what is usually defined as 'accountability'. This does not mean that only original systems develop mechanisms for accountability, but they are more

84 Robé, 'Multinational Enterprises'.

85 Dijk, 'The Implementation of the Final Act'.

86 OSCE, Common Responsibility: Commitments and Implementation, Report submitted to the OSCE Ministerial Council in response to MC Decision No. 17/05 on Strengthening the Effectiveness of the OSCE, 2006, para. 1, available at: www.osce.org/odihr/22681?download=true; Gheciu, *Securing Civilization?*, 118.

87 Dominguez, *The OSCE*.

88 OSCE, 'Common Responsibility' (n. 86); see also Steinbrück Platise, 'Legitimate Governance as a Privilege and Price for the Autonomy of International Organisations', Chapter 14 in this Volume.

inclined to adopt this notion for internal compliance. They are not based on the mechanism provided by international responsibility, but on the internal system of implementation.[89] For example, the immediate and most basic reaction to the breach of internal values would be expulsion from the community. The OSCE was the first regional institution to react to the crises in the western Balkans in June 1991, and already in 1992 suspended the participation of the Federal Republic of Yugoslavia in the Organization.[90]

In those years, the OSCE was also developing an internal dispute settlement system, consisting of different 'political' procedures: the so-called Valletta Mechanism, the CSCE Conciliation Commission, the Directed Conciliation and the Court of Conciliation and Arbitration.[91] The will to maintain a clear separation from international law is reflected in the academic commentaries written in those years. For example, scholars acknowledge that commitments are not part of international law and could therefore not be subject to international arbitration, since the Court of Conciliation and Arbitration decides arbitral cases in accordance with international law.[92] According to this reading, OSCE commitments can thus be submitted to the conciliation procedure only and not to the arbitration procedure, because the latter implies the application of international law.[93]

More contemporary interests are devoted to the Electoral Observation Missions deployed by the OSCE's Office for Democratic Institutions and Human Rights.[94] The issue here relates to the question under which legal framework these missions perform their functions, in absence of internationally binding norms. Again, systems of internal accountability, such as the reports on methodology published by the OSCE's Office for Democratic Institutions and Human Rights,[95] refer to the independence of the Organization, and they are often presented as the only way to grant the respect of 'non-legal' obligations. In this sense, accountability is a notion useful for isolating an internal system from international law.

Different issues arise when we look at the international responsibility of participating States for their conduct in the framework of the OSCE. In this case states

89 Ibid.

90 Stefanova, 'Institutionalist Theories'.

91 Jacobi, 'The OSCE Court'.

92 Condorelli, 'En attendant la "Cour de conciliation et d'arbitrage de la CSCE"'.

93 Convention on Conciliation and Arbitration within the OSCE, adopted by the Council of Ministers at its meeting held on 15 December 1992 in Stockholm, as part of the Decision on Peaceful Settlement of Disputes, 15 December 1992, Arts. 23 and 30, available at: www.osce.org/cca/111409?download=true.

94 Aaken and Chambers, 'Accountability and Independence'.

95 See, e.g., OSCE, ODIHR, *Common Responsibility Commitments and Implementation*.

may rely on their quality of organs of the Organization, hiding themselves under the institutional veil. As an original entity the Organization loses its transparent quality, resulting in the impossibility of piercing the institutional veil.

This consequence is not different from what is seen today in the context of multinational corporations, for example, in case of an attempt to sue the parent company for the conduct of subsidiaries.[96] Multinational corporations are a de facto entity not recognised by national or international law. Each subsidiary of the group is a singular entity incorporated in a state and is subject to the internal legal order of that state, with the result that the multinational entity constitutes a legal order of its own, with its own peculiarities.[97]

3.4 *The OSCE's Legal System Is Original, and It Possesses International Legal Personality*

Under the last conceptualisation, the OSCE has international legal personality to conclude international agreements and to bear responsibility for its wrongful conduct, but it is not derived from international law. This model is based on the idea that the legal personality of international organisations does not derive from the will of member states but from general international law.[98] Again, the ILC does not take a clear stance on this, limiting itself to an affirmation that '[t]he capacity of an international organisation to conclude treaties is governed by the relevant rules of that organisation'.[99] If the rules belong to international law, legal personality is limited by the will of member states;[100] if the rules belong to internal law, legal personality is inherent to the organisation.[101] Concerning the OSCE, Ryngaert considers the acquisition of legal personality through 'a norm of intra-institutional customary law' based on the duty of loyalty.[102] In the framework of our conceptualisations, this hypothesis is founded on the idea that international organisations possess an original legal system with international legal personality.

This circumstance resembles the status of states in international law, and, indeed, the OSCE would then not be different from a federal state.

96 Muchlinski, 'Multinational Enterprises'.

97 Robé, 'Multinational Enterprises'.

98 See, in general, Klabbers, *An Introduction to International Organizations Law*, 46.

99 Vienna Convention on the Law of Treaties Between States and International Organizations or Between International Organizations, 21 March 1986, Art. 6; Morgenstern, 'The Vienna Convention' 1989.

100 This is the most popular theory. See, e.g., UN, United Nations Juridical Yearbook, 1971, 215.

101 Seyersted, 'International Personality'; Seyersted, 'Objective International Personality'.

102 Ryngaert, 'Basing the Legal Status of the OSCE on Participating States' Duty of Loyalty' (n. 9).

To a certain extent this is what the EU demands for itself and for other regional (economic) integration organisations.[103] The European Commission has claimed that the ARIO is not applicable in the relationship between the EU and its member states.[104] Moreover, it demanded the application of ad hoc criteria of attribution of conduct, by reason of the exclusive competences that member states have delegated to the EU. The approach tends to consider member states as organs of the organisation and their conduct as the conduct of the organisation. Internal relations are no longer the domain of international law.

If international organisations are categorised by their level of integration, the OSCE and the EU would be situated on the opposite ends of the scale. However, their exceptionalisms are not that different, founded as they are on the unclear nature of their respective legal systems. For example, in both cases the protection of human rights has often been considered evidence of the creation of an internal community of values that necessitates exceptionalism and the presence of an original legal system.[105] Conversely, even if states have different internal levels of integration and none resembles the other, the formal equality that they enjoy in international law is one of the fundamental principles of the international community. Despite integration, the fundamental criterion to distinguish between entities is the relation that their legal systems have with the legal system in which they perform their functions as legal subjects. This relation resembles the concept of 'relevance' used by Santi Romano, and the distinction between original or derivative entities.[106]

The OSCE's human dimension shows well how an original legal system can isolate itself.[107] Since the Helsinki Final Act of 1975, human rights have been considered central to the CSCE and later the OSCE. During the same period in which the EU was starting to consolidate its internal legal system, the CSCE was imagined by participating States as a standard-setter for 'human rights and fundamental freedoms, the rule of law, democracy and democratic institution-building, the rights of persons belonging to national minorities, and human contacts'.[108] The fact was stressed that the human dimension goes beyond other human rights conventions, establishing 'a distinct CSCE order' capable of penetrating the internal legal order of states

103 Hoffmeister, 'Litigating Against the European Union'.

104 ILC, Responsibility of International Organizations Comments and Observations Received from International Organizations, 14 February 2011 (n. 8).

105 Roucounas, 'Remarques sur la portée juridique'.

106 See Section 2 of this chapter.

107 Buergenthal, 'The CSCE Rights System'.

108 Heraclides, 'The diplomatic process', 28.

because states are no longer allowed to invoke the non-intervention principle in the framework of the human dimension.[109] Today this finding is no longer debated and is accepted by every human rights treaty, but it is interesting to see how it was connected to the particular status of CSCE commitments. These are not international law, but still binding rules of a different normative order.[110]

If the OSCE is an original entity, it is more difficult to consider participating States responsible for their implementation of OSCE commitments. First, they themselves might not even be bound by the obligation. The OSCE, as an original entity with legal personality, would have the competence to conclude international agreements that benefit participating States without them being a (formal) party to the agreement. This is the case for EU member states in agreements concluded by the EU alone: even if member states materially breach the agreement, only the EU would be responsible for their conduct.[111] Second, the conduct of participating States would be regarded as the conduct of the Organization, and they would be considered as acting as a 'sub-organ' under the OSCE's 'ultimate authority and control'.[112] Organisations considered as original entities thus adopt a closed structure, developing an institutional veil that is opaque (using Dupuy's terminology) and not easily pierced.

4 CONCLUSION

Observers or involved actors often resort to the concept of international organisation that better suits their argumentative interest in the concrete circumstances. Indeed, the four concepts of the OSCE's legal status that I have described in this chapter are mutually exclusive as a matter of legal doctrine, but in practice can coexist. It is the context that leads participants in legal discourse to adopt one concept or the other. Due to this flexibility, organisations such as the UN are considered by some observers as the constitutional framework of the international community, whereas others see it as

109 Bloed, 'The CSCE Human Dimension Commitments'.

110 Dijk, 'The Final Act of Helsinki'; Barberini, *Sicurezza e Cooperazione*.

111 See, e.g., International Tribunal for the Law of the Sea, *Request for an Advisory Opinion Submitted by the Sub-Regional Fisheries Commission*, Advisory Opinion of 2 April 2015, Case No. 21.

112 See, e.g., European Court of Human Rights, *Behrami and Behrami* v. *France* and *Saramati* v. *France, Germany And Norway* [GC], Judgment of 2 May 2007 as to admissibility, Applications No. 71412/01 and No. 78166/01.

a forum for cooperation and therefore unable to bear the responsibility for its wrongful conduct.[113]

The OSCE is subjected to the same contestations, which do not arise (only) from the unsettled question of the Organization's international legal personality but, first and foremost, from the unclear nature of the legal system it develops. Even if competences and the level of integration of international organisations are different, they all face the same problems in reconciling their original and derived nature. This chapter does not provide an ultimate answer on what the OSCE is and how its legal responsibility is to be assessed, but rather illustrates the reasons for the OSCE's complexity from the perspective of international responsibility. Clarity cannot come from the claim that every organisation is an exception, but from a general theory on the nature of the diverse legal systems constituting the international community.

REFERENCES

Aaken, Anne van and Chambers, Richard, 'Accountability and Independence of International Election Observers', *International Organizations Law Review* 6 (2009), 541–80.

Abass, Ademola, *Regional Organisations and the Development of Collective Security: Beyond Chapter VIII of the UN Charter* (Oxford, Portland: Hart, 2004).

Ahlborn, Christiane, 'The Rules of International Organizations and the Law of International Responsibility', *International Organizations Law Review* 8 (2011), 397–482.

Amerasinghe, Felix, *Principles of the Institutional Law of International Organizations* (Cambridge: Cambridge University Press, 2005).

Anzilotti, Dionisio, 'Gli organi comuni alle società di stati', *Rivista di Diritto Internazionale* (1914), 156–64.

Balladore Pallieri, Giorgio, 'Le droit interne des organisations internationales', *Recueil des Cours de l'Académie de Droit International de La Haye* 127 (1969), 1–38.

Barberini, Giovanni, *Sicurezza e cooperazione da Vancouver a Vladivostok* (Torino: Giappichelli, 2004).

Bertrand, Christine, 'La nature juridique de l'Organisation pour la sécurité et la coopération en Europe (OSCE)', *Revue Général de Droit International Public* CII (1998), 365–406.

[113] Compare, Fassbender, *The United Nations Charter* and Mégret, 'La responsabilité des Nations unies'.

Bloed Arie, 'The CSCE Human Dimension Commitments: Present and Prospects', in Emmanuel Decaux and Linos-Alexandre Sicilianos (eds.), *La CSCE: dimension humaine et règlement des différends* (Paris: Montchrestien, 1993), 43–61.

Bohannan, Paul, 'The Differing Realms of the Law', *American Anthropologist* 67 (1965), 33–42.

Brander, Sonya, 'Making a Credible Case for a Legal Personality for the OSCE', *OSCE Magazine* (2009), 18–23.

Brander, Sonya and Martín Estébanez, María, 'The OSCE Matures: Time for Legal Status', *Helsinki Monitor: Security and Human Rights* 18 (2007), 2–5.

Brölmann, Catherine, *The Institutional Veil in Public International Law: International Organisations and the Law of Treaties* (Oxford: Hart, 2007).

'Member States and International Legal Responsibility: Developments of the Institutional Veil', *International Organizations Law Review* 12 (2015), 358–81.

Brölmann, Catherine and Nijman, Janne Elisabeth, 'Legal Personality as a Fundamental Concept of International Law', in Jean d'Aspremont and Sahib Singh (eds.), *Fundamental Concepts of International Law* (London: Elgar, 2017).

Buergenthal, Thomas, 'The CSCE Rights System', *George Washington Journal of International Law & Economics* 25 (1991–1992), 333–86.

Cahier, Philippe, 'L'ordre juridique interne des organisations internationales', in René-Jean Dupuy (ed.), *Manuel sur les organisations internationales* (Leiden: Brill, 1998), 377–96.

Condorelli, Luigi, 'En attendant la "Cour de conciliation et d'arbitrage de la CSCE": quelques remarques sur le droit applicable', in Christian Dominicé, Robert Patry and Claude Reymond (eds.), *Études de droit international en l'honneur de Pierre Lalive* (Bâle, Francfort-sur-le-Main: Helbing & Lichtenhahn, 1993), 457–67.

Decaux, Emmanuel, 'L'institutionalisation de la CSCE', in Emmanuel Decaux and Linos-Alexandre Sicilianos (eds.), *La CSCE: dimension humaine et règlement des différends* (Paris: Montchrestien, 1993), 125–59.

Decleva, Matteo, *Il diritto interno delle unioni internazionali* (Padova: CEDAM, 1962).

Dijk, Pieter van, 'The Final Act of Helsinki – Basis for a Pan-European System?' *Netherlands Yearbook of International Law* 11 (1980), 97–124.

'The Implementation of the Final Act of Helsinki: The Creation of New Structures or the Involvement of Existing Ones?', *Michigan Journal of International Law* 10 (1989), 110–26.

Dominguez, Roberto, *The OSCE: Soft Security for a Hard World: Competing Theories for Understanding the OSCE* (Brussels: P. I. E. Peter Lang, 2014).

Dominicé, Christian, 'Attribution of Conduct to Multiple States and the Implication of a State in the Act of Another State', in James Crawford, Alain Pellet and Simon Olleson (eds.), *The Law of International Responsibility* (Oxford: Oxford University Press, 2010), 281–9.

Dupuy, Pierre-Marie and Viñuales, Jorge E., *International Environmental Law* (Cambridge: Cambridge University Press, 2015).

Fassbender, Bardo, *The United Nations Charter as the Constitution of the International Community* (Leiden, Boston: Nijhoff, 2009).

Ferrari-Bravo, Luigi, 'Difficultés et perspectives de la nouvelle Europe', in Emmanuel Decaux and Linos-Alexandre Sicilianos (eds.), *La CSCE: dimension humaine et règlement des différends* (Paris: Montchrestien, 1993), 15–27.

Focsanenau, Lazar, 'Le droit interne de l'organisation des Nation Unies', *Annuaire français de droit international* 3 (1957), 315–49.

Forteau, Mathias, 'Régime général de responsabilité ou lex specialis?', *Revue belge de droit international* 46 (2013), 147–61.

Gaja, Giorgio, 'Note introductive de l'ancien rapporteur spécial', *Revue belge de droit international* 46 (2013), 9–17.

Gheciu, Alexandra, *Securing Civilization? The EU, NATO, and the OSCE in the Post-9/11 World* (Oxford: Oxford University Press, 2008).

Heraclides, Alexis, 'The diplomatic Process of Elaborating the CSCE Human Dimension Commitments: From Ideological Incompatibility to Community of Values', in Emmanuel Decaux and Linos-Alexandre Sicilianos (eds.), *La CSCE: dimension humaine et règlement des différends* (Paris: Montchrestien, 1993), 27–43.

Hoffmeister, Frank, 'Litigating Against the European Union and Its Member States – Who Responds Under the ILC's Draft Articles on International Responsibility of International Organizations?', *European Journal of International Law* 21 (2010), 723–47.

Jacobi, Susanne, 'The OSCE Court: An Overview', *Leiden Journal of International Law* 10 (1997), 281–94.

Kerchove, Michel van de and Ost, François, *Legal System Between Order and Disorder* (Oxford: Clarendon Press, 1994).

De la pyramide au réseau?: Pour une théorie dialectique du droit (Brussels: FUSL, 2002).

Klabbers, Jan, *An Introduction to International Organizations Law* 3rd edn (Cambridge: Cambridge University Press, 2015).

Klein, Pierre, *La responsabilité des organisations internationales dans les ordres juridiques internes et en droit des gens* (Brussels: Bruylant, 1998).

Ličková, Magdalena, 'European Exceptionalism in International Law', *European Journal of International Law* 19 (2008), 463–90.

Mégret, Frédéric, 'La responsabilité des Nations unies aux temps du choléra', *Revue belge de droit international* 46 (2013), 161–90.

Monaco, Riccardo, 'I regolamenti interni degli enti internazionali', *Jus Gentium, Annuario italiano di diritto internazionale* I (1938), 52–108.

Morgenstern, Felice, 'The Vienna Convention on the Law of Treaties Between States and International Organisations or between International Organisations', in Yoram Dinstein (ed.), *International Law at a Time of Perplexity: Essays in Honour of Shabtai Rosenne* (Dordrecht, Boston: Brill, 1989), 435–47.

Muchlinski, Peter, *Multinational Enterprises and the Law* (Oxford: Oxford University Press, 2007).

Nollkaemper, André and Plakokefalos, Ilias, *Principles of Shared Responsibility in International Law: An Appraisal of the State of the Art* (Cambridge: Cambridge University Press, 2014).

Oberschmidt, Randolf and Zellner, Wolfgang, 'OSCE at the Crossroads', Centre for OSCE Research: Institute for Peace Research and Security Policy at the University of Hamburg, CORE Working Paper 2 (2001).

Pellet, Alain, 'Les fondements juridiques internationaux du droit communautaire', Collected Courses of the Academy of European Law (1997), 193–271.

Prevost, Jean-François, 'Observations sur la nature juridique de l'Acte final de la Conférence sur la sécurité et la coopération en Europe', *Annuaire français de droit international* 21 (1975), 129–53.

Robé, Jean-Philippe, 'Multinational Enterprises: The Constitution of a Pluralistic Legal Order', in Gunther Teubner (ed.), *Global Law Without a State* (Farnham: Ashgate, 1997), 45–78.

Robilant, Anna di, 'Genealogy of Soft Law', *American Journal of Comparative Law* 54 (2006), 499–554.

Romano, Santi, *L'ordinamento giuridico* (Pisa: Spoerri, 1918).

Roucounas, Emmanuel, 'Remarques sur la portée juridique des engagements CSCE concernant la dimension humaine', in Emmanuel Decaux and Linos-Alexandre Sicilianos (eds.), *La CSCE: dimension humaine et règlement des différends* (Paris: Montchrestien, 1993), 89–115.

Sapiro, Miriam, 'Changing the CSCE into the OSCE: Legal Aspects of a Political Transformation', *American Journal of International Law* 89 (1995), 631–7.

Schermers, Henry and Blokker, Niels, *International Institutional Law: Unity within Diversity* (Boston, Leiden: Nijhoff, 2011).

Schultz, Thomas, *Transnational Legality: Stateless Law and International Arbitration* (Oxford: Oxford University Press, 2014).

Sereni, Angelo Piero, *Le organizzazioni internazionali* (Milano: Giuffré, 1959).

Seyersted, Finn, 'International Personality of Intergovernmental Organizations', *Indian Journal of International Law* 4 (1964), 1–75.

'Objective International Personality of Intergovernmental Organizations: Do Their Capacities Really Depend Upon the Conventions Establishing Them', *Nordisk Tidsskrift International Ret* 34 (1964), 1–112.

Stefanova, Boyka, 'Institutionalist Theories. The OSCE in the Western Balkans', in Roberto Dominguez, *The OSCE: Soft Security for a Hard World: Competing Theories for Understanding the OSCE* (Brussels: P. I. E. Peter Lang, 2014), chapter 3.

Stern, Brigitte, 'The Elements of an Internationally Wrongful Act', in James Crawford, Alain Pellet and Simon Olleson (eds.), *The Law of International Responsibility* (Oxford: Oxford University Press, 2010), 193–221.

Tichy, Helmut and Köhler, Ulrike 'Legal Personality or Not – The Recent Attempts to Improve the Status of the OSCE', in Isabelle Buffard, James Crawford, Alain Pellet and Stephan Wittich (eds.), *International Law Between Universalism and Fragmentation: Festschrift in Honour of Gerhard Hafner* (Leiden, Boston: Brill Nijhoff, 2008), 455–78.

Virally, Michel, *L'organisation mondiale* (Paris: Armand Colin, 1972).

White, Nigel, *The Law of International Organisations* (Manchester: Manchester University Press, 2017).

Wouters, Jan and Odermatt, Jed, 'Are All International Organizations Created Equal?', *International Organizations Law Review* 9 (2012), 7–14.

Zagorski, Andrei, 'Make the OSCE Institutions Less Dependent on Politics, Not More', *Helsinki Monitor* 209 (2005).

PART IV

THE LEGAL AND INSTITUTIONAL FRAMEWORK AS A GOVERNANCE ISSUE

12

The OSCE as a Case of Informal International Lawmaking?

Olivia Herman and Jan Wouters

1 INTRODUCTION

Informal normative processes and cross-border cooperation have drastically increased in recent decades, claiming an important place in global governance. In an attempt to study and critically analyse this phenomenon, a collaborative research project was set up between the Graduate Institute in Geneva, the Leuven Centre for Global Governance Studies and the University of Twente with the support of the Hague Institute for the Internationalisation of Law, focusing particularly on the concept of 'informal international lawmaking' (IN-LAW).[1] The IN-LAW research project resulted in two books: *Informal International Lawmaking*, which sets out in a comprehensive manner the conceptual framework of IN-LAW,[2] and *Informal International Lawmaking: Case Studies*, which bundles together case study research on a selection of IN-LAW networks active in a significant number of policy fields.[3] The OSCE was not included in the selection of case studies, arguably because the Organization was already too 'well known' at the time and did not display new regulatory dynamics or initiatives in the recent past. The focus was primarily upon new dynamics of IN-LAW. Moreover, the selected informal networks were preferably informal in all three dimensions, namely output, process and actor informality,[4] which at first glance may not be the case in relation to the OSCE. Examples of selected case studies included the G20, the Financial Stability Board and the Kimberley Scheme on Conflict Diamonds. Nevertheless, the OSCE constitutes a thought-provoking case to

[1] For a comprehensive study of the concept, see Pauwelyn, Wessel and Wouters, *Informal International Lawmaking*.
[2] See Pauwelyn, Wessel and Wouters, *Informal International Lawmaking*.
[3] See Berman *et al.*, *Informal International Lawmaking: Case Studies*.
[4] Berman *et al.*, *Informal International Lawmaking: Case Studies*, 7–8.

analyse from an IN-LAW perspective, especially due to its *sui generis* nature in comparison to other entities involved in global governance.

Throughout this chapter, an analysis of the OSCE as a norm-creator from an IN-LAW perspective will be undertaken. Considering the complex and specific nature of the Organization in terms of institutional structure, actor participation and output, the analysis will highlight those processes that are most interesting in an IN-LAW context. First, in order to provide a theoretical framework for our analysis, the essential characteristics of IN-LAW will be outlined and contrasted to the phenomenon of soft law (Section 2). Subsequently, we will examine the OSCE more closely, in particular it being a forum for political dialogue rather than a formal international organisation and the informal nature of certain of its decision-making processes (Section 3.1). Subsequently, the various actors included in the decision-making process of the OSCE will be considered. A particular focus will be on those actors that are distinct from the traditional diplomatic actors commonly associated with international cooperation (Section 3.2). Lastly, the miscellaneous output of the OSCE will be examined (Section 3.3). In our concluding remarks, we will gather the main findings from our IN-LAW analysis and develop some reflections in relation to accountability concerns (Section 4).

2 THE CONCEPT OF IN-LAW

The concept of IN-LAW has been defined as:

> Cross-border cooperation between public authorities, with or without the participation of private actors and/or international organizations, in a forum other than a traditional international organization (*process informality*), and/or as between actors other than traditional diplomatic actors (such as regulators or agencies) (*actor informality*) and/or which does not result in a formal treaty or other traditional source of international law (*output informality*).[5]

From this definition it becomes apparent that the concept of IN-LAW is applied in stark contrast to traditional international lawmaking, which usually takes place within the framework of an international organisation, with formal legal instruments as the output (e.g. a treaty). Conversely, IN-LAW dispenses with certain formalities that are commonly associated with the traditional lawmaking process and can in this sense be described as being informal. Such informality can manifest itself in different dimensions, namely in

[5] Pauwelyn, 'Informal International Lawmaking: Framing the Concept and Research Questions', 22.

relation to the output, process and actors involved. This entails that any activity can be considered as constituting IN-LAW when informal in any of the above three ways. As a result, the phenomenon of IN-LAW can display itself in various degrees. Moreover, informal lawmaking is international in the sense that it involves cooperation between two or more actors in different countries, which also may include cooperation between international organisations.

It is worth describing the three dimensions of IN-LAW a bit more closely. First, *process informality* involves international cooperation that occurs in a loosely organised network or forum rather than in an international organisation. However, it does not exclude the existence of detailed procedural rules, permanent staff or physical headquarters. Moreover, process informality can take place within the broader framework of a formal organisation. What is excluded are formal negotiations between governmental representatives for the adoption of an instrument, such as a treaty or resolution (which may be instruments of soft law, as will be discussed hereafter). Second, *output informality* refers to international cooperation that does not result in the adoption of a traditional instrument of international law, but rather of a guideline, declaration, standard or an even more informal policy coordination or exchange. This does not necessarily exclude the output being legally binding (and here IN-LAW may differ from soft law as well). The focus of IN-LAW is on the lack of certain formalities in the lawmaking process and not on the lack of a legally binding character per se. Yet, not all informal interactions that take place across borders amount to IN-LAW. A necessary condition is that the output is normative in nature, meaning that it steers behaviour or determines the freedom of actors.[6] Taking all this into account, one may wonder why IN-LAW incudes the term 'lawmaking'. The process of lawmaking is defined as 'norm-setting or public policy-making by public authorities' whereby the term 'law' is understood in a broad sense as including outputs that 'may not, strictly speaking, be part of law but merely have legal effects or fit in the context of a broader legal or normative process'.[7] The term 'law' is used in order to connote the involvement of public authorities in the process. While IN-LAW may include private actor participation, exclusive private cooperation is excluded. In this context, the notion of 'public authorities' refers to actors exercising any kind of governance activity that unilaterally determines or reduces the freedom of others. When defining lawmaking beyond *who* is acting (public authorities), of particular interest to us is the inclusion of informal networks or fora that

6 Ibid., 15–16.
7 Ibid., 21.

exercise international public authority and that may impact the freedom of others.[8] This brings us to the final dimension of IN-LAW, namely *actor informality*. The actors involved in international cooperation may be informal, in the sense that they do not constitute traditional diplomatic actors, such as heads of state, ministers of foreign affairs, ambassadors or accredited diplomats. Entities such as sectoral ministries, domestic regulators, independent or semi-independent agencies (e.g. food safety authorities), sub-federal entities (e.g. provinces or municipalities) or the judicial or legislative branch may also be engaged in the processes, even though it is commonly held that only traditional diplomatic actors can represent and bind a state.[9] In addition, private actors and international organisations may be actively involved next to public actors. Yet, purely private cooperation without public authority involvement is not covered by the concept of IN-LAW.[10] As a result, the process of IN-LAW remains state-based.[11]

From a first encounter with the concept of IN-LAW, one may wonder to what extent IN-LAW differs from the concept of soft law. Both have emerged as valuable tools of global governance by providing the actors involved with the desired flexibility often lacking in formal lawmaking processes.[12] However, while IN-LAW may include soft law, the concept of IN-LAW goes beyond this particular notion.

Soft law is not a strict legal concept with a clearly agreed-upon scope and content. Instead it is considered a catch-all category of non-legally binding instruments.[13] Examples include treaties with imprecise, subjective or indeterminate language; various UN General Assembly (UNGA) resolutions; and guidelines and recommendations issued by international organisations.[14] Generally, its non-legally binding nature is considered the key characteristic distinguishing soft law norms from hard law. Yet, as indicated above, what characterises IN-LAW norms is not so much their non-legally binding character, but rather the fact that they are outside traditional international law altogether. One of the key reasons thereof may arguably lie in the fact that IN-LAW actors often lack the capacity to create international law. In contrast, soft law instruments are commonly adopted in the traditional setting of an

8 Ibid., 21.

9 Vienna Convention on the Law of Treaties, 23 May 1969, 1155 UNTS 331, Article 7.

10 Pauwelyn, 'Informal International Lawmaking: Framing the Concept', 19.

11 Pauwelyn, Wessel and Wouters, 'Informal International Lawmaking: An Assessment and Template to Keep It Both Effective and Accountable', 504.

12 O'Connell, 'The Role of Soft Law in a Global Order', 109–10.

13 See Chinkin, 'Normative Development in the International Legal System', 21–42.

14 Ibid., 29.

international organisation with the involvement of diplomatic actors. A classic example thereof is the Universal Declaration of Human Rights, which was adopted through an UNGA resolution as a common standard of achievement. Nevertheless, in certain cases controversial claims to soft law status have been made for instruments not emanating from state actors, such as common international standards adopted by NGOs and expert groups. In this case the non-legally binding nature of the instrument in question does not arise from the lack of intent to be bound, but rather from the actors' lack of formal lawmaking capacity.[15] In this particular case, an overlap with the phenomenon of IN-LAW may be noted.[16] Yet, a nuance can be made here in relation to international organisations, which are considered as non-state entities in the sense of being distinct from their member states. Despite their non-state nature, international organisations may be entrusted with the international legal capacity and competence to adopt certain norms and even to conclude certain treaties.[17] Lastly, even though there can be an overlap of soft law and IN-LAW in certain instances, there is nothing soft – in the sense of vague, aspirational or deeply contested – about most IN-LAW norms developed in recent years. The norm-making process is typically based on consensus and the expectation of compliance is often higher than with traditional treaties. As a result, while soft law may in part overlap with the concept of IN-LAW, the latter takes a broader approach by encompassing the various informalities that may manifest itself in the international lawmaking process.[18]

3 AN IN-LAW ANALYSIS OF THE OSCE AS A NORM CREATOR

3.1 *Process Informality*

It is well known that the OSCE as a formalised institution originates from the Conference on Security and Co-operation in Europe (CSCE), or Helsinki Process, which played a pivotal role in bridging the East–West divide during and after the Cold War.[19] It was established as a forum for cross-border

15 Ibid., 29.

16 Wouters and Hamid, 'Custom and Informal International Lawmaking', 336.

17 ICJ, *Reparation for Injuries Suffered in the Service of the United Nations*, Advisory Opinion of 11 April 1949, ICJ Rep 1949, 174; A. Peters *et al.*, *Non-State Actors as Standard Setters*, 16.

18 Pauwelyn, Wessel and Wouters, 'Informal International Lawmaking: An Assessment and Template', 506; Wouters and Hamid, 'Custom and Informal International Lawmaking', 335–7.

19 Schlager, 'A Hard Look at Compliance with "Soft" Law: The Case of the OSCE', 360.

cooperation engaged in standard-setting in a wide array of security-related fields concerning human, socio-military and economic topics. Since its inception, the CSCE's, and later the OSCE's, organisational framework has drastically developed with the formation of various permanent decision-making bodies and offices, as well as field operations.[20]

Contrary to what the name suggests, the OSCE is generally not considered as constituting a traditional international organisation but rather a forum for informal political dialogue.[21] In 1995, when the CSCE transformed into the OSCE, the parties agreed that the term 'Organization' would not change the status of the forum into an organisation under international law.[22] Moreover, the Helsinki Final Act, which constitutes the backbone of the Organization's activities, explicitly excludes the possibility of registering the said Act under Article 102 of the Charter of the UN.[23] It has been argued that this demonstrates the intent of the participating States not to establish legally binding constitutional structures by way of treaty.[24] As a consequence, the regulation of the relations between the various participating States by the Helsinki Final Act is of a political rather than a legal nature. Accordingly, the OSCE may be considered a unique entity engaged in international cooperation. In legal scholarship, such non-treaty based institutions have also been referred to as 'soft law organizations'.[25]

In this sense, the OSCE satisfies the dimension of process informality, as international cooperation takes place in a forum rather than within the confines of a formal international organisation. Yet, when studying the organogram of the OSCE, one quickly takes note of its highly formalised nature, which to a large extent mirrors the structures of a traditional international organisation. The OSCE Handbook itself underscores the OSCE's unique status by indicating that, while having no legal status under international law, the OSCE 'possesses most of the normal attributes of an international organisation: standing decision-making bodies, permanent headquarters and institutions, permanent staff, regular financial resources and field offices'.[26]

20 For a discussion of the origin and development of the CSCE process from 1972–93, see Bloed, *The Conference on Security and Co-operation in Europe*.

21 Manton, 'The OSCE Human Dimension and Customary International Law Formation', 197–8.

22 Ulfstein, 'Institutions and Competences', 51.

23 CSCE, Helsinki Final Act, 1 August 1975, 59, available at www.osce.org/helsinki-final-act?download=true.

24 See Klabbers, 'Institutional Ambivalence by Design', 412.

25 See, e.g., ibid.; Ulfstein, 'Institutions and Competences', 51–5; Di Stasi, 'About Soft Law Organizations: An Open Question', 44–69.

26 OSCE, Press and Public Information Section, 'The OSCE Handbook' 2007.

Moreover, the broader OSCE family even includes a Parliamentary Assembly (an autonomous OSCE body) and a dispute settlement mechanism, the Court of Conciliation and Arbitration (an OSCE-related body).

In an attempt to describe the OSCE, Schweisfurth rejected the terminology of 'soft organisation' or '*sui generis* organisation'. He deemed it more helpful to consider the OSCE as an international organisation *in statu nascendi*, making a comparison to the early days of the Organization of American States.[27] As the debate on the transformation of the OSCE into a fully fledged international organisation continues, Schweisfurth's statement still holds regardless of the passing of time. Yet, its validity may be questioned. Klabbers, in turn, has argued that: 'if an entity looks like an international organization, functions like one, and is treated by outsiders as one then it is pretty unlikely that it is, all appearances notwithstanding, something other than an international organization'.[28] Still, in the case of the OSCE, the participating States had the clear intent of *not* establishing a formal international organisation in order to preserve the flexibility and effectiveness desired for the subject matter at hand (security-related matters) and the particular constellation of the participating States. In this sense, the states intended on keeping this informal forum for cooperation outside the realm of international law altogether.[29] Yet, such a decision comes with direct legal consequences, such as the lack of capacity to enter into treaties or adopt legally binding decisions, as well as the principal lack of privileges and immunities. The OSCE's legal ambivalence has led to an extensive debate. Still, as will be indicated later in this chapter, the OSCE is not entirely disconnected from international law, as there are some links with (hard) international law.

While the concept of IN-LAW does not exclude the existence of headquarters, permanent staff and detailed procedural rules, one may question whether the OSCE as a forum is informal at all, and particularly which mechanisms distinguish the OSCE on an institutional level from traditional international organisations.

Besides the formal decision-making bodies (i.e. Meeting of Heads of State or Government, or Summit; Ministerial Council; Permanent Council; and Forum for Security Co-operation), the OSCE consists of various informal subsidiary bodies and working groups open to all participating States. Such bodies do not have the capacity to take binding decisions, but rather function

27 Schweisfurth, 'Die juristische Mutation der KSZE', 228.

28 Klabbers, 'Institutional Ambivalence by Design', 415.

29 Bloed, *The Conference on Security and Co-operation in Europe*, 22; Klabbers, 'Institutional Ambivalence by Design', 408.

as an important framework for informal political dialogue whilst supporting the work of the formal decision-making bodies.[30] The Permanent Council consists, for example, of various informal subsidiary bodies, such as the Preparatory Committee and a three-committee structure representing the three OSCE security dimensions.[31] Decision-making bodies and informal subsidiary bodies, in close consultation with their superior decision-making body, may also set up ad hoc/thematic, open-ended informal working bodies.[32] For instance, in 2004, in response to the 2003 Maastricht Strategy,[33] an informal working group met and produced proposals for more intensely sharing OSCE norms, principles and commitments with the Mediterranean and Asian Partners.[34] Furthermore, ad hoc or informal meetings may be convened commonly in preparation of the formal decision-making process, which takes place in the permanent decision-making bodies.[35] During such meetings no formal decisions can be adopted.[36] Examples thereof are the Informal Ministerial Meetings organised on the margins of the Ministerial Council, such as the OSCE Informal Ministerial Meeting held in July 2017 in Mauerbach, Austria. The Informal Meeting was convened by Austria, which held the OSCE Chairmanship in 2017, and offered the fifty-seven participating States a platform for informal exchange with the aim of finding common ground on security-related matters. Another practical example is the Informal High-Level Meeting that was held in celebration of the fortieth anniversary of the Helsinki Final Act, during which the participating States discussed issues relating to the security situation in the OSCE area.[37]

It may be argued that the informality of such bodies is first of all reflected in their title (e.g. 'informal' working group). In reality, their informality is manifested in the procedural rules that regulate these bodies. More concretely, such bodies are informal in the sense that they constitute important

30 OSCE, Ministerial Council, 'OSCE Rules of Procedure', MC.DOC/1/06, 1 November 2006, 1–2 II. (A), para. 6 & 8.

31 OSCE, 'The OSCE Handbook' (n. 26).

32 OSCE, Ministerial Council, 'OSCE Rules of Procedure' (n. 30), 2 II. (A), para. 8.

33 In the Maastricht Strategy, the participating States committed themselves to intensifying cooperation with the OSCE Partners for Co-operation by identifying areas of common interest and concern, as well as possibilities for further coordination. The commitment was made against the backdrop of increasing threats in neighbouring regions. OSCE, Ministerial Council, 'OSCE Strategy Document for the Economic and Environmental Dimension', MC (11).JOUR/2, 2 December 2003, Annex I.

34 OSCE, 'The OSCE Handbook' (n. 26), 106.

35 OSCE, Ministerial Council, 'OSCE Rules of Procedure' (n. 30), 2 II. (A), para. 11.

36 Ibid., 14 VI. (A), para. 1.

37 OSCE, 'OSCE Annual Report 2015', 2016, available at: www.osce.org/annual-report/2015?download=true.

platforms for informal discussions between participating States on draft decisions and potential mediation efforts in preparation of the formal adoption of a given decision by the governing bodies.[38] Their informality is also reflected in the fact that as a rule no official records are kept for the meetings of informal subsidiary bodies and working groups; informal summaries or reports may under certain circumstances be issued.[39] Moreover, in contrast to the formal decision-making bodies, informal bodies are not provided with translations between the working languages.[40] Lastly, informal subsidiary bodies are not open to the press or public, thus keeping discussions behind closed doors.[41] One may note, however, that such informal subsidiary bodies/working groups are also utilised in traditional international organisations. An example is the UN ad hoc Open-ended Informal Working Group to study issues relating to the conservation and sustainable use of marine biological diversity beyond areas of national jurisdiction, established by the UNGA,[42] and the thirty-member Open Working Group of the UNGA that was tasked with the development of a set of sustainable development goals.[43]

A particular example of process informality is the nature of the OSCE Parliamentary Assembly (Assembly or OSCE PA). The Assembly is an autonomous OSCE body consisting of parliamentarians from the various participating States and maintains close relationships with other OSCE structures. Though the Assembly is mentioned in the OSCE Rules of Procedure, it is an independent body not formally part of the OSCE's decision-making processes.[44] This has led some to argue that from a strictly formal perspective, the Assembly is not part of the OSCE.[45] An expression thereof can be found in the notion of the broader 'OSCE family', which is used in relation to the Assembly.[46] This aspect adds to the informality of the OSCE at large and more specifically to the informality of the relationships between the

[38] OSCE, Ministerial Council, 'OSCE Rules of Procedure' (n. 30), 1–2 II. (A), para. 6 & 8.

[39] Ibid., 12 V. (A), para. 4; 13 V. (B), para. 2.

[40] Ibid., 12 V. (A), para. 5; 13 V. (B), para. 3.

[41] Ibid., 13 V. (A), para. 9; V. (B), para. 5.

[42] UN, General Assembly, 'Oceans and the Law of the Sea', UNGA/RES/68/70, 29 December 2014, para. 200.

[43] UN, General Assembly, 'Open Working Group of the General Assembly on Sustainable Development Goals', UNGA/67/L.48/Rev.1, 2013.

[44] OSCE, Ministerial Council, 'OSCE Rules of Procedure' (n. 30), 4 II. (C), para. 3.

[45] Habegger, 'Democratic Control of the OSCE: The Role of the Parliamentary Assembly', 135.

[46] The usage of the notion of 'OSCE family' can be found in documents of the OSCE PA. See, e.g., OSCE, Parliamentary Assembly, 'Our Common Vision for the OSCE Parliamentary Assembly: Supporting OSCE Principles and Facilitating Parliamentary Dialogue', 2016, available at: www.oscepa.org/documents/all-documents/annual-sessions/2016-tbilisi/reports-19/3362-osce-pa-vision-document/file; Christine Muttonen, 'Report of

Assembly and other OSCE bodies. As will be further discussed hereafter, an example of the latter is the nature of the cooperative relationship between the Assembly and OSCE governing bodies, which largely takes place on an informal basis. Despite its informal nature, their interactions have developed into an extended network of cooperation. This has contributed to a further integration of the Assembly into the workings of the OSCE, albeit in an informal manner.

The Assembly's mandate consists of assessing the implementation of OSCE objectives, discussing subjects addressed by OSCE governing bodies, developing and promoting mechanisms for the prevention and resolution of conflicts, supporting the strengthening and consolidation of democratic institutions in OSCE participating States and contributing to the development of the Organization's institutional structures and the relations between the existing institutions.[47] While the Assembly can only meet its objectives in close cooperation with the intergovernmental side of the OSCE, it has 'no bridge by which to cross to the inter-governmental process',[48] as there are no coordinating organs or mechanisms between the governmental and parliamentary sides of the OSCE.[49] Nor is there a formal agreement about the concrete role of the Assembly in the work of the OSCE.[50] As a result, cooperation has largely developed through practice and mutual agreement with the OSCE's governmental side.[51] In 2002 for instance, the Assembly and the Permanent Council intended to formalise their relations by concluding an agreement. This idea was eventually abandoned, as both parties realised that this attempt at formalisation could jeopardise many valuable forms of informal cooperation.[52] The example is a clear expression of the OSCE's preference to

The President of The OSCE Parliamentary Assembly, Twenty-Sixth Annual Session of the OSCE Parliamentary Assembly', July 2017, available at: www.oscepa.org/documents/annual-sessions/2017-minsk/reports-and-speeches-1/3554-closing-remarks-by-president-christine-muttonen-at-final-plenary-9-july-2017/file.

47 OSCE, Parliamentary Assembly, 'Rules of Procedure', 25 March 2017, Rule 2, available at: www.oscepa.org/documents/rules-of-procedure/1832-rules-of-procedure-english/file.

48 Buchsbaum, 'The 1993 Session of the CSCE Parliamentary Assembly', 33.

49 Habegger, 'Democratic Accountability of International Organizations', 194.

50 Some exceptions may be noted. These include: 'Memorandum of Understanding between the Assembly President and the OSCE Chairperson-in-Office', CIO.GAL/40/02/Rev.1, 26 June 2002; and the 'Co-operation Agreement on Election Monitoring between the OSCE Parliamentary Assembly and the Office for Democratic Institutions and Human Rights', CIO.GAL/7/97, 2 September 1997.

51 Spencer Oliver, 'The Parliamentary Assembly and Its Political Influence in the OSCE', 2005, 4–5, available at: www.oscepa.org/documents/all-documents/documents-1/955–2005-the-parliamentary-assembly-and-its-political-influence-in-the-osce/file.

52 Habegger, 'Democratic Accountability of International Organizations', 195.

work on an informal basis.[53] Accordingly, the institutional relations between OSCE governing bodies and the Assembly are primarily of an informal nature but have, over time, developed into quite a dense network of contacts and cooperation.[54]

The informal cooperation and interactions between the intergovernmental and interparliamentary side of the OSCE take place in both directions and have incrementally increased over the years.[55] On the one hand, representatives of the Assembly can participate in the meetings of OSCE institutions during which oral statements may be made. Although they cannot participate in the drafting of documents, they may comment on drafts that directly concern them.[56] The results of the Assembly's Annual Session, particularly the final declaration and resolutions containing various recommendations, are also transferred to the OSCE leadership.[57] Moreover, the Assembly's President plays a particularly active role. Usually, she or he delivers a speech at, for example, the meetings of the OSCE Summits or the Ministerial Councils.[58] The Assembly President has also taken part in the meetings of the Troika, which consists of the current, previous and incoming Chairperson-in-Office.[59] On the other hand, OSCE governmental representatives may participate in the plenary sessions of the Assembly. Thus, the OSCE Chairperson-in-Office participates on a regular basis in the Assembly's annual meetings, answers parliamentarians' questions and communicates their views to the Ministerial Council. Members of the Ministerial Council in turn have the right to attend the Assembly's sessions and speak in debates.[60] In addition, even though not obligated to, many leading OSCE representatives partake in the Assembly's meetings, offering parliamentarians the opportunity to engage in a political dialogue. The Assembly's representatives also have the option to ask questions to participating OSCE representatives, which transforms the Assembly into a platform for internal political dialogue. However, due to the absence of a formal link between both, no strict obligations can result from this informal

53 Ibid., 142.

54 Ibid., 134–5; Beqiraj, 'The OSCE: The Difficult Path of Survival', 52.

55 Spencer Oliver, 'The Parliamentary Assembly and Its Political Influence in the OSCE', 5, 7 (n. 51).

56 OSCE, Ministerial Council, 'OSCE Rules of Procedure' (n. 30), 8 IV. 1 (D), para. 1.

57 Nothelle, 'The OSCE Parliamentary Assembly – Driving Reform', 348.

58 OSCE, Ministerial Council, 'OSCE Rules of Procedure' (n. 30), 10 IV.2 (A)-(B), paras. 8; Habegger, 'Democratic Control of the OSCE: The Role of the Parliamentary Assembly'.

59 OSCE, Report of the Chairman-in-Office to the Lisbon Summit, 'Report of Working Group 2', REF.S/91/96, 1996, para. 4; Degn, 'The OSCE Parliamentary Assembly – Growth in Recent Years', 366; Habegger, 'Democratic Accountability of International Organizations', 195.

60 OSCE, Parliamentary Assembly, 'Rules of Procedure' (n. 47), Rules 27(5) and 42(2).

dialogue.[61] The same holds true for the Assembly's declarations, resolutions and recommendations: there are no formal mechanisms to guarantee that OSCE governing institutions will take them into consideration.[62] In addition, the Assembly does not contain any genuine control mechanisms vis-à-vis the intergovernmental side, besides the aforementioned questioning of OSCE representatives and the agreement that the result of the Annual Session will be sent to the OSCE leadership.[63] Yet, even without strictly formalised relations between the parliamentary side and OSCE governing bodies, the Assembly contributes informally to the Organization's political development.[64]

In a panel discussion held in Vienna in 2017 on the current challenges for the OSCE and the role that the Assembly could play in this regard, it was noted that the Assembly plays a crucial role as it provides the opportunity for parliamentarians to meet their counterparts and to discuss and find compromises together, including within the setting of informal meetings and seminars.[65] Moreover, the 1999 Istanbul Summit Declaration recognised the Assembly as 'one of the most important OSCE institutions continuously providing new ideas and proposals'.[66] This statement was described by Victor-Yves Ghebali as an 'unusual tribute from an intergovernmental body towards an interparliamentary organ'.[67] The statement brought more clarity to the nature of the relationship between the Assembly and other OSCE institutions and it meant that the OSCE leadership accepted the Assembly as their partner, albeit on an unequal footing. Yet, as Helle Degn, former Assembly President, noted, this does not take away the OSCE's democratic deficit, which includes the fact that the Assembly has no formal status in the decision-making process.[68] The Assembly deems democratic oversight important, as OSCE activities directly impact the people that OSCE parliamentarians

61 Habegger, 'Democratic Accountability of International Organizations', 194.

62 Spencer Oliver, 'The Parliamentary Assembly and Its Political Influence in the OSCE', 2005, 4 (n. 51); Beqiraj, 'The OSCE: The Difficult Path of Survival', 52–3.

63 Nothelle, 'The OSCE Parliamentary Assembly – Driving Reform', 347–8.

64 Habegger, 'Democratic Control of the OSCE: The Role of the Parliamentary Assembly', 142.

65 See, in particular, statements by Christine Mutton, President of the OSCE Parliamentary Assembly, and Doris Barnett, Treasurer of the OSCE Parliamentary Assembly. Julien Pinaudeau, 'The Challenges for the OSCE and the Role of the Parliamentary Assembly, Summary of the panel discussion on Wednesday, 22 February 2017', 7 March 2017, available at: https://www.iipvienna.com/new-blog/2017/3/14/f6076n7in2t9lbbzt3gkq4hu90e2b6.

66 OSCE, 'Charter for European Security', November 1999, para. 17, available at: www.osce.org /mc/17502?download=true.

67 Ghebali, 'The Contribution of the Istanbul Document 1999 to European Security and Co-operation', 294.

68 Degn, 'The OSCE Parliamentary Assembly – Growth in Recent Years', 370.

represent.[69] Degn's successors, and other involved individuals, continue the struggle for greater 'transparency and accountability'.[70] In its 2013 Istanbul Final Declaration, the Assembly adopted a resolution on enhancing trust, transparency and accountability within OSCE institutions, noting that the current status of the Assembly continues to result in a democratic deficit within OSCE institutions. One of the proposals included the possibility for the Assembly to oversee all OSCE institutions, policies and practices, which would imply, inter alia, that the Assembly could organise fact-finding missions. A further recommendation stated that the Assembly would be closely associated with the decision-shaping and decision-making processes to provide the governing bodies with greater input, as well as to enhance the capacities of OSCE parliamentarians to report about OSCE issues and policies to their national parliaments.[71] These calls were reiterated in the 2016 Final Declaration, whilst welcoming the progress made in establishing procedures in the cooperation between the Assembly and the governing structures of the OSCE.[72]

3.2 *Actor Informality*

As mentioned before, actor informality refers to international cooperation between actors other than traditional diplomatic actors, such as regulatory agencies, sectoral ministries, sub-federal entities or the judicial or legislative branches of government. In addition, private actors and international organisations may be actively involved in the lawmaking process. The concept of IN-LAW excludes purely private cooperation without public authority involvement and thus the lawmaking process remains state-based. Whilst the OSCE

69 OSCE, Parliamentary Assembly, 'Our Common Vision for the OSCE Parliamentary Assembly: Supporting OSCE Principles and Facilitating Parliamentary Dialogue', 2016, 7, available at: www.oscepa.org/documents/all-documents/annual-sessions/2016-tbilisi/reports-19/3362-osce-pa-vision-document/file.

70 Nothelle, 'The OSCE Parliamentary Assembly – Driving Reform', 357; e.g., in 2001, the ad hoc Committee on Transparency and Accountability, now known as the ad hoc Committee on Strengthening OSCE Engagement Through Transparency and Reform, was established with the aim of strengthening the interaction between the parliamentarian and governmental side of the OSCE in order to encourage more transparency within the OSCE and increase effectiveness and efficiency.

71 OSCE, Parliamentary Assembly, 'Istanbul Declaration and Resolutions', AS (13) D E, 29 June to 3 July 2013, 18–19, paras. 10 and 12, available at: www.oscepa.org/documents/all-documents/annual-sessions/2013-istanbul/declaration/1801-istanbul-declaration-eng-1/file.

72 OSCE, Parliamentary Assembly, 'Tbilisi Declaration and Resolutions', AS (16) D E, 1–5 July 2016, 18–19, available at: www.oscepa.org/documents/all-documents/annual-sessions/2016-tbilisi/declaration-24/3371-tbilisi-declaration-eng/file.

is clearly a product of a multilateral diplomatic process, a number of non-traditional actors have gradually manifested themselves in different degrees within the OSCE decision-making process.[73]

The participating States play the biggest role in terms of agenda setting at the OSCE, with a particular role for the OSCE Chairmanship headed by the Chairperson-in-Office (always the foreign minister of the state holding the Chairmanship). The Chairmanship coordinates the decision-making process and sets the priorities for the Organization's activities during its year in office on behalf of the formal decision-making bodies. As a result, it can place an emphasis on particular issues that it deems important when setting the draft agendas.[74] In this sense, primarily traditional actors play a decisive role in the process of agenda setting. Yet, as will be shown, the involvement of non-traditional actors in the OSCE may indirectly feed into the larger decision-making process.

The OSCE constitutes in the first place a forum for political dialogue between traditional diplomatic actors active within the various formal decision-making bodies.[75] For instance, it is the Chairmanship or participating States that may initiate proposals for draft decisions.[76] Nonetheless, the participating States can generally invite, on a regular or case-by-case basis, the Partners for Co-operation and representatives of other international organisations, institutions and initiatives, as well as NGOs, academia and businesses to attend certain meetings of decision-making bodies and make oral and/or written contributions, however, without the right to participate in the drafting of the documents.[77] Let us take the example of the Meeting of Heads of State or Government (or Summit), which is the highest decision-making body of the OSCE. It takes decisions, sets priorities and provides orientation for the Organization.[78] Whilst decisions are made at the highest political level, the Summits are also open to the Mediterranean and Asian Partners for Co-operation, as well as other international organisations and NGOs, which, as mentioned, are allowed to make oral and/or written contributions and can in this sense participate in the decision-making process.[79] The same holds true

73 Schlager, 'A Hard Look at Compliance with "Soft" Law: The Case of the OSCE', 346.

74 OSCE, Ministerial Council, 'OSCE Rules of Procedure' (n. 30), 4–5 III; 7–8 IV.1 (C), para. 1–4; 12 V. (A), para. 3; OSCE, 'The OSCE Handbook' (n. 26), 19–21.

75 See ibid., 5–6 IV.1 (A).

76 Ibid., 5 IV.1 (A), para. 1.

77 Ibid., 8–9 IV.1 (D), paras. 1–6; see, for informal subsidiary bodies and working groups, ibid., 13 V. (A), para. 7–9; (B), para. 5.

78 Ibid., 3 II. (B), para. 2.

79 OSCE, Ministerial Council, 'OSCE Rules of Procedure' (n. 30), 9 IV.2, para. 6–10; OSCE, 'The OSCE Handbook' (n. 26), 13.

for the Ministerial Council, which is the central decision-making and governing body between Summits. Although it constitutes a forum for negotiation between traditional diplomatic actors, that is, the ministers of foreign affairs of the participating States, consultations among smaller groups involving, for example, the Mediterranean and Asian Partners for Co-operation or other international organisations, may be conducted at the margins of the Ministerial Council meetings.[80]

The dimension of actor informality manifests itself as well in relation to the OSCE Parliamentary Assembly, which was created in 1991 in response to the Paris Summit's call for greater involvement of parliamentarians in the CSCE.[81] As already mentioned, the Assembly is an autonomous body consisting of parliamentarians from the various participating States. It aims at promoting their involvement in the activities of the OSCE and facilitating interparliamentary dialogue and cooperation on OSCE-related issues.[82] Moreover, the Assembly cooperates closely with various external parliamentary bodies: the Parliamentary Assembly of the Council of Europe, the Inter-Parliamentary Union, the European Parliament, the Inter-parliamentary Assembly of the Commonwealth of Independent States and the NATO Parliamentary Assembly.[83] All bodies have observer status in the Assembly.[84] In addition, parliaments of states that are Partners for Co-operation may be admitted as observers.[85] Accordingly, the Assembly can be regarded as a primary example of a body involving unconventional actors in international cooperation. In general, different positions may be noted among states on the involvement of nationally elected parliamentarians in global governance. Some states oppose their involvement, mainly because they themselves lack democratic legitimacy and therefore do not attach any importance to increasing transparency and accountability in the work of international forums. Other states support the involvement of parliamentarians as a matter of principle, but are internally divided on the extent to which this should take place in practice. Proponents of a traditional diplomatic approach try to

80 OSCE, Ministerial Council, 'OSCE Rules of Procedure' (n. 30), 3 II. (B), para. 3; OSCE, 'The OSCE Handbook' (n. 26), 15.

81 CSCE, 'Charter of Paris for a New Europe', 21 November 1990, 13, available at www.osce.org/mc/39516?download=true; OSCE, 'The OSCE Handbook' (n. 26), 6.

82 OSCE, Ministerial Council, 'OSCE Rules of Procedure' (n. 30), 4 II. (C), para. 3; OSCE, 'The OSCE Handbook' (n. 26), 36.

83 OSCE, 'The OSCE Handbook' (n. 26), 37; OSCE, Parliamentary Assembly, 'The OSCE Parliamentary Assembly: Factsheet', www.oscepa.org/documents/factsheet/669-factsheet-english/file.

84 OSCE, Parliamentary Assembly, 'Rules of Procedure' (n. 47), Rule 45(1).

85 Ibid., Rule 45(2).

minimise their involvement, as they consider foreign policy the main prerogative of the executive branch, whilst proponents for greater involvement of parliamentarians argue that increased decision-making at the international level requires involvement of non-traditional actors, such as parliamentarians and civil society.[86] It is held that parliamentary involvement may increase openness, transparency and public visibility; ultimately, it would contribute to democratic accountability. Yet, as was discussed above under process informality, the extent to which the OSCE Parliamentary Assembly can effectively check the governmental side is quite limited.[87]

Besides the OSCE Parliamentary Assembly, other examples may be given at the level of the specialised OSCE bodies that reveal a certain degree of actor informality. A first example are the annual Human Dimension Implementation Meetings hosted by the Office for Democratic Institutions and Human Rights (ODIHR), during which a variety of actors convene (e.g. government representatives, non-governmental organisations, international experts and human rights activists) in order to discuss the implementation of the human dimension commitments to which the participating States agreed.[88] While such meetings do not have a decision-making capacity and are not mandated to produce any negotiated text, their recommendations may feed directly into the OSCE's decision-making process through, for instance, a subsequent Ministerial Council meeting.[89] The same may be argued in relation to the recommendations stemming from Human Dimension Seminars organised by the ODIHR. Such Seminars aim at discussing and exchanging information about human dimension issues of importance to the participating States. In addition to governmental officials, international organisations and, as of 1994, NGOs participate as well.[90] An example thereof is the Seminar organised in 2015 on the role of national human rights institutions (NHRIs) in promoting and protecting human rights in the OSCE area, in which inter alia twenty-five NGOs and various NHRIs participated. Key recommendations addressing the participating States, the OSCE, its institutions and field operations were formulated and circulated. In this regard, the final report explicitly stated that 'conclusions and recommendations have no official status and are not based on consensus; however, they should serve as useful indicators for the OSCE in setting priorities and planning its

86 Habegger, 'Democratic Control of the OSCE: The Role of the Parliamentary Assembly', 142
87 Ibid., 142–3.
88 OSCE, 'The OSCE Handbook' (n. 26), 29.
89 OSCE, Ministerial Council, 'OSCE Rules of Procedure' (n. 30), 14 VI. (A), para. 1; OSCE, 'The OSCE Handbook' (n. 26), 92.
90 OSCE, 'The OSCE Handbook' (n. 26), 93.

programmes',[91] thus indicating that such recommendations may have a particular influence on the OSCE's priority-setting and decision-making process.

It has been asserted that although the role of civil society has dramatically increased in most international forums whilst having an important influence on the decision-making process, this development has manifested itself to a lesser degree in the OSCE due to its particular governmental nature.[92] Yet, in relation to the work of the High Commissioner for National Minorities (HCNM), it has been argued that civil society (in particular minority representatives, human and minority rights organisations and academia)[93] constitutes one of its essential components.[94] The elaboration of general sets of recommendations constitutes one of the specific areas in which the involvement of civil society is of particular importance to the work of the HCNM (see further below).[95] In relation to NGOs, their involvement in the OSCE takes place through various channels and especially in relation to the human dimension. These are primarily in Summit Meetings, the review conferences and implementation meetings, seminars on particular security-related issues and in meetings of the HCNM and the Media Representative.[96]

To some extent, one can also argue that expert groups have a role to play. The HCNM has, for example, convened various expert groups to develop a series of thematic recommendations and guidelines that assist the HCNM in formulating advice to governments, clarify the content of international standards and guide states when resolving inter-ethnic problems.[97] The role of the experts is twofold. On the one hand, they assist in identifying the relevant normative principles and make sure that all standards are referred to and interpreted correctly. On the other hand, they contribute to the legitimacy of the recommendations.[98] An example is The Hague Recommendations Regarding the Educational Right of National Minorities, for which a variety of independent

91 OSCE, Human Dimension Seminar, 'The Role of National Human Rights Institutions (NHRIs) in Promoting and Protecting Human Rights in the OSCE Area: Consolidated Summary', 2015, 4, available at: www.osce.org/odihr/210256?download=true.

92 Zellner, 'The OSCE Network of Think Thanks and Academic Institutions: Baby Steps', 274.

93 Altenhoener and Palermo, 'Civil Society Contributions to the Work of the OSCE High Commissioner on National Minorities', 203.

94 Ibid., 202.

95 Ibid., 211, 213–16.

96 Tudyka, 'Non-Governmental Organizations and the OSCE', 470. See, for a discussion on the interaction of the OSCE and the NGO Human Rights Watch, Andersen, 'The OSCE and Human Rights Watch', 391–401.

97 CSCE, 'Helsinki Document: The Challenges of Change', 9–10 July 1992, paras. 31–6, available at: www.osce.org/mc/39530?download=true; OSCE, 'The OSCE Handbook' (n. 26), 33.

98 Altenhoener and Palermo, 'Civil Society Contributions to the Work of the OSCE High Commissioner on National Minorities', 215.

experts from different disciplines were consulted.[99] Other thematic areas that have been the focus of expert participation are, amongst others, linguistic rights of minorities, minority participation in public life, media broadcasting in minority languages, policing practices in multi-ethnic societies and national minorities in interstate relations. The latter set of recommendations are technically speaking the HCNM's own recommendations in the sense that they have been mainly drafted in-house and later endorsed by international experts, and not the other way around.[100] Another example is the OSCE Network of Think Thanks and Academic Institutions, which was set up in 2013. It is an autonomous and informal OSCE-related track II initiative bringing together research institutions from OSCE participating and partner States engaged in academic research and policy analysis on the OSCE.[101] Even though not formally part of the OSCE structure, its work may inform the OSCE decision-making process. It also constitutes an effort to include in a more systematic manner civil society actors in the work of the OSCE.[102]

Lastly, the OSCE serves as a forum for intense external cooperation with other international organisations.[103] Apart from the ability of the OSCE to invite such organisations to attend certain of its meetings (see above), the OSCE cultivates close cooperative relationships with particular international organisations.[104] The UN is, for instance, one of the OSCE's closest partners. In 1992, the participating States declared the CSCE a regional arrangement under Chapter VIII of the Charter of the UN.[105] Moreover, in 1993, a Framework for Cooperation and Coordination between the UN Secretariat and the CSCE was agreed upon, and the CSCE was granted observer status at the UN.[106] Both organisations engage in political dialogue, coordination and

99 OSCE, High Commission of National Minorities, 'The Hague Recommendations Regarding the Educational Right of National Minorities & Explanatory Note', 1996, available at: www.osce.org/hcnm/32180?download=true.

100 Altenhoener and Palermo, 'Civil Society Contributions to the Work of the OSCE High Commissioner on National Minorities', 214, note 17.

101 Track II initiatives aim at promoting unofficial dialogue with non-governmental actors, such as NGOs and academics, which are normally not included in the formal decision-making processes.

102 See Zellner, 'The OSCE Network of Think Thanks and Academic Institutions: Baby Steps'.

103 See Zannier, 'Strength in Numbers: Co-operating with Other International Organizations', 383–90.

104 On this issue, see Boisson de Chazournes and Gadkowski, 'The External Relations of the OSCE', Chapter 10 in this Volume.

105 CSCE, 'Helsinki Document: The Challenges of Change' (n. 97), para. 25.

106 UN, General Assembly, 'Framework for Cooperation and Coordination Between the United Nations Secretariat and The Conference on Security and Cooperation in Europe', UNGA/48/185, Annex II, Appendix, 1993; UN, General Assembly, 'Observer Status for the

information exchange at the political and expert levels.[107] It has, for instance, become common for the OSCE Chairperson-in-Office to address the UN Security Council in order to highlight the Chairmanship's priorities for greater collaboration with the UN. In addition, regular meetings take place between high-ranking officials, for instance at the Secretary-General level. Every year around a dozen senior UN officials are invited to speak at the meetings of the OSCE Permanent Council or Forum for Security Co-operation.[108] Since 1992, the CSCE/OSCE, the UN and the Council of Europe have held annual Tripartite High-level Meetings, which have expanded to include the EU, the International Organization for Migration and the International Committee of the Red Cross.[109] The aim is to facilitate cooperation in conflict prevention and democratic institution building, as well as to share information and to improve cooperation by drawing on each other's expertise and know-how.[110] Another example is the OSCE's longstanding and close cooperation with the EU. The EU is represented in all OSCE decision-making bodies. Until the Treaty of Lisbon, the EU was represented by the delegation of the country holding the Presidency of the Council of the EU and by the European Commission.[111] As the EU's external representation system changed with the entry into force of the Lisbon Treaty, the EU Delegation has taken over this task.[112] Cooperation takes place in various policy areas, such as democratisation, institution-building and human rights.[113]

To conclude in terms of actor informality, the OSCE remains primarily state-based through the involvement of traditional diplomatic actors in the decision-making process. Nevertheless, there is also a great involvement of a variety of non-traditional actors in the OSCE's decision-making processes, which may feed into formal decision-making processes. These include, amongst others, international organisations, NGOs and independent experts,

Conference on Security and Cooperation in Europe in the General Assembly', UNGA/RES/48/5, 1993.

107 Zannier, 'The OSCE and Chapter VIII of the United Nations Charter – Contributing to Global Peace and Security', 101.

108 Ibid., 102.

109 Galbreath, *The Organization for Security and Co-operation in Europe (OSCE)*, 126; OSCE, 'The OSCE Handbook' (n. 26), 101.

110 Council of Europe, 'The Council of Europe and the OSCE: Enhancing Co-operation and Complementarity through Greater Coherence', 23 March 2012, para. 5.7, available at: https://rm.coe.int/1680472b8d.

111 OSCE, Ministerial Council, 'OSCE Rules of Procedure' (n. 30), 8 IV.1 (C), para. 11; 10 IV.2 (A)-(B), para. 7.

112 See further, Niels van Willigen, 'Effective Multilateralism Between Unequal Partners', 136–52.

113 Paunov, 'Assessing the Success of EU–OSCE Cooperation: A Case of Mutualism?', 339.

as well as national parliamentarians sitting in the OSCE Parliamentary Assembly.

3.3 *Output Informality*

The OSCE has had very active days of standard setting. Yet, as Schlager noted in 2000: '[a]fter 1990, participating states generally agreed that the days of standards setting in the OSCE had passed and that they should focus attention on achieving compliance with already agreed norms'.[114] Moreover, over the past decade it has been increasingly difficult for the participating States to achieve the consensus generally required to adopt formal decisions and address key issues in the OSCE region.[115] Regardless of these observations, the OSCE is still actively involved in standard setting through, for example, the recommendations issued by the HCNM.[116]

One of the essential features of the OSCE is the fact that its decision-making process does not result in the adoption of formal treaties or other traditional sources of international law, but produces politically, and not legally, binding decisions and documents.[117] Consequently, participating States make commitments to which they can only be held to account in a political, and possibly moral, manner but not before a court of law. Some have questioned the binding force of such political commitments. In response, many have noted that the political character of the decisions does not result in the lack of binding force, as the distinction is between legal and political, and not between binding and non-binding.[118] Therefore, OSCE decisions retain their normative and obligatory character but differ in their consequences in cases of non-compliance. As such, the violation of a politically binding agreement is as inadmissible as any violation of legally binding norms of international law.[119] The reasons the participating States opted for politically rather

114 Schlager, 'A Hard Look at Compliance with "Soft" Law: The Case of the OSCE', 365.

115 See Commission on Security and Cooperation in Europe (US–Helsinki Commission), 'Consensus Denied? Challenges for OSCE Decision-Making in 2017', 2017, available at: www.csce.gov/international-impact/publications/consensus-denied-challenges-osce-decision-making-2017.

116 See Farahat, 'Regulating Minority Issues through Standard-Setting and Mediation', 1453–80.

117 OSCE, Ministerial Council, 'OSCE Rules of Procedure' (n. 30), 1 II. (A), paras. 1 & 3.

118 OSCE, Office of Democratic Institutions and Human Rights, 'OSCE Human Dimension Commitments: Thematic Compilation, 3rd edition, volume 1', 2011, XVIII, available at: www.osce.org/odihr/76894?download=true.

119 For the OSCE context, see Bloed, *The Conference on Security and Co-operation in Europe*, 22; Berger, 'OSCE and International Law', 43; Manton, 'The OSCE Human Dimension and Customary International Law Formation', 199–200.

than legally binding decisions may be found in their belief that it would provide for a more dynamic and flexible decision-making process tailored to the particular security-related issues with which the OSCE deals, and not in the denial of binding force as such.[120] The OSCE would essentially not be burdened with the bureaucratic and lengthy processes associated with traditional lawmaking processes and would be able to respond in a swift manner to urgent situations.[121]

Whilst OSCE decisions have generally been placed in the soft law basket, it is argued that their non-legal nature does not necessarily affect their binding force. Reisman has identified three components in lawmaking that make the binding nature of an instrument a matter of degree rather than a binary distinction between hard and soft law. These components are: policy content, authority of the prescriber, and implementation and enforcement mechanisms.[122] The hardness of the policy content will depend upon the language used in a particular instrument (mandatory versus permissive) and on the degree of precision and substance.[123] As a result, the hardness of this component may vary amongst OSCE documents. For instance, many OSCE Human Dimension documents use mandatory language. An example thereof is the Copenhagen Document, which includes compelling phrases such as 'reaffirm their commitment to implement fully', 'commit themselves' and 'will ensure that'.[124] Manton holds that in terms of policy content the Copenhagen Document is considered harder than other human rights instruments.[125] In relation to the authority of the prescriber, the fact that OSCE decisions are adopted by consensus gives such decisions great authority and

[120] Manton, 'The OSCE Human Dimension and Customary International Law Formation', 205.

[121] Klabbers, 'Institutional Ambivalence by Design', 408 & 410–12; OSCE, ODIHR, OSCE Human Dimension Commitments: Thematic Compilation (n. 118), XVIII.

[122] Michael Reisman uses the following terms: 'policy statements couched in normative mood, expectations of authority, and communications of control intention' (Reisman, 'The Concept and Functions of Soft Law in International Politics', in Emmanuel G. Bello and Bola A. Ajibola S.A.N. (eds.), *Essays in Honour of Judge Taslim Olawale Elias*, Contemporary International Law and Human Rights, vol. 1 (Dordrecht; Boston; London: Martinus Nijhoff Publishers, 1992), 135–6).

[123] Manton, 'The OSCE Human Dimension and Customary International Law Formation', 208–9.

[124] CSCE, 'Document of the Copenhagen Meeting of The Conference on the Human Dimension of the CSCE', 29 June 1990, see paras. 22.2, 40.2 & 24, available at: www.osce.org/odihr/elections/14304?download=true; Ratner, 'Does International Law Matter in Preventing Ethnic Conflict?', 612–13.

[125] Manton, 'The OSCE Human Dimension and Customary International Law Formation', 209.

thus a high degree of binding force, strengthened further by the level at which they are made (head of state or foreign minister).[126] Lastly, the binding nature of OSCE decisions manifests itself in the various procedures, mechanisms and institutions that have been set up in order to ensure compliance and accountability. Examples thereof are the Vienna and Moscow Mechanisms, which provide platforms to raise questions and concerns about human dimension commitments undertaken by participating States.[127] Other mechanisms include, amongst others, election-monitoring missions in order to evaluate compliance with commitments to free and fair elections and the HCNM.[128] It has been argued that the OSCE would be no more successful were it established on the basis of a hard law framework.[129] This boils down to acknowledging that in reality legal agreements, especially in the human rights field, have only a few meaningful consequences in the event of non-compliance and that compliance is primarily linked to effective monitoring mechanisms rather than the legally binding or non-binding nature of a norm.[130] Yet, the crisis in Ukraine has provided us with a mixed picture. It has, on the one hand, confirmed the OSCE's reputation as an international security organisation, but, on the other hand, unveiled a troublesome example of clear violations of several foundational OSCE principles by one of its main participating States (Russia).[131] In sum, the binding nature of OSCE decisions can be considered as being generally of a high degree, which, however, may be tempered in certain instances.

[126] OSCE, Ministerial Council, 'OSCE Rules of Procedure' (n. 30), 1 II. (A), para. 2; Ratner, 'Does International Law Matter in Preventing Ethnic Conflict?', 614; Manton, 'The OSCE Human Dimension and Customary International Law Formation', 209.

[127] The Vienna Mechanism was established in the CSCE, 'Concluding Document of the Third Follow-up Meeting, Vienna, 4 November 1986 to 19 January 1989', 19 January 1989, available at: www.osce.org/mc/40881?download=true; the Moscow Mechanism, however, was agreed upon at the last meeting of the Conference on the Human Dimension of the CSCE held in Moscow in 1991, CSCE, 'Document of the Moscow Meeting of the Conference on the Human Dimension of the CSCE', 4 October 1991, available at: www.osce.org/odihr/elections/14310?download=true.

[128] See, in relation to High Commissioner of National Minorities, Ratner, 'Does International Law Matter in Preventing Ethnic Conflict?'; Packer, 'Making International Law Matter in Preventing Ethnic Conflict: A Practitioner's Perspective', 715–24.

[129] Börzel and I. Peters, '"It's Politics, Stupid": An International Relations Perspective on Strengthening the Legal Framework of the OSCE', Chapter 5 in this Volume. See also Schlager, 'A Hard Look at Compliance with "Soft" Law: The Case of the OSCE', 371–2.

[130] Schlager, 'A Hard Look at Compliance with "Soft" Law: The Case of the OSCE', 351; Shelton, 'Commentary and Conclusions', 462.

[131] Bloed, 'OSCE Chronicle', 145–51; Bloed, 'OSCE Principles: Which Principles?, 210–20.

Even though the OSCE's political decision-making process has generally been contrasted with (hard) international law, various links with formal sources of law and formal lawmaking may be identified. Some have even questioned whether it is possible to enter at all into a politically binding commitment that is not at the same time legally binding.[132] First of all, OSCE commitments are often drafted using legal language or referring to international law and are analysed by using standard techniques of international law.[133] As a result, they mirror the output of traditional international organisations.[134] Furthermore, the Decalogue of Principles of the Helsinki Final Act, which guides the relations between the participating States, is in part binding upon the participating States as fundamental principles of customary international law.[135] Another illustration is the fact that several treaties have been negotiated within the framework of the OSCE.[136] These include the Treaty on Conventional Armed Forces in Europe and the Open Skies Treaty, as well as the Convention on Conciliation and Arbitration within the OSCE. In relation to the first two treaties, the link between their negotiation process and the CSCE/OSCE as such was rather weak, while with regard to the latter treaty one may speak of the first OSCE convention in the proper sense of the word. However, these treaties only apply to those participating States that have ratified them and constitute in this sense a deviation from the principle of universalism of OSCE commitments.[137] Another interesting example is that from time to time CSCE/OSCE documents have been relied upon before the International Court of Justice (ICJ). For instance, the ICJ referred in its judgment in the *Nicaragua Case* to the Helsinki Final Act as evidence of *opinion juris*.[138] Similarly, certain treaties under international law have referred to CSCE–OSCE documents, transforming political obligations into legal ones.[139]A last example is the argument that OSCE decisions can contribute to the development of customary international law.[140] Accordingly,

132 Klabbers, 'Institutional Ambivalence by Design', 412.
133 Berger, 'OSCE and International Law', 39–40.
134 Klabbers, 'Institutional Ambivalence by Design', 410.
135 Bloed, *The Conference on Security and Co-operation in Europe*, 23; Berger, 'OSCE and International Law', 38–9.
136 OSCE, 'The OSCE Handbook' (n. 26), 97.
137 Bloed, *The Conference on Security and Co-operation in Europe*, 24–5; OSCE, 'The OSCE Handbook' (n. 26), 97–9.
138 ICJ, *Case Concerning Military and Paramilitary Activities in and against Nicaragua (Nicaragua* v. *USA)*, Judgment of 27 June 1986, ICJ Reports 1986, 14, paras. 189, 204 & 264.
139 Fastenrath, 'The Legal Significance of CSCE/OSCE Documents', 417.
140 Ibid., 422–3; Manton, 'The OSCE Human Dimension and Customary International Law Formation'.

it has been asserted that although the participating States chose a non-legally binding form for OSCE documents, these may still play an important role in the processes of international lawmaking.[141]

When conducting an IN-LAW analysis, one question in particular arises: to what extent do OSCE decisions and documents correspond to output informality? As they do not constitute a formal treaty or any other traditional source of international law, this would prima facie be the case. Yet, one may challenge the extent to which such decisions and documents are part of a lawmaking process, as they are politically but not legally binding. However, as explained in the context of IN-LAW (Section 2), 'law' is to be understood in a broad sense, namely 'norm-setting or public policy making by public authorities' whereby the output 'may not, strictly speaking, be part of law but merely have legal effects or fit in the context of a broader legal or normative process'.[142] Understood in this manner, the mere fact that OSCE decisions and documents are not law in a strict sense, as they are not traditional sources of international law, does not exclude them from being part of a broader normative process. A further condition is that the informal output is normative in nature in the sense that it determines or reduces the freedom of others. This is clearly the case, as their non-legally binding character does not take away that they generally have a high degree of 'bindingness', as discussed above, and thus steer the behaviour of the participating States. Moreover, OSCE decisions and documents may impact the freedom of non-state actors such as individuals and businesses that find themselves within the OSCE area. Accordingly, the OSCE's decisions and documents represent a clear case of output informality.

Besides OSCE decisions and documents concluded by the formal decision-making bodies, other types of outputs can be identified. The three specialised bodies of the OSCE (ODIHR, HCNM and the Representative on Freedom of the Media) monitor compliance with OSCE principles and commitments by the participating States in their respective field of specialisation and provide assistance, inter alia, by issuing recommendations and guidelines. Such instruments provide for an interesting case to analyse from an IN-LAW perspective. A closer look at the output of the HCNM will now be taken.

The HCNM may, in addition to its other activities, issue recommendations on possible policy and legislative steps that could be taken to implement minority protection standards. Such recommendations are considered as one of the central

141 Bloed, *The Conference on Security and Co-operation in Europe*, 23.

142 Pauwelyn, 'Informal International Lawmaking: Framing the Concept', 21.

and most effective instruments of the HCNM.[143] They serve as standards, understood as commitments and responsibilities below the level of formally binding decisions.[144] The recommendations can be either general or country-specific. The latter are directed to a particular country; they contain detailed proposals to deal with certain issues and are as a rule not made public. General recommendations, by contrast, set standards for all participating States; these are public documents that bring together existing international standards, comparative practices and HCNM experiences when dealing with a specific issue. As mentioned above under actor informality, the recommendations are usually drafted with the assistance of independent experts and other civil society actors.[145]

The HCNM may be considered as exercising public authority in two ways: first by acting as a standard-setter by particularising international rights and standards, and secondly by monitoring the compliance of the participating States with these standards.[146] Moreover, in order for the standards to be considered as being part of informal lawmaking, they need to be normative in nature. The HCNM does not have a formal decision-making capacity and is strictly speaking not even tasked with the elaboration of standards. The institution was originally established as a mechanism for conflict prevention but quickly took up an important role in standard setting.[147] Although HCNM recommendations serve as suggestions and do not impose any obligations on the participating States,[148] they can be considered as constituting important and effective instruments of persuasion, particularly due to their legitimacy emanating as they do from the involvement of renowned experts in their respective fields, civil society and the HCNM as a highly respected institution.[149] In this sense, they may steer the behaviour of the participating States and contribute to the further development of international standards on the matter at hand. Nevertheless, the participating States may at the same time overlook these practical guidelines, as their implementation is entirely

143 Farahat, 'Regulating Minority Issues through Standard-Setting and Mediation', 1458.

144 Ibid., 1455.

145 Altenhoener and Palermo, 'Civil Society Contributions to the Work of the OSCE High Commissioner on National Minorities', 213–15.

146 Farahat, 'Regulating Minority Issues through Standard-Setting and Mediation', 1456.

147 CSCE, 'Helsinki Document: The Challenges of Change' (n. 97), sec. II; Ratner, 'Does International Law Matter in Preventing Ethnic Conflict?', 620; Farahat, 'Regulating Minority Issues through Standard-Setting and Mediation', 1458; Altenhoener and Palermo, 'Civil Society Contributions to the Work of the OSCE High Commissioner on National Minorities', 215.

148 CSCE, 'Helsinki Document: The Challenges of Change' (n. 97), para. 34.

149 Altenhoener and Palermo, 'Civil Society Contributions to the Work of the OSCE High Commissioner on National Minorities', 215–16.

dependent upon the discretion of states.[150] Yet, this may be different in relation to those standards that reflect existing international law or OSCE decisions. The references to international obligations on minority protection in both types of recommendations are quite extensive. They include relevant OSCE documents, the Framework Convention on National Minorities, the European Convention on Human Rights, UN documents concerning minorities, etc. Whilst the general recommendations translate these various standards into concrete standards, the country-specific recommendation applies the general recommendations to a concrete situation.[151] Interestingly, one of the main consequences is that the HCNM not only functions as a mediative monitoring mechanism for OSCE commitments relating to minority protection but also for international treaties external to the OSCE.[152] Even though the standards set by the HCNM are in principle non-binding, a large body of scholarship has asserted that they are at least as effective as formal international law.[153] Taking all of this into account, the standards set by the HCNM may be identified as being normative in nature and as a manifestation of output informality.

Lastly, the output of the OSCE Parliamentary Assembly provides for an interesting case to analyse from an informal output perspective. In order to pursue its responsibilities and objectives, the Assembly adopts, by majority vote, declarations and resolutions containing recommendations addressed to OSCE bodies and institutions and OSCE participating States. Notably, due to the adoption of decisions by majority vote, the Assembly has the ability to address more controversial issues in comparison to the governing bodies, which govern by consensus.[154]

The Assembly's output may inform the work of the OSCE and national parliaments. For instance, the Declarations adopted by the Assembly at the Annual Sessions are commonly transferred to the Ministerial Council, Permanent Council and the OSCE Chairmanship. Such Declarations set out the common view of the parliamentarians on a variety of political matters that are on the OSCE agenda and may provide valuable input into the formal

[150] Farahat, 'Regulating Minority Issues through Standard-Setting and Mediation', 1470–1.

[151] Ratner, 'Does International Law Matter in Preventing Ethnic Conflict?', 624–36; Farahat, 'Regulating Minority Issues through Standard-Setting and Mediation', 1467–8.

[152] Farahat, 'Regulating Minority Issues through Standard-Setting and Mediation', 1471.

[153] Packer, 'Making International Law Matter in Preventing Ethnic Conflict: A Practitioner's Perspective'; Ratner, 'Does International Law Matter in Preventing Ethnic Conflict?'; Farahat, 'Regulating Minority Issues through Standard-Setting and Mediation', 1471–3.

[154] OSCE, Parliamentary Assembly, 'Rules of Procedure' (n. 47), Rule 33; Degn, 'The OSCE Parliamentary Assembly – Growth in Recent Years', 365.

decision-making process.[155] Still, the governing bodies are not compelled to take the opinion of the Assembly into consideration. Its output is neither legally nor politically binding. Nonetheless, over the years, the recommendations of the Assembly have, for example, led to the establishment of the Representative on Freedom of the Media and to increased attention to gender issues within the work of the OSCE.[156] Despite this, the governmental side only rarely makes direct references to the Assembly in its decisions and documents.[157] Accordingly, some have asserted that the influence of the Assembly's recommendations in the decision-making process should not be overestimated.[158]

Whilst the output of the OSCE Parliamentary Assembly may influence the behaviour of both the OSCE and the participating States, its normative nature is of a significantly lower degree than the politically binding decisions adopted by the formal decision-making bodies of the Organization. This does not ignore that the Assembly's resolutions and recommendations may in an informal manner influence the OSCE's policies. Moreover, they constitute important instruments for informal policy coordination and exchange between the various parliaments of the participating States, taking into account that it is the only regionally based parliamentary assembly that includes representatives from Europe, Asia and North America. It is, however, left to the parliamentarians themselves to translate the Assembly's policy recommendations to the domestic political level in order to provide for a follow-up in the national parliaments.[159] In this regard, the OSCE Parliamentary Assembly has acknowledged that efforts to institutionalise follow-up procedures within the Assembly have not received sufficient support from parliamentarians, which is necessary in order to ensure an actual impact of the Declarations.[160] To conclude, even though the output of the Assembly may play an influential role, it does not fall within the category of output informality, as it lacks the necessary normative content in the sense of unilaterally determining or reducing the freedom of others, that is at the level of the OSCE and on the domestic political level.

155 OSCE, Parliamentary Assembly, 'Our Common Vision for the OSCE Parliamentary Assembly' (n. 69), 3.

156 Degn, 'The OSCE Parliamentary Assembly – Growth in Recent Years', 369–70.

157 Spencer Oliver, 'The Parliamentary Assembly and Its Political Influence in the OSCE', 2005, 4 (n. 51).

158 Habegger, 'Democratic Control of the OSCE: The Role of the Parliamentary Assembly', 140.

159 Ibid., 143.

160 OSCE, Parliamentary Assembly, 'Our Common Vision for the OSCE Parliamentary Assembly' (n. 69), 7.

4 CONCLUDING REMARKS

The IN-LAW analysis of the OSCE as a norm-creator has provided us with an interesting and multifaceted case of IN-LAW, especially due to the OSCE's particular nature in comparison to other entities involved in global governance. As the OSCE displays many features that are characteristic for traditional intergovernmental organisations, one may not easily recognise the Organization as a case of IN-LAW, especially in all its three dimensions. The question was even raised as to whether the OSCE as a forum is informal at all, given its highly formalised institutional nature and it being referred to as 'one of the most governmental international organisations'.[161] In the context of the IN-LAW project, we are open to counting any activity as IN-LAW when informal in any of the three dimensions. In this sense, IN-LAW can be informal in different ways and to different degrees.[162] Even though the OSCE is of a highly formalised nature involving, in the first instance, traditional diplomatic actors, we have given throughout this chapter various examples of process, actor and output informality, which have shown us a more nuanced picture of the OSCE as a case of IN-LAW.

To be sure, the qualification of certain processes as IN-LAW was not a goal in its own right for us. However, as part of the IN-LAW project we have found that informal international cooperation can considerably affect individual freedom. As a result, one of the most pressing problems emerging from this is the potential lack of *democratic accountability*. Our normative threshold was that any exercise of public authority must be kept accountable. Accordingly, we developed a calibrated and sophisticated approach to counter this issue, taking into account that accountability can be organised at different levels,[163] invoked by different actors[164] and function in various ways (i.e. democratic, constitutional and learning). Moreover, we found that accountability entails more than only *ex post* accountability in the form of an institutional relation between an actor and a forum. It also entails an *ex ante* responsiveness towards stakeholders, which includes a willingness to take their views into account and

161 Altenhoener and Palermo, 'Civil Society Contributions to the Work of the OSCE High Commissioner on National Minorities', 202.

162 Pauwelyn, 'Informal International Lawmaking: Framing the Concept', 21.

163 Namely on the international (e.g. participatory decision-making, transparency and the existence of a complaint mechanism) and domestic level (e.g. domestic administrative or political control).

164 Internally by those who entrusted the makers of IN-LAW with the power to do so (e.g. the participating States or the parliament who elected the responsible representatives) and externally by those who are outside but affected by the IN-LAW network (e.g. private individuals).

to reconcile conflicting interests, both in terms of substance and procedure, and questions of ongoing control. Lastly, we found that there is no one-size-fits-all mechanism to keep informal cooperation accountable. Rather, it depends on various factors, such as the organisational structure, output and legal mandate of the entity in question. As mentioned, one of the main attractions of IN-LAW is the fact that it dispenses with certain formalities commonly associated with the traditional lawmaking process and as a consequence could offer greater effectiveness. While an increase in effectiveness is often presumed as requiring a reduction in accountability, we identified accountability and effectiveness as going hand-in-hand on various occasions.[165]

Even though this chapter did not delve into a discussion on accountability within the OSCE, as this is the subject of another chapter,[166] on a number of occasions attention was drawn to the role, or rather potential role, of the OSCE Parliamentary Assembly in this regard. While the Assembly could play a useful function in securing and increasing domestic democratic accountability, it appears that the Assembly's lack of formal status contributes to a so-called democratic deficit within the OSCE. On the other hand, our discussion has shown that considerable proposals and efforts are being made for greater transparency and accountability by assigning the Assembly a greater role to that end.

REFERENCES

Altenhoener, Charlotte and Palermo, Francesco, 'Civil Society Contributions to the Work of the OSCE High Commissioner on National Minorities', *International Journal on Minority and Group Rights* 18 (2) (2011), 201–18.

Andersen, Elizabeth, 'The OSCE and Human Rights Watch: From Norm-Setting to Implementation and Enforcement', in Institute for Peace Research and Security Policy at the University of Hamburg (ed.), *OSCE Yearbook 2000* (Baden-Baden: Nomos Verlagsgesellschaft, 2001), 391–401.

Beqiraj, Julinda, 'The OSCE: The Difficult Path of Survival', *The Whitehead Journal of Diplomacy and International Relations* 13 (2) (2012), 45–61.

Berger, Christian, 'OSCE and International Law', *International Journal of Legal Information* 24 (1) (1996), 36–47.

165 See further Pauwelyn, Wessel and Wouters, *Informal International Lawmaking*.

166 The question of accountability in the legal and institutional framework of the OSCE will be discussed by Moser, 'Conceptualising Accountability in the Legal and Institutional Framework of the OSCE', Chapter 13 in this Volume.

Berman, Ayelet, Duquet, Sanderijn, Pauwelyn, Joost, Wessel, Ramses and Wouters, Jan (eds.), *Informal International Lawmaking: Case Studies*, Law of the Future Series 3 (The Hague: Torkel Opsahl Academic EPublisher, 2012).

Bloed, Arie (ed.), *The Conference on Security and Co-operation in Europe: Analysis and Basic Documents, 1972–1993* (Dordrecht, Boston, London: Martinus Nijhoff Publishers, 1993).

'OSCE Chronicle', *Security and Human Rights* 25 (1) (2014), 145–51.

'OSCE Principles: Which Principles?', *Security and Human Rights* 25 (2) (2014), 210–220.

Buchsbaum, Thomas, 'The 1993 Session of the CSCE Parliamentary Assembly', *Helsinki Monitor* 4 (4) (1993), 26–35.

Chinkin, Christine, 'Normative Development in the International Legal System', in Dinah Shelton (ed.), *Commitment and Compliance: The Role of Non-Binding Norms in the International Legal System* (Oxford: Oxford University Press, 2000), 21–42.

Degn, Helle, 'The OSCE Parliamentary Assembly – Growth in Recent Years', in Institute for Peace Research and Security Policy at the University of Hamburg (ed.), *OSCE Yearbook 2001* (Baden-Baden: Nomos Verlagsgesellschaft, 2002), 365–72.

Di Stasi, Angela, 'About Soft Law Organizations: An Open Question', in Roberto Virzo and Ivan Ingravallo (eds.), *Evolutions in the Law of International Organizations*, Legal Aspects of International Organizations, vol. 54 (Leiden, Boston: Brill Nijhoff, 2015), 44–69.

Farahat, Anuscheh, 'Regulating Minority Issues through Standard-Setting and Mediation: The Case of the High Commissioner on National Minorities', *German Law Journal* 9 (11) (2008), 1453–80.

Fastenrath, Ulrich, 'The Legal Significance of CSCE/OSCE Documents', in Institute for Peace Research and Security Policy at the University of Hamburg (ed.), *OSCE Yearbook 1996* (Baden-Baden: Nomos Verlagsgesellschaft, 1997), 411–27.

Galbreath, David, *The Organization for Security and Co-operation in Europe (OSCE)* (New York: Routledge, 2007).

Ghébali, Victor-Yves, 'The Contribution of the Istanbul Document 1999 to European Security and Co-operation', in Institute for Peace Research and Security Policy at the University of Hamburg (ed.), *OSCE Yearbook 2000* (Baden-Baden: Nomos Verlagsgesellschaft, 2001), 289–305.

Habegger, Beat, 'Democratic Accountability of International Organizations: Parliamentary Control within the Council of Europe and the OSCE and the Prospects for the United Nations', *Cooperation and Conflict* 45 (2) (2010), 186–204.

'Democratic Control of the OSCE: The Role of the Parliamentary Assembly', *Helsinki Monitor* 17 (2) (2006), 133–43.

Klabbers, Jan, 'Institutional Ambivalence by Design: Soft Organizations in International Law', *Nordic Journal of International Law* 70 Issue 3 (2001), 403–21.

Manton, Eric, 'The OSCE Human Dimension and Customary International Law Formation', in Institute for Peace Research and Security Policy at the University of Hamburg (ed.), *OSCE Yearbook 2005* (Baden-Baden: Nomos Verlagsgesellschaft, 2006), 1–20.

Nothelle, Andreas, 'The OSCE Parliamentary Assembly – Driving Reform', in Institute for Peace Research and Security Policy at the University of Hamburg (ed.), *OSCE Yearbook 2006* (Baden-Baden: Nomos Verlagsgesellschaft, 2007), 347–73.

O'Connell, Mary Ellen, 'The Role of Soft Law in a Global Order', in Dinah Shelton (ed.), *Commitment and Compliance: The Role of Non-Binding Norms in the International Legal System* (Oxford: Oxford University Press, 2000), 100–14.

Packer, John, 'Making International Law Matter in Preventing Ethnic Conflict: A Practitioner's Perspective', *New York University Journal of International Law and Politics* 32 (2000), 715–24.

Paunov, Dimitar, 'Assessing the Success of EU–OSCE Cooperation: A Case of Mutualism?', in Institute for Peace Research and Security Policy at the University of Hamburg (ed.), *OSCE Yearbook 2015* (Baden-Baden: Nomos Verlagsgesellschaft, 2016), 339–52.

Pauwelyn, Joost 'Informal International Lawmaking: Framing the Concept and Research Questions', in Joost Pauwelyn, Ramses Wessel and Jan Wouters (eds.), *Informal International Lawmaking* (Oxford, New York: Oxford University Press, 2012), 13–34.

Pauwelyn, Joost, Wessel, Ramses and Wouters, Jan, 'Informal International Lawmaking: An Assessment and Template to Keep It Both Effective and Accountable', in Joost Pauwelyn, Ramses Wessel and Jan Wouters (eds.), *Informal International Lawmaking* (Oxford, New York: Oxford University Press, 2012), 500–38.

Peters, Anne, Koechlin, Lucy, Förster, Till and Fenner Zinkernagel, Gretta (eds.), *Non-State Actors as Standard Setters* (Cambridge: Cambridge University Press, 2009).

Ratner, Steven, 'Does International Law Matter in Preventing Ethnic Conflict?', *New York University Journal of International Law and Politics* 32 (2000), 591–698.

Reisman, Michael, 'The Concept and Functions of Soft Law in International Politics', in Emmanuel Bello and Bola A. Ajibola S. A. N. (eds.), *Essays in Honour of Judge Taslim Olawale Elias*, Contemporary International Law and Human Rights, vol. 1 (Dordrecht; Boston, London: Martinus Nijhoff Publishers, 1992), 135–44.

Schlager, Erika, 'A Hard Look at Compliance with "Soft" Law: The Case of the OSCE', in Dinah Shelton (ed.), *Commitment and Compliance: The Role of Non-Binding Norms in the International Legal System* (Oxford: Oxford University Press, 2000), 346–71.

Schweisfurth, Theodor, 'Die juristische Mutation der KSZE: eine internationale Organisation in statu nascendi', in Ulrich Beyerlin, Michael Bothe, Rainer Hofmann and Ernst-Ulrich Petersmann (eds.), *Recht zwischen Umbruch und Bewahrung: Festschrift für Rudolf Bernhardt* (Berlin, Heidelberg: Springer, 1995), 213–28.

Shelton, Dinah, 'Commentary and Conclusions', in Dinah Shelton (ed.), *Commitment and Compliance: The Role of Non-Binding Norms in the International Legal System* (Oxford: Oxford University Press, 2000), 449–61.

Tudyka, Kurt, 'Non-Governmental Organizations and the OSCE', in Institute for Peace Research and Security Policy at the University of Hamburg (ed.), *OSCE Yearbook 2001* (Baden-Baden: Nomos Verlagsgesellschaft, 2002), 465–74.

Ulfstein, Geir, 'Institutions and Competences', in Jan Klabbers, Anne Peters and Geir Ulfstein (eds.), *The Constitutionalization of International Law* (Oxford: Oxford University Press, 2011).

Willigen, Niels van, 'Effective Multilateralism Between Unequal Partners: The EU in the OSCE', in Edith Drieskens and Louise G. van Schaik (eds.), *The EU and Effective Multilateralism: Internal and External Reform Practices, Routledge Studies in European Security and* Strategy (London, New York: Routledge, 2014), 136–52.

Wouters, Jan and Hamid, Linda, 'Custom and Informal International Lawmaking', in Curtis Bradley (ed.), *Custom's Future: International Law in a Changing World* (Cambridge: Cambridge University Press, 2016), 332–59.

Zannier, Lamberto, 'Strength in Numbers: Co-operating with Other International Organizations', in Institute for Peace Research and Security Policy at the University of Hamburg (ed.), *OSCE Yearbook 2012* (Baden-Baden: Nomos Verlagsgesellschaft, 2013), 383–90.

'The OSCE and Chapter VIII of the United Nations Charter – Contributing to Global Peace and Security', in Institute for Peace Research and Security Policy at the University of Hamburg (ed.), *OSCE Yearbook 2014* (Baden-Baden: Nomos Verlagsgesellschaft, 2015), 97–109.

Zellner, Wolfgang, 'The OSCE Network of Think Thanks and Academic Institutions: Baby Steps', in Institute for Peace Research and Security Policy at the University of Hamburg (ed.), *OSCE Yearbook 2013* (Baden-Baden: Nomos Verlagsgesellschaft, 2014), 269–75.

13

Conceptualising Accountability in the Legal and Institutional Framework of the OSCE

Carolyn Moser

1 POWER WITHOUT ACCOUNTABILITY?[*]

The OSCE is a crucial part of the European security edifice. Through its manifold activities – including election observation, early warning, conflict prevention, crisis management and post-conflict rehabilitation – the OSCE has become a key player in maintaining peace and promoting stability in Europe.[1] This operational vigour unfolds, however, within an unsettled legal and institutional framework: even though the OSCE possesses most of the attributes typically ascribed to an international institution, it lacks a constitutive act under international law and has no established international legal personality.[2] In other words, the OSCE is an international organisation by name and by practice, but not by law. It has been said, therefore, to constitute a 'soft organisation' based on non-binding instruments.[3]

So far, discussions on the unsettled legal status of the OSCE have revolved around two interrelated issues, namely the implications of the Organization's informality for (staff at) its Headquarters, permanent institutions and field operations, and the possible adoption of legal instruments to formalise existing structures.[4] With a view to providing an additional stimulus to the debate, this

* This chapter draws on (accountability) conceptualisations developed in Moser, *EU Civilian Crisis Management – Law and Practice of Accountability*.

1 An overview of core OSCE activities can be found in Fastenrath and Weigelt, 'Organization for Security and Cooperation in Europe', 43–73.

2 Ibid., 37; see also Blokker and Wessel, 'Revisiting Questions of Organisationhood, Legal Personality and Membership in the OSCE: The Interplay between Law, Politics and Practice', Chapter 7 in this Volume; and Ryngaert, 'The OSCE's Domestic Legal Status: An Exploration of Relevant International Law Sources', Chapter 8 in this Volume.

3 Klabbers, 'Institutional Ambivalence', 403, 405.

4 See, for instance, Tichy and Köhler, 'Legal Personality or Not'; see further Tabassi, 'The Role of the Organisation in Asserting Legal Personality: The Position of the OSCE Secretariat on the OSCE's Legal Status', Chapter 3 in this Volume.

chapter adopts a broader governance perspective on the topic: it sets out to conceptualise accountability in the legal and institutional framework of the OSCE. To date, accountability mechanisms involving different decision-making and implementing entities of the OSCE on the one hand, and accountability fora on the other hand, have barely played a role in the debate on the (reform of the) legal and institutional framework of the OSCE. In the rare event that OSCE accountability was addressed, the discussion's scope was restricted to legal issues – in particular, responsibility and liability – and did not extend to institutional matters.[5] Only the OSCE Parliamentary Assembly has been advocating for an increase of accountability arrangements *within* the OSCE.[6] This chapter intends to fill this important conceptual gap.

Understanding accountability as a core governance principle, this chapter underscores that the formality – or *in*formality – of an international institution cannot be considered the decisive criterion for its accountability. Rather, it is the actual exercise of public power that is significant for determining whether an institution needs to be accountable for its actions or omissions.[7] The OSCE undoubtedly wields public power, regardless of whether the institution is codified or enjoys international legal personality; an expression of its exercise of public power is – not least – the implementation of various activities and field operations whose mandates cover central public functions such as election observations, rule of law programmes or capacity building of law enforcement agencies. Yet, there are currently only a few accountability arrangements in the legal and institutional framework of the OSCE. This chapter therefore reasons that it is crucial to enhance further the accountability of power-wielders – both collective and individual actors – within the governance structures of the OSCE, especially through political and administrative accountability mechanisms tackling both strategic and operational functions.

The accountability-centred argumentation unfolds in three interrelated steps. The chapter starts by outlining some general conceptual underpinnings of the reflection (Section 2). Building on this conceptual framework, the analysis then goes on to contextualise accountability in the broader governance scheme of international cooperation (Section 3). In a third step, the assessment concentrates on accountability in the OSCE framework, drawing, where appropriate, on insights from other institutions entrusted with similar functions and tasks, namely the UN and the EU (Section 4). After elaborating

5 See ibid.

6 For a detailed account on the stance of the Parliamentary Assembly, see Nothelle, 'The OSCE Parliamentary Assembly', 357–60.

7 *Public power* is understood as the power vested in an individual or entity performing functions of the state – be they legislative, judicial or executive in nature.

on the risks tied to insufficient or inappropriate accountability mechanisms, the chapter ends with some concluding remarks on OSCE accountability (Section 5).

2 UNPACKING ACCOUNTABILITY

The content of accountability is in the eye of the beholder. As a 'buzzword of modern governance',[8] accountability is often used as a conceptual umbrella covering an array of concepts.[9] It is frequently mentioned together with or as a synonym for transparency, responsibility, participation, control or integrity. This multiplicity of meanings and understandings derives, at least partly, from the etymological origins of accountability: it made its appearance as a medieval Anglo-Norman notion and has no obvious corresponding expression in other European and many non-European languages.[10] Given these semantic differences, policy makers and academics alike have diverging views on the precise content of accountability, since their understanding is shaped by the expressions, including connotations, offered by their respective language(s).

The reflection developed in this chapter is based on the widely shared assumption in democratic systems that accountability provides a counterweight to the exercise of public power on the basis of both formal and informal procedural and institutional arrangements. Since the Enlightenment, power and accountability have been construed as a conceptual dyad in which accountability is the corollary of the exercise of public power. Thus, there is a power–accountability nexus. In the words of the International Law Association '[p]ower entails accountability, that is the duty to account for its exercise'.[11] Accordingly, those holding and exercising public power in liberal democratic systems are expected to explain and justify the use of that power.[12] This power-centred comprehension of accountability translates a constitutional perspective on accountability,[13] which links accountability to key concepts of constitutional law – in particular the rule of law doctrine(s).[14] Following this

8 Bovens, Schillemans and Goodin, 'Public Accountability', 1.

9 Bovens, Curtin and 't Hart, 'Real World of EU Accountability', 32.

10 Harlow, *Accountability in the European Union*, 13–18; Bovens, Curtin and 't Hart, 'Real World of EU Accountability', 32; Bovens, Schillemans and Goodin, 'Public Accountability', 2–3.

11 International Law Association, Committee on Accountability of International Organisations, Final Report on the Accountability of International Organisations 2004, 5.

12 Bovens, 'Analysing and Assessing Accountability', 447, 450. On this point, see also Schedler, 'Conceptualizing Accountability', 15.

13 Bovens, Curtin and 't Hart 'Real World of EU Accountability', 51–2.

14 Other elements described in the literature entail the separation of powers and the independence of the judiciary. See Harlow, 'Accountability and Constitutional Law', 198–205.

line of reasoning, this chapter focuses on the legal framework and institutional setting in which accountability mechanisms are embedded (or not), including when revisiting the framework of the OSCE.

2.1 *Defining Accountability: a Three-Stage Account Giving Process*

In reference to Mark Bovens, accountability is defined as 'a relationship between an actor and a forum, in which the actor has an obligation to explain and to justify his or her conduct, the forum can pose questions and pass judgement, and the actor may face consequences'.[15] The accountability mechanism thus unfolds in three interconnected stages. In the first stage, the actor shares information with the forum. Providing information is the *sine qua non* condition for accountability as it enables the (in)action of the power-holder to be scrutinised.[16] The key role of information is also reflected in the three-stage model employed: as information-sharing is the very first step, the mechanism depends on the provision of information between the actor and the forum. While information is necessary for accountability, it is by itself insufficient. Hence, in the second stage scrutiny by the forum occurs: the information provided by the actor is closely assessed by the forum. Characterised by a dialectic interaction, this stage of accountability is about being responsible or answerable *to* another person or institution for one's actions. In the third and last stage, the forum then goes on to pass judgement on the conduct or performance (in terms of procedures and/or outcomes) of the actor, with the possibility of sanctions in the event of a negative judgement.[17] As the consequences prevail over the explanatory interplay between the actor and the forum, this aspect of accountability is about an actor being responsible *for* one's conduct or performance to another person or institution.

At this juncture, it is judicious to make three clarifying remarks on (1) actor–forum constellations, (2) the nature of the accountability relationship and (3) timing. First, accountability obviously needs two entities to work: only if there is an actor *and* a forum can we speak of an accountability relationship. Indeed, accountability essentially consists of an interaction between the power-wielder and the accountability-demander. Therefore, there has to be a certain distance and/or distinction between the *who* (actor) and the *whom*

[15] Bovens, 'Analysing and Assessing Accountability', 450.

[16] Curtin, 'Holding (Quasi-)Autonomous EU Administrative Actors to Public Account', 523, 532; Dyrberg, 'Accountability and Legitimacy', 83.

[17] 'Judgement' is used here in the broader sense of *evaluation* or *assessment* and not in the narrow legal sense of a court judgement.

(forum). This is also why self-control – for instance in the form of (self-imposed) compliance procedures monitored by the actor – cannot qualify as accountability.[18] Secondly, the accountability relationship between the actor and the forum can be of a formal or an informal nature, or both. It need not be codified by law or regulated by some other procedure but can be based on informal arrangements. The (in)formality relates to all elements – the obligation incumbent upon the actor to be held to account, the scrutiny and judgement of the forum and the potential consequences. Thirdly, accountability takes place *ex post facto*. This retrospective character, however, does not preclude the accountability mechanism from having potential *ex ante* effects, since 'the line between retrospective accounting and proactive policy making can be thin in practice'.[19] The threat or shadow of sanctions can indeed influence the behaviour of actors who are aware of the fact that their conduct or performance will be analysed and eventually evaluated by an accountability forum.

2.2 *Detailing Accountability: Types, Constellations, Dimensions*

There are also different types of accountability relationships based on different criteria (e.g. the nature of the forum, the actor, the conduct and the obligation). As previously outlined, this chapter adopts a constitutional perspective on accountability. As accountability-demanders play a vital role in this perspective, the *nature of the forum* is the one core categorising parameter that will be analysed in more detail. This means that the 'to whom' (forum) is essential for the adjective qualifying the accountability relationship – legal, political or administrative – and not the 'who' (actor), or 'for what' (obligation). The categorisation of accountability based on the nature of the forum is judicious as it puts the analytical focus on the account-giving process and, furthermore, embeds actors in a dense web of accountability arrangements. The very same actor (who) can be held to account for a specific action or omission (for what) by a variety of fora (to whom) according to different yardsticks. The methods used to evaluate the conduct of the actor are indeed context-dependent. While parliamentarians will, for instance, scrutinise their own access to government-held information according to the (informal and subjective) yardstick of political salience – does the information provided enable them to exert political influence through debate or decision-making? – a judge will have recourse to codified rules and

[18] Dann, 'Accountability in Development Aid Law', 381, 384, 398.
[19] Bovens, 'Analysing and Assessing Accountability', 453.

procedures as well as jurisprudence, for instance, when ascertaining whether a request to access certain documents should have been granted (in full or in part) to an individual or entity.

In the event that the forum is of a political nature, one can speak of *political* accountability. This type of accountability is the most prominent in liberal democratic systems. Parliamentarians, political parties, the electorate, the media and increasingly civil society organisations play the role of the forum. They exercise their function in a framework of formal and informal accountability arrangements, and operate at times separately and at times concomitantly. A classic example of political accountability is when government representatives (often ministers) have to explain their policy choices to parliament. Elections are another typical case of political accountability: the voter (the forum) can sanction the elected representative (the actor) for his or her performance. A further example of political accountability, taken in a wider sense, is the involvement of NGOs and other civil society actors. By 'accessing, interpreting, and distributing information to multiple stakeholders in usable and accessible formats', they directly and indirectly increase demands for the accountability of power-holders.[20] If the forum is a judicial body, namely a court, the accountability arrangement can be qualified as *legal* accountability.[21] The scrutiny undertaken by courts takes place in a defined framework as the procedures and applicable laws or precedents are known. The obligation incumbent upon the actor to be held to account is formal: it is codified in civil, penal or administrative law. Also, a court's sentence in the third stage of the accountability process is of a formal nature, as are most of the consequences. Hence, while political accountability can leave the actor with formal but also informal consequences stemming from his or her conduct, legal accountability generally implies formal consequences – be they positive or negative for the actor. Another important type of accountability is *administrative* accountability. Here, the forum is of a quasi-legal nature, and exercises administrative and/or financial oversight. Courts of auditors, inspectors, ombudspersons and controllers fall under this category of accountability fora. With the rise of New Public Management techniques, the importance of these actors has considerably increased. Analogous to legal fora (courts), such quasi-legal entities act on the basis of statues, specific standards and norms. Nonetheless,

[20] Zyl, 'Civil Society Organizations and Accountability', 347.

[21] Aspects of legal accountability are analysed in detail in the third part of this Volume. See, in particular, Lorenzo Gasbarri, 'The International Legal Responsibility of the OSCE', Chapter 11 in this Volume.

the scrutiny of ombudspersons can, according to the mandate, go beyond legality and cover improper (though not necessarily illegal) behaviour. The forum's judgement can be both formal or informal in nature, depending on the institutional anchorage of the body at stake. While the decision of an ombudsperson is in many systems non-binding, the report of an auditing body can comprise compulsory recommendations.

Most forms of political accountability can be qualified as principal–agent constellations, the forum being the principal and the actor being the agent.[22] The chain of accountability then follows precisely the inverted pattern of the chain of power delegation, starting from the other end of the chain. Yet, chains of delegation tend to be very long because policy documents or bills run through many hands prior to approval. Responsibilities can therefore be somewhat blurred: there is the 'problem of many hands'[23] on the actor side and the 'problem of many eyes'[24] on the forum side. This combined hands–eyes *problématique* is particularly present in a multi-level setting, a setting characteristic of OSCE decisional and operational activities. However, the principal–agent model mostly does not fit legal, quasi-legal or administrative accountability mechanisms. The institutional independence of the respective fora (especially courts), implying that the forum is precisely *not* part of the chain of delegation, renders the principal–agent model unsuitable.

In addition, accountability mechanisms can cover different dimensions of the exercise of public power: while policy choices are made and agendas set at the strategic level, steering and implementation are the central tasks at the operational level. Actors tend to vary across these levels. Executive actors (mostly high-ranking national representatives) are in the majority when it comes to strategic choices, while single rather than collective actors (often, albeit not always, civil servants of lower rank) are more prominent for operational issues. In addition, accountability related to strategic issues tends to be political in nature, whereas accountability arrangements covering operational aspects are more diverse, covering political, administrative and legal issues. In order to prevent a power–accountability gap, accountability mechanisms – be they political, legal or administrative in nature – need to be adapted to this two-dimensional situation.

22 Bovens, 'Analysing and Assessing Accountability', 455.
23 Thompson, 'Moral Responsibility', 905.
24 Bovens, 'Analysing and Assessing Accountability', 455–7.

3 CONTEXTUALISING ACCOUNTABILITY IN INTERNATIONAL RELATIONS

What happens when the above-described conceptual framework regarding accountability – a three-stage mechanism involving an actor and a forum – is applied to the international realm? In the international arena, policy problems and their solutions are transnational in nature. The institutional and procedural blueprint of national (constitutional) systems not being easily transposable to the international arena, the fundamental question remains: *sed quis custodiet ipsos custodes?*[25]

3.1 *Prevalent Executive Governance*

In the multi-layered and multi-dimensional international system, the exercise of public power takes place in a governance context where executive agenda setting and decision-making prevails. This asymmetrical allocation of public power on the international plane derives, to a considerable extent, from the prerogatives granted to the executive in foreign-policy issues on the national plane. These prerogatives are reinforced in an interstate and intergovernmental scheme created by and for the interaction of national executives (at least initially).[26]

In the past decades, international cooperation has considerably increased – as has the number of international institutions as well as their powers and significance.[27] This enhanced internationalisation has changed governance patterns,[28] and has shaped a new order that 'is dominated by executive powers who jump the fence of their national constitutional and democratic systems and who exercise public power over an increasing range of politically and socially salient issues'.[29] Enhanced international or, more precisely, inter*state* and trans*governmental* cooperation leads to the creation of various overlapping and/or superposed 'executive orders'.[30] These executive orders are often characterised by informal procedures, leading to a lack of transparency.[31]

25 'Who guards the guardians themselves?' On this aspect, see Reinisch, 'Accountability of International Organizations', 131, 132.

26 The reinforcement of executive governance, however, is not limited to the international level. In the domestic sphere, too, the internationalisation of policy issues relocates political resources from legislative to executive actors. See Moravcsik, 'Why the European Union Strengthens the State'.

27 Blokker, 'Proliferation of International Organizations', 2–11.

28 Rosenau, 'Governance in the Twenty-First Century', 13.

29 Curtin, Papadopolous and Mair, 'Accountability in European Governance', 929, 932.

30 Ibid., 933.

31 See, in this context, the analysis of Yannis Papadopolous on network governance: Papadopolous, 'Accountability in Network and Multilevel Governance', 472–83.

This informality–opacity nexus, in turn, bears the risk of unlashing executive power above the nation state in the absence of appropriate control mechanisms. Despite some eclectic pockets of accountability in international politics,[32] there are by design no legal or institutional safeguards built into the international system ensuring that the exercise of power above territorial units is subject to monitoring or scrutiny. As a result, 'most collectivities in globalised space [including international institutions] are not accountable for their actions in the sense required even by a minimalist theory of democratic governance'.[33] In other words, the shift in governance to the international level has not been followed by a shift in accountability mechanisms.[34] Indeed, in the international realm both the 'problem of many hands'[35] on the actor side and the 'problem of many eyes'[36] on the forum side are aggravated by the intricacy and multi-dimensionality of the system, which then results in international politics – and especially international institutions – functioning at a safe distance from accountability.

3.2 *Going beyond Responsibility and Liability*

This observation reposes on a conceptualisation of accountability that is broader than the traditional legal and institutional perspective. Instead of restricting accountability to justiciable matters, accountability is regarded in this chapter as a crucial component of governance: it is a mechanism the objective of which is to constrain, and by this to prevent the abuse of power. Yet, the control of international institutions is, from a legal perspective, often approached under the heading of responsibility and/or liability, both of which presuppose a violation by the international institution of its international (or domestic) law obligations.[37] A classic legal approach imposes four limitations on accountability. First, accountability is construed as narrowly relating to legal (and justiciable) issues only. Secondly, the actor under examination needs to have international legal personality to fit the categories of international responsibility and liability, which excludes informal actors from scrutiny. Thirdly, there needs to be a jurisdiction that has the competence to

[32] Expression inspired by Robert O. Keohane, 'Global Governance and Democratic Accountability', 25, available at: http://citeseerx.ist.psu.edu/viewdoc/download?doi=10.1.1.610.6432&rep=rep1&type=pdf.

[33] Rosenau, 'Governance in Globalizing Space', 192.

[34] Curtin and Nollkaemper, 'Conceptualizing Accountability', 6.

[35] Thompson, 'Moral Responsibility'.

[36] Bovens, 'Analysing and Assessing Accountability', 455–7.

[37] Dekker, 'Accountability in International Institutional Law', 85–6.

adjudicate the disputed case, which, in the international arena, can be far from evident. Fourthly, the accountability mechanism is triggered as a matter of exception and on an ad hoc basis in cases of misconduct.

Is this traditional international legal perspective, incrementally developed for an interstate international system, still suited for a scheme where 'the exercise of power has transcended the boundaries of the nation state'?[38] Can it grasp the complexities of a system where public power is no longer confined to formal entities but also exercised by informal institutions stretching across governance levels (e.g. the OSCE)? The answer is no. It is difficult to capture new governance patterns as well as multi-dimensional and multi-level power constellations by employing only the traditional (and narrow) legal concepts.[39] First, as both formal and informal entities exercise public power in the international realm,[40] it would be outdated to construe accountability as a dependent variable of international legal personality or capacity.[41] Therefore, the legal status of an actor – in our case the OSCE – is only of secondary importance for accountability; the core question is whether that actor actually exercises public power in the international realm.[42] The OSCE perfectly illustrates that a lack of legal personality does not hamper an institution from actually exercising public power (e.g. through its field operations). Moreover, because of the specificities of the (exercise of) public power in the international realm, accountability needs to extend beyond justiciable matters – as has been outlined above. Therefore, it is argued here that accountability needs to be thought of with new categories: in addition to legal elements, it needs to cover political and administrative (including financial) aspects, both from a procedural and institutional perspective, so as to ensure that there is no power–accountability gap above the nation state. The idea is not to replicate national constitutional solutions, as this would obviously lead to misplaced analogies, but to imagine 'functional equivalences of domestic procedures' providing for accountability mechanisms that are anchored in the respective legal-institutional framework.[43]

38 Fisher, 'Age of Accountability', 495.

39 Curtin and Nollkaemper, 'Conceptualizing Accountability', 6–7.

40 Kingsbury, Krisch and Steward, 'The Emergence of Global Administrative Law', 17; Bogdandy, Dann and Goldmann, 'Publicness of Public International Law', 15.

41 Berman and Wessel, 'Informal International Lawmaking Bodies', 57–60.

42 Rosenau, 'Governance in Globalizing Space', 189. Paradoxically, the successful avoidance of external accountability by an international actor can also be a sign of power. Keohane, 'Global Governance and Democratic Accountability', 16.

43 Rosenau, 'Governance in Globalizing Space', 192.

3.3 *Accountability Intensifiers and Impairments*

Several elements are particularly salient with regard to the abovementioned functional equivalences because they impact on the effectiveness of the accountability process. As they feed into the accountability equation, these elements can be either intensifiers of accountability or – to the contrary – obstacles to accountability. The first element is related to institutional design. The exercise of power does not take place in a vacuum but unfolds in a given framework, be that framework formal or informal in nature. Institutional design choices determine the allocation of strategic and/or operational power, which in turn impacts on the precise modes of interaction within this framework. It not only relates to determining which body or entity is in charge of what, but furthermore concerns procedural (e.g. decision-making and voting procedures) and staffing questions. Policy choices will be prepared and taken differently in a purely intergovernmental setting dominated by national representatives deciding on a consensual basis than in a transnational regulatory body composed of experts where majority voting might apply. In addition, long and intricate chains of accountability make it more difficult to determine who is accountable to whom in international institutions. Finding the appropriate power-wielder is indeed a challenging task as the 'problem of many hands' is acute. In the international arena, decision makers and agenda setters are often high-ranking national representatives acting on the basis of consensus or unanimity; in many cases their decisions are prepared by semi-bureaucratic structures also composed of national envoys. It is difficult, therefore, to disentangle the decision *maker* from the decision *preparer*. An eye will be kept on this important aspect when assessing accountability arrangements in the OSCE framework.

Intrinsically linked to the element of institutional design is the question of how accountability arrangements are structured in a multi-level setting. Will accountability be exercised through traditional national channels (e.g. national parliaments and courts), or will accountability mechanisms be raised to the international arena to match the transnational exercise of power, or both? The former solution is attractive as it seemingly rests on existing accountability structures – at least in some nation states. But there are several reasons to advocate the latter solutions. First, traditional national accountability mechanisms might not fit the new governance patterns and therefore be inadequate. Whereas decisions are taken collectively at the international level, only the representative of a given state can be held to account by the institutions of that state. Secondly, using nationally anchored accountability mechanisms for the exercise of public power on the international plane leads to a fragmented accountability environment, which reposes on constitutional provisions as well as institutional structures and resources of the respective territorial states. Eventually, this results in a patchwork of accountability, unequal in breadth and depth across the different national systems. Thirdly, channelling accountability for international cooperation through national institutions misses a very crucial point: the shift in governance. In international cooperation, the exercise of strategic and often operational functions is de facto and/or de jure relocated to the international level. Therefore, it is necessary to establish accountability mechanisms adapted to this post-national situation in which power is leaking away and dispersed.[44] Put differently, the increased internationalisation of policy issues also enhances the salience of novel (transnational) accountability mechanisms, operating in parallel or cumulatively to the existing national mechanisms.[45] This point also plays an essential role in the case of the OSCE.

This ties in with another important aspect: information-sharing arrangements. Information asymmetries are a core element of the international system. These asymmetries derive from the very scheme of international cooperation and stretch across governance levels. As executive actors dominate the international arena, they are not only *power* holders but, by extension, also *information* holders. Therefore, both at the international and at the national level (potential) fora – such as parliamentary bodies, judicial actors, the media or public opinion, which could hold the power holders to account – structurally face a shortage of information. This is why it is particularly important to include information circuits in the institutional design shaping the governance framework, not least because '[h]iding information is endemic to organizations, even when their leaders do not engage in systematic deceit'.[46] It goes without saying that this finding extends to international institutions: here, too, 'the lack of transparency is accompanied by a loss of accountability'.[47] In world politics, procedural and institutional arrangements ensuring that information is shared

44 Curtin and Nollkaemper, 'Conceptualizing Accountability', 7.

45 In substance, then, this understanding of accountability comes close to what the International Law Association called the *first level of accountability* (internal and external scrutiny in general), and more precisely to the sub-components of the principle of good governance, namely 'transparency in both the decision-making process and the implementation of the ensuing institutional and operational decisions; a large degree of democracy in the decision-making process; access to information open to all potentially concerned and/or affected by the decisions at stake; the well-functioning of the international civil service; sound financial management; and appropriate reporting and evaluation mechanisms'. ILA, Committee on Accountability of International Organisations, Final Report, 2004.

46 Keohane, 'Accountability in World Politics', 84.

47 Nothelle, 'The OSCE Parliamentary Assembly', 348.

on a regular basis by power-wielders – simultaneously being information-holders – are key. Improving information flows is indeed crucial both for strategic and operational accountability, also in the OSCE context.

4 THE OSCE AND ACCOUNTABILITY: TAKING STOCK

Taking into consideration, on the one hand, the importance of accountability in the broader governance scheme and, on the other hand, the specificities of accountability in the international arena, this section will take stock of accountability arrangements in the OSCE framework, particularly those of a political and administrative nature. The analysis will address *who* is currently *accountable to whom, for what* and *how*. Where appropriate, reference will be made to two other international institutions with similar tasks and activities operating in comparable environments, namely the UN and the EU.

4.1 *Active versus Passive Accountability: Determining the Who and for What*

The most pressing question regarding accountability relates to *who* is accountable and *for what*. Concerning the quest for the accountable actor, it is an interesting observation that many international institutions adopt an *active* stance on accountability,[48] according to which it is the international institution holding another entity or individual to account. In this constellation the international institution is the forum, not the actor. A prime example in this respect is the UN Security Council, which increasingly makes reference to accountability in its resolutions. Not only is accountability used as an umbrella term in a panoply of situations, stretching from general socio-political issues (e.g. the fight against corruption and the promotion of good governance) to questions of individual responsibility (e.g. criminal liability for serious crimes).[49] More importantly, in its resolutions mentioning accountability, the UN Security Council calls other entities (e.g. member states) to

[48] On active and passive accountability, see Bovens, 'Two Concepts of Accountability', 946, 949, 951. The European Commission is an exception in this regard as it counts accountability among the ingredients of European institutional governance and highlights its procedural nature, for instance in its 2001 White Paper on Governance. For a detailed analysis of the said White Paper, see Wincott, 'The Governance White Paper, the Commission and the Search for Legitimacy'.

[49] Farrall, 'Rule of Accountability or Rule of Law?', 389.

account, for instance on human rights violations or a lack of governance. Its own legal and political accountability is, however, severely limited.[50]

Similarly, the OSCE tends to adopt an active stance on accountability. When searching the publicly available documents on different topics produced by the Secretariat, the OSCE institutions and diverse field operations, one will find that OSCE policy papers and publications generally employ accountability when describing the institution's outreach and activities: the Organization tries to foster the accountability of other actors (mostly state institutions or offices), for example, through its field activities.[51] This implies, first, that the OSCE sees itself as an accountability forum so that, secondly, accountability is conceived as a mission statement rather than as an organising governance principle of the institution.

Yet, in the contemporary understanding of public accountability, the power-wielder is the actor, not the forum. Even though, originally, accountability meant that it was the powerful sovereign who held their subjects to account (financially), this initial logic has been reversed over the course of centuries.[52] Nowadays, '[a]ccountability concerns agents, not subjects. It concerns those who exercise power, not those who are subordinate to it'.[53] Accountability, thus, coveys a *passive* dimension: someone is held *to* account. As a result, accountability can be part of the mandate ascribed to an international institution, meaning that this international institution can find itself playing the role of the forum entitled to an account (active), but it does not preclude this very same international institution from also being an actor subject to accountability mechanisms itself (passive). As previously stated, self-policing – in the form of compliance procedures, for instance – does not amount to accountability because it lacks the interaction between the power-holder and the accountability-demander.[54] The passive dimension of accountability therefore implies that there be meaningful fora which can hold the power-wielder to account, since accountability only works if there is both an actor and a forum.

Who then is the actor in the case of the OSCE? It is submitted here that the *who* ought to include those structures vested with power, that is both decisional bodies (at the strategic level) and agents with implementing functions (at

50 Henderson, 'Authority without Accountability?', 489.

51 A search for the term *accountability* on the OSCE's central website is telling in this regard.

52 Bovens, 'Analysing and Assessing Accountability', 449; Mulgan, 'Accountability', 563; Bovens, 'Two Concepts of Accountability', 955.

53 Schedler, 'Conceptualizing Accountability', 20.

54 A critical account of internal oversight policies and mechanisms with regard to international financial institutions can be found in Tan, 'Mandating Rights and Limiting Mission Creep'.

the operational level). Depending on the level at which functions are exercised, accountability will cover *processes*, that is, the conformity with decision-making modalities at the strategic level, whereas more *outcome*-related aspects are likely to be scrutinised at the operational level (e.g. field operations).[55]

4.2 *Measuring the Field: Identifying to Whom and How*

Given the predominantly active stance on accountability, what do accountability arrangements in the OSCE currently look like? *To whom* must account be rendered and *how*? In the absence of a constitutive act under international law, accountability arrangements are programmed or facilitated by documents laying down the rules and procedures of an institution. According to the OSCE Rules of Procedure, 'informal subsidiary bodies' report and account to the relevant 'superior decision-making body'; and 'informal working groups', as well as 'executive structures', report and account to the respective 'superior authority'.[56] In short, subordinated units report *and* account to their respective hierarchy, which also established them. Lines of reporting and chains of accountability are thus the same – and they run in reverse to delegation. At the top end of the line of reporting/chain of accountability are the so-called 'OSCE decision-making bodies', namely the Meeting of Heads of State or Government (Summit), the Ministerial Council and the Permanent Council – all distinctively intergovernmental structures. The pertinent OSCE documents thus translate a classical principal–agent model in which the principal (participating State) holds the agent (the OSCE) to account.

This structure supporting hierarchical accountability, in turn, leads to a limited scope of accountability arrangements: accountability primarily concerns operational actors belonging to the bureaucracy who have to account for their conduct to their superiors, whereas the higher ranks in charge of strategic questions and agenda setting are not subject to accountability requirements at the OSCE level. The Secretary General, for instance, is responsible and accountable to the Permanent Council according to the OSCE Staff Regulations and Staff Rules.[57] At the same time there is no mention of the

55 A comprehensive description regarding *process* accountability and *outcome* accountability can be found in Patil, Vieider and Tetlock, 'Process versus Outcome Accountability', 69–89.

56 OSCE, Ministerial Council, 'Rules of Procedure of the Organization for Security and Co-operation in Europe', MC.DOC/1/06, 1 November 2006, pt II.

57 OSCE, Permanent Council, Staff Regulations and Staff Rules of the Organization for Security and Co-operation in Europe, Decision N. 1128, DOC.SEC/3/03, endorsed in September 2003 and last amended on 17 July 2014, Regulation 1.05.

accountability of the members of the aforementioned superior decisional body, namely the Permanent Council. In line with the general principal–agent model, one can assume that the members of the intergovernmental 'decision-making bodies' are accountable to their respective domestic institutions (i.e. national parliaments and courts) in accordance with the pertinent national regulations. Yet, the use of purely hierarchical accountability arrangements for operational matters, and the reliance on national mechanisms for strategic issues, has some significant conceptual, procedural and substantive lacunae.[58] Most importantly, it leads to a fragmented accountability environment that potentially undermines effective accountability for both the strategic and operational conduct of OSCE instances.

Of particular interest in this respect are the current arrangements for political accountability, which continue to rely on national structures solely as decision makers remain formally accountable to institutions of their respective participating State and not the OSCE Parliamentary Assembly.[59] Indicative hereof is that the OSCE Parliamentary Assembly is primarily involved in parliamentary diplomacy,[60] while it has only rudimentary oversight and control mechanisms at its disposal. It is also evident, inter alia, in that the only intergovernmental entities taking consensual decisions are listed as originators of OSCE decisions and OSCE documents, and that the involvement of the OSCE Parliamentary Assembly in drafting these decisions and documents is expressly excluded by the Rules and Procedure of the Organization.[61]

The budgetary powers of the OSCE Parliamentary Assembly are indeed very limited.[62] In contrast, the UN General Assembly has to approve the budget of the UN and apportion the expenses for UN peace operations.[63] The European Parliament, too, has to approve future expenditure and give its discharge for past expenditure of the Union budget, including costs for civilian missions (which fulfil similar functions as OSCE field operations).[64] In addition, appointments

58 See above ('Going beyond Responsibility and Liability').

59 Nothelle, 'The OSCE Parliamentary Assembly', 347–73.

60 The term *parliamentary diplomacy* is borrowed from ibid., 347.

61 'Rules of Procedure of the Organization for Security and Co-operation in Europe', MC.DOC/1/06, 1 November 2006, pt II.A paras. 1; 3; pt IV.D para. 1; pt V.A para. 6.

62 Nothelle, 'The OSCE Parliamentary Assembly', 362.

63 Article 17 Charter of the United Nations, 1 UNTS XVI, 24 October 1945.

64 Treaty on the Functioning of the European Union (TFEU), 25 March 1957, OJ C 326, Article 319 read in conjunction with Section E of the Interinstitutional agreement of 2 December 2013 between the European Parliament, the Council and the Commission on budgetary discipline, on cooperation in budgetary matters and on sound financial management, 2 December 2013, OJ C 373/01.

of high-ranking personnel within the OSCE, including the Secretary General and the Heads of Institutions and Missions, depend on intergovernmental actors (e.g. the Ministerial Council and the Chairmanship) and not on a vote by the OSCE Parliamentary Assembly.[65] In line with its role to 'contribute to the development of the institutional structures of the OSCE and of relations and co-operation between the existing OSCE institutions',[66] the OSCE Parliamentary Assembly has issued a range of resolutions on the accountability of the OSCE,[67] in particular calling decisional OSCE structures to account for their actions. In addition, the OSCE Parliamentary Assembly has established an ad hoc Committee on Transparency and Accountability in 2001 (renamed 'Committee on Transparency and Reform of the OSCE' in the meantime). With a view to revisiting the OSCE's legal and institutional framework, it would be worth considering the different institutional and procedural proposals made by the OSCE Parliamentary Assembly aiming at improving the OSCE's overall accountability.

These institutional questions tie in with another issue, this time of a procedural nature, namely the sharing of information. Information is key to accountability but in the context of peacekeeping and peacebuilding activities, information is often scarce. On the one hand, bodies entrusted with steering and implementation – including the Headquarters and field operations – are located in scattered and faraway places. This geographic span can be an obstacle to the establishment of information-sharing circuits. In addition, especially in the case of seconded personnel, this situation leads to intricate and often diluted reporting lines. On the other hand, the disclosure of information is mostly scarce because of the nature (confidential) and content (security-related) of information. This shortage of information available to potential accountability fora can, however, be remedied by introducing innovative information-sharing mechanisms. In this regard, the OSCE could draw inspiration from the EU, where an agreement has been reached between the Council of the EU and the European Parliament (EP) on the

65 Permanent Council, Staff Regulations and Rules, 2003, Regulation 3.02 and 3.03.

66 OSCE Parliamentary Assembly, Rules of Procedure of the OSCE Parliamentary Assembly, 25 March 2017, Rule 2.

67 OSCE Parliamentary Assembly, Resolution on correcting the democratic deficit of the OSCE, 10 July 1999; OSCE Parliamentary Assembly, Resolution on strengthening transparency and accountability in the OSCE, 10 July 2001; OSCE Parliamentary Assembly, Resolution on reform of the OSCE, 1–5 July 2005; OSCE Parliamentary Assembly, Resolution on transparency and further OSCE reform: reinforcement of parliamentary participation in the Organization, 29 June–3 July 2008; OSCE Parliamentary Assembly, Resolution on enhancing trust, transparency and accountability within the OSCE institutions, 29 June–3 July 2013.

access to sensitive information in the field of security and defence.[68] According to this agreement, access to information is confined to a restricted number of Members of the European Parliament (MEPs) and subject to specific rules. In compliance with those security and secrecy requirements, the agreement allows MEPs to receive more information, including on ongoing and future activities.[69] The arrangement is said to improve discursive interaction and enhance accountability.[70] In the context of the OSCE, an information-sharing arrangement would also likely foster the flow of information between decision-making bodies (power-wielders) and potential accountability fora (accountability-demanders) – in particular the Parliamentary Assembly – and thereby could improve the institution's accountability.

4.3 *Indispensable Accountability? On Reputational Aspects*

But *why* should the OSCE bother about enhancing its internal accountability? In the absence of a world parliament, a global public and (compulsory) international jurisdiction, what reasons could influence the OSCE to take steps to enhance its own accountability? The answer is that accountability is a significant factor for the success of the OSCE. A disconnect between the institution's mandate (and rhetoric), on the one hand, and its institutional realities, on the other hand, can indeed negatively affect the OSCE's legitimacy and, eventually, have an impact on the ground. This legitimacy–impact nexus concerns the functions and activities of the institution: the OSCE fulfils diplomatic tasks and, at the same time, is a key operational player in the field of peacekeeping and peacebuilding.[71] In both cases, its success relies on its standing (in the sense of *rayonnement*) as an international actor. Indeed, in the absence of coercive means, the extent to which the propelled principles, standards and mechanisms are espoused, for instance in the host state of an

68 Interinstitutional Agreement of 20 November 2002 between the European Parliament and the Council concerning access by the European Parliament to sensitive information of the Council in the field of security and defence policy, 20 November 2002, OJ C 298/01.

69 Huff, 'Parliamentary Scrutiny'; Barbé and Herranz Surralés, 'European Parliament in Security Policies'.

70 Rosén, 'EU Confidential', 385.

71 While peace*keeping* aims to help the implementation of peace agreements through an array of measures both military and civilian in nature, peace*building* is concerned with creating and consolidating the conditions necessary for sustainable peace through a panoply of activities in a post-conflict environment. United Nations, Secretary General, An Agenda for Peace. Preventive diplomacy, peacemaking and peace-keeping, A/47/277-S/24111, 17 June 1992, 21; United Nations, Department of Peacekeeping Operations and Department of Field Support, 'United Nations Peacekeeping Operations Principles and Guidelines' 2008, pt 2.1.

OSCE field operation, largely depends upon the Organization's persuasiveness, which in turn rests to a large degree on its legitimacy.[72] Legitimacy and impact can hence be understood as interrelated elements, the connecting element being soft power (which rests on attraction and persuasiveness, in contrast to coercion).[73] Providing for accountability mechanisms is a way to lead by example and to thereby sustain one's reputation.[74] This also holds true for the OSCE: it is important that there is a correspondence – at least in part – between what the Organization *is* and what it *does*. How credible and legitimate can the OSCE be in propelling governance standards if these very standards, including accountability, are not met by the Organization itself?[75]

The lack of appropriate accountability mechanisms can indeed have severe reputational consequences. A prominent example hereof is the cholera case concerning Haiti. It has been proved by an internal UN report that the 2010 cholera outbreak on the island, devastated by an earthquake prior to the dispatch of a UN peacekeeping unit, was caused by UN peacekeeping troops from Asia.[76] So far the UN has, however, refused to acknowledge any legal obligation to compensate the numerous victims,[77] invoking the institution's immunity. This accountability stance, however, has been roundly criticised, including by several Special Rapporteurs whose views are shared by many advocates for the end of political impunity.[78] Eventually, the absence of appropriate accountability mechanisms leads to a deterioration in the UN's legitimacy and impacts its effectiveness on the ground.[79] This underscores the

72 For a general analysis of the impact of governance/rule of law-related activities (anti-corruption measures) and stakeholder reception, see Mungiu-Pippidi, 'Contextual Choices in Fighting Corruption', available at: https://norad.no/en/toolspublications/publications/2011/contextual-choices-in-fighting-corruption-lessons-learned/. The point has also specifically been made with regard to EU security and defence activities in Whitman, 'Norms, Power and Europe', 15–16.

73 Nye defines *soft power* as 'the ability to shape the preferences of others'. Nye, *Soft Power: The Means to Success in World Politics*, 5.

74 Busuioc and Lodge, 'Reputational Basis of Public Accountability', 248.

75 Grant and Keohane, 'Accountability and Abuses of Power', 29.

76 Information released by international media having seen the report in question. See, for instance, Clarke and Pilkington, 'Leaked UN reports faults sanitation at Haiti bases at time of cholera outbreak', 5 April 2016, available at: www.theguardian.com/world/2016/apr/05/leaked-un-report-sanitation-haiti-bases-cholera-outbreak.

77 According to statistics of the Haitian ministry for health, 9,202 people have died and another 769,080 have received treatment since 2010. See Ministère de la Santé publique et de la population, 'Rapport de Cas', 31 January 2016, available at: http://mspp.gouv.ht/site/downloads/Rapport%20cholera%2031%20janvier%202016.pdf.

78 United Nations, Office of the High Commissioner for Human Rights, Letter of five Special Rapporteurs to the UN Secretary-General Ban Ki-moon, 23 October 2015, available at: https://assets.documentcloud.org/documents/2745778/Haiti-2nd-Rapporteur-Letter-Oct-2015.pdf.

79 On this issue, see Daugirdas, 'Reputation and Responsibility'.

importance of accountability in the context of peacebuilding activities, a context in which the OSCE is a prominent institution.

5 CONCLUSIONS

The present chapter has demonstrated that accountability is crucial for the OSCE – independently of the conferral of legal personality. As the corollary of wielding public power, accountability is an indispensable element of governance. Its field operations indicate that the OSCE has been entrusted with decision-making and implementing tasks in the public sphere. The institution hence needs to account for its conduct – both at the strategic and operational level. If the OSCE does not want to imperil its long-term success, it should work towards supplementing its efforts to foster the accountability of other actors by arrangements providing for its own administrative and political accountability. The otherwise strictly hierarchical accountability scheme could indeed be complemented by accountability arrangements – both political and administrative ones – between OSCE entities or affiliated bodies, including the OSCE Parliamentary Assembly. The current informality of the institution could prove beneficial to this endeavour as both political and administrative accountability arrangements could be introduced by small procedural changes (in contrast to an overhaul of legal instruments) affecting the current institutional practice. In the end, the OSCE's accountability will significantly depend upon the political will demonstrated by the participating States as they are the ones driving institutional change. The lack of political consensus over general governance issues, though, is likely to hamper reforms aimed at enhancing the OSCE's accountability.[80] Yet, the perpetuation of the current situation poses a risk to the OSCE's legitimacy and, eventually, could have repercussions for its impact on the ground. This in turn would be regrettable given the Organization's role in assuring Europe's stability and security.

REFERENCES

Barbé, Esther and Herranz Surralés, Anna, 'The Power and Practice of the European Parliament in Security Policies', in Dirk Peters, Wolfgang Wagner and Nicole Deitelhoff (eds.), *The Parliamentary Control of European Security Policy* (Oslo: ARENA, 2008), 77–107.

80 See Börzel and I. Peters, '"It's Politics, Stupid": An International Relations Perspective on Strengthening the Legal Framework of the OSCE', Chapter 5 in this Volume.

Berman, Ayelet and Wessel, Ramses A., 'The International Legal Form and Status of Informal International Lawmaking Bodies: Consequences for Accountability', in Joost Pauwelyn, Ramses A. Wessel and Jan Wouters (eds.), *Informal International Lawmaking* (Oxford: Oxford University Press, 2012), 35–61.

Blokker, Niels, 'Proliferation of International Organizations: An Exploratory Introduction', in Niels Blokker and Henry Schermers (eds.), *Proliferation of International Organizations: Legal Issues* (The Hague: Kluwer Law International, 2001), 1–49.

Bogdandy, Armin von, Dann, Philipp and Goldmann, Matthias, 'Developing the Publicness of Public International Law: Towards a Legal Framework for Global Governance Activities', in Armin von Bogdandy, Rüdiger Wolfrum, Jochen von Bernstorff, Philipp Dann and Matthias Goldmann (eds.), *The Exercise of Public Authority by International Institutions: Advancing International Institutional Law* (Heidelberg: Springer, 2010), 3–32.

Bovens, Mark, 'Analysing and Assessing Accountability: A Conceptual Framework', *European Law Journal* 13 (2007), 447–68.

'Two Concepts of Accountability: Accountability as a Virtue and as a Mechanism', *West European Politics* 33 (2010), 946–67.

Bovens, Mark, Curtin, Deirdre and 't Hart, Paul, 'Studying the Real World of EU Accountability: Framework and Design', in Mark Bovens, Deirdre Curtin and Paul 't Hart (eds.), *The Real World of EU Accountability* (Oxford, New York: Oxford University Press, 2010), 31–62.

Bovens, Mark, Schillemans, Thomas and Goodin, Robert E., 'Public Accountability', in Mark Bovens, Robert E. Goodin and Thomas Schillemans (eds.), *The Oxford Handbook of Public Accountability* (Oxford, New York: Oxford University Press, 2014), 1–20.

Busuioc, Madalina E. and Lodge, Martin, 'The Reputational Basis of Public Accountability', *Governance* 29 (2015), 247–63.

Curtin, Deirdre, 'Holding (Quasi-)Autonomous EU Administrative Actors to Public Account', *European Law Journal* 13 (2007), 523–41.

Curtin, Deirdre, Papadopolous, Yannis and Mair, Peter, 'Positioning Accountability in European Governance: An Introduction', *West European Politics* 33 (2010), 929–45.

Curtin, Deirdre and Nollkaemper, André, 'Conceptualizing Accountability in International and European Law', *Netherlands Yearbook of International Law* 36 (2005), 3–20.

Dann, Philipp, 'Accountability in Development Aid Law: The World Bank, UNDP and Emerging Structures of Transnational Oversight', *Archiv Des Völkerrechts* 44 (2006), 381–404.

Daugirdas, Kristina, 'Reputation and the Responsibility of International Organizations', *European Journal of International Law* 25 (2015), 991–1018.

Dekker, Ige F., 'Making Sense of Accountability in International Institutional Law', *Netherlands Yearbook of International Law* 36 (2005), 83–118.

Dyrberg, Peter, 'Accountability and Legitimacy: What is the Contribution of Transparency', in Anthony Arnull and Daniel Wincott (eds.), *Accountability and Legitimacy in the European Union* (Oxford, New York: Oxford University Press, 2002), 81–96.

Farrall, Jeremy M., 'Rule of Accountability or Rule of Law? Regulating the UN Security Council's Accountability Deficits', *Journal of Conflict and Security Law* 19 (2014), 389–408.

Fastenrath, Ulrich and Weigelt, Katja, 'Organization for Security and Cooperation in Europe (OSCE)', in Rüdiger Wolfrum (ed.), *Max Planck Encyclopedia of Public International Law* (Oxford: Oxford University Press, 2012), VII: 1040–55.

Fisher, Elizabeth, 'The European Union in the Age of Accountability', *Oxford Journal of Legal Studies* 24 (2004), 495–515.

Grant, Ruth W. and Keohane, Robert O., 'Accountability and Abuses of Power in World Politics', *American Political Science Review* 99 (2005), 29–43.

Harlow, Carol, 'Accountability and Constitutional Law', in Mark Bovens, Robert E. Goodin and Thomas Schillemans (eds.), *The Oxford Handbook of Public Accountability* (Oxford, New York: Oxford University Press, 2014), 195–210.

Accountability in the European Union (Oxford, New York: Oxford University Press, 2002).

Henderson, Christian, 'Authority without Accountability? The UN Security Council's Authorization Method and Institutional Mechanisms of Accountability', *Journal of Conflict and Security Law* 19 (2014), 489–509.

Huff, Ariella, 'Problems and Patterns in Parliamentary Scrutiny of the CFSP and CSDP', *OPAL Online Paper Series* 14 (2013), 1–28.

Keohane, Robert O., 'Accountability in World Politics', *Scandinavian Political Studies* 29 (2006), 75–87.

'Global Governance and Democratic Accountability', Miliband Lecture at the London School of Economics and Political Science, 17 May 2002.

Kingsbury, Benedict, Krisch, Nico and Steward, Richard B., 'The Emergence of Global Administrative Law', *Law and Contemporary Problems* 68 (2005), 15–61.

Klabbers, Jan, 'Institutional Ambivalence by Design: Soft Organizations in International Law', *Nordic Journal of International Law* 70 (2001), 403–21.

Moravcsik, Andrew, 'Why the European Union Strengthens the State: Domestic Politics and International Cooperation', Working Paper 52, in CES Working Paper Series (Harvard University: Centre for European Studies, 1994), 1–78.

Moser, Carolyn, *EU Civilian Crisis Management – Law and Practice of Accountability* (Utrecht: Utrecht University, 2018)

Mulgan, Richard, '"Accountability": An Ever-Expanding Concept?', *Public Administration* 78 (2000), 555–73.
Mungiu-Pippidi, Alina, 'Contextual Choices in Fighting Corruption: Lessons Learned', Study Report 4/2011, Oslo: Norwegian Agency for Development Cooperation (NORAD), 2011.
Nothelle, Andreas, 'The Parliamentary Assembly: Driving Reform', in University of Hamburg, Institute for Peace Research and Security Policy (ed.), *OSCE Yearbook 2006* (Baden-Baden: Nomos Verlagsgesellschaft, 2007), 347–73.
Nye, Joseph S., *Soft Power: The Means to Success in World Politics* (New York: PublicAffairs, 2004).
Papadopolous, Yannis, 'Problems of Democratic Accountability in Network and Multilevel Governance', *European Law Journal* 13 (2007), 469–86.
Patil, Shefali V., Vieider, Ferdinand and Tetlock, Philip E., 'Process versus Outcome Accountability', in Mark Bovens, Robert E. Goodin and Thomas Schillemans (eds.), *The Oxford Handbook of Public Accountability* (Oxford, New York: Oxford University Press, 2014), 69–89.
Reinisch, August, 'Securing the Accountability of International Organizations', *Global Governance* 7 (2001), 131–49.
Rosén, Guri, 'EU Confidential: The European Parliament's Involvement in EU Security and Defence Policy', *Journal of Common Market Studies* 53 (2015), 383–98.
Rosenau, James N., 'Change, Complexity, and Governance in Globalizing Space', in Jon Pierre (ed.), *Debating Governance: Authority, Steering, and Democracy* (Oxford, New York: Oxford University Press, 2000), 167–200.
'Governance in the Twenty-First Century', *Global Governance* 1 (1995), 13–43.
Schedler, Andreas, 'Conceptualizing Accountability', in Andreas Schedler, Larry Diamond and Marc F. Plattner (eds.), *The Self-Restraining State: Power and Accountability in New Democracies* (London: Lynne Rienner Publishers, 1999), 13–28.
Tan, Celine, 'Mandating Rights and Limiting Mission Creep: Holding the World Bank and the International Monetary Fund Accountable for Human Rights Violations', *Human Rights and International Legal Discourse* 2 (2008), 79–116.
Thompson, Dennis F., 'Moral Responsibility of Public Officials: The Problem of Many Hands', *American Political Science Review* 74 (1980), 905–16.
Tichy, Helmut and Köhler, Ulrike, 'Legal Personality or Not – The Recent Attempts to Improve the Status of the OSCE', in Isabelle Buffard, James Crawford, Alain Pellet and Stephan Wittich (eds.), *International Law between Universalism and Fragmentation: Festschrift in Honour of Gerhard Hafner* (Leiden, Boston: Martinus Nijhoff Publishers, 2008), 455–78.

Whitman, Richard G., 'Norms, Power and Europe: A New Agenda for Study of the EU and International Relations', in Richard G. Whitman (ed.), *Normative Power Europe: Empirical and Theoretical Perspectives* (Houndsmills, New York: Palgrave Macmillan, 2011), 1–22.

Wincott, Daniel, 'The Governance White Paper, the Commission and the Search for Legitimacy', in Anthony Arnull and Daniel Wincott (eds.), *Accountability and Legitimacy in the European Union* (Oxford, New York: Oxford University Press, 2002), 379–98.

Zyl, Albert van, 'How Civil Society Organizations Close the Gap between Transparency and Accountability', *Governance* 27 (2014), 347–56.

14

Legitimate Governance as a Privilege and Price for the Autonomy of International Organisations

Mateja Steinbrück Platise

1 INTRODUCTION

The notion of autonomy has long been deployed by different disciplines and has been used to describe different legal, political and social relations between different public and private actors. Yet, in international institutional law it has attracted more attention only in recent decades, when international organisations started to display increasing independence from their member states and to exercise in their place ever more public authority over individuals and peoples at large. Today, organisations determine core standards in policy fields as vital and as diverse as food safety, regional and global security, financial assistance, education and environmental protection; they authorise military interventions, manage migration flows and engage in democratisation processes; indeed, some may even act as a substitute for a state. The exercise of powers by international organisations can therefore amount to a kind of governance activity that determines the legal and factual position of states and other public institutions, as well as individuals and other private parties, and consequently calls for a legal framework that regulates the legitimate exercise of such public authority.[1]

In that context, the autonomy of international organisations becomes a proxy for sovereignty.[2] This function of autonomy can be understood in descriptive and normative terms. Descriptively, autonomy manifests the status and independence that an international organisation enjoys under international law; normatively, autonomy gives rise to normative demands for

[1] For a full argument and supporting literature concerning the requirement of the legitimate governance, see Section 5 of the present chapter.

[2] See also A. Peters, 'Membership', 208–10; some authors go even a step further and attribute sovereign powers to organisations; see Sarooshi, *International Organizations*; whereas for a political science conception, see Cooper, Hawkins, Jacoby and Nielson, 'Yielding Sovereignty'.

legitimate governance of the organisation over peoples and individuals.[3] Therefore, this chapter argues that the trigger for such normative demands is not the organisation's international legal personality as traditionally considered, but the organisation's capacity to exercise public authority autonomously, by which it can adversely affect the individual.

This trend heralds a conceptual shift in the standards that regulate the governance of international organisations, since the application of such standards has long been viewed as being conditioned by the international legal personality of the organisation and by its legal capacity to acquire rights and obligations under international law, rather than by its more or less autonomous functioning. The relevance of such a shift cannot be overstated, considering that not all organisations are granted international legal personality, and that states in fact increasingly prefer to engage in less formal types of international cooperation rather than to pursue their aims through classical international organisations.[4]

The present chapter aims to examine both descriptive and normative features of the autonomy of international organisations and seeks to analyse how autonomy is related to the international legal personality, responsibility and legitimacy of international organisations. The findings are tested in particular on the example of the Organization for Security and Co-operation in Europe (OSCE) as probably the most prominent organisation without international legal personality, although the chapter is clearly relevant also for other international organisations regardless of their legal status under international law.

The structure of the chapter roughly follows the above-sketched research questions: after outlining certain conceptual aspects of the notion of autonomy in Section 2, autonomy is first used as a descriptive label in Section 3 to analyse the relationship between the notions of autonomy and international legal personality, and to show how organisations like the OSCE can enjoy a certain level of autonomy without having been granted international legal personality. Section 4 draws some legal consequences from the distinction between the autonomy and international legal personality of international organisations, in particular those relating to the responsibility of the organisation and its members (or in OSCE jargon, 'participating States') under international law. While these legal consequences indicate that organisations like

[3] For a growing interest in international organisations as autonomous actors and the efforts to articulate the normative demands applicable to their exercise of public authority, see Venzke, 'International Bureaucracies from a Political Science Perspective', 1424.

[4] Pauwelyn, Wessel and Wouters, 'When Structures Become Shackles'.

the OSCE cannot be held responsible for an internationally wrongful act, Section 5 reveals why and how such organisations nevertheless need to meet certain normative standards for legitimate governance, and spells out some of the standards that have been elaborated in that respect by scholarship and practice. Section 6 concludes with a general assessment of the longstanding political efforts to strengthen the legal framework of the OSCE, exposing their potential strengths and shortcomings.

2 CONCEPTUAL ASPECTS OF AUTONOMY

In constitutional and international law, the notion of autonomy has in the past been commonly associated with the functioning of the state and sub-state entities, and has typically been used to describe various degrees of an entity's independence from the state.[5] Such an understanding of autonomy broadly corresponds to the term's use in political science, where autonomy is often used in the context of federal states and stands for the limits on the exercise of power by the federal government vis-à-vis particular federal units.[6] Autonomy may range from a mere right to act upon one's own discretion in certain matters, to the exercise of legislative, administrative and/or adjudicative powers in defined areas.[7] In all these variants, however, autonomy is consistently used as a concept that describes the relationship between two entities, whereby one entity can possess more or less independence from the other. Autonomy is, therefore, often understood as a matter of degree rather than kind.[8]

In the context of sub-state entities and the self-determination of peoples, such an understanding of autonomy as a graduated concept has led to the arguments about 'the runaway nature of autonomy', based essentially on concerns that the more autonomy is granted, the more it will be demanded.[9]

5 Suksi, 'Autonomy'.

6 See, e.g., Braun, 'Dezentraler und unitarischer Föderalismus'; Jensen, 'Federal Authority vs. State Autonomy'; Clinton, 'Isolated in Their Own Country'.

7 For a classic approach, see Hannum and Lillich, 'The Concept of Autonomy in International Law'; in that context, autonomy is also used to describe different levels of discretion entrusted to the administrative branch, see Huber and Shipan, *Deliberate Discretion?*

8 Compare Suksi, 'Autonomy'; Foldvary, 'Political Autonomy', 853; Hannum and Lillich, 'The Concept of Autonomy in International Law', 859; for autonomy as a matter of degree in the context of international institutional law see further below the references under footnotes n. 16 and n. 30; for a different approach, see e.g., A. Peters, 'Membership', 210, where the author points out that autonomy can be conceived either as a graduated or as an all-or-nothing concept.

9 Burri, 'Secession in the CIS', 147.

Kosovo might be one of the more-quoted examples to that end, in that it enjoyed different degrees of autonomy within the former Socialist Federal Republic of Yugoslavia (SFRY),[10] was later granted under the UN Interim Administration Mission in Kosovo (UNMIK) a 'substantial' degree of autonomy and self-government within the Federal Republic of Yugoslavia (FRY),[11] and eventually proclaimed itself independent from Serbia.[12]

With the rise in number, power and independence of international organisations, autonomy has become used also for describing a specific position that organisations enjoy in relation to other entities on the international plane, in particular towards their members. In that new context, autonomy is applied to different internal and external relations in which international organisations may engage, which leads to different conceptual understandings of the term. For the purposes of the present chapter, three different understandings of autonomy of international organisations deserve special attention.

Probably the most common understanding of the autonomy of international organisations relates to the relationship between the organisation and its members, signifying the level of independence that an organisation enjoys from its members. In International Relations (IR) scholarship, this type of autonomy is often studied as part of the principal–agent theory, according to which states (making up the collective principal) establish an international organisation (agent) to pursue certain goals and perform certain functions that will in turn generate benefits for the principal.[13] Such a conceptual understanding implies, on the one hand, that the organisation has to act in the principal's best interest, enabling states to realise gains that follow from the organisation's specialisation. On the other hand, by delegating their decision-making authority to the organisation, states allow it to pursue those goals with a certain degree of autonomy.[14]

In that sense, autonomy can be considered as inversely proportional to the control and influence that members can exercise over their organisation. Since such an understanding of autonomy tends to be state-centric, as it conceives of organisations as intergovernmental actors dominated by their

10 Summers, 'Kosovo', 237.

11 UN, Security Council, Resolution 1244, S/RES/1244, 10 June 1999, operative clauses 10 & 11.

12 For some controversies surrounding the unilateral proclamation of independence, see ICJ, Accordance with International Law of the Unilateral Declaration of Independence in Respect of Kosovo, Advisory Opinion of 22 July 2010, ICJ Reports 2010, 403.

13 For a classic approach, see Abbott and Snidal, 'Why States Act through Formal International Organizations'.

14 Compare Hawkins, Lake, Nielson and Tierney, 'Delegation Under Anarchy', 7, and Rittberger, Zangl and Staisch, *International Organization*, 6–8.

members, in the past it was rare for IR scholars to take the autonomy of international organisations seriously and to admit that 'many international organisations have clearly succeeded in formulating, and sometimes implementing, policies that cannot be described as the simple product of interstate bargaining'.[15]

International legal scholarship, on the other hand, has traditionally ascribed to international organisations a higher level of autonomy from their members, focusing on organisations' legal and institutional autonomy from members, rather than on organisations' political autonomy. A particularly substantial degree of autonomy is ascribed to those organisations that possess an international legal personality of their own, separate from the international legal personalities of their members.[16] For many, such a degree of autonomy is even a prerequisite for an entity to be considered an international organisation at all.[17] Still, the legal autonomy of an organisation can also manifest itself in other forms, especially by majority voting in its decision-making and by the organisation's capacity to unilaterally adopt acts through which it regulates the respective activities of its members.[18] Correspondingly, organisations such as the OSCE, as well as the early EU and the Association of Southeast Asian Nations (ASEAN), have been able to regulate relatively autonomously their policy fields without having been (explicitly) granted international legal personality.[19]

Clearly, different organisations enjoy legal and political autonomy from their members to different degrees. Moreover, within each organisation different internal layers of institutional autonomy towards members can be observed with respect to the organisation's organs and bodies. For example, while the plenary and executive organs of organisations are typically composed of member states' representatives and thus display several features of an intergovernmental action, organisations usually possess also secretariats, expert bodies, judicial organs or other bodies that are composed of

15 Reinalda and Verbeek, *Autonomous Policy-Making*, 3.

16 Gazzini, 'The Relationship', 208.

17 See, for detail, the following Section 3.

18 For unilateral acts of international organisations, see concisely Klein, 'International Organizations'; for various forms of an organisation's legal autonomy, see in constitutionalist terms A. Peters, 'Membership', 209–10.

19 For the consensus rule within the OSCE and for exceptions to the rule, see OSCE Handbook 2007, OSCE Press and Public Information Section, 14. For the evolution and eventual recognition of international legal personality to the EU, see Wessel, 'Revisiting the International Legal Status of the EU'; for the gradual development and recognition of the ASEAN international legal personality, see Phan, 'The Association of Southeast Asian Nations'.

international legal servants and other personnel not acting on behalf of any member, and therefore enjoy greater institutional autonomy from members. The strictest requirements for autonomy and independence apply to international tribunals and international judges, albeit an autonomous functioning is a prerequisite for many other international positions and bodies as well.[20]

The second broad concept of autonomy, which is much less debated and is commonly assumed under the above-analysed concept, is that which can be established in the relationship between an organisation and other legal subjects, including third states, other international organisations and private parties. In that context, autonomy is understood as the organisation's capacity to act on the international and domestic plane independently from other actors, not only from its members. The most prominent legal form of such autonomy is, similar to the above-discussed concept, demonstrated by the recognition of the organisation's own legal personality vis-à-vis third parties. Such legal personality was famously defined by the International Court of Justice (ICJ) as 'objective' and is enjoyed towards all other international legal subjects, including non-member states.[21] No rule, however, seems to exist under international law that would oblige non-members to recognise international organisations.[22]

On the international plane, having objective international legal personality gives an organisation the capacity to conclude treaties with third parties, bring international claims against third parties and incur responsibility under international law for any breach of an international obligation that it owes to other legal subjects, including private parties. On the domestic plane, such autonomy is recognised by the grant of legal personality to an organisation within the domestic legal system of a (non-member) state.[23] In the function of protecting the autonomy of international organisations from control or interference by other legal subjects, including by non-members and private parties, organisations are regularly granted immunities before domestic courts.[24] Such protection seems particularly relevant for organisations that carry out their activities in part within non-member countries: the 1999 NATO air strike

20 For general standards, see International Commission of Jurists, 'International Principles on the Independence and Accountability of Judges, Lawyers and Prosecutors – Practitioner's Guide No 1', 2007, available at: www.icj.org/no-1-international-principles-on-the-independence-and-accountability-of-judges-lawyers-and-prosecutors/#!lightbox/0/.

21 ICJ, *Reparation for Injuries Suffered in the Service of the United Nations*, Advisory Opinion of 11 April 1949, ICJ Reports 1949, 174, 185.

22 Schmalenbach, 'International Organizations or Institutions'.

23 See Cedric Ryngaert, 'The OSCE's Domestic Legal Status: An Exploration of Relevant International Law Sources', Chapter 8 in this Volume.

24 Reinisch, 'Privileges and Immunities'.

against the FRY is a notorious example, the OSCE field operation in Kosovo another.[25]

A third type of autonomy can be used to conceptualise the relationship between an organisation's internal legal order and other legal orders, including international law. Such autonomy connotes the organisation's power to make rules for its own internal legal order, which emanates from the organisation's constitutive instrument. Since the constitutive instrument normally regulates the functioning of the organisation only in general terms, more detailed provisions must be made by the organisation itself.[26] The resulting rules of the organisation are deemed to become part of an autonomous legal order that is separated from any other legal order.[27] Typically, the organisation's internal law is considered a new branch of international law and is regarded as *lex specialis*,[28] at least to the extent that it regulates the legal consequences of a member's breach of such law. That allows members to resort to the general law of state responsibility if the relevant rules of the organisation are ineffective or non-existent (*lex specialis derogat legi generali*).[29] Also this type of autonomy can be manifested to various degrees,[30] with the highest degree exhibited by the organisation's competence on competence (*Kompetenz-Kompetenz*).[31]

Indeed, the former European Community (EC) was initially considered by the European Court of Justice (ECJ, later renamed as the Court of Justice of the European Union, CJEU) to constitute 'a new legal order of international law'.[32] Particularly high levels of autonomy can however eventually transform

25 For the special position of the field operation in Kosovo, see Niedobitek, 'OSCE and Kosovo'.

26 Schermers and Blokker, *International Institutional Law*, 755, with further references.

27 See also Bernhardt, 'International Organisations, Internal Law and Rules', 1314–18.

28 See, in particular, Article 64 (*Lex specialis*) ARIO (UN, International Law Commission, Draft Articles on the Responsibility of International Organizations, A/66/10, 9 November 2011); for a more general application of the rule in international institutional law, see UN, International Law Commission, Fragmentation of International Law: Difficulties Arising from the Diversification and Expansion of International Law, Report of the Study Group of the International Law Commission, A/CN.4/L.682, 13 April 2006, 56, discussing the distinction between 'weak' and 'strong' forms of *lex specialis* when dealing with self-contained regimes.

29 For divergences in academic discourse compare, e.g., Simma and Pulkowski, 'Of Planets and the Universe', esp. 492–3; and Lagrange, *La représentation institutionnelle dans l'ordre international*, 46, where the author seems to distinguish partial legal orders of international organisations from self-contained regimes.

30 Wessel and Blockmans, 'Between Autonomy and Dependence', 1–9.

31 The competence on competence is thus generally not viewed as a necessary element for an autonomous legal order and is not to be understood in absolute terms even within the EU context; see, among many other authorities, Weiler and Haltern, 'The Autonomy of the Community Legal Order'.

32 CJEU, Case 26/62 *Van Gend & Loos* v. *Netherlands Inland Revenue Administration* [1963] EU:C:1963:1, II.B.

an international organisation into a supranational one, as seen in the case of EU. Hence, today the CJEU interprets the autonomy of the EU order more broadly: it signifies the independence of EU law from both domestic and international law and, above all, as rendering the CJEU a monopoly over the authoritative interpretation of EU law.[33] Quite tellingly, some observers have therefore started to use the notion of autonomy in the EU context to describe the autonomy that member states enjoy from the organisation, and not vice versa.[34]

At the other end of the spectrum, the OSCE *acquis* cannot be regarded as enjoying autonomy from international law, since it is considered merely politically and not legally binding.[35] Consequently, to the extent that OSCE commitments lack a legal nature, they cannot alter international law applicable to the Organization and its participating States.[36]

3 THE AUTONOMY AND LEGAL PERSONALITY OF INTERNATIONAL ORGANISATIONS

Although autonomy and legal personality are related concepts, they have often attracted different disciplines of study: in political science (and IR scholarship more particularly), being primarily interested in the distribution of power and resources between different political actors, the concept of autonomy is deemed a core criterion for studying the influence and control exercised over an international organisation and the corresponding independence of the organisation from its members and other political actors. For legal scholars, the principal criterion for establishing the independence of an

[33] See, in particular, the CJEU, Opinion 2/13 of the Court of 18 December 2014 [2014] EU:C:2014:2454; for a nuanced analysis of the opinion against many critical voices, see Halberstam, 'It's the Autonomy, Stupid!', 105–46; the CJEU concern with its autonomy vis-à-vis other judicial courts and tribunals can, however, be traced much further back in time; see CJEU, Opinion 1/76 of the Court of 26 April 1977 [1977] EU:C:1977:63; CJEU, Opinion 1/91 of the Court of 14 December 1991 [1991] EU:C:1991:490; CJEU, Opinion 2/94 of the Court of 28 March 1996 [1996] EU:C:1996:140; CJEU, Case C-459/03 *Commission* v. *Ireland* [2006] EU:C:2006:345; CJEU, Opinion 1/09 of the Court of 8 March 2011 [2011] EU:C:2011:123.

[34] Young, 'Protecting member state autonomy'.

[35] CSCE, *Towards a Genuine Partnership in a New Era*, Budapest Decisions attached to the Budapest Document, 21 December 1994, Decision X para. 39, available at: www.osce.org/mc/39554?download=true, and OSCE, Ministerial Council, 'Rules of Procedure of the Organization for the Security and Co-operation in Europe', MC.DOC/1/06, 1 November 2006, General Provisions A(1).

[36] Legally non-binding acts of an organisation can, however, still bind internally; see Schermers and Blokker, *International Institutional Law*, 755 and the following, esp. at 768 with further references.

organisation is rather the concept of legal personality. The different scholarly approaches can therefore result in different assessments as to whether and to what extent an organisation can be considered an independent actor.

International law defines an international legal person – international legal subject – as an entity capable of possessing rights and duties under international law and of invoking and being subject to international claims.[37] Such a *capacity of being an addressee* of rights and duties under international law and of pursuing these rights by invoking them vis-à-vis other legal persons does not, however, say anything about the scope of the entity's *capacity to perform legal acts* on the international plane. Not all international legal persons have the same capacity to act, for example to conclude treaties or to defend their rights before international forums. In fact, the legal standing of international legal persons before international forums is granted only sparingly and is regulated by the procedural rules of the respective forum, rather than derived from legal personality as such.[38]

A further distinction must be drawn between domestic and international legal personality. International legal personality does not automatically imply domestic legal personality, and vice versa. They relate to different legal status and capacities that an entity such as an international organisation can exercise on the international and on the domestic plane, and are awarded in accordance with the rules that regulate the status of legal subjects in the respective legal system. The answer to the question of whether, for example, an international organisation possessing international legal personality will also be recognised as a legal person in a domestic legal system lies therefore in the laws of the various jurisdictions involved. Thus, the International Tin Council (ITC) was considered before the UK courts as an entity that 'as an international persona, had no status under the laws of the United Kingdom'.[39]

However, the domestic legal personality of a particular organisation can also be foreseen on the international – or supranational – level. The EU is endowed with international legal personality under Article 47 of the Treaty on European Union (TEU), whereas the member states commit themselves in Article 335 of the Treaty on the Functioning of the EU to grant the EU

37 Crawford, *Brownlie's Principles*, 115.

38 International instruments accordingly regulate separately the international legal personality and legal capacity of an international organisation; see to that end also OSCE, Fifteenth Meeting of the Ministerial Council, Draft Convention on the international legal personality, legal capacity, and privileges and immunities of the OSCE, Annex to MC.DD/28/07, 29 November 2007.

39 UK, House of Lords, *JH Rayner Ltd* v. *Department of Trade and Industry*, [1989] 3 WLR 969, 708; such outcomes are especially likely in dualistic legal systems that do not incorporate treaties as part of domestic law, like the UK; see Higgins, *Problems & Processes*, 48.

domestic legal personality within their own legal systems. The OSCE, conversely, has merely been granted domestic legal personality in a number of domestic jurisdictions, whereas political efforts to endow it with international legal personality have only recently been resumed.[40]

While the autonomy of an international organisation is viewed as one of the essential elements of international and domestic legal personality, it is broader in scope and is enjoyed also by organisations without legal personality. Henceforth, if the autonomy of international organisations can be understood as a matter of degree, in that organisations can be more or less autonomous, legal personality features a binary character: an organisation either possesses legal personality or not.[41] As noted above, organisations possessing international legal personality thereby enjoy a relatively high level of autonomy.

Conversely, international organisations with no legal personality enjoy a lower level of autonomy and depend heavily on the action of their members/participating States, be it in terms of their international relations, implementation of their decisions or their daily functioning.[42] Though such organisations are commonly regarded as 'informal' or 'soft law' organisations,[43] a general observation has it that they may regulate their policy fields as effectively as classical international organisations possessing international legal personality.[44]

The OSCE has probably been one of the most quoted examples of an informal organisation of this type, since in the majority view it lacks international legal personality,[45] whereby some of its organs exercise a considerable degree of autonomy and adopt acts that are distinguishable from the acts of its participating States. The more obvious examples are the OSCE Secretariat and the OSCE Office for Democratic Institutions and Human Rights, which

40 For the milestones in that development, see Tichy, 'The Role of the Participating States in Reforming the Legal Framework of the OSCE – Past Developments, Status Quo and Future Ambitions', Chapter 4 in this Volume; for political controversies of the project see Börzel and I. Peters, '"It's Politics, Stupid": An International Relations Perspective on Strengthening the Legal Framework of the OSCE', Chapter 5 in this Volume.

41 Gazzini, 'The Relationship'.

42 For the example of the OSCE external relations, see Boisson de Chazournes and Gadkowski, 'The External Relations of the OSCE', Chapter 10 in this Volume.

43 Klabbers, 'Institutional Ambivalence', 403–21.

44 Benvenisti, *The Law of Global Governance*, 37 and the following.

45 See, e.g., White, *The Law of International Organisations*, 50–3; Gazzini, 'Legal Personality of International Organizations', 40; Wenig, 'Der völkerrechtliche Status der OSZE'; Bertrand, 'La nature juridique'; for the official position of the OSCE Chairmanship concerning the lack of international legal personality of the OSCE, see OSCE, 'The Legal Framework of the OSCE', 1 December 2010, available at: www.osce.org/mc/87192; see, however, Tabassi, 'The Role of the Organisation in Asserting Legal Personality: The Position of the OSCE Secretariat on the OSCE's Legal Status', Chapter 3 in this Volume.

manifest a particularly high level of independence from participating States. But a certain degree of autonomy can also be observed in other organs and bodies, including those composed of state representatives that adopt decisions by consensus, since it suffices that no votes are cast against in order for the decision to be adopted as an OSCE act and thus to become applicable also to those participating States that have abstained from voting.[46]

The distinction between the autonomy and international legal personality of an international organisation was introduced in international institutional law in the aftermath of the ICJ *Reparations* case,[47] in which the Court established for the first time that an international organisation *can* possess international legal personality distinct from the personality of its member states and that the organisation in question – the UN – in fact does possess international legal personality.[48] Thus, although all organisations necessarily depend on their members in terms of creation, functioning and extinction, and that one can speak of their autonomy only in relative terms, certain organisations became considered by legal scholarship and practice as being able to possess a will of their own (*volonté distincte, der eigene Wille*).[49]

More than that, possessing its own will represents today one of the main requirements for an entity to be granted international legal personality. An organisation without international legal personality may therefore be subject to assertions that it is not an international organisation at all[50] and considered, formally speaking, a states' agent. On the other hand, an organisation possessing such personality is recognised as an international legal subject capable of acquiring its own rights and obligations under international law and pursuing its aims and purposes in its own legal right. Thus, once an organisation is granted international legal personality, acts performed by the organisation are attributable, as a rule, to the organisation itself and not to its members.

The rules on attribution of conduct to organisations (relevant with regard to their primary obligations as well as possible secondary obligations concerning legal responsibility, if the primary obligations have been breached) have been most comprehensively spelled out in the work of the Institut de Droit

46 See also OSCE, Press and Public Information Section, *OSCE Handbook 2007* (n. 19), 14, available at: www.osce.org/files/documents/b/3/22624.pdf; Wessel, 'Revisiting the International Legal Status of the EU'; Phan, 'The Association of Southeast Asian Nations'.

47 ICJ, *Reparation for Injuries* (n. 21).

48 Ibid., 178–9.

49 For the theoretical underpinnings see Blokker, 'Constituent Instruments', 951.

50 Schermers and Blokker, *International Institutional Law*, 44–6; see also Blokker and Wessel, 'Revisiting Questions of Organisationhood, Legal Personality and Membership in the OSCE: The Interplay between Law, Politics and Practice', Chapter 7 in this Volume.

international,[51] the International Law Association (ILA)[52] and the UN International Law Commission (ILC), by relying on the Vienna Convention on the Law of Treaties between States and International Organisations or between International Organisations, and other instruments governing international organisations.[53] The ILC Draft Articles on the Responsibility of International Organisations for Internationally Wrongful Acts (ARIO) accordingly provide that the conduct of an organ or agent of an international organisation carried out in the performance of functions of that organ or agent shall be considered an act of that organisation under international law, whatever position the organ or agent holds in respect of that organisation.[54] The recognition of international legal personality to an organisation therefore functions as an institutional veil behind which activities carried out within the framework of that organisation by its members are considered, as a rule, activities of the organisation itself, regardless of how high the degree of autonomy of the organisation really is.[55]

4 THE AUTONOMY AND RESPONSIBILITY OF AN INTERNATIONAL ORGANISATION

The question of whether an international organisation enjoys international legal personality is not only relevant for the determination of the actor to whom acts adopted by the organisation are to be attributed, but also for determining which actor is to be held responsible for any wrongful act that may result from such acts. Strictly speaking, an organisation without international legal personality cannot even commit a wrongful act, as no obligation binding upon the organisation exists that the organisation could breach in the first place. Any act carried out by such an organisation is therefore to be attributed to its members/participating States, which will also bear

51 Institut de Droit international, '[Resolution on] The Legal Consequences for Member States of the Non-fulfilment by International Organizations of their Obligations toward Third Parties', Annuaire de l'Institut de Droit international, Session de Lisbonne 66-II (1995), 447.

52 International Law Association, 'Final Report on Accountability of International Organisations', Berlin Conference (2004), available at: www.ila-hq.org/index.php/committees?committeeID=5.

53 ARIO (n. 28), see, e.g., Article 2 (*Use of Terms*) with the accompanying commentary, especially para. 16 and the following; for the Vienna Convention, see Vienna Convention on the Law of Treaties, 23 May 1969, 1155 UNTS 331.

54 Art. 6 ARIO (n. 28); compare also with the definition of state agents as adopted by the UN, International Law Commission, Draft Articles on Responsibility of States for Internationally Wrongful Acts, A/56/10, 2001, Articles 4 & 5.

55 For challenges thereby arising for legal scholarship and practice, see Brölmann, *The Institutional Veil.*

responsibility for any breach of international law that may have been committed by that act.

Conversely, if the organisation has been granted international legal personality, an act carried out by an organ or agent of the organisation that violates international law will, as a rule, give rise to the organisation's responsibility and not its members.[56] An act by a member state done in accordance with the rules of the organisation will therefore in principle not engage the responsibility of that state.[57] When the ILA adopted the Final Report on the Accountability of International Organisations it thus specified from the outset that their focus has been on 'intergovernmental organisations in the traditional sense, i.e. created under international law by an international agreement amongst states, possessing a constitution and organs separate from its Member States'.[58] The ILC has similarly provided for the ARIO to apply to international organisations 'established by a treaty or other instrument governed by international law and possessing its own international legal personality'.[59]

A separate legal personality therefore forms the legal basis for a separate responsibility of an international organisation under international law. When state responsibility has been invoked before domestic or international courts for the acts adopted by an international organisation, member states have successfully claimed that the challenged acts were to be attributed to the organisation, which was also the subject to be held responsible for any wrongdoing caused by such acts. In the field of human rights, the concept of the separate responsibility of an organisation from the responsibility of its members has most notably been developed in the case law of the European Court of Human Rights (ECtHR).

For instance, the ECtHR considered the fact that a state hosting the headquarters of an international organisation is insufficient ground for attributing to that state any wrongful act committed by that organisation.[60] Complaints were also invoked against the Netherlands, which hosts the seat and premises

[56] Art. 58(2) ARIO (n. 28); see also Institut de droit international, 'Resolution on the Legal Consequences' (n. 51), Article 6, together with the background report by Higgins, 'The Legal Consequences'.

[57] For exceptions, see further below; for an ongoing critical scholarly discussion, see Hartwig, *Die Haftung der Mitgliedstaaten*, 298–306; Seidl-Hohenveldern, *Liability of Member States*; Barros, Ryngaert and Wouters, *International Organizations*; for specific concerns whether concurrent responsibility of members could undermine legal personality and independence of the organisation, see Stumer, 'Liability of Member States'.

[58] ILA, Report, 2004 (n. 52), 4.

[59] Art. 2 ARIO (n. 28).

[60] ECtHR, *Lopez Cifuentes* v. *Spain*, ECtHR Decision of 7 July 2009, No. 18754/06.

of international criminal tribunals, for human right violations that allegedly arose from the operation of those tribunals, but these complaints were likewise declared inadmissible.[61] In the same vein the ECtHR dealt with complaints relating to the acts and omissions of UNMIK and NATO Forces (KFOR) that were operating in Kosovo pursuant to a UN Security Council resolution, and refused to establish responsibility for human rights violations by France, Norway and Germany merely on the basis of their membership of these organisations and their contributing personnel to the field operations.[62] The ECtHR based its conclusion on the finding that the actions of the armed forces acting pursuant to the UN Security Council authorisations were attributable to the UN, which exercised 'ultimate authority and control' over the impugned action.[63] It is worth noting, however, that the scholarship and practice heavily criticised the decision for misinterpreting the rules of attribution in the present case, suggesting that the ECtHR should have reviewed the cases also in light of possible simultaneous attribution of the challenged acts and responsibility to the respondent states.[64]

In such cases, a different approach to the analysis of responsibility and accountability of international organisations and their members becomes apparent between IR and legal scholarship. Since members may play an important role in the organisation committing a wrongful act, especially when the organisation or a particular organ displays a low level of autonomy, IR scholars easily ascribe such an act to the control, influence and power of (particular) members. In legal terms, though, the act of the organisation's organs, bodies and agents will be attributed to the organisation itself as soon as it has been granted international legal personality, and the organisation alone will normally be held responsible for the consequences arising from the wrongful act.

Nonetheless, legal scholarship and practice increasingly acknowledge that states may sometimes seek to hide behind the organisation's institutional veil while in fact exercising substantial influence over the commission of an act. Probably the most debated example has been the targeted sanctions of the UN

61 For the International Criminal Court, see ECtHR, *Djokaba Lambi Longa* v. *The Netherlands*, Decision of 9 October 2012ECtHR; for the International Criminal Tribunal for Yugoslavia, see ECtHR, *Galić* v. *The Netherlands*, Decision of 9 June 2009, No. 22617/07 and ECtHR, *Blagojević* v. *The Netherlands*, Decision of 9 June 2009, No. 49032/07.

62 ECtHR, *Behrami and Behrami* v. *France; Saramati* v. *France, Germany and Norway*, Decision of 2 May 2007, Nos. 71412/01 and 78166/01.

63 Ibid., para. 133.

64 See the commentary to Art. 7 ARIO (Conduct of organs of a State or organs or agents of an international organization placed at the disposal of another international organization), together with further references.

Security Council, which gave rise to a number of proceedings before domestic, international and supranational courts and in which individuals complained that the UN financial and travel sanctions as implemented by the member states violated their human rights.[65] Once the CJEU and the ECtHR established that the implementation of the challenged UN sanctions by the respondent states could result in human rights breaches and was therefore incompatible with the European Convention on Human Rights (ECHR) and EU law respectively, the implementation of the UN resolution by a member state was considered as potentially giving rise to the responsibility of that state, and not (only) the UN.[66]

In the *Nada* case, the ECtHR found that while the applicant's listing by the Sanctions Committee of the UN Security Council was attributable to the UN, the implementation of the sanctions by Switzerland was attributable to Switzerland itself.[67] The ECtHR then recalled its previous case law holding that it would be incompatible with the object and purpose of the ECHR if the contracting states were absolved from their responsibility under the ECHR in a particular policy field once they transferred in that field certain competencies onto an international organisation.[68] The ECtHR therefore reviewed the challenged domestic measures that aimed at implementing the UN sanctions against the applicant and found them disproportionate and depriving the applicant of effective means of redress, and as such violating the ECHR.[69]

The ECtHR thereby explicitly sided with the CJEU in the *Kadi* case,[70] quoting the CJEU that 'it is not a consequence of the principles governing the international legal order under the UN that any judicial review of the *internal lawfulness* of the contested regulation in the light of fundamental freedoms is excluded by virtue of the fact that that measure is intended to give effect to a

65 For the CJEU, see Joined Cases CJEU, C–584/10 P, C–593/10 P, C–595/10 P, *European Commission and the Council of the European Union* v. *Yassin Abdullah Kadi* [2013] EU: C:2013:518; for the ECtHR, see ECtHR, *Nada v. Switzerland*, GC Judgment of 12 September 2012, No. 10593/08; and ECtHR, *Al-Dulimi and Montana Management Inc.* v. *Switzerland*, GC Judgment of 21 June 2016, No. 5809/08.

66 For the scholarly support, see, among many others, de Wet, 'From Kadi to Nada'; d'Aspremont, 'Abuse of the Legal Personality'; Giegerich, 'Verantwortlichkeit und Haftung'.

67 ECtHR, *Nada* v. *Switzerland* (n. 65), para. 121.

68 For the line of case law see European Commission of Human Rights, *M & Co* v. *the Federal Republic of Germany*, Decision of 9 February 1990, No. 13258/87; ECtHR, *Waite and Kennedy* v. *Germany*, GC Judgment of 18 February 1999, No 26083/94; ECtHR, *Matthews* v. *the United Kingdom*, GC Judgment of 18 February 1999, No. 24833/94; ECtHR, *Bosphorus Hava Yollary Turizm ve Ticaret Anonim Sirketi* v. *Ireland*, GC Judgment of 30 June 2005, No. 45036/98.

69 ECtHR, *Nada v. Switzerland* (n. 65), paras. 199, 214.

70 CJEU, Case C–402/05 P and C–415/05 *P. Kadi and Al Barakaat International Foundation* v. *Council and Commission* [2008] ECLI:EU:C:2008:461.

resolution of the Security Council adopted under Chapter VII of the Charter of the United Nations'.[71]

In addition to the shared responsibility of an organisation and its members, the same wrongful act can give rise to the responsibility of the particular individuals who were involved in the commission of that act. Hence, when complaints were brought before the Dutch courts against the UN and the Netherlands for the alleged failure of the Dutch peacekeeping forces of the UN Protection Force (UNPROFOR) to prevent the genocide in Srebrenica, the Dutch courts conducted parallel proceedings and reviewed the question of the Netherland's responsibility separately from the question of responsibility of the UN for the same event,[72] whereas the question of individual responsibility of Dutch UNPROFOR personnel was in turn part of a separate civil and criminal proceedings.[73]

Legal scholarship and practice therefore acknowledge that in certain cases the institutional veil of the organisation needs to be pierced and the level of influence and control of particular members as well as individuals over the commission of a wrongful act examined. That view has been reflected in the ARIO, which elaborates in Part Five the conditions under which states can be held responsible for the acts of an international organisation. Thus, although the challenged conduct is to be attributed to the organisation, and the organisation may be held responsible for it, members can likewise incur responsibility if their influence over such conduct amounts to aiding, assisting, directing or controlling the commission of that act by the organisation, or even to coercing the organisation to commit such an act.[74] Moreover, the ARIO provides for the responsibility of members if they take advantage of the organisation's separate international legal personality, by making the organisation committing an act that would, if committed by a member, result in a breach of a rule of international law.[75] Such responsibility of members can

[71] Ibid., para. 299, emphasis added; for the ECtHR reference to the CJEU case, see ECtHR; *Nada* v. *Switzerland* (n. 65), paras. 212–13; for the scholarly account on state responsibility in the context of their membership in international organisations, see generally Crawford, *State Responsibility*; for responsibility of international organisations in such situations, see the following Section 5.

[72] Compare van Alebeek, 'Stichting Mothers of Srebrenica and Others v. Netherlands and the United Nations'; and Boutin, 'Ministry of Defence and Ministry of Foreign Affairs v. Nuhanović'; see also ECtHR, *Stichting Mothers of Srebrenica and Others* v. *The Netherlands*, Decision of 11 June 2013, No. 65542/12.

[73] For a summary of the domestic proceedings concerning the individual responsibility and for the subsequent review of these proceedings by the ECtHR, see ECtHR, *Mustafić-Mujić and Others* v. *The Netherlands*, Decision of 30 August 2016, No. 49037/15.

[74] ARIO, Arts. 58–60.

[75] Ibid., Art. 61.

arise even if the organisation is itself not bound by the international rule in question.[76]

But international law, contrary to IR, takes equally into account cases in which international organisations, in particular those with a high degree of autonomy, may exercise undue influence and control over (particular) members.[77] Such a risk has likewise been acknowledged in the ARIO, which provides for different degrees of control and influence that an organisation can exercise over its members and thereby make them violate international law, ranging from the organisation's aid and assistance to direction, control or even coercion of its members.[78] An organisation can therefore be held responsible for adopting a decision *binding* upon its members which they cannot fulfil without violating some rule of international law.

Similarly, an international organisation can incur responsibility when it merely *authorises* members to commit an act that would be wrongful if committed by the organisation itself, if a member in fact implements that act due to the authorisation.[79] Thus, even where some discretion is left to members – which is the case in a growing number of non-binding resolutions or other non-binding instruments adopted by organisations – the organisation can still be held responsible if a member actually utilises the authorisation given and implements the decision resulting in a wrongful act.[80]

Such responsibility and autonomous action by international organisations is not easily accommodated within IR scholarship, which has been long dominated by a state-centric understanding of the functioning of international organisations and IR more generally. As such it seems particularly well fitted to explain the functioning of those organisations that enjoy a higher level of autonomy and enjoy the status of an international legal subject. Organisations without international legal personality however fall out of reach of international responsibility regime, including the OSCE.

Thus, although some OSCE organs and bodies certainly enjoy a considerable degree of autonomy, OSCE acts are to be attributed not to the

76 ARIO thereby incorporates the principle developed by the ECtHR in the context of human rights protection and gives it general application; compare ECtHR, *Waite and Kennedy* v. *Germany* (n. 68), para. 67, and ECtHR, *Bosphorus Hava Yollary Turizm ve Ticaret Anonim Sirketi* v. *Ireland* (n. 68), paras. 53–5.

77 That issue was hotly discussed in the wake of the NATO intervention in Kosovo, given the absence of explicit authorisation by the UN Security Council; see, e.g., Pellet, 'L'imputabilité d'éventuels actes illicites'.

78 ARIO, Articles 14–16.

79 Ibid., Art. 17.

80 For the great practical relevance of this provision, in particular in terms of remedies, see Nedeski and Nollkaemper, 'Responsibility of International Organizations'.

Organization but to the participating States collectively, which will also bear responsibility for any wrongful act that may arise from OSCE activities. Similarly, OSCE members of staff are formally to be considered as state agents acting on behalf of participating States rather than international civil servants, although they are allowed neither to seek nor accept instructions from any participating State but must comply with the principles of the international civil service.[81] Correspondingly, a number of voices have called for the OSCE to gain international legal personality in terms of the need to grant the OSCE and its staff the autonomy and independence that participating States expect of them.[82] In terms of this section, the granting of international legal personality would therefore facilitate the attribution of acts adopted within the OSCE to the Organization itself and provide a clear legal basis for binding the OSCE to international law.[83]

5 THE AUTONOMY AND LEGITIMACY OF AN INTERNATIONAL ORGANISATION

If only those international organisations that possess international legal personality have the capacity to be bound by international law and held responsible for a wrongful act under international law, the question arises whether issues relating to the accountability and legitimacy of organisations matter only once an organisation has been endowed with legal personality. Or, in other words, can those organisations that are functioning below the threshold

81 Compare the position of the OSCE staff as regulated under the CSCE, Charter of Paris for a New Europe, Supplementary document to give effect to certain provisions contained in the Charter of Paris for a New Europe, November 1990, available at: www.oscepa.org/documents/all-documents/documents-1/historical-documents-1/673–1990-charter-of-paris-for-a-new-europe/file, point I H, which reads that '[s]taff will be accredited by the seconding State to the host country where they will enjoy full diplomatic status'; and OSCE, Permanent Council, 'OSCE Code of Conduct for Staff/Mission Members', Appendix 1 to the OSCE Staff Regulations and Staff Rules, Permanent Council Decision 550/Corr.1, 27 June 2003, available at: www.osce.org/secretariat/31781?download=true, which states in Regulation 2.01 (Conduct of OSCE Officials) (a) that 'OSCE officials shall conduct themselves at all times in a manner befitting the status of an international civil servant'.

82 International Secretariat of the OSCE, Parliamentary Assembly/OSCE, Secretariat for Legal Services, 'Helsinki +40 Project Food-for-Thought Paper: The OSCE's Lack of an Agreed Legal Status–Challenges in Crisis Situations', April 2015, available at: www.oscepa.org/documents/all-documents/helsinki-40/seminar-4-diis/2814-helsinki-40-food-for-thought-paper-the-osce-s-lack-of-an-agreed-legal-status-challenges-in-crisis-situations/file, 3.

83 See also UN, International Law Commission, First report on responsibility of international organizations, UN Doc. A/CN.4/532, 15; see, however, for a different reading OSCE, Irish Chairmanship to the Ministerial Council, Chairmanship Food-for-Thought Paper, Strengthening the Legal Framework of the OSCE, 18 May 2012, CIO.GAL/63/12, 1.

of international legal personality, but nevertheless act at least to a certain degree as autonomous actors, indeed escape all international normative standards that otherwise apply to organisations with international legal personality and regulate the exercise of their public authority?

In this case, one could suggest that no international normative standards govern the manner in which organisations without international legal personality may exercise their mandate, powers and functions, or the remedies that those adversely affected by the organisations' activities would be entitled to claim. Such a conception would allow for a legal gap in international law under which an international organisation, possibly one as prominent as the OSCE, acting more or less autonomously in the fields as significant as the use of force and being capable of adversely affecting other public and private actors, including individuals, could not be held accountable for any wrongful act under international law. Such an understanding could however hardly find support in scholarship and practice.

5.1 A *Sketch of Theoretical Foundations*

In the liberal tradition, a specific legitimacy standard flows from the rule of law: the principle that any exercise of public authority needs to be constituted, and limited, by law.[84] Moreover, international legal scholarship has well established that the exercise of public authority by international organisations and other international institutions corresponds to the kind of governmental activity that needs to be based on international law, and be controlled and limited by substantive and procedural standards.[85] Both legal and political science have thereby identified certain normative standards against which the accountability and legitimacy of a particular organisation can be measured, regardless of the organisation's legal status or its international legal personality more specifically. Most commonly, these standards are defined in terms of requiring the organisation to respect certain basic human rights and the rule of law standards, as well as certain minimum standards of representative and participatory decision-making on the international level.[86]

84 For distinction between legitimacy that is based on legality and legitimacy that goes beyond the proceduralist understanding of the law, see powerfully Habermas, *Between Facts and Norms*, 135 and 450; for the purposes of the present chapter I focus primarily on the first type of legitimacy, in order to show that acts of international organisations sometimes fail to satisfy already such a narrow legalistic understanding of legitimacy.

85 For a comparative analysis of the argument, see von Bogdandy, Dann and Goldmann, 'Developing the Publicness of Public International Law', 1375–8; see also further below.

86 See, among many other authorities, Wouters, Brems, Smis and Schmitt, *Accountability for Human Rights Violations by International Organisations*; Zürn, Nollkaemper and Peerenboom, *Rule of Law Dynamics*; Grote and Gbikpi, *Participatory Governance*.

While there exist different scholarship approaches that explore the theoretical underpinnings and scope of application of such legitimacy standards, they essentially seem to share the premise that the trigger for applicability of such standards to an international organisation is not its possible possession of international legal personality, but its capacity to exercise public authority, in particular over individuals and peoples.[87] These findings are therefore valid also for organisations like the OSCE, under which the exercise of public authority may even include the use of military force, and thus most evidently affect individuals *directly*.

Indeed, it may be hard for an observer to interpret such legitimacy standards as generally binding even upon international organisations possessing international legal personality, in particular due to the lack of organisations' accession to human rights treaties. An act of an organisation that conflicts with such standards is therefore not automatically considered illegal. Yet, it can be considered illegitimate. A failure of an organisation to respect certain basic legitimacy standards may thereby not only harm the reputation of the respective organisation,[88] but, as the practice of domestic, international and supranational institutions demonstrates, also hinder the implementation and enforcement of the challenged act of the organisation at the domestic, international and supranational level.

5.2 *Formation of Practice by Domestic, International and Supranational Institutions*

The contested targeted sanctions of the UN Security Council referred to in Section 4 provide a paramount lesson to international organisations with international legal personality as well as to those without: once the CJEU established in the *Kadi* case[89] that the implementation of the contested UN Security Council resolution could result in a violation of certain fundamental human rights as guaranteed by the EU Charter of Fundamental Rights, in particular the judicial protection of the individual, the Court annulled the regulation of the Council of the EU which aimed to implement the UN resolution.[90] Similarly, once the ECtHR

87 Compare, e.g., von Bogdandy, Dann and Goldmann, 'Developing the Publicness of Public International Law', esp. 1380–6; A. Peters, 'Membership', esp. 208–15; Kingsbury, Krisch and Steward, 'The Emergence of Global Administrative Law', esp. 37–41.

88 Daugirdas, 'How and Why International Law Binds International Organizations'.

89 CJEU, *P. Kadi and Al Barakaat International Foundation* v. *Council and Commission* (n. 70).

90 For a lively debate among international and EU scholars see, e.g., Kokott and Sobotta, 'The Kadi Case'; De Búrca, 'The European Court of Justice'; and Fassbender, 'Triepel in Luxemburg'.

found in the *Nada* case[91] that the implementation of the UN sanctions by Switzerland contravened the ECHR, it effectively prevented the UN sanctions from being implemented by the respondent state.[92] International legal scholarship has thereby openly supported, if not paved the way for, the development of such practice.[93]

Such practice of international and supranational courts suggests that the crucial question for the ECtHR and the CJEU, but also for a domestic court in reviewing the implementation of an act adopted by an international organisation, will not be whether the respective organisation enjoys legal personality under international, EU or domestic law, but rather whether the legal consequences that would arise from the implementation and enforcement of such an act could conflict with the human rights and the rule of law standards that the respective court is obliged to protect. If so, the court may – and would in certain cases be obliged to – refuse to uphold the implementation of the act, if it is to comply with its *own* obligations under domestic, international or EU law, respectively. The question of whether the organisation is itself formally bound to respect such obligations does not even necessarily need to be examined. Even if the organisation is not bound as a matter of law (for example, because it lacks international legal personality), a domestic court, the CJEU or the ECtHR can still find that a particular act of the organisation should not be implemented if the implementation of such an act could result in violation of the standards that the court is bound to protect.[94]

Non-compliance of an international organisation with legitimacy standards such as certain fundamental human rights may also result in the organisation being deprived of its immunities before domestic courts. That can particularly be the case if the organisation does not provide for any alternative dispute settlement mechanism where complaints against the organisation by private

91 ECtHR, *Nada* v. *Switzerland* (n. 65); see also ECtHR, *Al-Dulimi et Montana Management* v. *Switzerland* (n. 65).

92 For a comparative analysis of the respective CJEU and ECtHR jurisprudence, see de Wet, 'From Kadi to Nada'.

93 See, e.g., ILA, 'Final Report' (n. 52), the part concerning the member states' implementation of acts adopted by international organisations.

94 The ECtHR for example reviews the compliance of domestic measures aiming to implement EU law with the ECHR despite the fact that by now both the EU members as well as the EU itself are formally bound to protect fundamental human rights; for a recent case law, see ECtHR, *Avotiņš v. Latvia*, GC Judgment of 23 May 2016, No. 17502/07; for the ECtHR principled approach, see ECtHR, *Bosphorus Hava Yollary Turizm ve Ticaret Anonim Sirketi v. Ireland* (n. 68); for the human rights standards binding upon the EU, see esp. the Charter of Fundamental Rights of the European Union, 7 December 2000 (ratified), OJ 2000/C 364/01 and Treaty of Lisbon amending the Treaty on European Union and the Treaty establishing the European Community, 13 December 2007, OJ 2007/C 306/01, Article 6(1).

parties could be heard, which in effect deprives the claimants of their right of access to justice.[95] Domestic courts may therefore condition their abstention from review of acts by international organisations with the availability of some other settlement procedure to which the victim can have recourse, either in the form of an internal mechanism established within the organisation or some other international dispute settlement procedure subjected to by the organisation.[96] In that way, the court fulfils its own obligation to protect the individual's right of access to justice, which today forms part of the basic human rights and the rule of law standards as established in constitutional democracies and protected under international and EU law. Such an interpretation can be reconciled also with the agreements granting privileges and immunities to international organisations, which as a rule oblige the respective organisation to waive immunities granted to its personnel when the immunity would interfere with the administration of justice.[97]

In Europe such practice became even more evident after the ECtHR proclaimed that states parties to the ECHR are obliged to ensure that their grant of immunities to an organisation will not deprive claimants of their right to a fair trial and the right to a remedy.[98] Thus, in *Siegler* v. *Western European Union*, the Belgian Court of Appeals expressly relied on the jurisprudence of the ECtHR and ultimately denied the organisation its entitlement to immunities.[99]

Moreover, these legitimacy standards become increasingly established also in general international law and a number of international organisations have already responded to these developments by establishing alternative means of redress, and even by calling upon other states and international organisations

95 For a seminal work, see Reinisch, *International Organisations.*

96 For a pioneering domestic courts' practice, see the judgment of the German Federal Constitutional Court in BVerfG, *Hetzel* v. *EUROCONTROL*, Second Chamber Judgment of 10 November 1981, 2 BvR 1058/79, 63; the Swiss Supreme Court in *Groupement d'Entreprises Fougerolle et consorts* v. *CERN*, 1ère Cour civile du tribunal fédéral Suisse, 21 décembre 1992, ATF 118 Ib 562; the Criminal Court of the City of New York, *People* v. *Mark S. Weiner*, 378 N.Y.S.2d 966, N.Y. County, 19 January 1976, UNJYB 249; and the Argentinian Supreme Court in *Duhalde, Mario Alfredo* v. *Organisatión Panamericana de la Salud-Officina Sanitaria Panamericana*, D.73.XXXIV, Accidente-ley 9688, CSJN, 31 August 1999; for a recent comparative analysis, see Reinisch, *The Privileges and Immunities*, 123–31.

97 For a model treaty, see the Convention on the Privileges and Immunities of the United Nations, 13 February 1946, 1 UNTS 15, esp. Articles V & VI; for OSCE immunities in the host countries, see Cogen, *An Introduction to European Intergovernmental Organisations*, 148–9; generally on the OSCE privileges and immunities see Pingel, 'Privileges and Immunities of the OSCE', Chapter 9 in this Volume.

98 ECtHR, *Waite and Kennedy v. Germany* (n. 68); ECtHR, *Beer and Regan* v. *Germany*, GC Judgment of 18 February 1999, No. 28934/95.

99 Vidal, 'Siedler v. WEU'.

to respect these standards. Probably the most prominent has been the response of the UN General Assembly, which in 2012 adopted the UN Declaration of the High-Level Meeting on the Rule of Law at the National and International Levels, stating that:

> the rule of law applies to all states equally, *and to international organisations, including the United Nations and its principal organs*, and that respect for and promotion of the rule of law and justice should guide all of their activities and accord predictability and legitimacy to their actions. We also recognise that all persons, institutions and entities, public and private, including the state itself, are accountable to just, fair and equitable laws and are entitled without any discrimination to equal protection of law.[100]

The Parliamentary Assembly of the Council of Europe (CoE) soon followed their lead. While embracing the relevant jurisprudence of the ECtHR, it recommended, inter alia, that international organisations 'examine the quality and effectiveness of mechanisms aimed at ensuring compliance with their human rights obligations and to further develop standards in this area.[101] The Assembly also recommended that member states 'examine the status of international organisations within their national legal systems and ensure that arrangements are in place for the waiver of immunity when this is required', and called for a number of further measures to be implemented by states and international organisations, including the adoption of binding mechanisms for monitoring organisations' compliance with human rights standards.[102]

Hence, even the UN Security Council, for its part, has progressively introduced several human rights guarantees into its targeted sanctions regime, including the Office of the Ombudsperson.[103] Other prominent human rights mechanisms that have been established for monitoring the compliance of

100 UN, General Assembly, Resolution adopted by the UNGA on 24 September 2012, A/RES/67/1 para. 2 (emphasis added).

101 See CoE, Parliamentary Assembly (PA), Accountability of International Organisations for Human Rights Violations, Recommendation 2037, 31 January 2014), para. 2.2 together with CoE, PA, Committee on Legal Affairs and Human Rights, Report, Doc. 13370, 17 December 2013; for the general trend, see Steinbrück Platise, 'The Development of the Immunities'.

102 CoE, PA, Accountability of International Organisations, 2014, para. 2.1; see also Council of Europe, Parliamentary Assembly, Accountability of International Organisations for Human Rights Violations, Resolution 1979, 31 January 2014, and the Council of Europe, Parliamentary Assembly, Committee of Ministers' Reply to the Recommendation, Doc. 13581, 10 July 2014.

103 See, e.g., UN, Security Council, Resolution 1452, S/Res/1452 20 December 2002 providing for a 'humanitarian exemption' allowing the targeted individuals to keep the funds necessary for their basic living expenses; the UN, Security Council, Resolutions 1730, S/Res/1730, 19 December 2006 and 1735, S/Res/1735, 22 December 2006) enabling the targeted individuals and entities to submit a request for de-listing; and UN, Security Council, Resolution 1904, S/

organisations with their human rights obligations and for allowing individuals to seek redress for human rights violations include the World Bank Inspection Panel, the use of human rights advisory panels to monitor the activities of UNMIK, and the EU Rule of Law Mission in Kosovo (EULEX).[104]

The present trend in international institutional law demonstrates that, first of all, international organisations are entrusted with a certain mandate and public authority which they may exercise in a more or less autonomous way, without necessarily being granted international legal personality. That does not mean that international law does not govern the exercise of public authority by organisations without international legal personality or does not protect human rights and the rule of law standards that thereby need to be observed. It simply means that the conduct adopted by such an organisation and the responsibility for any wrongful act that might arise from such a conduct will be attributed to the states that established the organisation.[105]

5.3 *The OSCE: out for Autonomy, out of Legitimacy?*

It seems that these developments have not yet been properly addressed in the debates on how to strengthen the legal framework of the OSCE, although the above-discussed practice of domestic, international and supranational institutions is relevant for international organisations with, as well as without, international legal personality. The OSCE clearly relies on the implementation of its decisions by participating States; it also enjoys immunities,[106] which have been granted to the OSCE on the basis of the domestic law of particular states in which the OSCE enjoys domestic legal personality.[107] Nevertheless, the

Res/1904, 17 December 2009 establishing the Office of the Ombudsperson to ensure the targeted persons an 'independent and impartial' review of their requests concerning the de-listing; for the gradual development of human rights standards with respect to the targeted sanctions, see Genser and Barth, 'Targeted Sanctions'.

104 See, however, an observation on the availability and effectiveness of these mechanisms by the CoE, Parliamentary Assembly, Accountability of International Organisations for Human Rights Violations, Resolution 1979, 2014 (n. 102).

105 See also Higgins, *Problems & Processes*, 46–8, preferring accordingly the term 'participants' to 'subjects' of international law; for a critical view on such denomination, see Walter, 'Subjects of International Law'.

106 For particular privileges and immunities of the OSCE in domestic legal orders, see Pingel, 'Privileges and Immunities of the OSCE', Chapter 9 in this Volume.

107 Several participating States adopted the domestic laws granting privileges and immunities upon the (non-binding) 1993 recommendation of the then CSCE Council; see 'CSCE and the New Europe – Our Security Is Indivisible', CSCE/4-C/Dec.2, 1 December 1993; yet, not all participating States implemented that decision; see also Ryngaert, 'The OSCE's Legal Status: An Exploration of Relevant International Law Sources', Chapter 8 in this Volume.

OSCE still lacks internal human rights and the rule of law standards that would regulate the activities of the Organization and its personnel and provide appropriate means of redress in case such standards were breached, including dispute settlement mechanisms that would be available to the affected third parties.[108]

The present situation therefore exposes the OSCE to the risk of non-implementation of some of its *acquis*, when that could lead to a breach of fundamental human rights and the rule of law standards. Similarly, the OSCE and its staff are exposed to the risk of being deprived of their immunities before domestic courts as long as a domestic court can establish that the OSCE does not provide for private claimants any alternative means of redress. Complaints against the OSCE may thereby arise not only from its disputes with third private parties, but also from employment disputes with its staff especially in light of the fact that internal dispute settlement mechanisms available to OSCE staff could hardly meet international standards of an effective remedy granted by an independent forum.[109] The recent security incident in Ukraine in which a member of the OSCE Special Monitoring Mission to Ukraine died and two others were injured, after their vehicle drove over a mine in Donbass, reveals all too well the nature and scale of the disputes in which the OSCE as an employer could get entangled.[110]

Such risks for the OSCE seem particularly high before the domestic courts of those states that are parties to the ECHR, since in case of a conflict between their obligation to grant immunities to the OSCE on the one hand, and their obligation to protect the claimant's right of access to justice on the other hand, the domestic courts are obliged by the ECHR to give priority to human rights protection. The only exception so far was recognised by the ECtHR with respect to immunities of the UN, in accordance with Article 103 of the UN Charter providing that the obligations under the UN Charter take precedence

108 See also Boisson de Chazournes and Gadkowski, 'The External Relations of the OSCE', Chapter 10 in this Volume.

109 The Regulation 11.02 of the OSCE Staff Regulations and Staff Rules (OSCE, Permanent Council, Staff Regulations and Staff Rules of the Organization for Security and Co-operation in Europe, Decision No. 1128, DOC.SEC/3/03, endorsed in September 2003 and last amended on 17 July 2014) merely provides that '*[i]n exceptional cases and in the interest of the* OSCE, the Secretary General, or *the respective head* of institution/mission in consultation with the Secretary General, shall be empowered to conclude mutually agreed settlements with staff/mission members, in relation to separation from service or disputes about working conditions, *provided that they renounce all right of appeal*' (emphasis added).

110 OSCE, 'OSCE Special Monitoring Mission to Ukraine patrol member killed in explosion near Luhansk', 23 April 2017, available at: www.osce.org/special-monitoring-mission-to-ukraine/312951.

over obligations under all other (regional) treaties and in accordance with the special position that the UN enjoys within the international system.[111]

Risks are involved for the OSCE participating States as well. First, every OSCE act is ultimately attributed to participating States, which can therefore be held responsible for any violation of international law caused by an OSCE act, including any pecuniary and non-pecuniary damages arising thereof. Secondly, domestic measures aiming at implementation of an OSCE *acquis* that would not conform to the basic human rights and the rule of law standards, or a domestic grant of immunities to the OSCE and its staff that would result in a claimant's deprivation of access to justice, may pose serious constitutional problems in many domestic legal systems. Thirdly, state implementation of an OSCE *acquis* or the grant of immunity to the OSCE that could result in violation of such standards would need to face the scrutiny of any international and supranational mechanisms that are competent to monitor the protection of human rights or the rule of law standards by the respective state, including the judicial review by the ECtHR and the CJEU. It is therefore worth noting that of the fifty-seven OSCE participating States, forty-seven are parties to the ECHR and twenty-seven are EU members, which means that these participating States are subject to the monitoring by the respective international and supranational courts.[112]

However, since privileges and immunities are necessary for the protection of the Organization's independent functioning, a denial of immunities to the OSCE or its staff could possibly result in state interference with their autonomy and subject them to frivolous actions by third parties. Such interference would be especially detrimental to those OSCE institutions and staff members whose autonomy and independence from the participating States are essential for their effective functioning, including the High Commissioner on National Minorities, the Office for Democratic Institutions and Human Rights, and the Secretariat. And yet the OSCE will only be able to rely on its privileges and immunities, and on the implementation of its *acquis* by participating States, if

[111] ECtHR, *Stichting Mothers of Srebrenica* v. *The Netherlands* (n. 72); see, however, for the concerted challenge by scholars and media to the absolute immunities of the UN that emerged from the UN invocation of immunities before the US courts in the Haiti case and that has been manifested in particular through the numerous *amici curie* briefs in US District Court, Southern District of New York, *Delama Georges et al.* v. *The United Nations et al.*, opinion and order of 9 January 2015, 13-cv-7146 (JPO); for the decision on the appeal, see US Court of Appeals for the Second Circuit, *Delama Georges et al.* v. *The United Nations et al.*, decision of 18 August 2016, No. 15–455-cv.

[112] For the relevant comparative and international studies, see only Cappelletti, *The Judicial Process in Comparative Perspective*; Wellens, *Remedies against International Organisations*; Reinisch, *International Organizations* and Reinisch, *The Privileges and Immunities*.

it is able to show that it complies with certain basic legitimacy standards, including the rule of law and fundamental human rights.

6 CONCLUSION

International organisations become formally bound by international law only once they have been granted international legal personality, which affords them the capacity to incur rights and obligations under international law, including standards for legitimate governance that apply to international organisations under international law. These standards include the obligation to respect certain fundamental human rights, the rule of law and increasingly also some basic standards of participatory decision-making. The granting of international legal personality to an international organisation therefore enables the organisation to become formally bound by the standards of legitimate governance.

However, international organisations can be endowed with a certain mandate and public authority, which they may exercise in a more or less autonomous way, without being necessarily granted international legal personality. That does not mean that such international organisations are not actors on the international plane, nor that international law does not govern their status, exercise of public authority or legal effects of their acts, including implementation of their acts on the domestic, international and EU level. It simply means that the conduct adopted by the organisation and in particular the responsibility for any wrongful act that might arise from such conduct is to be attributed solely to the members (or participating States) that established the organisation.

This chapter has therefore tried to show that normative demands to respect certain standards for legitimate governance can and do exist also with respect to those organisations that do not possess international legal personality and hence display a lower degree of autonomy and independence from their members. The trigger for such legitimate expectations is not the organisation's international legal personality, but its capacity to autonomously exercise public authority, by which it can adversely affect individuals and peoples at large. The normative standards for legitimate governance therefore apply also to organisations like the OSCE, which, despite futile political efforts to award it international legal personality, possesses institutions and bodies that have managed to gain a relatively high level of autonomy.

Some of these normative standards have been developed by the practice of domestic, international and supranational institutions and elaborated by scholarly work. In line with this trend, an act of an organisation may – or in certain cases *shall* – remain unimplemented if that could result in a violation of certain basic human rights and the rule of law standards as granted under domestic, international and EU law, irrespective of the organisation's personality under international law. Similarly, domestic courts may – and are in certain cases *obliged* to – deny immunities to an international organisation that does not provide the claimant with any alternative means of redress and thereby violates her human right of access to justice. And since privileges and immunities can be granted under domestic law also to the organisations that lack international legal personality, such practice is also valid for international organisations without international legal personality, such as the OSCE.

These findings reveal the missing debate in the political efforts to reform the OSCE's legal framework, which largely overlook how vulnerable the OSCE is: on the one hand, the engagement in activities by which the Organization can adversely affect peoples and individuals, including OSCE personnel, is on the rise and covers tasks ranging from monitoring of ceasefires or the destruction of dangerous ammunitions to combatting human trafficking and managing migration and refugee flows. On the other hand, the OSCE's internal standards and compliance mechanisms for an accountable and legitimate governance vis-à-vis those potentially affected by OSCE activities are still at a nascent stage.

That trend increases the legitimacy gap between the public authority exercised by the OSCE and the lack of accountability mechanisms, which puts at risk the implementation of the OSCE *acquis*, as well as the enjoyment of immunities by the OSCE and its personnel. The ultimate obligation to ensure that the OSCE abides by certain basic human rights and the rule of law standards thereby lies with the participating States, which should therefore strive to strengthen the OSCE's legal framework, not simply for the sake of the Organization's greater international empowerment, but for the sake of its greater legitimacy.

REFERENCES

Abbott, Kenneth W. and Snidal, Duncan, 'Why States Act through Formal International Organizations', *Journal of Conflict Resolution* 42 (1998), 3–32.

Alebeek, Rosanne van, 'Stitching Mothers of Srebrenica and Others v Netherlands and United Nations, Final appeal judgment, LJN: BW1999, ILDC 1760 (NL 2012), 13th April 2012, Netherlands; Supreme Court [HR]', Oxford Reports on International Law in Domestic Courts (2012).

Barros, Ana Sofia, Ryngaert, Cedric and Wouters, Jan, *International Organizations and Member State Responsibility: Critical Perspectives* (Leiden, Boston: Brill Nijhoff Publishers, 2015).

Benvenisti, Eyal, *The Law of Global Governance* (The Hague: The Hague Academy of International Law, 2014).

Bernhardt, Rudolf, 'International Organisations, Internal Law and Rules', in Rudolf Bernhardt (ed.), *Encyclopedia of Public International Law*, vol. II (Amsterdam: North Holland Publishing Company, 1995), 1314–18.

Bertrand, Christine, 'La nature juridique de l'Organisation pour la Sécurité et la Coopération en Europe (OSCE)', *Revue Générale de Droit International Public* 98 (1998), 365–406.

Blokker, Niels, 'Constituent Instruments', in Jan Klabbers and Asa Wallendahl (eds.), *Research Handbook on the Law of International Organizations* (Cheltenham: Edward Elgar, 2011), 943–61.

Bogdandy, Armin von, Dann, Philipp and Goldmann, Matthias, 'Developing the Publicness of Public International Law: Towards a Legal Framework for Global Governance Activities', *German Law Journal* 9 (2008), 1376–1400.

Boutin, Bérénice, 'Netherlands (Ministry of Defence and Ministry of Foreign Affairs) v Nuhanović, Final appeal judgment, ECLI/NL/HR/2013/BZ9225, ILDC 2061 (NL 2013), 12/03324, 6th September 2013, Netherlands; Supreme Court [HR]', Oxford Reports on International Law in Domestic Courts (2013).

Braun, Dietmar, 'Dezentraler und unitarischer Föderalismus. Die Schweiz und Deutschland im Vergleich', *Swiss Political Science Review* 9 (2003), 57–89.

Brölmann, Catherine, *The Institutional Veil in Public International Law: International Organisations and the Law of Treaties* (Oxford: Hart Publishing, 2007).

Burri, Thomas, 'Secession in the CIS: Causes, Consequences and Emerging Principles', in Christian Walter, Antje von Ungern-Sternberg and Kavus Abushov (eds.), *Self-determination and Secession in International Law*, (Oxford: Oxford University Press, 2014), 138–56.

Cappelletti, Mauro, *The Judicial Process in Comparative Perspective* (Oxford: Clarendon Press, 1989).

Clinton, Robert N., 'Isolated in Their Own Country: A Defence of Federal Protection of Indian Autonomy and Self-Government', *Stanford Law Review* 33 (6) (1981), 979–1068.

Cogen, Marc, *An Introduction to European Intergovernmental Organisations* (London, New York: Routledge, 2016).

Cooper, Scott, Hawkins, Darren, Jacoby, Wade and Nielson, Daniel, 'Yielding Sovereignty to International Institutions: Bringing System Structure Back In', *International Studies Review* 10 (2008), 501–24.

Crawford, James, *Brownlie's Principles of Public International Law* 8th edn (Oxford: Oxford University Press, 2012).

State Responsibility: The General Part (Cambridge: Cambridge University Press, 2013).

D'Aspremont, Jean, 'Abuse of the Legal Personality of International Organisations and the Responsibility of Member States', *International Organizations Law Review* 4 (2007), 91–119.

Daugirdas, Kristina, 'How and Why International Law Binds International Organizations', *Harvard International Law Journal* 57 (2016), 325–81.

de Búrca, Gráinne, 'The European Court of Justice and the International Legal Order after Kadi', *Harvard International Law Journal* 51 (2010), 1–49.

de Wet, Erika, 'From Kadi to Nada: Judicial Techniques Favouring Human Rights over United Nations Security Council Sanctions', *Chinese Journal of International Law* 12 (2013), 787–807.

Fassbender, Bardo, 'Triepel in Luxemburg. Die dualistische Sicht des Verhältnisses zwischen Europa- und Völkerrecht in der "Kadi-Rechtsprechung" des EuGH als Problem des Selbstverständnisses der Europäischen Union', *Die öffentliche Verwaltung* 63 (2010), 333–41.

Foldvary, Fred E., 'Political Autonomy', in Deen K. Chatterjee (ed.), *Encyclopedia of Global Justice* (Berlin: Springer, 2011), 853–4.

Gazzini, Tarcisio, 'Legal Personality of International Organizations', in Jan Klabbers (ed.), *Research Handbook on the Law of International Organizations* (Cheltenham: Edward Elgar, 2011), 33–55.

'The Relationship Between International Legal Personality and the Autonomy of International Organisations', in Nigel D. White and Richard Collins (eds.), *International Organizations and the Idea of Autonomy, Institutional Independence in the International Legal Order* (Routledge, 2011), 196–212.

Genser, Jared and Barth, Kate, 'Targeted Sanctions and Due Process of Law', in Jared Genser and Bruno Stagno Ugarte (eds.), *The United Nations Security Council in the Age of Human Rights* (Cambridge: Cambridge University Press, 2014), 195–246.

Giegerich, Thomas, 'Verantwortlichkeit und Haftung für Akte internationaler und supranationaler Organisationen', *Zeitschrift für vergleichende Rechtwissenschaft* 104 (2005), 163–91.

Grote, Jürgen R. and Gbikpi, Bernard (eds.), *Participatory Governance: Political and Societal Implications* (Berlin: Springer, 2002).

Habermas, Jürgen, *Between Facts and Norms: Contributions to a Discourse Theory of Law and Democracy* (Cambridge, MA: MIT Polity Press, 1996).

Halberstam, Daniel, 'It's the Autonomy, Stupid! A Modest Defence of Opinion 2/13 on EU Accession to the ECHR, and the Way Forward', *German Law Journal* 16 (2015), 105–46.

Hannum, Hurst and Lillich, Richard B., 'The Concept of Autonomy in International Law', *The American Journal of International Law* 74 (1980), 858–89.

Hawkins, Darren G., Lake, David A., Nielson, Daniel and Tierney, Michael J., 'Delegation Under Anarchy: States, International Organizations and Principal Agent Theory', in Darren G. Hawkins, David A. Lake, Daniel Nielson and Michael J. Tierney (eds.), *Delegation and Agency in International Organizations* (Cambridge: Cambridge University Press, 2006), 3–38.

Higgins, Rosalyn, 'The Legal Consequences for Member States of the Non-fulfilment by International Organisations of their Obligations toward Third Parties', *Annuaire de l'Institut de Droit international* 66-I (1995), 375–420.

Problems & Processes: International Law and How We Use It (Oxford: Clarendon Press, 2001).

Huber, John D. and Shipan, Charles R., *Deliberate Discretion? The Institutional Foundations of Bureaucratic Autonomy* (Cambridge: Cambridge University Press, 2002).

Jensen, Laura S., 'Federal Authority vs. State Autonomy: The Supreme Court's Role Revisited', *Public Administration Review* 59-II (1999), 97–9.

Kingsbury, Benedict, Krisch, Nico and Steward, Richard B., 'The Emergence of Global Administrative Law', *Law and Contemporary Problems* 68 (2005), 15–61.

Klabbers, Jan, 'Institutional Ambivalence by Design: Soft Organizations in International Law', *Nordic Journal of International Law* 70 (2001), 403–21.

Klein, Pierre, 'International Organizations or Institutions, Decision-Making Process', in Rüdiger Wolfrum (ed.), *Max Planck Encyclopedia of Public International Law*, vol. V (Oxford: Oxford University Press, 2012), 403–21.

Kokott, Juliane and Sobotta, Christoph, 'The Kadi Case – Constitutional Core Values and International Law – Finding the Balance?', *The European Journal of International Law* 23 (2012), 1015–24.

Lagrange, Evelyne, *La représentation institutionnelle dans l'ordre international: Une contribution à la théorie de la personnalité morale des organisations internationales* (The Hague: Kluwer, 2002).

Hartwig, Matthias, *Die Haftung der Mitgliedstaaten für internationale Organisationen* (Berlin, New York, London: Springer, 1993).

Nedeski, Nataša and Nollkaemper, André, 'Responsibility of International Organizations in Connection with Acts of States', *International Organizations Law Review* 9 (2012), 33–52.

Niedobitek, Matthias, 'OSCE and Kosovo', in Peter Hilpold (ed.), *Kosovo and International Law: The ICJ Advisory Opinion of* 22 July 2010 (Leiden, Boston: Martinus Nijhoff Publishers, 2012), 139–56.

Pauwelyn, Joost, Wessel, A. Ramses and Wouters, Jan, 'When Structures Become Shackles: Stagnation and Dynamics in International Lawmaking', *European Journal of International Law* 25 (2014), 733–63.

Pellet, Allain, 'L'imputabilité d'éventuels actes illicites: Responsabilité de l'OTAN ou des Etats membres', in Christian Tomuschat (ed.), *Kosovo and the International Community: A Legal Assessment* (The Hague: Kluwer Law International, 2002), 193–202.

Peters, Anne, 'Membership in the Global Constitutional Community', in Jan Klabbers, Anne Peters and Geir Ulfstein, *The Constitutionalization of International Law* 2nd edn (Oxford: Oxford University Press, 2011), 153–262.

Phan, Hao Duy, 'The Association of Southeast Asian Nations: International Legal Personality and its Treaty-Making Power', *International Organizations Law Review* 13 (2016), 273–307.

Reinalda, Bob and Verbeek, Bertjan (eds.), *Autonomous Policy-Making by International Organisations* (London; New York: Routledge, 1998).

Reinisch, August (ed.), *International Organisations before National Courts* (Cambridge: Cambridge University Press, 2000).

The Privileges and Immunities of International Organisations in Domestic Courts (Oxford: Oxford University Press, 2013).

'Privileges and Immunities', in Jacob Katz Cogan, Ian Hurd and Ian Johnstone (eds.), *The Oxford Handbook of International Organizations* (Oxford: Oxford University Press, 2016), 1048–68.

Rittberger, Volker, Zangl, Bernhard and Staisch, Matthias, *International Organization Polity, Politics and Policies* (New York: Palgrave Macmillan, 2006).

Sarooshi, Dan, *International Organizations and Their Exercise of Sovereign Powers* (Oxford: Oxford University Press, 2005).

Schermers, Henry G. and Blokker, Niels M., *International Institutional Law: Unity within Diversity* 5th edn (Leiden, Boston: Martinus Nijhoff Publishers, 2011).

Schmalenbach, Kirsten, 'International Organizations or Institutions: General Aspects', in Rüdiger Wolfrum (ed.), *Max Planck Encyclopedia of Public International Law* (Oxford: Oxford University Press, 2012), 1126–53.

Seidl-Hohenveldern, Ignaz, 'Liability of Member States for Acts or Omissions of an International Organization', in Sabine Schlemmer-Schulte and Ko-Yung Tung (eds.), *Liber Amicorum Ibrahim F. I. Shihata: International Finance & Development Law* (The Hague: Kluwer Law International, 2001), 727–39.

Simma, Bruno and Pulkowski, Dirk, 'Of Planets and the Universe: Self-Contained Regimes in International Law', *The European Journal of International Law* 17 (2006), 483–529.

Steinbrück Platise, Mateja, 'The Development of the Immunities of International Organizations in Response to Domestic Contestations', in Machiko Kanetake and André Nollkaemper (eds.), *The Rule of Law at the National and International Levels: Contestations and Deference, Studies in International Law* (Oxford: Hart Publishing, 2016), 67–97.

Stumer, Andrew, 'Liability of Member States for Acts of International Organizations: Reconsidering the Policy Objections', *Harvard International Law Journal* 48 (2007), 553–80.

Suksi, Markku, 'Autonomy', in Rüdiger Wolfrum (ed.), *Max Planck Encyclopedia of Public International Law*, vol. I (Oxford: Oxford University Press, 2012), 754–68.

Summers, James, 'Kosovo', in Christian Walter, Antje von Ungern-Sternberg and Kavus Abushov (eds.), *Self-Determination and Secession in International Law* (Oxford: Oxford University Press, 2014), 235–54.

Venzke, Ingo, 'International Bureaucracies from a Political Science Perspective – Agency, Authority and International Institutional Law', *German Law Journal* 9 (2008), 1401–28.

Vidal, Maarten, 'Siedler v. Western European Union, Appeal Judgment, JT 2004, 617, ILDC 53 (BE 2003), 17th September 2003, Belgium; Brussels; Labour Court of Appeal; 4th Chamber', Oxford Reports on International Law in Domestic Courts (2006).

Walter, Christian, 'Subjects of International Law', in Rüdiger Wolfrum (ed.), *Max Planck Encyclopedia of Public International Law*, vol. IX (Oxford: Oxford University Press, 2012), 634–43.

Weiler, Joseph H. H. and Haltern, Ulrich 'The Autonomy of the Community Legal Order - Through the Looking Glass', *Harvard International Law Journal* 37 (1996), 411–48.

Wellens, Karel, *Remedies against International Organisations* (Cambridge: Cambridge University Press, 2004).

Wenig, Marcus, 'Der völkerrechtliche Status der OSZE – Gegenwärtiger Stand und Perspektiven', *OSZE-Jahrbuch* 3 (1997), 393–411.

Wessel, Ramses A. and Blockmans, Steven, 'Between Autonomy and Dependence: The EU Legal Order Under the Influence of International Organisations – An Introduction', in Ramses A. Wessel and Steven Blockmans (eds.), *Between Autonomy and Dependence: The EU Legal Order Under the Influence of International Organisations* (The Hague: T. M. C. Asser Press; Springer, 2013), 1–9.

Wessel, Ramses A., 'Revisiting the International Legal Status of the EU', *European Foreign Affairs Review* 5 (2000), 507–37.

White, Nigel, *The Law of International Organisations* (Manchester: Manchester University Press, 2005).

Wouters, Jan, Brems, Eva, Smis, Stefaan and Schmitt, Pierre (eds.), *Accountability for Human Rights Violations by International Organisations* (Antwerp: Intersentia, 2010).

Young, Ernest A., 'Protecting Member State Autonomy in the European Union: Some Cautionary Tales from American Federalism', *New York University Law Review* 77 (2002), 1612–737.

Zürn, Michael, Nollkaemper, André and Peerenboom, Randy, *Rule of Law Dynamics: In an Era of International and Transnational Governance* (Cambridge: Cambridge University Press, 2012).

PART V

CONCLUSIONS

15

Transformation of the OSCE's Legal Status

Mateja Steinbrück Platise and Anne Peters

1 THE OSCE IN CONTEXT

1.1 *The OSCE as a Cold War Instrument in Demand*

The growing confrontation and distrust between the USA and Russia has reached the point at which the United Nations (UN), as the prime organisation responsible for securing international peace and security, regularly fails to respond to some of the most serious global security threats, including the Ukraine crisis, the Syrian conflict and nuclear confrontations.[1] Bitter divisions block effective decision-making within the UN Security Council, which led the UN Secretary-General, António Guterres, in 2018 to say that 'the Cold War is back with a vengeance'.[2]

But he did not stop there. He further warned that, contrary to our past experiences with the Cold War, 'the mechanisms and the safeguards to manage the risks of escalation that existed in the past no longer seem to be present'.[3] Therefore, the hopes of the international community have turned now towards the OSCE to do its old tricks again – right at the time when the OSCE is seeking to reform its legal framework. One of the aims of the present book, therefore, is to distinguish between those traditional characteristics of the OSCE's legal framework that remain vital for the Organization's success and those characteristics that can or even should be subject to reform if the Organization is to function in an effective and legitimate way.

[1] For deep divisions between some of the permanent members of the UN Security Council enabling protracted conflicts in Europe, see the address to the UN Security Council by the OSCE Chairperson-in-Office, Angelino Alfano, of 8 March 2018; UN Security Council 8200th Meeting (PM), SC/13241.

[2] BBC News, 'Syria Crisis: UN Chief Says Cold War Is Back', 13 April 2018, available at: www.bbc.com/news/world-middle-east-43759873.</u

[3] Ibid.

The first hints come from the chapters by Petri Hakkarainen and Christian Nünlist,[4] and from Tanja Börzel and Ingo Peters,[5] who from political and historical perspectives explain how and why the OSCE as a non-legal platform for political dialogue enjoys certain comparative advantages over other international organisations that are active in the field of security and defence, in particular the UN, the EU and NATO. First, the non-binding nature of political commitments adopted within the OSCE framework has traditionally facilitated negotiations between opposing sides, and compromises were more easily reached in times of deep ideological and political divisions. Second, in comparison to the EU and NATO, the OSCE is a more inclusive organisation, allowing Russia and its European allies to participate in discussions on regional security matters, and therefore can bring all the key actors of European security together. Third, the fall of the USSR Communism has evidenced the transformative power of the OSCE's broad definition of security, which goes beyond political and military dimensions and includes economic development and environmental and human rights protection. This broad concept remains central in our current era of economic crises, climate change, increased migration flows and, most importantly, of secessionist and irredentist wars on European soil.

1.2 *The OSCE as an Informal Mode of Governance by Participating States*

The OSCE is no traditional international organisation.[6] Even after participating States decided in 1994 to strengthen a number of CSCE institutions and to rename it from 'Conference' to 'Organization', they solemnly declared that the change in name 'has no effect on the character of its commitments nor the status of the CSCE and its institutions'.[7] They also determined in the Helsinki Final Act of 1975 and in the Paris Charter of 1990 that the two documents are not eligible for registration under Article 102 of the UN Charter, consistent with the assertion that the two constitutive Acts are not treaties under international law. Moreover, as Helmut Tichy meticulously records in his chapter,[8]

4 Hakkarainen and Nünlist, 'Political Dynamics and Institutional Reforms in the OSCE', Chapter 2 in this Volume.

5 Börzel and I. Peters, '"It's Politics, Stupid": An International Relations Perspective on Strengthening the Legal Framework of the OSCE', Chapter 5 in this Volume.

6 For the concept of an international organisation, see Moser and A. Peters, 'Legal Uncertainty and Indeterminacy – Immutable Characteristics of the OSCE?', Chapter 1 in this Volume.

7 CSCE, *Towards a Genuine Partnership in a New Era*, Budapest Decisions attached to the Budapest Document, 21 December 1994, available at: www.osce.org/mc/39554?download=true, point 29.

8 Tichy, 'The Role of the Participating States in Reforming the Legal Framework of the OSCE – Past Developments, Status Quo and Future Ambitions', Chapter 4 in this Volume.

the idea of granting the OSCE an international legal personality has long been rejected by several participating States. The 2007 Draft Convention on the International Legal Personality, Legal Capacity and Privileges and Immunities of the OSCE (2007 Draft Convention), proposed by an informal working group, remains 'a sleeping beauty', as Niels Blokker and Ramses Wessel call it.[9] The current deadlock in attempts to consolidate and formalise the status of the OSCE under international law indeed seems to mirror the rise and fall of the overall process of legalisation of international relations that had been observed in the 1990s but which currently seems to have come to a standstill.[10]

Most authors in the present book, both legal and IR scholars, therefore begin their analyses from the premise that, first and foremost, the OSCE is an intergovernmental forum for regional cooperation between participating States.[11] This function as an agora is reflected especially in the structure of the OSCE's decision-making bodies, which are all duly composed of representatives of all participating States,[12] as well as in the rules of procedure, which afford each state one vote in accordance with the sovereign equality of states and which provide for consensus-based decision-making.[13]

For the IR scholars, the OSCE is primarily an informal platform for political dialogue between participating States. Thus, as regards the research methods, approaches and outcome assessments, the IR analysis of the OSCE does not differ significantly from the analysis of any other informal network of interstate cooperation. Moreover, their main focus is on the Organization's overall performance, measuring the quality of its performance against the participating States' interests. Tanja Börzel and Ingo Peters,[14] as well as Christian Nünlist and

9 Blokker and Wessel, 'Revisiting Questions of Organisationhood, Legal Personality and Membership in the OSCE: The Interplay between Law, Politics and Practice', Chapter 7 in this Volume.

10 Goldstein, Kahler, Keohane and Slaughter, 'Introduction: Legalization and World Politics'.

11 In Gasbarri's Chapter 11 of this Volume, 'The International Legal Responsibility of the OSCE', the author sketches out various legal models in order to test different legal consequences.

12 The OSCE Summits are held by Heads of State or Government; the OSCE Ministerial Council by foreign ministers; and the OSCE Permanent Council by other state representatives such as ambassadors (similarly with the OSCE Forum for Security and Cooperation). The OSCE Chairmanship is held on a rotation basis by a different participating State through its foreign minister and is assisted by foreign ministers of the participating states holding the preceding and future OSCE Chairmanships (Troika).

13 OSCE, Ministerial Council, 'Rules of Procedure of the Organization for Security and Co-operation in Europe', MC.DOC/1/06, 1 November 2006.

14 Börzel and I. Peters, '"It's Politics, Stupid": An International Relations Perspective on Strengthening the Legal Framework of the OSCE', Chapter 5 in this Volume.

Petri Hakkarainen,[15] therefore consider the informal mode of cooperation by participating States *through* the OSCE as one of the main assets of the Organization, in historical as much as in contemporary terms.

Legal scholars and some legal practitioners seem to hesitate in qualifying the OSCE as enabling mere interstate cooperation. That is remarkable, considering the fact that they generally agree that the Organization does not possess international legal personality. Clearly, they regard the OSCE, first of all, as an informal mode of governance and analyse different facets of such organisations' informality. For example, Niels Blokker and Ramses Wessel show how the informal mode of intergovernmental cooperation is mirrored in the informal status of states within the OSCE: they are called 'participating' States, instead of 'member' states, which should underline that their cooperation rests on a voluntary basis, free of legal obligations towards the Organization and the other states.[16] Olivia Herman and Jan Wouters expose how the informal mode of intergovernmental cooperation creates process informality and output informality, especially in the informal and legally non-binding status of decisions taken by OSCE bodies.[17] Mateja Steinbrück Platise demonstrates how the lack of international legal personality results in OSCE activities being ultimately attributable to participating States, together with any responsibility that might arise under international law for any wrongful conduct carried out under the framework of the OSCE.[18] Isabelle Pingel analyses how the OSCE's lack of international legal personality results in the OSCE's lack of privileges and immunities under international law.[19] Lisa Tabassi critically outlines how such informality brings about legal uncertainty and operative difficulties that the Organization and its staff encounters in its daily functioning.[20]

However, the interstate dimension is only one of several dimensions relevant for the OSCE, as expressly argued by Lorenzo Gasbarri.[21] Most, if not all

15 Hakkarainen and Nünlist, 'Political Dynamics and Institutional Reforms in the OSCE', Chapter 2 in this Volume.

16 Blokker and Wessel, 'Revisiting Questions of Organisationhood, Legal Personality and Membership in the OSCE: The Interplay between Law, Politics and Practice', Chapter 7 in this Volume.

17 Herman and Wouters, 'The OSCE as a Case of Informal International Lawmaking?', Chapter 12 in this Volume.

18 Steinbrück Platise, 'Legitimate Governance as a Privilege and Price for the Autonomy of International organisations', Chapter 14 in this Volume.

19 Pingel, 'Privileges and Immunities of the OSCE', Chapter 9 in this Volume.

20 Tabassi, 'The Role of the Organisation in Asserting Legal Personality: The Position of the OSCE Secretariat on the OSCE's Legal Status', Chapter 3 in this Volume.

21 Gasbarri, 'The International Legal Responsibility of the OSCE', Chapter 11 in this Volume.

legal scholars therefore consider also the institutional dimension of the OSCE, by recognising it as a global actor in its own right – despite lacking legal status under international law. The following section aims to disclose why and how the OSCE is viewed as a global governance actor by legal scholars and searches for some common findings by legal and IR scholars.

1.3 *The OSCE as a Global Governance Actor in Its Own Right*

As the OSCE's practice evidences, a loosely organised political forum can have detailed procedural rules, permanent staff, regular financial resources and physical headquarters. The OSCE thus developed its own institutional characteristics in addition to its informal channels of communication between states. True, the whole OSCE institutional design rests on legally non-binding constitutive documents, yet it is by no means a house of cards. The documents establishing the OSCE effectively fulfil the same function as any other founding document establishing an international organisation: they prescribe the aims and policy fields of the entity, provide for the institution to act in those fields and determine the states that participate in the entity's undertaking.

Furthermore, the policy fields and areas of state participation are broadly defined. The comprehensive approach of the OSCE to the notion of security speaks of the broad mandate that it has been given. It encompasses politico-military, economic, environmental and human aspects that enable the OSCE to adopt policies in a wide range of security-related matters, including arms control, confidence- and security-building measures, human rights, national minorities, democratisation, counter-terrorism and economic and environmental activities. All this happens between fifty-seven participating States, which shows the global reach of the Organization.

The main governance instruments of the OSCE are decisions, recommendations and other OSCE documents that are adopted by the OSCE bodies and institutions, such as the OSCE Permanent Council. Decision-making is consensus-based, with several exceptions to the rule. Niels Blokker and Ramses Wessel argue that the OSCE possesses decision-making organs and institutions that are able to produce a 'corporate' will, as opposed to a mere 'aggregate' of the wills of the member/participating States, which makes the whole more than just the sum of its parts.[22] Mateja Steinbrück Platise

[22] Blokker and Wessel, 'Revisiting Questions of Organisationhood, Legal Personality and Membership in the OSCE: The Interplay between Law, Politics and Practice', Chapter 7 in this Volume.

concludes that the OSCE has managed to establish a certain degree of autonomy from participating States, regardless of its lacking a constitutive treaty and international legal personality.[23] Carolyn Moser likewise identifies the OSCE as an actor distinguishable from its participating States.[24]

The insights showing the OSCE as an actor in its own right seem to be at least partly in line with those of other IR scholars who, while analysing the OSCE under the paradigm of a mere political cooperation between states, agree that the OSCE imposes standards on participating States and monitors compliance with such standards, for example through the Office for Democratic Institutions and Human Rights (ODIHR). As Tanja Börzel and Ingo Peters recall, such activities sometimes meet opposition by particular participating States. They mention Russia as the state that has most commonly voiced concerns about the scope of the OSCE's operations, in particular those aiming at the protection and promotion of free and fair elections and the rule of law within participating States. The Russian government deems such action an interference in a state's domestic affairs and a violation of Russian national sovereignty – even though such OSCE actions are legally non-binding, and the OSCE and its institutions lack a legal status under international law.

Some legal scholars and practitioners go further. Cedric Ryngaert underlines that while the *international* legal status of the OSCE may be unsettled, it is often regulated *de lege lata* on the level of *domestic* law. Several states afford legal capacity, privileges and immunities to the OSCE in their domestic legal systems, though incoherently and often on an ad hoc basis. From that legal basis, Ryngaert then derives more general rights and obligations for participating States and the OSCE, in particular their duty of loyal cooperation, which includes the duty of participating States to grant the OSCE the international legal status it needs in order to attain its objectives.[25]

His understanding can find some support in state practice. As revealed by Helmut Tichy,[26] Austria and Poland, as the two states hosting the OSCE Headquarters and the ODIHR respectively, recently concluded host agreements with the OSCE as a treaty party, thereby recognising the OSCE as an international legal subject in its own right. That in turn corresponds to the

[23] Steinbrück Platise, 'Legitimate Governance as a Privilege and Price for the Autonomy of International Organisations', Chapter 14 in this Volume.

[24] Moser, 'Conceptualising Accountability in the Legal and Institutional Framework of the OSCE', Chapter 13 in this Volume.

[25] Ryngaert, 'The OSCE's Domestic Legal Status: an Exploration of Relevant International Law Sources', Chapter 8 in this Volume.

[26] Tichy, 'The Role of the Participating States in Reforming the Legal Framework of the OSCE – Past Developments, Status Quo and Future Ambitions', Chapter 4 in this Volume.

self-understanding of the OSCE (at least its Secretariat) as possessing international legal personality.[27] Lisa Tabassi advocates for a high degree of independence for the Organization from participating States and views the OSCE as an employer to which she assigns the duty of care vis-à-vis its staff members, by drawing parallels between the OSCE and the UN.[28]

Mateja Steinbrück Platise shows that not only are the OSCE instruments distinguishable from the acts of participating States but may also feature as instruments for the exercise of public authority vis-à-vis participating States and non-state actors, including individuals. Public authority is here understood as the capacity to determine the scope of those others' freedom of action, directly and indirectly, for better or worse.[29] The OSCE's capacity to *directly* affect the freedom of other actors is best illustrated by Lisa Tabassi, who warns that the OSCE's engagement in numerous field operations can expose everyone involved (including the OSCE's own staff) to high risks.

The OSCE's capacity to *indirectly* determine the scope of freedom of action of other state and non-state actors is convincingly explained by Olivia Herman and Jan Wouters.[30] They conclude that despite being regarded as mere political commitments, the OSCE's decisions do not necessarily lack binding force. The distinction, they argue, exists between legal and political, and not between binding and non-binding decisions. Put differently: political but nevertheless binding decisions are conceivable. The lack of international legal personality therefore does not prevent the OSCE from acting as a global governance actor or from exercising public authority in the sense just explained towards state and non-state actors alike.

2 TRANSFORMATION OF INTERESTS

2.1 *The Changing Interests of Participating States*

Over the past decades, many participating States, including some of the major players, have changed their official positions with respect to the legal status that

27 See also Tabassi, 'The Question of Legal Status for the OSCE and Implications for Ukraine', 27 April 2015, available at: www.oscepa.org/documents/all-documents/helsinki-40/seminar-4-diis/2919-presentation-by-lisa-tabassi-for-helsinki-40-seminar-27-april-2015/file.

28 Tabassi, 'The Role of the Organisation in Asserting Legal Personality: The Position of the OSCE Secretariat on the OSCE's Legal Status', Chapter 3 in this Volume.

29 See von Bogdandy, Dann and Goldmann, 'Developing the Publicness of Public International Law', 1375, 1381; compare also Pauwelyn, Wessel and Wouters, 'The Exercise of Public Authority through Informal International Lawmaking'.

30 Herman and Wouters, 'The OSCE as a Case of Informal International Lawmaking?', Chapter 12 in this Volume.

should in their view be awarded to the OSCE. The USA, most notably, was long convinced that the Organization should remain nothing but an informal platform for political dialogue. It continuously rejected the proposals to grant the OSCE legal personality, privileges and immunities on the international level and preferred to keep the Organization's activities below the radar of international law. That seems to be consistent with the traditional US attitude towards the CSCE/OSCE. As ascertained by Christian Nünlist and Petri Hakkarainen, the USA has always been unwilling to give the Organization a leading role in the European security system, preferring instead to entrust that role to NATO. Helmut Tichy highlights that it was not until 2006 that the USA withdrew its objections and allowed the informal working group to resume the work on the text that became the 2007 Draft Convention.

Similarly, many European states only recently accepted a more institutional approach to the OSCE and, one after another, accepted that the Organization's legal personality, privileges and immunities under international law could be recognised so as to replace the current patchwork of different national legal regimes regulating the OSCE's legal status. Countries as diverse as Germany, Finland, Greece, Kazakhstan, Spain and Lithuania meanwhile maintain that the Organization should be afforded the legal status it needs in order to fulfil its mandate more effectively and to operate in an international environment with a higher degree of legal certainty.[31]

Since 2010, a voice of support for awarding the OSCE with international legal personality arose also from within the EU, when the European Parliament raised the concern that 'the OSCE is the sole organisation among those dealing with security issues in the European region that lacks an international legal personality; whereas this situation has a number of political and practical legal implications'.[32] Such a backing from the EU for a stronger OSCE is anything but taken for granted, given the geographical and functional overlap between the two organisations.[33]

31 For Germany, see the inaugural speech by Foreign Minister Frank-Walter Steinmeier to the OSCE Permanent Council to mark the start of Germany's OSCE Chairmanship, Federal Foreign Office Press Release, 14 January 2016, available at: www.osce.org/cio/212506; for other countries, see Ministry for Foreign Affairs of Finland, 'Chairmanship Countries Pledge Enhanced Co-ordination to Strengthen OSCE', Press Release, 6 February 2008, available at: www.finland.org.au/public/default.aspx?contentid=114849&nodeid=35606&contentlan=2&culture=en-US.

32 European Parliament, 'European Parliament Resolution on Strengthening the OSCE – A Role of the EU', 11 November 2010, available at: www.europarl.europa.eu/sides/getDoc.do?type=MOTION&reference=B7-2010-0603&language=EN, point E.

33 For a revealing analysis, see Paunov, 'Assessing the Success of the EU–OSCE Cooperation: A Case of Mutualism?', 373–91.

Austria and Poland, the hosts of the OSCE's Headquarters and the ODHIR respectively, have gone a step further. As noted above, the two states recently recognised – from their perspective – the international legal personality of the OSCE. In order to manifest their new position on the OSCE as an international legal person capable of entering into treaties on its own, they concluded Headquarters Agreements with the OSCE that replaced their old national measures regulating the legal status of particular OSCE institutions (but not the OSCE as such) in their countries.[34]

The enthusiasm across Europe for strengthening the institutional side of the Organization by no means ends there. Though most European states, including several eastern European ones, consider the 2007 Draft Convention sufficient to settle the Organization's legal status, Russia and some of its allies are striving for nothing less than the adoption of an OSCE Charter, which would give the Organization legal foundations. In their official statements, Russian representatives invoke domestic constitutional requirements that ostensibly prevent Russia from granting international legal personality to an organisation that does not possess an international legal founding document.

However, as Gleb Bogush's legal analysis reveals, the Russian stance can hardly be explained on the basis of the Russian constitutional order.[35] Russia's motives for strengthening the legal framework of the OSCE might be strategic rather than legal. Yet, in times of shifting state positions, Russia seems to remain consistent: as recalled by the IR scholars in this book, Russia has traditionally advocated for an institutionally stronger OSCE that could serve as a counterpart to the NATO alliance and curb the influence of the USA in Europe more generally.

2.2 *The Changing Interests of the OSCE Institutions*

Interesting trends and changes in official positions can be traced also within the OSCE institutions. When the UN International Law Commission (UN

[34] OSCE press release of 14 June 2017, available at: www.osce.org/chairmanship/322916. Compare this state practice in particular with the older official Austrian position, according to which the OSCE did not have legal personality and, from the point of view of public international law (as Austria saw it), did not enjoy the status of an international organisation. On these grounds Austria was unable to define the legal status of the OSCE institutions on its territory by means of a Headquarters Agreement but instead adopted the Federal Act on the legal status of OSCE institutions in Austria, 30 July 1993, amended 1995 and 2002, Federal Law Gazette (*Bundesgesetzblatt*) No. 511/1993.

[35] Bogush, 'Domestic Implications of the OSCE's Legal Personality under Russian Constitutional Law', Chapter 6 in this Volume.

ILC) was drafting the Articles on Responsibility of International Organizations (ARIO), the OSCE, like Austria at that time, objected to the proposal that the Organization would be considered an international organisation and maintained that it does not possess a legal personality of its own and is not governed by international law.[36] Consequently, the final commentary to Article 2 of ARIO, which defines an international organisation for the purposes of the project, no longer makes reference to the OSCE.[37] Lorenzo Gasbarri points out that such a situation may well suggest that the OSCE escapes responsibility for any wrongful conduct arising out of OSCE activities – at least as far as the ARIO concept of the responsibility of international organisations is concerned.[38]

In recent years, however, one can observe a diversification of needs, interests and official positions among different OSCE institutions. On the one hand, the OSCE Summit and the OSCE Ministerial Council, being composed of participating States' representatives, have so far failed to achieve the necessary consensus to adopt the 2007 Draft Convention that would recognise the Organisation international legal personality. On the other hand, some other OSCE institutions and bodies support the adoption of the 2007 Draft Convention. What is more, the OSCE Secretariat espoused the view, as submitted by Lisa Tabassi, that the OSCE already possesses de facto international legal personality and enjoys functional privileges and immunities on the basis of customary international law. The principal political argument is that the Organization has such a legal status under international law *because* it needs it. And it needs it urgently. In addition to the reasons well known from the national agendas of several participating States, including increased legal certainty and more efficient functioning of the Organization on the operational level, the OSCE Secretariat expects to gain a better reputation for the Organization, and in particular better security and conditions of work for OSCE staff, as a result of a settled international legal status.[39]

36 United Nations, International Law Commission, 'Responsibility of International Organizations: Comments and Observations Received from International Organizations', A/CN.4/637, 14 February 2011, 18; compare with 'Comments and Observations Received from Governments', A/CN.4/636, 14 February 2011.

37 United Nations, International Law Commission, 'Draft Articles on the Responsibility of International Organizations', A/66/10, 9 November 2011.

38 Gasbarri, 'The International Legal Responsibility of the OSCE', Chapter 11 in this Volume.

39 See Tabassi, 'The Role of the Organisation in Asserting Legal Personality: The Position of the OSCE Secretariat on the OSCE's Legal Status', Chapter 3 in this Volume; see also Tabassi, 'The Question of Legal Status for the OSCE and Implications for Ukraine'.

The diversity in positions and statements of particular OSCE institutions raise the question of who is entitled to speak on the OSCE's behalf. The answer of course depends on the regulation of the OSCE's representation in internal and international affairs and is as such related to the issue of the Organization's legal personality and the legal framework in which it operates. At least for the time being, however, it is the OSCE Chairmanship that plays a central role in managing the Organization's work and in its external representation.[40]

2.3 *The Emerging Interests of the Governed?*

In the peak period of nineteenth-century legal positivism, when the ground for contemporary international law was laid, states became the sole subjects of international law and possessors of international legal personality. It was not until after World War II that other actors re-entered the sphere of international law and were considered eligible for international legal personality – most notably international organisations and, more recently, individuals.[41] These developments heralded the shift in international law from a system of interstate cooperation to a system of global governance in which rights and obligations under international law are not solely attributed to states, and international regulation is no longer based exclusively on the expression of a sovereign will.

Nevertheless, states remain the most important subjects of international law. After all, they are indispensable for the activities of the other two types of international legal persons on the international plane: for international organisations, states form a constitutive part of their institutional structure as their members;[42] for individuals, states are instrumentally valuable to the extent that they represent the interests of the governed and as such officially act as their legal representatives.[43]

Ideally, states therefore speak for their people, that is, for 'the whole people belonging to the territory without distinction of any kind', as stated in the UN Vienna Declaration and Programme of Action, adopted by the World

40 See OSCE, 'Rules of Procedure' 2006, Section III. Chairmanship and Troika.

41 A. Peters, *Beyond Human Rights*, 11–34.

42 This holds true even if the membership of some international organisations is partly, or even wholly constituted by other organisations, since these are again constituted by states.

43 A. Peters, 'Humanity as the A and Ω of Sovereignty', 513–44; for a broader concept, see Benvenisti, 'Sovereigns as Trustees of Humanity', 300.

Conference on Human Rights in 1993.[44] The transformation of the role of the state on the international plane to one of representing peoples and individuals is to some extent reflected in state practice, in particular in the context of the international recognition of the newly established states in central and eastern Europe in the early 1990s.[45] During most of the twentieth century, the international recognition of states was based on the judgment, pronounced by other states, that a given entity fulfilled the factual criteria for statehood – territory, people and an effective government exercised over that territory and people. Starting in the 1990s, however, the existence of a representative government, institutions allowing for political participation, and the protection of human rights and minority rights became a relevant consideration for a number of recognising states when pronouncing or implying the recognition of new states, including more recently East Timor (2002), Kosovo (2008) and South Sudan (2011).[46]

The function of the state as the representative of the interests of peoples and individuals in global governance is crucial also in the context of state participation in and states' membership of international organisations, including the OSCE. Thus, it is first of all for participating States to represent the interests of the governed in the Organization's decision-making processes. However, many governments are not representative of their people or do not adhere to democratic practices. The lack of inclusion of groups and individuals in national political processes leads to a deficient representation of their interests on the international level, too. Moreover, even the interests of the governed in advanced democracies may not always be properly represented in international organisations: first, there is no chain of election and recall running from citizens through their governments to the state delegates that take the political decisions in the various fora of international organisations; secondly, some states may have a weak position in the organisation's decision-making structures; thirdly, the

44 United Nations, World Conference on Human Rights, 'Vienna Declaration and Programme of Action', UN Doc. A/CONF. 157/23, 25 June 1993.

45 The 'conditions' attached to the recognition of new states have at least a de facto influence on the international legal concept of the state, even on the premise that the legal act of recognition merely has a declaratory effect and does not create states.

46 See, in particular, the Preamble of the European Commission, 'Declaration of Guidelines on Recognition of New States in Eastern Europe and in the Soviet Union', 16 December 1991. For a nuanced assessment of the ambiguous and mixed practice, see A. Peters, 'Membership in the Global Community', 180–2; A. Peters 'Dual Democracy', 276–7. For comprehensive legal analyses of the new trend, see Fabry, *Recognizing States: International Society and the Establishment of New States Since 1776*; Vidmar, *Democratic Statehood in International Law: The Emergence of New States in Post-Cold War Practice*; Högger, *The Recognition of States*.

organisations' decision-making is often so opaque that democratic oversight is difficult; and finally, the actions and omissions of many international organisations regularly produce externalities (military, economic or financial) for individuals who are not citizens of member states and thus not represented by them.[47]

For all these reasons, the legitimacy of an international organisation cannot rest on the sources of legitimacy of its member states alone. Consequently, multi-level governance structures need to feed on multiple sources of legitimacy.[48] The highest standards for international organisations are demanded by international scholars who call for dual democratic mechanisms in global governance structures.[49] These mechanisms should, on the one hand, relate to governments within nation states and, on the other hand, relate to governance structures 'above' states, such as international organisations.[50] International organisations themselves, including the OSCE, have increasingly realised how important it is to include the governed into global governance structures.[51] As Laurence Boisson de Chazournes and Andrzej Gadkowski explain, the OSCE has developed multiple types of cooperation and partnership with civil society, in which local communities, NGOs and other civil society representatives are able to participate in limited yet diverse OSCE activities, such as environmental protection, anti-corruption and disarmament.[52]

In the present Volume, the interests of the governed have also been identified in the context of the privileges and immunities of the OSCE, which may hinder judicial protection for those individuals that suffer from a wrongful act carried out by the Organization or its staff. Isabelle Pingel proposes to balance the Organization's interests against the interests of individuals. In particular, she recalls the Organization's obligation to waive immunity under certain conditions, and concludes her chapter

[47] See, on the oligarchy in international organisations and on their further nondemocratic features, A. Peters, 'Dual Democracy', 286–9, 291–3; see also Stewart, 'Remedying Disregard in Global Regulatory Governance', 220; Benvenisti, *The Law of Global Governance*, 18.

[48] See, for the concept of 'legitimacy', see Section 4 of this Chapter.

[49] See seminally Eric Stein, 'International Integration and Democracy: No Love at First Sight', *American Journal of International Law* 95 (2001), 489–534.

[50] A. Peters, 'Dual Democracy'; for the context of international courts and tribunals, see also von Bogdandy and Venzke, *In wessen Namen?*, 128–36.

[51] See, on the participation of civil society actors in the work of international organisations and on their democratic deficit, A. Peters, 'International Organizations and International Law', 50–2, 56–8; for civil society participation in international security organisations, see Mayer, 'Civil Society Participation in International Security Organizations', 116–39.

[52] Boisson de Chazournes and Gadkowski, 'The External Relations of the OSCE', Chapter 10 in this Volume.

with a powerful message: 'without balance there is no justice'.[53] Mateja Steinbrück Platise supports that finding by providing examples from the practice of states and international organisations, which increasingly demonstrates that immunity for an international organisation should be complemented with effective alternative remedies available to victims in case a national judge should refuse to hear the case.[54] Laurence Boisson de Chazournes and Andrzej Gadkowski report that such an approach has been advocated also by the OSCE itself, in particular in the context of immunities granted to the UN Interim Administration Mission in Kosovo (UNMIK), part of which was the OSCE mission in Kosovo. In that regard, the OSCE Advisory Panel supported the creation of an effective alternative remedy against KFOR and UNMIK and persuasively stated that 'no one, especially a governmental authority (UNMIK) is above the law'.[55]

It should therefore be welcomed that Article 18 of the 2007 Draft Convention provides for the waiving of immunities granted to OSCE staff and other persons performing tasks for the OSCE. Particularly noteworthy is Article 18(3), which specifies that a participating State not only has the right but also a *duty* to waive the immunity of its representative if the immunity would impede the course of justice and could be waived without prejudice to the functioning of the OSCE. Similarly to other treaties establishing immunities of international organisations, Article 20 of the 2007 Draft Convention requires that the OSCE provide alternative modes of dispute settlement in situations where the immunity of persons performing tasks for the OSCE has not been waived. Regrettably, the 2007 Draft Convention does not contain a similar clause with respect to the immunity that would be awarded to the OSCE itself.[56]

[53] Pingel, 'Privileges and Immunities of the OSCE', Chapter 9 in this Volume.

[54] Steinbrück Platise, 'Legitimate Governance as a Privilege and Price for the Autonomy of International Organisations', Chapter 14 in this Volume. See also, on the restrictions of the immunities of international organisations, A. Peters, 'International Organizations', 56; more generally, see Steinbrück Platise, 'The Development of the Immunities of International Organizations in Response to Domestic Contestations', 67–97.

[55] Nowicki, Chinkin and Tulkens, 'Final Report of the Human Rights Advisory Panel', 80; the Human Rights Advisory Panel (HRAP) was created by the United Nations, UNMIK, 'Establishment of the Human Rights Advisory Panel to examine alleged violations of human rights by the United Nations Interim Administration in Kosovo (UNMIK)', Regulation No. 2006/12, 23 March 2006, available at: www.unmikonline.org/hrap /Documents%20HRAP /Regulations%20Eng/RE2006_12.pdf.

[56] For the lack of guidance and regulation in that field of international law, see von Bogdandy and Steinbrück Platise, 'ARIO and Human Rights Protection', 67–76.

3 TOWARDS THE POLITICISATION AND REGULATION OF INFORMAL GLOBAL GOVERNANCE ACTORS

3.1 *The Myth of an Apolitical Organisation*

In the absence of democratic modes of legitimation or justification, the legitimacy of international organisations[57] has been commonly considered as resting on the successful performance of highly complex and technical tasks of global governance, which in turn rest on expert knowledge.[58] The emphasis on 'technical' functions traditionally shielded organisations against reproaches that they might encroach upon state sovereignty.[59] Indeed, the organisations' expert bodies are freed from many diplomatic constraints that otherwise dictate decision-making at the political level. This leads some observers to conclude that international organisations depoliticise international regulation.[60] Various chapters in this book demonstrate that conviction. Helmut Tichy describes a dialectic relationship between different OSCE expert bodies and state representatives working on strengthening the OSCE's legal framework and writes that while experts seem to have been much more result-oriented, flexible and able to agree on various legal solutions concerning the OSCE's legal status, none of the proposed solutions have so far successfully passed diplomatic negotiations.[61] Along the same line (confirming the image of international organisations as apolitical actors), Lisa Tabassi regrets the politicised debate that blocks progress and describes the efforts of the OSCE Secretariat as being 'purely based on the serious operational need to protect OSCE officials and assets'.[62] Niels Blokker and Ramses Wessel similarly consider the practice of the OSCE as pursued by the OSCE Secretariat as taking place outside or

57 For the concept of legitimacy, see Section 4 of this Chapter.

58 Littoz-Monnet, *The Politics of Expertise in International Organizations*; Venzke, 'International Bureaucracies in a Political Science Perspective – Agency, Authority and International Institutional Law', 1401–28; see, on the doctrine of functionalism (associated with the technicality and apolitical nature of international organisations), A. Peters, 'International Organizations', 35–7.

59 A. Peters and Peter, 'International Organizations: Between Technocracy and Democracy', 182–6, 193–6.

60 For an overview of such claims, see Petiteville, 'Do International Organizations Depoliticize International Relations?', 113–29.

61 Tichy, 'The Role of the Participating States in Reforming the Legal Framework of the OSCE – Past Developments, Status Quo and Future Ambitions', Chapter 4 in this Volume.

62 Tabassi, 'The Role of the Organisation in Asserting Legal Personality: The Position of the OSCE Secretariat on the OSCE's Legal Status', Chapter 3 in this Volume.

beyond politics, with politics being apparently reserved for the state domain.[63]

A second, competing view on international organisations sees them – especially those operating in fields such as global security or economic affairs – as being controlled by the most powerful states and/or other strong economic actors. According to this 'political' view, the institutional veil of international organisations is merely masking the underlying power dynamics and political agendas of particular states that are pursued as the agenda of the organisation itself.[64] That should hold true even more so with respect to the OSCE, given that it was not established by a treaty and has no recognised international legal personality. Indeed, all the OSCE decision-making bodies are essentially used as a forum for interstate bargaining and power politics, in which great powers play the leading role. In one of his alternative conceptualisations of the OSCE, Lorenzo Gasbarri pushes this argument to the extreme and points out that the Organization's institutional veil could be completely ignored, if such a veil exists at all.[65] Some elements of the image of the OSCE as a purely political actor can also be found in the chapter by Tanja Börzel and Ingo Peters,[66] as well as in Gleb Bogush's contribution.[67] They recall that for a state like Russia, not only the central decision-making bodies but also other OSCE institutions, including those claiming independence, are merely political instruments in the hands of participating States, or more specifically, in the hands of some of the most powerful western states. From that perspective, OSCE institutions such as the ODIHR are political in nature, in the sense that they are captured by national political interests.

Thirdly, there is the view that international organisations can operate as autonomous actors capable of pursuing political agendas and interests of their own.[68] In this framework, the term 'political' is used in a broad sense. The word here does not refer to decision-making based on national

[63] Blokker and Wessel, 'Revisiting Questions of Organisationhood, Legal Personality and Membership in the OSCE: The Interplay between Law, Politics and Practice', Chapter 7 in this Volume. See also Klabbers, 'What Role for International Organizations in the Promotion of Community Interests?', 86–100.

[64] Bernstein and van der Ven, 'Best Practices in Global Governance', 534. See also Stewart, 'Remedying Disregard in Global Regulatory Governance'; Benvenisti, 'Global Governance'.

[65] Gasbarri, 'The International Legal Responsibility of the OSCE', Chapter 11 in this Volume.

[66] Börzel and I. Peters, '"It's Politics, Stupid": An International Relations Perspective on Strengthening the Legal Framework of the OSCE', Chapter 5 in this Volume.

[67] Bogush, 'Domestic Implications of the OSCE's Legal Personality under Russian Constitutional Law', Chapter 6 in this Volume.

[68] The qualifier of 'autonomy' for international organisations is often used as a proxy for 'sovereignty'. The more 'autonomous', quasi-sovereign and 'political' an organisation appears, the more it seems to be in need of constitutional constraints. See A. Peters, 'Membership in the Global Community', 208–210; on the autonomy of international organisations see also

considerations or subject to political processes at the domestic level. Rather, decision-making and standard setting is called 'political' when it refers to a common or public good (such as safety and security), the allocation of public resources (such as those concerning education or environmental protection) or policy prioritisations, which all require choices (as opposed to purely 'automatic' reactions) about the appropriate collective action, institutions and procedures to regulate the social condition and shared problems. Crucially, this kind of 'political' activity can happen at the international level, within organisations, just as in the national realm.[69] A characterisation of the OSCE as a 'political' actor in this sense can be traced in the chapters by Olivia Herman and Jan Wouters, Mateja Steinbrück Platise, Carolyn Moser and, finally, Niels Blokker and Ramses Wessel.

The co-existence of these three perspectives undergirds the persisting diversity of proposals regarding whether and how to strengthen the OSCE's legal framework. Competing proposals persevere because each of the three perspectives carries some truth – though not the whole truth. Many scholars and experts, especially those with a legal background, may find the first perspective (the apolitical OSCE) most attractive. It allows them to discuss legal reform with a sense of law de-coupled from politics, to benevolently appreciate the OSCE as a source of expertise rather than a new centre of public (political) authority. This view bolsters the demand for constraining participating States for the benefit of the Organization, for example with the help of a legal duty of loyalty of OSCE participating States towards the Organization, as Cedric Ryngaert suggests.[70]

The first perspective – of the OSCE as an apolitical actor – also flatters the OSCE's bureaucracy, which prefers to see itself in the duty of furnishing expertise and pursuing the common interest, rather than being exposed as following its own interests and benefits. For example, the need to establish an alternative means of redress as a *quid pro quo* for granting the Organization and its staff international privileges and immunities, advocated in several contributions to the present Volume, is absent in Lisa Tabassi's chapter, which instead focuses on the risks and burdens experienced by OSCE staff members.[71]

Steinbrück Platise, 'Legitimate Governance as a Privilege and Price for the Autonomy of International Organisations', Chapter 14 in this Volume.

69 Zürn, 'The Politicization of World Politics and Its Effects', 47–71. Along a similar line on international organisations as 'public collectives' ('collectivités publiques') pursuing a global public interest, see Lagrange, 'Chapitre 2: La catégorie "Organisation internationale"', 64, 67.

70 Ryngaert, 'The OSCE's Domestic Legal Status: An Exploration of Relevant International Law Sources', Chapter 8 in this Volume; see also Russo, 'Implementation of the Duty of Care by the OSCE', 265–92.

71 Tabassi, 'The Role of the Organisation in Asserting Legal Personality: The Position of the OSCE Secretariat on the OSCE's Legal Status', Chapter 3 in this Volume.

The second perspective (the Organization as a vehicle for national interests) is probably favoured by IR scholars and politicians. It allows them to disregard the legal implications of the proposed reforms of the OSCE and to consider law as an instrument of politics, though not as an instrument that can itself constrain political choices. The discussions around strengthening the OSCE's legal framework are thereby reduced to the power politics between the USA and Russia, or more broadly between western states and Russia and its allies, with the two great powers or alliances fighting for dominance within Europe. Both the chapter by Tanja Börzel and Ingo Peters and the nuanced historical analysis by Christian Nünlist and Petri Hakkarainen highlight this perspective as decisive for the future development of the OSCE.

The third perspective (the Organization as an autonomous political actor) might offer shelter for more sceptical international scholars with legal or political backgrounds. For them, strengthening the OSCE's legal framework should bring more legal certainty to the individual who is affected by the OSCE activities and make the Organization's functioning more transparent, accountable and legitimate. Carolyn Moser, Mateja Steinbrück Platise, and Olivia Herman and Jan Wouters exemplify the approach that seeks to clarify the legal status of the Organization first and foremost in order to regulate the OSCE and/or its activities. Legalisation of the OSCE should, from this perspective, be undertaken for the sake of those substantially affected by such activities, be it states or non-state actors including individuals, and not only or mainly for the sake of the OSCE itself and its personnel.

3.2 *The Law under Pressure*

In terms of the above-described diverse interests of states, OSCE officials, civil society, and individuals more particularly, one can identify different understandings of some of the most basic concepts of international institutional law. It is worth examining whether and how these different legal understandings accommodate the interests of various actors in the context of the OSCE reform debate.

One understanding centres on the concept of what constitutes an international organisation. As noted in the introduction to the present Volume,[72] the dominant view in legal scholarship, expressed also through the collective work of the UN ILC and the International Law Association, is that an entity is an international organisation when it has been established by a treaty or other

[72] Moser and A. Peters, 'Legal Uncertainty and Indeterminacy – Immutable Characteristics of the OSCE?', Chapter 1 in this Volume.

instrument governed by international law and possesses international legal personality.[73] Such a narrow definition hinders the OSCE's ability to claim treatment as an organisation at the international and the domestic level. It therefore seems no coincidence that the political efforts to adopt the 2007 Draft Convention have been accompanied by a growing number of voices arguing that neither of the two traditional elements (founding treaty and international legal personality) are constitutive elements of an international organisation. This view is manifest in the recent practice of Austria and Poland, as well as the OSCE Secretariat, and finds some support in scholarship.[74]

Another concept under scrutiny is that of international legal personality, in particular its acquisition. The traditional mode and procedure of acquiring international legal personality by an international organisation relies on the will of its members (the so-called subjective theory). That approach is mirrored in the *Reparations* case of the International Court of Justice (ICJ), in which the Court relied on the UN Charter and on the Convention on the Privileges and Immunities of the United Nations for inferring the intent of UN members to create an organisation with an international legal personality.[75] With this approach, the OSCE cannot gain international legal personality if participating States fail to adopt a treaty to that end.

However, the so-called 'objective' theory is gaining ground, proposing that the acquisition of international legal personality by an international organisation is not a matter of agreement among members but a matter of fact. That would mean that organisations acquire *ipso iure* international legal personality as soon as certain objective criteria required by international law are met. The recognition of their international legal personality therefore would have a merely declaratory and not a constitutive effect.[76] This scholarly view is probably ahead of the law as it currently stands. But general international law already seems to contain a presumption in favour of the international legal personality of stable interstate bodies.[77]

73 United Nations, International Law Commission, 'Draft Articles on the Responsibility of International Organizations', A/66/10, 9 November 2011, Art. 2 lit. a.

74 These are, in particular, the authors who espouse a broad definition of an international organisation; see, e.g., Lagrange, 'Chapitre 2: La catégorie "Organisation internationale"', 35–70.

75 ICJ, *Reparation for Injuries Suffered in the Service of the United Nations*, Advisory Opinion, ICJ Reports 1949, 174 at 178.

76 In the past, this theory was supported by only a few scholars, most notably Finn Seyersted, Angelo Piero Sereni and Manuel Rama-Montaldo; for comparisons, see Portmann, *Legal Personality in International Law*, 101–2.

77 Klabbers, 'Presumptive Personality', 231–53.

The objective approach minimises states' say in the creation of international organisations as international legal persons and concomitantly boosts the relevance of the organisation's actual practice and functioning at the international level. It is therefore not surprising that those actors who advocate granting international legal personality to the OSCE and who are frustrated by the absence of a treaty to that effect increasingly promote the objective theory of international legal personality. Among the most visible proponents is Austria, as a particularly organisations-friendly state. As Helmut Tichy writes, Austria views the 'recognition' of the OSCE's international legal personality as a matter of acknowledging an already objective reality.

The objective approach ultimately boils down to the idea that the Organization could gain international legal personality as a matter of customary international law when a number of participating States treat the Organization as an international legal person and recognise its international legal personality by concluding bilateral treaties with it. The approach seems to rest on the assumption that by such state practice the OSCE's international legal personality would no longer need to be based on a multilateral treaty, as initially planned with the 2007 Draft Convention, but on a rule of customary international law that would emerge from international practice, as embraced most evidently by Austria and Poland.

However, on the traditional assumption that a rule of customary international law emerges from a general, consistent and representative state practice if supported by *opinio iuris*,[78] the new approach raises at least three questions. The first concerns the generality of the practice, since so far only a few participating states have recognised international legal personality of the OSCE. The second question concerns the representativeness of the practice. We can hardly affirm a representative state practice when one of the two most important participating States of the OSCE – Russia – challenges the acquisition of international legal personality by the OSCE if not coupled with the adoption of a constitutive treaty. Indeed, the lack of a general and representative state practice might also have been Austria's concern when it asked the UN ILC to include a note in the project on the identification of customary international law, stating that a single state is not in a position to prevent the creation of a new customary rule.[79] This note raises the question of whether

78 See United Nations, International Law Commission, 'Draft Conclusions on Identification of Customary International Law', UN Doc. A/71/10), Chapter V: Identification of Customary International Law, Conclusions 2–4.

79 Permanent Mission of Austria to the United Nations, 71st Session of the General Assembly, Sixth Committee, Report of the International Law Commission on the Work of its 68th Session, 25 October 2016; International Law Commission, 68 sess. of 2 May–10 June and

Russia and its satellites could indeed be viewed merely as persistent objectors within the OSCE's legal framework or whether they could form a rule of customary international law of their own.[80]

Another question concerns the degree of legal effect from such a new rule of customary international law vis-à-vis persistent objectors. If international legal personality of the OSCE, together with privileges and immunities of the Organization and its staff, could not be invoked against persistent objectors, the solution would still leave the Organization and its staff without the necessary legal status and protection in certain countries. Considering that these might be the countries in which the Organization and its staff need such status and protection most, the solution is sub-optimal. The reflections on a customary international legal personality highlight once again the importance of keeping the Organization inclusive and open to antagonistic states and interests so that it can continue serving as a forum for dialogue, as it did during the Cold War.

4 BY WAY OF CONCLUSION: FROM EFFECTIVENESS TO LEGITIMACY AND BACK

This book examines the calls for the transformation of the OSCE's legal status from a mere domestic to an international one. It provides some empirical insights and explains the normative foundations of the proposed change. The book is not limited to the proposals that have so far been shaped primarily by political considerations brought forward by OSCE participating States and that have ended up in a stalemate. Instead, the book aims at opening up the topic to a wider scholarly debate, proposing further necessary changes and passing on the findings to a broader international audience of scholars and practitioners, politicians and international civil servants, NGOs and other civil society representatives alike. After all, the OSCE has grown into a major global governance actor in fields as vital for human flourishing as security, economic development, democratisation and environmental and human rights protection.

4 July–12 August 2016 (UN Doc. A/71/10), Supplement No. 10, Conclusion 15 together with the commentary. See also Helmut Tichy, 'The Role of the Participating States in Reforming the Legal Framework of the OSCE – Past Developments, Status Quo and Future Ambitions', Chapter 4 in this Volume.

80 That question has been debated also in the context of the USA's status as a persistent objector state in relation to certain customary norms reflected in the UN Convention on the Law of the Sea; see, e.g., Green, *The Persistent Objector Rule in International Law*, 266–7.

The book aspires to insert new and valuable arguments into the previously rather politically driven debate. But the scholarly debate, like the political one, makes conflicting proposals as to whether and how to settle the OSCE's legal status. In particular, there is a tension between the arguments advocating for a more effective Organization and those advocating for a more legitimate Organization. Authors seeking effectiveness worry that strengthening the legal framework of the OSCE could deprive the Organization of its advantageous informality and flexibility. In contrast, authors concerned about legitimacy propagate such changes as indispensable for the Organization to be accountable and legitimate. The proposals pull in opposite directions, suggesting that the effectiveness and legitimacy of the OSCE are conflicting aims.

These concerns reveal a belief among many scholars and politicians that the effectiveness and legitimacy of international organisations dictate different sets of priorities, in which one aim cannot be achieved without trade-offs with respect to the other. Nevertheless, there is sufficient ground for reconciling the two. More so, we argue that these two aims can be complementary and mutually reinforcing.[81]

Before finally addressing the OSCE's legitimacy and effectiveness, we need to clarify our understanding of these two concepts. 'Legitimacy' is both an empirical and a normative concept. Social (empirical) legitimacy means recognition or acceptance by the persons concerned.[82] In contrast, normative legitimacy is worthiness to be recognised.[83] In the context of international and European governance, the legitimacy of an organisation is commonly understood in normative terms.[84] The question then is whose perspective matters, and who needs to deem the organisation worthy of recognition. It is increasingly acknowledged that what matters is not only the perspective of states but also non-state actors, including individuals. The effectiveness of an organisation, on the other hand, relates to its actual achievements and problem-solving outputs.

The legitimacy and effectiveness of an international organisation are closely related and interdependent. An institution that does not perform effectively will not earn recognition and will not be deemed worthy of recognition.

81 On the interconnection between the effectiveness and accountability of organisations, see A. Peters, 'International Organizations', 59; see also Daugirdas, 'Reputation and the Responsibility of International Organizations', 991.

82 Weber, *Economy and Society*, 212 *et seq*.

83 Habermas, *Communication and the Evolution of Society*, 178.

84 Buchanan and Keohane, 'The Legitimacy of Global Governance Institutions', 25–62; von Bogdandy, 'Globalization and Europe: How to Square Democracy, Globalization, and International Law', 885–906.

The effective functioning of the OSCE should therefore be of central concern also to those calling for a more legitimate Organization.

But to which aspects should the effectiveness of the Organization be related? The reflections in this book reveal that both the OSCE's day-to-day functioning and its overall performance are assessed. Several authors described the OSCE's daily work and particular field operations as suffering from the lack of a settled legal status, which results in less effective performance. We conclude that an effective functioning of the Organization requires, inter alia, some degree of legal certainty in the environment in which it operates. If this is lacking, as in the case of the OSCE Special Monitoring Mission to Ukraine, the Organization cannot carry out in a timely and satisfactory way the tasks entrusted to it, which risks a potential loss of life. In that light, strengthening the OSCE's legal status could contribute to and not hamper its effectiveness.

The Organization's overall performance may be assessed differently. The yardstick here is its capacity to accomplish its core mission, which is to serve as a forum for political dialogue between antagonistic states, especially when international cooperation through other international organisations is impeded. When witnessing the current decay of international cooperation between the most powerful states, the achievements of the OSCE should therefore be assessed in terms of its ability to remain inclusive, to attract antagonistic states and accommodate their conflicting interests. One might conclude that establishing the OSCE's international legal status only among similar-minded states while isolating the other states might in the long run prove detrimental to the Organization's effective functioning; more than that, it can also compromise its legitimacy.

This finding brings us to the second part of our argument, which rests on the premise that the effective functioning of an organisation cannot be achieved without it enjoying a certain level of legitimacy. Commentators often distinguish between input and output legitimacy.[85] Input legitimacy refers to institutional arrangements that allow for an inclusive, transparent and accountable decision-making process in which the interests, values and concerns of stakeholders are fed into the political process. Output legitimacy, on the other hand, relates to policy results and is generally associated with the effectiveness of an organisation, which is in line with the reflection above.[86]

85 Scharpf, *Demokratietheorie zwischen Utopie und Anpassung*, 21–8.

86 For a critical analysis of the distinction between input and output legitimacy, see Steffek, 'The Output Legitimacy of International Organizations and the Global Public Interest', 263–93.

In global governance, stakeholders relevant for legitimacy are states and, ultimately, the individuals who are governed, directly or indirectly, by the respective organisation.[87] If they do not perceive the organisation's activity as worthy of recognition, they might not accept it and thus obstruct the effective implementation of its tasks. Members/participating States are especially relevant here and can obstruct the functioning of the organisation by calling into question the attribution of competences to the organisation, by disrupting the decision-making process, and by refusing to implement particular acts adopted by the organisation.[88] Other organisations and institutions can also obstruct an organisation's action. A case in point is the contestation of UN-imposed sanctions by the Organization of American States (OAS), the European Court of Human Rights (ECtHR) and the Court of Justice of the EU (CJEU). Those who strive for an effective OSCE should therefore not turn a blind eye to the standards of legitimacy of international organisations, which are in themselves contested but are increasingly understood to encompass participatory decision-making processes, transparency, access to justice, and respect for human rights and the rule of law.

These standards of legitimacy are problematised notably in research on Global Constitutionalism. The OSCE is as yet far from being 'constitutionalised' in the sense of satisfying the said standards. The adoption of a fully-fledged 'OSCE Charter',[89] as demanded by Russia, could be seen as one step in that direction because such a founding document would be both a treaty and a constitution.[90] The ICJ described this hybridity of the founding documents of international organisations as follows: 'From a formal standpoint, the constituent instruments of international organisations are multilateral treaties (...). But the constituent instruments of international organisations are also treaties of a particular type', with a 'character conventional and at the same time institutional.'[91] In the debate on the legal framework of the OSCE, both

87 A. Peters, 'International Organizations', 45–6; for a case study with respect to individuals, see Smrkolj, 'International Institutions and Individualized Decision-Making', 165–93.

88 For the lack of implementation of decisions by an international organisation by member states due to the organisation's disregard for human rights, see De Schutter, 'Human Rights and the Rise of International Organisations', 55–129.

89 OSCE, Permanent Council, Draft Decision on the Charter of the OSCE, PC.DEL/897/07, 18 September 2007, submitted to the Permanent Council on 18 May 2007 (PC.DEL/444/07).

90 A. Peters, 'Das Gründungsdokument internationaler Organisationen als Verfassungsvertrag', *Zeitschrift für öffentliches Recht* 68 (2013), 1–57. See also A. Peters, 'The Constitutionalisation of International Organisations', 253–85.

91 ICJ, *Legality of the Use by a State of Nuclear Weapons in Armed Conflict*, Advisory Opinion, ICJ Reports 1996, 66, para. 19. This qualification related to the WHO constitution. On the UN Charter as 'a treaty having *certain special characteristics*' see ICJ, *Certain Expenses of the*

motives for the sectoral constitutionalisation of international organisations[92] are visible. A Charter would perform both a constitutive and enabling function ('constitutionalism 1.0'), as well as the function of constraining and checking the OSCE ('constitutionalism 2.0').[93]

These insights have so far been neglected by high politics in the debates about whether and how to strengthen the OSCE's legal framework. The present book seeks to fill this gap and thereby complements research on global governance, including projects on Global Administrative Law,[94] Global Constitutionalism,[95] International Public Authority[96] and IN-Law,[97] which plead for more inclusive global governance structures and seek to tie international actors to human rights and the rule of law.

The results of this study are thus relevant also for other informal governance structures in which states seek to negotiate outside formal decision-making procedures, to enter into political commitments allegedly free of any legal constraints, and to walk out of deals whenever they no longer correspond to the state's foreign policy interests. Indeed, this model of international cooperation appears especially attractive today, when states need to govern fast-changing and increasingly diverse societies. Yet, as the present book shows, denying an international legal existence to an organisation in an effort to keep it outside the scope of international law by simply using different terms ('participating' States, 'legally non-binding' decisions) is not only futile but can in the long run endanger the organisation's effective and legitimate functioning.

United Nations (Article 17, paragraph 2 of the Charter), Advisory Opinion of 20 July 1962, ICJ Reports 1962, 151 (157).

92 The sectoral constitutionalisation of specific international organisations is both in line and in some tension with the overall constitutionalisation of international law. See n. 95 below.

93 See, for the two rationales of the sectoral constitutionalisation of international organisations, A. Peters, 'International Organizations' .

94 Kingsbury, Krisch and Stewart, 'The Emergence of Global Administrative Law', 15–62; Cassese, 'Administrative Law Without the State? The Challenge of Global Regulation', 663–94.

95 See Klabbers, Peters and Ulfstein, *Constitutionalisation*; A. Peters, 'Global Constitutionalism'; A. Peters, 'Constitutionalisation'.

96 von Bogdandy, Wolfrum, von Bernstorff, Dann and Goldmann, *The Exercise of Public Authority* 2010.

97 Pauwelyn, Wessel and Wouters, 'Informal Lawmaking'.

REFERENCES

Benvenisti, Eyal, 'Sovereigns as Trustees of Humanity: On the Accountability of States to Foreign Stakeholders', *The American Journal of International Law* 107 (2013), 295–333.

The Law of Global Governance (Leiden: Brill, 2014).

Bernstein, Steven and van der Ven, Hamish, 'Best Practices in Global Governance', *Review of International Studies* 43 (2017), 534–56.

Bogdandy, Armin von, 'Globalization and Europe: How to Square Democracy, Globalization and International Law', *European Journal of International Law* 15 (2004), 885–906.

Bogdandy, Armin von and Steinbrück Platise, Mateja, 'ARIO and Human Rights Protection: Leaving the Individual in the Cold', *International Organizations Law Review* 9 (2012), 67–76.

Bogdandy, Armin von, Dann, Philipp and Goldmann, Matthias, 'Developing the Publicness of Public International Law: Towards a Legal Framework for Global Governance Activities', *German Law Journal* 9 (2008), 1375–400.

Bogdandy, Armin von and Venzke, Ingo, *In wessen Namen? Internationale Gerichte in Zeiten globalen Regierens* (Berlin: Suhrkamp Verlag, 2014).

Buchanan, Allen and Keohane, Robert O., 'The Legitimacy of Global Governance Institutions', in Rudiger Wolfrum and Volker Röben (eds.), *Legitimacy in International Law* (Berlin: Springer, 2008), 25–62.

Cassese, Sabino, 'Administrative Law Without the State? The Challenge of Global Regulation', *New York University Journal of International Law and Politics* 37 (2005), 663–94.

Daugirdas, Kristina, 'Reputation and the Responsibility of International Organizations', *European Journal of International Law* 25 (2015), 991–1018.

De Schutter, Olivier, 'Human Rights and the Rise of International Organisations: The Logic of Sliding Scales in the Law of International Responsibility', in Eva Brems, Jan Wouters, Pierre Schmitt and Stefaan Smis (eds.), *Accountability for Human Rights Violations by International Organizations* (Antwerp: Intersentia, 2011), 55–129.

Fabry, Mikulas, *Recognizing States: International Society and the Establishment of New States Since 1776* (Oxford: Oxford University Press, 2010).

Fassbender, Bardo, *The United Nations Charter as the Constitution of the International Community* (Leiden: Martius Nijhoff, 2009).

Goldstein, Judith, Kahler, Miles, Keohane, Robert O. and Slaughter, Anne-Marie, 'Introduction: Legalization and World Politics', *International Organization* 54 (2000), 385–399.

Green, James, *The Persistent Objector Rule in International Law* (Oxford: Oxford University Press, 2016).

Habermas, Jürgen, *Communication and the Evolution of Society* (Boston: Beacon, 1979).

Högger, Daniel, *The Recognition of States: A Study on the Historical Development in Doctrine and Practice with a Special Focus on the Requirements* (Berlin: LIT Verlag, 2014).

Kingsbury, Benedict, Krisch, Nico and Stewart, Richard, 'The Emergence of Global Administrative Law', *Law and Contemporary Problems* 68 (2005), 15–62.

Klabbers, Jan, 'Presumptive Personality: The European Union in International Law', in Martti Koskenniemi (ed.), *International Law Aspects of the European Union* (The Hague: Kluwer Law International, 1998), 231–53.

'Setting the Scene', in Jan Klabbers, Peters, Anne and Ulfstein, Geir, *The Constitutionalization of International Law* 2nd edn (Oxford: Oxford University Press, 2011), 1–44.

'What Role for International Organizations in the Promotion of Community Interests? Reflections on the Ideology of Functionalism', in Eyal Benvenisti and Georg Nolte (eds.), *Community Interests Across International Law* (Oxford: Oxford University Press, 2018).

Klabbers, Jan, Peters, Anne and Ulfstein, Geir, *The Constitutionalisation of International Law* 2nd edn (Oxford: Oxford University Press, 2011).

Lagrange, Evelyne, 'Chapitre 2: La catégorie "Organisation internationale"', in Evelyne Lagrange and Jean-Marc Sorel (eds.), *Droit des Organisations Internationales* (Paris: LGDJ, 2013), 35–70.

Littoz-Monnet, Annabelle (ed.), *The Politics of Expertise in International Organizations: How International Bureaucracies Produce and Mobilize Knowledge* (London: Routledge, 2017).

Mayer, Peter, 'Civil Society Participation in International Security Organizations: The Cases of NATO and the OSCE', in Jens Steffek, Claudia Kissling and Patrizia Nanz (eds.), *Civil Society Participation in European and Global Governance: A Cure for the Democratic Deficit?* (Hampshire, New York: Palgrave Macmillan, 2008), 116–39.

Nowicki, Marek, Chinkin, Christine and Tulkens, Francoise, 'Final Report of the Human Rights Advisory Panel', *Criminal Law Forum* 28 (2017), 77–97.

Paunov, Dimitar, 'Assessing the Success of the EU–OSCE Cooperation: A Case of Mutualism?', *Security and Human Rights* 24 (2013), 373–91.

Pauwelyn, Joost, Wessel, Ramses and Wouters, Jan, 'The Exercise of Public Authority Through Informal International Lawmaking: An Accountability Issue?', Jean Monnet Working Paper 06/11 (2011), available at: https://papers.ssrn.com/sol3/papers.cfm?abstract_id=2873365&download=yes.

Peters, Anne and Peter, Simone, 'International Organizations: Between Technocracy and Democracy', in Bardo Fassbender and Anne Peters (eds.), *Oxford Handbook of the History of International Law* (Oxford: Oxford University Press, 2012), 170–97.

Peters, Anne, 'Humanity as the A and Ω of Sovereignty', *European Journal of International Law* 20 (2009), 513–44.

'Dual Democracy', in Jan Klabbers, Anne Peters and Geir Ulfstein, *The Constitutionalisation of International Law* 2nd edn (Oxford: Oxford University Press, 2011), 263–341.

'Membership in the Global Community', in Jan Klabbers, Anne Peters and Geir Ulfstein, *The Constitutionalisation of International Law* 2nd edn (Oxford: Oxford University Press, 2011), 153–262.

'The Constitutionalisation of International Organisations', in Neil Walker, Jo Shaw and Stephen Tierney (eds.), *Europe's Constitutional Mosaic* (Oxford: Hart, 2011), 253–85.

'Das Gründungsdokument internationaler Organisationen als Verfassungsvertrag', *Zeitschrift für öffentliches Recht* 68 (2013), 1–57.

'Global Constitutionalism', in Michael T. Gibbons (ed.), *The Encyclopedia of Political Thought* (London: Wiley-Blackwell, 2015), 1484–7.

Beyond Human Rights (Cambridge: Cambridge University Press, 2016).

'International Organizations and International Law', in Jacob Katz Cogan, Ian Hurd and Ian Johnstone (eds.), *The Oxford Handbook of International Organizations* (Oxford: Oxford University Press, 2016), 33–59.

'Constitutionalisation', in Jean d' Aspremont and Sahib Singh (eds.), *Concepts for International Law – Contributions to Disciplinary Thought* (Cheltenham: Edward Elgar, 2019), 141–153.

Petiteville, Franck, 'Do International Organizations Depoliticize International Relations?', *Gouvernement et action publique* 3 (2016), 113–29.

Portmann, Roland, *Legal Personality in International Law* (Cambridge: Cambridge University Press, 2010).

Russo, Deborah, 'Implementation of the Duty of Care by the OSCE', in Andrea de Guttry, Micaela Frulli, Edoardo Greppi and Chiara Macchi (eds.), *The Duty of Care of International Organizations Towards Their Civilian Personnel – Legal Obligations and Implementation Challenges* (The Hague: TMC Asser Press, 2018), 265–292.

Scharpf, Fritz, *Demokratietheorie zwischen Utopie und Anpassung* (Konstanz: Universitätsverlag, 1970).

Smrkolj, Maja, 'International Institutions and Individualized Decision-Making: An Example of UNHCR's Refugee Status Determination', in Armin von Bogdandy, Rüdiger Wolfrum, Jochen von Bernstorff, Philipp Dann and Mathias Goldmann (eds.), *The Exercise of Public Authority by International Institutions* (Berlin: Springer, 2010), 165–93.

Steffek, Jens, 'The Output Legitimacy of International Organizations and the Global Public Interest', *International Theory* 7 (2015), 263–93.

Stein, Eric, 'International Integration and Democracy: No Love at First Sight', *American Journal of International Law* 95 (2001), 489–534.

Steinbrück Platise, Mateja, 'The Development of the Immunities of International Organizations in Response to Domestic Contestations', in Machiko Kanetake and André Nollkaemper (eds.), *The Rule of Law at the National and International Levels: Contestations and Deference, Studies in International Law* (Oxford: Hart, 2016), 67–97.

Stewart, Richard, 'Remedying Disregard in Global Regulatory Governance: Accountability, Participation, and Responsiveness', *American Journal of International Law* 108 (2014), 211–70.

Venzke, Ingo, 'International Bureaucracies in a Political Science Perspective – Agency, Authority and International Institutional Law', *German Law Journal* 9 (2008), 1401–28.

Vidmar, Jure, *Democratic Statehood in International Law: The Emergence of New States in Post-Cold War Practice* (London: Hart, 2013).

Weber, Max, *Economy and Society*, eds. Guenther Roth and Claus Wittich (New York: Bedminster Press, 1968).

Zürn, Michael, 'The Politicization of World Politics and Its Effects: Eight Propositions', *European Political Science Review* 6 (2014), 47–71.

Index